Spring

London
Berlin
Heidelberg
New York
Barcelona
Budapest
Hong Kong
Milan
Paris
Santa Clara
Singapore
Tokyo

International Programme Committee:

R. Bloomfield (Chair EWICS, UK)
S. Anderson (UK)
P. Bishop (UK)
S. Bologna (I)
G. Cleland (UK)
A. Coombes (UK)
F. Dafelmair (D)
G. Dahll (N)
W. Ehrenberger (D)
R. Genser (A)
J. Gorski (PL)
D. Inverso (USA)
J. Järvi, (F)
K. Kanoun (F)
F. Koornneef (NL)

P. Daniel (IPC Chairman, UK)
V. Maggioli (USA)
Ch. Mazuet (F)
J. McDermid (UK)
M. van der Meulen (NL)
A. Pasquini (I)
G. Rabe (D)
J. Ranier (A)
F. Redmill (UK)
B. Runge (DK)
I. Smith (UK)
G. Sonneck (A)
A. Weinert (D)
Z. Zurakowski (PL)

Local Organising Committee:

John McDermid (General Chair)
Ginny Wilson (Administration Chair)
Jonathan Moffett (Treasurer)
Andrew Vickers (Local Arrangements Chair)
Darren Buttle (Exhibitions Chair)
Bob Fields (Publicity Chair)
Peter Daniel (Programme Committee Liaison)

SAFE COMP 97

The 16th International Conference on Computer Safety, Reliability and Security

York, UK
September 7-10, 1997

Edited by
PETER DANIEL

THE UNIVERSITY *of York*

Springer

Peter Daniel, PhD, BSc, MSc
GEC-Marconi Secure Systems Ltd, Wavertree Boulevard,
Wavertree Technology Park, Liverpool L7 9PE, UK

ISBN 3-540-76191-8 Springer-Verlag Berlin Heidelberg New York

British Library Cataloguing in Publication Data
Safecomp '97 : proceedings of the 16th International
   Conference on Computer Safety, Reliability and Security,
   York, 8-10 September 1997
   1.Computers - Reliability - Congresses   2.Computer security
   - Congresses
   I.Daniel, Peter   II.International Conference on Computer
   Safety, Reliability and Security (16th : 1997 : York,
   England)
   629.8'9
ISBN 3540761918

Library of Congress Cataloging-in-Publication Data
International Conference on Computer Safety, Reliability, and Security
   (16th : 1997 : York, England)
   SAFECOMP 97 : the 16th International conference on Computer
   Safety, Reliability and Security, York, UK, September 8-10, 1997 /
   edited by Peter Daniel.
        p.   cm.
   Includes bibliographical references.
   ISBN 3-540-76191-8 (pbk. : alk. paper)
   1. Computer software- -Reliability- -Congresses.   2. Electronic
   digital computers- -Reliability- -Congresses.   3. Computer security-
   -Congresses.   4. Industrial safety- -Congresses.   I. Daniel, Peter,
   1950-   .   II. Title.
   QA76.76.R44I55   1997   97-26958
   005.1- -dc21   CIP

© Springer-Verlag London Limited 1997
Printed in Great Britain

Typesetting: Camera ready by editors
Printed and bound at the Athenæum Press Ltd., Gateshead, Tyne and Wear
34/3830-543210 Printed on acid-free paper

Preface

The safe and secure operation of computer systems continues to be the major issue in many applications where there is a threat to people, the environment, investment or goodwill. Such applications include medical devices, railway signalling, energy distribution, vehicle control and monitoring, air traffic control, industrial process control, telecommunications systems and many others.

This book represents the proceedings of the 16th International Conference on Computer Safety, Reliability and Security, held in York, UK, 7-10 September 1997. The conference reviews the state of the art, experience and new trends in the areas of computer safety, reliability and security. It forms a platform for technology transfer between academia, industry and research institutions. In an expanding world-wide market for safe, secure and reliable computer systems SAFECOMP 97 provides an opportunity for technical developers, users and legislators to exchange and review the experience, to consider the best technologies now available and to identify the skills and technologies required for the future. The papers were carefully selected by the Conference International Programme Committee. The authors of the papers come from twelve different countries. The subjects covered include safe software, safety cases, management & development, security, human factors, guidelines standards & certification, applications & industrial experience, formal methods & models and validation, verification and testing.

SAFECOMP '97 continues the successful series of SAFECOMP conferences first held in 1979 in Stuttgart. SAFECOMP is organised by the European Workshop on Industrial Computer Systems, Technical Committee 7 on Safety, Security and Reliability (EWICS TC7). EWICS TC7 membership represents a broad coverage of industry, manufacturers and users as well as Universities, Research Centres. Licensing and Standardisation Authorities. The current subgroups include security of industrial systems, industrial applications of formal methods, programmable logic controllers, system integrity. New subgroups have been formed to deal with the safety and security of medical devices, using IEC1508, future programmable controllers, use of PCs in safety systems, Risk and Hazard Analysis and subgroups on Social and Cognitive Aspects and Safety Aspects of Advisory Systems are being considered. More information can be obtained from the EWICS TC7 chairman Robin Bloomfield on +44 (0) 181 983 0217 or by email at reb@adelard.co.uk.

The Call for Papers, this year, asked for full papers rather than abstracts, requested in previous years. The response produced many more good papers than could be included in the programme. As chairman of the International Programme Committee (IPC), I would like to thank all the authors who submitted their work, the presenters of the papers, the session chairmen, the IPC, the Local Organising Committee, in particular Ginny Wilson and David Hull in the production of these proceedings, and the Sponsors for their efforts and support. Through their strong motivation and hard work, the conference and this book was realised.

Peter Daniel   *Liverpool, UK*
June 1997

Contents

Guidelines, Standards and Certification

Formal Methods and Models

Applications and Industrial Experience

Testing, Validation and Verification

List of Contributors

Stephen Barker
Lloyd's Register
Safety Integrity & Risk
    Management
Lloyd's Register House
29 Wellesley Road
Croydon CR0 2AJ
UK

Philippe Baufreton
SNECMA - Elecma
77550 Moissy-Cramayel
France

M Bowell
Health and Safety Laboratory
Broad Lane
Sheffield S3 7HQ
UK

Jens Braband
Siemens AG Transportation
    Systems Group
D-38023 Braunschweig
Germany

M Cepin
Reactor Engineering Division
"Jozef Stefan" Institute
Ljubljana
Slovenia

C Chambers
Department of Computer Science
The University of Sheffield
Sheffield
UK

P W H Chung
Department of Chemical
    Engineering
Loughborough University of
    Technology
Loughborough
Leicestershire
UK

P R Croll
Department of Computer Science
The University of Sheffield
Sheffield
UK

Gustav Dahll
OECD Halden Reactor Project
PO Box 173
N-1751 Halden
Norway

Anthony Darlison
Lloyd's Register
Safety Integrity & Risk
    Management
Lloyd's Register House
29 Wellesley Road
Croydon CR0 2AJ
UK

Andrew M Dearden
Department of Computer Science
University of York
York YO1 5DD
UK

P D Edwards
Rover Group Ltd
2nd Floor
Advanced Technology Centre
University of Warwick
Coventry CV4 7AL
UK

Richard C Eldridge
Safety Integrity and Risk
    Management
Lloyd's Register of Shipping
Lloyd's Register House
29 Wellesley Road
Croydon CR0 2AJ
UK

Klaus Gotthardt
Department of Electrical
    Engineering
Fernuniversitdt-GH-Hagen
58084-Hagen
Germany

S Gritzalis
Department of Informatics
University of Athens
TYPA Buildings
Athens GR-15771
Greece
and
Department of Informatics
Technological Educational
    Institute (TEI) of Athens
Ag. Spiridonos St.
Aegaleo GR-12210
Greece

Yong-Fei Han
National University of Singapore
Republic of Singapore

Michael D Harrison
Department of Computer Science
University of York
York YO1 5DD
UK

Maritta Heisel
Technische Universität Berlin
Franklinstraße 28/29
Sekr. FR 5-6
10587 Berlin
Germany

David Jenkins
University of Paisley
Paisley
Scotland
UK

T P Kelly
Rolls-Royce Systems and
    Software Engineering
    University Technology Centre
Department of Computer Science
University of York
York YO1 5DD
UK

Ian Kendall
Jaguar Cars
Abbey Road
Whitley
Coventry CV3 4LF
UK

P M Kirkham
Department of Computer Science
University of York
York YO1 5DD
UK

John C Knight
Department of Computer Science
University of Virginia
Charlottesville
VA 22903-2442
USA

Kwork-Yan Lam
National University of Singapore
Republic of Singapore

K Lano
Department of Computing
Imperial College
180 Queens Gate
London SW7 2BZ
UK

Yahia Lebbah
École des Mines de Nantes
Nantes
France

Clive Lee
Safety Integrity and Risk
    Management
Lloyd's Register of Shipping
Lloyd's Register House
29 Wellesley Road
Croydon CR0 2AJ
UK

Brian Lees
University of Paisley
Paisley
Scotland
UK

R de Lemos
Department of Computing Science
University of Newcastle upon Tyne
Newcastle upon Tyne
UK

Reiner Lichtenecker
Department of Electrical
    Engineering
Fernuniversität-GH-Hagen
58084-Hagen
Germany

Peter A Lindsay
Software Verification Research
    Centre
School of Information Technology
The University of Queensland
Australia

Daniel Livingstone
University of Paisley
Paisley
Scotland
UK

Thomas Maier
Daimler-Benz AG
F1M/IV
Stuttgart
Germany

Marcelo Masera
Joint Research Centre
Institute for Systems, Informatics
    and Safety
TP210 - 21020
Ispra (VA)
Italy

B Mavko
Reactor Engineering Division
"Jozef Stefan" Institute
Ljubljana
Slovenia

G F McCall
Ford Motor Company Ltd
UK

John A McDermid
Rolls-Royce Systems and
    Software Engineering
    University Technology Centre
    and High Integrity Systems
    Engineering Group
Department of Computer Science
University of York
York YO1 5DD
UK

Xavier Méhaut
TNI
29608 BREST Cedex
France

Bruno Mermet
CRIN-CNRS URA 262
BP 239
54506 Vand□uvre-lhs-Nancy
France

Dominique Méry
Université Henri Poincaré
Nancy 1
France
and
CRIN-CNRS URA 262
BP 239
54506 Vandœuvre-lès-Nancy
France

Ian T Nabney
Neural Computing Research Group
Aston University
Birmingham B4 7ET
UK

Luís G Nakano
Department of Computer Science
University of Virginia
Charlottesville
VA 22903-2442
USA

Hélène Papini
Alcatel Alsthom Recherche
Route de Nozay
91460 Marcoussis
France

Mickael J S Paven
Neural Computing Research Group
Aston University
Birmingham B4 7ET
UK

Despina Polemi
Institute of Communications and
    Computer Systems
National Technical University of
    Athens
Athens
Greece

C H Pygott
Defence Evaluation and
    Research Agency
Malvern
UK

Andrew Reglinski
University of Paisley
Paisley
Scotland
UK

S Riddle
Department of Computing Science
University of Newcastle upon Tyne
Newcastle upon Tyne
UK

R S Rivett
Rover Group Ltd
2nd Floor
Advanced Technology Centre
University of Warwick
Coventry CV4 7AL
UK

Éric Rutten
IRISA/INRIA
35042 RENNES Cedex
France

A Saeed
Department of Computing Science
University of Newcastle upon Tyne
Newcastle upon Tyne
UK

Francesca Saglietti
Institute for Safety Technology
    (ISTec)
Forschungsgelände
Garching
Germany

Stefan Scheer
Joint Research Centre of the EC
Institute for Systems, Informatics
    and Safety
Ispra
Italy

François Simon
Alcatel Alsthom Recherche
Route de Nozay
91460 Marcoussis
France

D Spinellis
Department of Mathematics
University of the Aegean
Samos GR-83200
Greece
and
SENA SA
Byzantiou 2
N Ionia GR-14234
Greece

Carsten Sühl
GMD FIRST
Rudower Chaussee 5
12489 Berlin
Germany

Henrik Thane
Mechatronics Laboratory
The Royal Institute of Technology
Stockholm
Sweden

D J Tombs
Defence Evaluation and Research
Agency
Malvern
UK

Konstantinos Tourlas
Laboratory for the Foundations of
    Computer Science
Department of Computer Science
University of Edinburgh
The King's Buildings
Edinburgh EH9 3JZ
UK

Davide Vallero
Politecnico di Torino
Italy

B A Wichmann
National Physical Laboratory
Teddington
Middlesex TW11 0LW
UK

Marc Wilikens
Joint Research Centre
Institute for Systems, Informatics
    and Safety
TP210 - 21020
Ispra (VA)
Italy

S P Wilson
Department of Computer Science
University of York
York YO1 5DD
UK

Xun Yi
National Communication
    Research Laboratory
Southeast University
Nanjing
People's Republic of China

Safe Software

Software-based Safety-critical Systems: a Taxonomy.

Hélène Papini

François Simon

Alcatel Alsthom Recherche

Route de Nozay, 91460 Marcoussis, France

e-mail: {papini || simon}@aar.alcatel-alsthom.fr

Abstract

Railway control systems are designed to ensure the safe behaviour of the Railway systems. While any existing railway control system has to ensure safety, each system is different from others, by difference of architecture, and difference of development process. This paper proposes a general presentation of safety related/critical systems based on software. It presents a classification of the development processes, and a classification of the architectures, and qualifies architectures and development processes. Each architecture has a set of undetectable errors that constitutes its weakness. And each development process is oriented towards a set of avoided faults. The use of a development process associated to an architecture is a way to reduce as far as possible the set of undetectable errors (through fault avoidance). This analysis leads to associate to each architecture the required development process.

1   Introduction

A Railway control system is designed to ensure the safe behaviour of a Railway system. A Railway control system is characterized by:

· a set of **signalling rules**, that are the property of the customer; roughly speaking, the specifications of the Railway control system are obtained by the definition of the signalling rules, and the layout,

· a **development process**, to avoid as far as possible the introduction of faults,

· an **architecture** (information coding, replication of components, or the diversification), that leads to the definition of a fail-safe system for fault tolerance.

The aim of the Railway control system has to comply with the signalling rules, either when properly functionning or when failed. The different states of a system are the following:

· The system behaves as specified: this is associated to a **correct state** of the system, that is supposed to be safe.

· The system does not behave as specified, but does not endanger the controlled process: this is associated to a **safe failed state** of the system.

· The system does not behave as specified, and may endanger the controlled process: this is associated to a **unsafe failed state** of the system.

The aim of a fail-safe system is to canalise any erroneous state into a safe state.

To define the safe behaviour of a system, two purposes have to be reached:

· The **functional safety**: the functions of the system have to comply with the signalling rules defined by the customer.

· The **technical safety**: the system must be resilient to impairments due to any fault. This is obtained by a suitable development process (see part 3) that allows the translation from the requirements to the implementation of the system, and by suitable safety mechanisms (see part 4) that provide run-time error detection.

This paper only addresses the problem of the technical safety. We assume that the functional safety of the system is well defined and validated.

2 Fail-Safe System Analysis

2.1 Fail-Safe System Model

The taxonomy proposed in this paper is based on a general model of software-based safety critical systems presented hereafter.

The functional specification of the control system, defined from the signalling rules and the track layout, is modelled as a function noted g. This function is specified such that it fulfills the safety requirements defined by the customer. Inputs of the g function are noted x, and outputs are noted y. The technical implementation of this function has to be such that in case of an error, the behaviour of the system has to be led to a state that does not endanger the safety: a safe state.

Technical safety relies on error detection. The results produced by the safe implementation of g are submitted to a check which is a consistency criterium. Any consistency criterium applied on data can be viewed as obtained from adding information to data: the detection is given by the inconsistency between the result information, and the added information. This is called **information redundancy**.

This results in a technical implementation that fulfills the customers requirements - that behaves as the function g - and that handles information redundancy.

The information redundancy is first given by the input module of the system. This input module has to encode the input information in a code that allows in the sequel error detection: the input module is modelled as an encoding function u.

The technical implementation of g has to be tuned to coded input data. This implementation of g is modelled by a function G. The aim of G is to produce encoded outputs, i.e., outputs which can be submitted to a consistency check. This check is modelled as a decoding output stage which is a decoding function v^{-1}. This error detecting code has to detect as far as possible any error that could occur during the computation of G. This decomposition leads to: $g = v^{-1} \circ G \circ u$. The general model of a fail-safe system is given by the figure 1. A safe system is thus considered as made of a fail-safe encoding input stage, a computing stage handling redundant information called a self-checking computation and a fail-safe decoding output stage in charge of checking the consistency of the computed data.

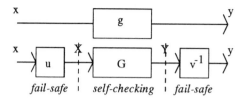

Figure 1: Fail-Safe System Architecture.

2.2 Error Analysis of a System

2.2.1 Fault Classification

A system is made of two kinds of components, hardware and software ones. They may be both be affected by faults. Errors coming from hardware or software may lead to errors which in turn may affect the system behaviour (failure). The errors that affect the hardware component have an effect on the software behaviour.

While only hardware can be affected by transient faults (mainly coming from external perturbations), both hardware and software can know permanent faults[1]. Permanent faults are introduced during the development/production of hardware and software components. Hardware components can be affected by permanent faults coming from ageing.

The figure 2 summarizes the different faults that can disturb a software based system.

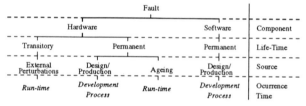

Figure 2: Fault Classification.

2.2.2 Fault Dependency from Development Process to Execution

The error analysis of a system is considered from its development process to its operational life (execution). In fact, for instance, in case of software component, errors can be introduced due to a misunderstanding of the specification, or due to an erroneous compiler that does not translate the source code into a correct executable code. These errors result in an erroneous behaviour of the system. The figure 3 summarizes the dependency between the development process and execution errors.

Development Process | fault ⟶ error

Run-Time | fault ⟶ error

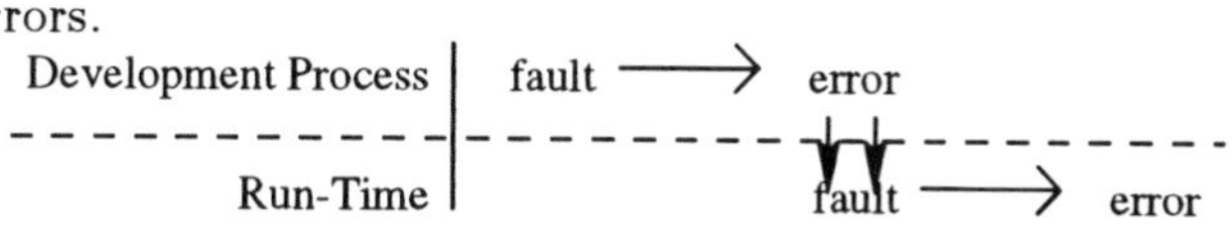

Figure 3: Dependency between Development Process and Execution Errors.

---

[1] The authors consider that errors like heisenbugs are not considered as transitory errors, as they are the result of faults introduced during the development process (for instance due to dimensioning), and then these faults are permanent [1].

2.2.3 Error Model

The different faults that have been presented in the part 2.2.2 lead to errors. The error is defined by a discrepancy between the expected behaviour of the system, and the actual behaviour of a system. If the g algorithm is considered, the expected behaviour is defined by: if g is provided at the time t with the input vector $x = [x_1 \cdots x_n]$ then g has to provide the output sequence $y = [y_1 \cdots y_m]$ during the time interval $[t + \Delta_{min}, t + \Delta_{max}]$. Then not only the output values have to be correct, but also, they have to be provided at an expected time interval. Then errors are qualified regarding two criteria: **value errors**, and **timing errors**.

2.3 Information Redundancy

An erroneous value can be due to either only a value error, or only a timing error, or a timing and a value error. Then the error detecting code that has been defined in the part 2.1 has to deal with value and timing errors.

This leads to define the information redundancy handled by the u and the v^{-1} functions as depending on respectively (x, t), and (y, t). For the detection of the timing errors, the t value is checked against an expected value. One way is to define a periodical execution of the software. Then the value of t has to be consistent with the predefined period.

3 Development Processes Taxonomy

3.1 Presentation of the Taxonomy Criteria

The development process is composed by a sequence of step and translation that translate the functional requirements into an executable form. The development process is modelled by the following steps (figure 4):

· **Specification**[2]: expression of functional requirements associated to the system. These requirements include the safety properties of the system. This is in paper form.
· **Source**: first electronical expression of the specification.
· **Executable**: electronical form that can be executed.

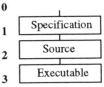

Figure 4: Development Process.

The development process has to guarantee the integrity of the software from its specification (assumed functionally safe) until the self checking implementation, i.e. G. The aim of a development process is to lead to an executable form that fulfills the requirements given by the step 0. Each translation from one step to the next one has to keep the integrity of the previous one. Different kinds of translation exist. The next enumeration allows to classify translations:

· **incremental development** (figure 5): the result of one step is progressively obtained from the previous one. This considers intermediate steps. No fault can be introduced by this development. For instance, formal methods have this

---

[2]The requirements express the functional safety of the system. We have previously specified that the functional safety of the system is supposed to be validated. Then the requirements of the system are supposed to be already validated.

policy from specification to source code production.

· **feedback development** (figure 6): the result of one translation is undone and checked for consistency with the input of translation. This is for instance the policy of decompilation.

· **tested development** (figure 7): the result of one translation is tested and checked for consistency against the input of the translation. This is for instance classical test.

The different translations are presented by figures 5, 6, and 7.

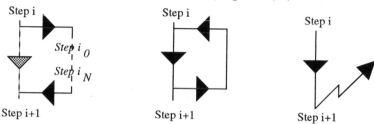

Figure 5: Incremental Development. Figure 6: Feedback Development. Figure 7: Tested Development.

The choice of a development process depends on the architecture of the system. The safety mechanisms used by the system ,cover a set of detectable errors. The development process has to behave as a complement, meaning that it has as far as possible to avoid the introduction of the faults that are not covered by the safety mechanisms.The fault avoidance and the fault tolerance give the completness.

This leads to the figure 8 that summarises all the different development processes. The grey squares are associated to steps that have to be validated, the grey arrows are associated to transitions that have to be validated. One transition is validated according to the use of a specific translation: this can be due to an incremental translation, a feedback translation, or a tested translation. A step is considered to be validated if the previous step is validated, and if the translation that has been used to generate this step is validated too. In fact as the part 4 presents, the architecture of the system can include either one instance of the software component, or two different instances of the software component.

3.2 Single Software Development Process

The single software development process is associated to type α. Single software development is used for system based on one self-checking software , or based on replication .

The type α_1 is the minimum required for any Safety critical system. The specification is the first input of the development process and then has to be checked for consistency against the customers requirements. The specification is the image of the functional safety, whatever the technical safety that will be applied in the next steps.

The type α_2 is for instance the B method [2]. The B method leads to the source form of the software, with an incremental approach. Roughly, each increment

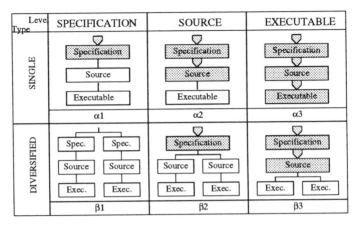

Figure 8: Development Process Taxonomy.

has to verify invariants, defined at the specification level of the development process.

The type α_3 is for instance the decompilation used for the SSI system [3], and applying the desk check operation. This allows to check the correctness between the decompilation result, and the source of the software.

3.3 Diversified Software Development Process

The diversified software development process is associated to type β. The diversification of a software component can be made at different levels of the development process. The steps that are defined before the level of diversification, have to be checked, and validated. In fact at the diversification level each different instance of the produced level constitute the check of the other instance. This check is only performed during the execution phase. Before the level of diversification there is no way (if no other mechanisms are provided) to check the consistency of the produced levels. This is the reason why an added check of the non-diversified level has to be provided. In the figure 8, this is represented by a grey square. Moreover the translation from the non-diversified step until the level of diversification have to be checked and validated (this is represented in the figure 8 by a grey arrow).

The diversification at the specification level (β_1) is for instance the policy of the safety bag technique. This technique is used for the Elektra system ([9]

The diversification at the source level (β_2) is the policy of N-version programming.

The diversification at the executable level (β_3) is for instance the policy of the use of diversified compiler.

4 Architecture Taxonomy

4.1 Presentation of the Taxonomy Criteria

Considering a software based system, two components can be highlighted: the software component(s), and the hardware component(s). Different ways are possible to define an architecture with these components:

· **Single component**: the software or the hardware is considered to be a single component of the system, if there is only one instance of this software or hardware component in the system.

· **Replicated component**: the software or the hardware is considered to be a replicated component of the system, if there is at least two instances of this software or hardware component in the system.

· **Diversified component**: the software or the hardware is considered to be a diversified component of the system, if there is at least two diversified instances of this software or hardware component in the system. In the part 3, the way to diversify a software is presented. The diversification of hardware is provided by the use of different technologies of hardware components.

The figure 9 summarises these different cases.

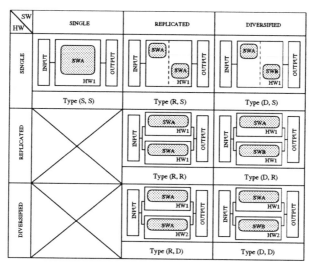

Figure 9: Architecture Taxonomy.

Each architecture defines an error detection mechanism. This induces a set of detectable errors, and moreover, a set of undetectable errors. This set of detectable errors iscompletely defined by the system architecture. To reduce the probability of undetectable errors occurrence, the definition of an associated development process is required. Next parts present the features of each architecture, the set of undetectable errors that remains, and the development process that allows to avoid the fault leading to undetectable errors. The analysis is led regarding the software axis.

4.2 Single Software Architecture

4.2.1 General Statement of a System based on Single Software

The single software architecture is supported by a single hardware. The general statements are given by the figure 10. The self-checking property is given by the definition of a code that allows errors detection.

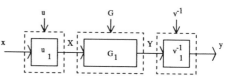

Figure 10: Single Software Principle.

Different approaches are distinguished:

· Algorithm Based Fault Tolerant: One of the example of this approach is [4]. The operations applied to matrix are self-checking. This property is provided by the use of enlarged matrices that are built with additional checksum lines, and checksum columns. Operations are extended to handle the added information. The result of an operation has to have consistent checksum lines, and checksum columns. One point to consider is the robustness of this approach. In fact a slight change of the operation may induce a complete redesign of the operation. To the authors best knowledge, no safe system uses ABFT.

· Decomposition in self-checking sub-components[3]: In this case the function G is defined by the composition of several functions that handle coded information. These functions do not use the same error detecting code. One characteristic of this approach is the use of transcoder. A transcoder (noted T_{12} in the figure 11) allows to translate informations from one error detecting code to another error detecting code. This allows to manipulate only coded informations.

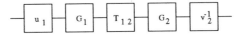

Figure 11: Decomposition of a self-checking algorithm into self-checking sub-algorithms.

4.2.2 Undetectable Errors of a System based on Single Software

In case of single software architecture, the set of undetectable errors that remains, is mainly given by the power of the code. However, they are:

· An intermediate sub-algorithm produces an erroneous value belonging to its output code.

· An out-of-code erroneous intermediate result is transformed by a correct sub-algorithm into an erroneous value belonging to the expected code.

· An out-of-code erroneous intermediate result is transformed by an erroneous operation into an erroneous value belonging to the expected code.

4.2.3 Development Process required for Single Software

The software is single, only one instance exists. Then the development process is of type α. In case of decomposition of the algorithm into sub-algorithm, or in case of the ABFT, the self-checking software is defined regarding a set of detectable errors. The development process that is oriented towards the fault avoidance is then associated to the set of undetectable errors that remains despite the self-checking algorithm. At this level of the analysis there is no way to define the minimum level of validation that has to fulfil the development process of a single software architecture. We can consider that the minimum type is in general the α_2 type.

The single coded processor is an example of single software system. The self-checking property is provided by the use of coded operations, that handles

---

[3]This is for instance the single coded processor system [5], where the sub-algorithms are the coded elementary functions of the algorithm.

coded information. The single coded processor's development process ensures the validation until the production of the source code by the use of the B method. It is supposed that the errors that can be introduced during the generation of the executable software (from the source code), are covered by the error detection mechanisms that are involved.

4.3 Replicated Software Architecture

4.3.1 General Statement of a System based on Replicated Software

The replicated software system is based on the execution of two or more instances of a single software. This execution can be either sequential, or concurrent, or interleaved pseudo-parallelism. The general statements are given by the figure 12. The output module computes the majority voting of the different provided results of the different instances of the software.

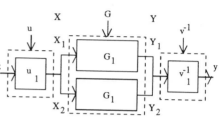

Figure 12: Replicated Software Statement.

The SMILE system [6] is an example of replicated system. In SMILE the output module computes a 2 out of 3 vote. The ESTWL90 [8] is based on Triple Modular Redundancy.

4.3.2 Undetectable Errors of a System based on Replicated Software

The information redundancy is $u(x) = (x, ..., x)$. The undetectable errors are exactly common mode errors for both value and timing. The common mode errors are mainly due to faults introduced during the development process. It is generally assumed that the probability that an external perturbation or an ageing fault disturbs all the replica in the same erroneous way is very low.

4.3.3 Development Process required for Replicated Software

The software is replicated, but only one instance exists. Then the development process is of type α. In case of architecture types (R,S), and (R,R) as the hardware is the same for each replica, then common modes due to hardware have to be avoided during the development process. For these architectures the hardware components have to be validated. The replication of the software induces that the software has to be validated until the production of the executable. This is only to detect potential common mode error that can be introduced until the production of the executable software. This leads to require a development process that is α_3 type.

4.4 Diversified Software Architecture

4.4.1 General Statement of a System based on Diversified Software

The general statements are given by the figure 13. This is for instance the Elektra system [9], where the two instances are: on one hand the safety critical application, and on the other hand the safety bag that has to monitor the application execution. The VIPER [7] is another example of diversification of the software. The diversification is provided by the use of on-line tests. In

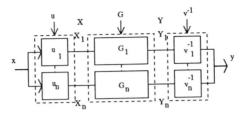

Figure 13: Diversified Software Statement.

case of the Erilock system [10], the diversification is provided by the use of one software using the positive logic, and the other one using the negative logic.

4.4.2 Undetectable Errors of a System based on Diversified Software

It is not possible to give a general characterisation of undetectable errors for diversified software as they depend on the peciliar sofware under concern. But, it is generally assumed that the most probable undetectable errors are common mode timing errors. One can cite, in case of an architecture type (D,S), hardware permanent errors that lead to a timing error (a clock derating, unexpected halt, $\cdots$), in case of architecture type (D,R), a hardware fault permanent or transitory, that leads to a timing error. In case of an architecture type (D,D) the diversification of the hardware and the software, allows to assume that the probability of common mode errors is very low.

4.4.3 Development Process required for Diversified Software

The development process is β type. There is no technical reason that imposes the use of one level of diversification. One point is that the diversification of the executable is due to the hardware diversification. Mainly the level of diversification is given by a cost consideration. Moreover, the way to reduce the probability of undetectable errors is to validate the hardware components to ensure that they are fault free.

5 Conclusion

A Railways signalling system is defined by the signalling rules that are the property of the customers, an architecture that has to ensure the safety mechanisms, and that is independent of the signalling rules, and a companion development process. The choice of the safety mechanisms, and the companion development process are given by complementary approaches. The safety mechanisms cover a set of detectable errors, however a set of undetectable errors remains. The fault avoidance is given by the development process. A safety strategy for a given system is mainly dependent on the technical choices that have been made. These choices give a set of components that are required during the operational life of the system (this can be a choice of the hardware component technology, $\cdots$), and during the development process (for instance a specific compiler that is validated, $\cdots$). The different architectures that exist are either a single software supported by a single hardware, or a replicated software supported either by a single hardware, a replicated or a diversified hardware, or a diversified software that is supported by a single or replicated or diversified hardware.

The development processes that are associated to these architectures are either the development of a single software with a certain level (specification, source, or executable) of validation, or a diversified development process, the diversification of the level depending on the technology to be used.

References

[1] J.N.Gray, "Why computers stop and what can be done about it?", Proc. 5th. Symposium on Reliability in Distributed Software and Database Systems, Los Angeles (USA), Jan. 1986

[2] J.R. Abrial, M.K.O. Lee, D.S. Neilson, P.N. Scharbach, I.H. Sorensen, "The B-method", VDM'91, Formal Software Development Methods, vol.2, tutorials 552, pp.398-405

[3] A.H. Cribbens, "Solid-state Interlocking(SSI): an integrated electronic signalling system for mainline Railways", IEE Proc., vol.134, pp.148-158

[4] K.H. Huang, J.A. Abraham, "Algorithm-Based Fault Tolerance for Matrix Operations", IEEE Transactions on Computers, June 1984, pp.518-528

[5] J. Martin,"Vital processing by single coded unit", Proceedings of SAFECOMP'92, Zürick, Switzerland, 1992, pp.147-152

[6] K. Akita, "Practical use of computerised interlocking system "SMILE" in JNR", Japanese Railway Engineering, N°94, June 1985, pp.21-24

[7] J. Kershaw, "VIPER", IEE Colloquium on VLSI Architectures, vol.32, March 1987, pp.6-13

[8] D. Weiniger, "Elektronische stellwerk in modulbauweise-bauart ESTWL90", Signal und Draht, N°87, 1995, pp.43-46

[9] A. Erb, "Safety measures of the eletronic interlocking system "Elektra"", Proceedings of SAFECOMP'89, Vienna, Austria, 1989, pp.49-52 electronic

[10] D. Nordenfors, A. Sjöberg, "Computer-controlled electronic interlocking system, Erilock 850", Ericsson Review, N°1, 1986, pp.11-17

Safety Assessment of Software Based Systems.

Gustav Dahll -
OECD Halden Reactor Project
P.O. Box 173, N-1751 Halden, Norway
E-mail: Gustav.Dahll@hrp.no

Abstract

Based on the experience gained during the licensing process of a computer based protection system, a framework for the safety assessment process of software based systems is formulated. The framework is made in the form of an influence net, where the top nodes in the graph represent the basic information sources. This information is penetrated through the net down to the bottom node representing the final acceptance of the system. A particular investigation is made on the possibility to apply FMECA on proprietary software modules.

Keywords: Safety assessment, Safety critical software, Configurable software, FMECA.

1. Introduction.

During the recent years there has been a trend to replace conventional electro-mechanical systems for the control of industrial plants with computer based systems. This also includes the use of computers in safety related tasks, e.g. in nuclear power plants and traffic control. There are many clear advantages of using programmable equipment in safety related systems in NPPs, compared to conventional equipment: But there has also been a certain reluctance to use programmable equipment in safety critical systems. A reason for this has been the complexity of safety assessment and the licensing of these systems, and in particular of the embedded software.

For a final acceptance of a system (computer based or other) with safety critical application, a thorough safety assessment of the system is necessary. In some fields, as e.g. in nuclear power, this is regulated by law, and a safety case must be put forward for the licensing authorities for each safety critical application.

The OECD Halden Project is an international institution with participation from 19 countries. A main research topic has been software dependability. Particular emphasis has been placed on software in safety critical systems. One of the activities has been to produce a guideline for reviewing and assessing safety critical software in nuclear power plants for the Swedish Nuclear Power Inspectorate (SKI). These Guidelines were applied in the licensing of the exchange of an analog protection system with a functionally equivalent programmable system (REPAC), in the Swedish nuclear power plant Ringhals. The new system is developed in what can be called a *configurable software system*. The program is build up by a tailor made application program, in a form similar to the graphical representation of the old analog system, and a set of standard software modules with the same functionality as the hardware components in the old system.

The Halden Project took part as consultants in the licensing process, and the experience gained from this work formed a basis for further considerations about the safety assessment process of a system partly based on proprietary software modules. This has been the basis for this paper.

A pragmatic approach concerning software based system is to combine all available information about the system into a framework for the safety assessment, and thereby for the final approval of the system. A such framework is discussed in section 2.

One method which was recommended, but not actually applied in the assessment of REPAC, was to apply Fault Tree Analysis (FTA) and Failure Mode, Effect and Criticality Analysis (FMECA) to the software. The application of these methods was, however, investigated later, as a research activity. The application of FMECA on proprietary software modules is discussed in section 3.

2. Safety Assessment Based on Multiple Evidences.

Figure 1 gives an illustration of the acceptance process for the software embedded in a computer based safety critical system. It has the form of an 'influence net', i.e. a directed graph where each node represents an aspect in the total assessment process. To each aspect there is associated an assessment (or belief or probability or a similar concept), and the strength of this is influenced by the strength of the nodes adjacent to the incoming edges.

The top nodes in the graph (rectangles) represent the basic information sources which are used in the acceptance process. This information is penetrated through the net down to the bottom node which represents the final acceptance of the system. The latter is mainly influenced by the safety assessment of the system, although there may also be other acceptance criteria. The safety assessment is influenced by a reliability assessment of the of the system, as well as by an evaluation of whether a failure in the system will jeopardise safety. This can be achieved through a hazard analysis of potential risks to plant and environment. Safety defences (both against hardware and software failures) may be implemented as an additional barrier against consequences of failures. A commonly used principle in this respect is diversity, i.e. to obtain the same functional goal through different means. The highest degree of diversity can be obtained if the same functional goal can be reached with completely different functions. This is essential to reach the safety goals of a safety critical system. For example, the REPAC protection system is divided into a number of protection channels which each performs a protective function, as e.g. a reactor trip, triggered by an initiating event, like e.g. loss of feedwater. The system is designed so that each initiating event is handled by at least two protection channels. As each protection channel is performed by a distinct processor one has obtained a complete functional diversity.

2.1 Reliability Assessment.

Reliability is according to standard terminology defined in probabilistic terms as the probability of failure free operation of a system over a specified time period. This definition may be adequate for hardware systems, where it can be estimated on the basis of statistical failure data of the components of the system. For software, however, such an estimation method is conceptually more complicated. A simple

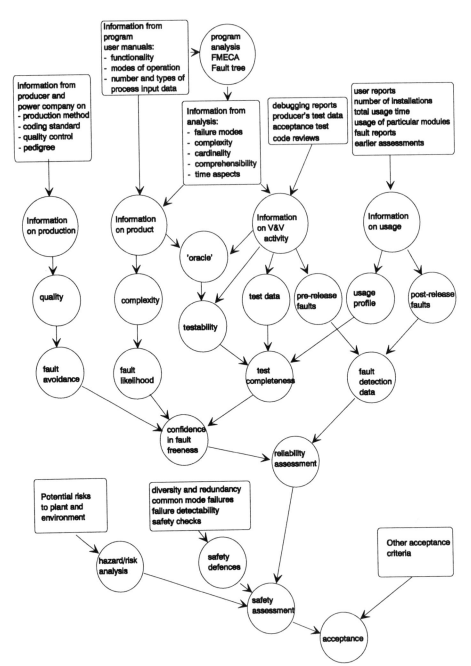

Fig. 1 Influence graph of a safety assessment and acceptance process.

estimate of the reliability could be based on a program test by dividing the number of failed tests with the number of executed tests. However, if a fault is revealed, the program would probably be corrected, and thus the reliability changed. And if no faults are found, such an estimate would not differentiate between no failures in 10 tests and no failures in a million tests.

There are, however, developed a variety of *reliability growth models*, which, based on the sequence of times between observed and repaired failures, calculate the reliability and current failure rate, and predict the time to next failure and required time to remove all faults. The general assumption of these models is that a single system is followed chronologically with recording of times to failure, and that the faults are corrected. This may be easy to achieve in the debugging and testing phase. However, the reliability figure obtained in this way estimates the failure probability if the real input profile is the same used in the testing. It is questionable, however, whether this gives a realistic estimate of the reliability in real applications, with a different input distribution.

A more realistic estimate is obtained if the data are collected during real operation. This could be obtained from user experience and failure reports on standard software modules in the post release period. A problem is that it is difficult to identify the chronological order of failures from such reports. Different faults are found by different users, who report them back to the producers. The same faults may also be found by different users. The producers will then usually collect the error reports and correct all the reported faults in the next program release, whereas the users will continue to use the faulty program, and possibly find new faults, until they get a new program release. None of the models take into account this realistic scenario.

Another problem with these methods is that they do not distinguish between different types of faults, e.g. between real faults and more cosmetic faults. It is of course a possibility to only take into account a particular class of faults. In this case, however, one may easily get an insignificant number of faults, in particular when one only takes into account critical faults. An alternative way to measure the reliability of a program with respect to a certain class of faults is to perform the reliability estimation with all types of faults and multiply this with the ratio between the number of faults in the particular class and the total number of faults.

A computer program implemented in a safety critical system contains presumably no known faults. There is, however, a possibility that it contain unknown faults, and an alternative reliability measure is the confidence in fault freeness of the program, or more generally in the upper limit of the 'bug-size'. Such a measure can be made on statistical basis from data obtained during testing of the complete program, as well as of the different modules. One set of data can be gained through a controlled testing combined with a coverage measure. The latter requires a fairly detailed knowledge about the program structure, which is not always available when proprietary software modules are used. For these, however, there may be an additional large set of 'test' data obtained from information about the usage of the system (see below).

A more qualitative type of measure is expressed as a subjective judgement, as a 'belief' in fault freeness. A methodology has been proposed to use Bayesian networks and engineering judgement to combine evidences from different information sources for a quantitative assessment of this belief [3], [4]. Some of these information sources are discussed in the following.

2.2 Information About Producer and Development Process.

The avoidance of faults in the program is clearly related to the quality of the development process of the software system. A lousy made program can of course be correct, but a well documented production procedure, in accordance with accepted standards, enhances the assessor's confidence in the reliability of the product. This confidence is also enhanced if the producer can document a history of producing high quality products.

To obtain a sufficiently high confidence in the quality, one should require that all parties involved in the development follow a quality assurance policy based on well-known standards for safety related systems (e.g. IEC 880 [1]). This may, however, be difficult when the proprietary software modules are concerned, since they are often delivered without appropriate information on the development process as well as on the final product itself. It may thus be difficult to assess whether the system has been developed according to the standards required for safety critical software. The experience from the REPAC project was that the system used was a fairly old system, which were developed before the presently available standards for safety related software were established. The development procedure was, however, documented, and a retrospective comparison of this procedure with several standards was documented, although the conformance with IEC-880 [1], which is very detailed, is hard to obtain in a retrospective analysis.

2.3 Information About the Programs.

Detailed information about the software is needed to assess the reliability of its application. One aspect is to identify structural properties of the program which makes it vulnerable to programming errors. Complexity is obviously one of these, i.e. the more complex a module is, the more likely it is that it contains coding faults. A main source of information about complexity can be gained through an analysis of the program listing. However, for proprietary software such listings are in general not available. It may be difficult to assess the complexity without this, but an indication on the complexity of the module can be seen from the complexity of the specification. A well structured and comprehensible explanation of the use of the module is also an indication of a well structured program.

A characteristic for the proprietary modules in a configurable software system is that they often have several modes of operation. A large number of operation modes will increase the complexity of the module as a whole. However, in an actual application only one operation mode is used, so one could ask whether only the complexity of the used mode is relevant. This depends upon how the selection of operation modes are coded in the module. Since one does not know the code it is difficult to know how it is done, but information about the producer's coding standard could be used in this respect.

A third aspect is the inherent complexity of the actual function itself. It is intuitively obvious that an adaptive controller is more complex to make, and therefore more error prone, than an AND gate, to take two extremes. One way to measure the inherent complexity of a module where one does not have access to the source code is to write it in a formal way, either as a program in high level language, or as a formal specification, and define a metric to measure the complexity.

Another way to analyse proprietary software modules is to apply FMECA (Failure Mode, Effect and Criticality Analysis) on them. This is discussed in more detail in section 3.

2.4. Information About Usage

'Proven design' is often used as an argument for high reliability by the producers of proprietary software system. This means that the system has been used by a wide range of users over a long period, with no, or few, reported faults. The idea behind this claim is that long user experience should reveal all inherent faults, if they exists. So if no faults have been reported over a long period, this should be a strong indication on error freeness. It is questionable, however, whether this argument is sufficient. A configurable software system has often a quite general purpose, and consists of many standard modules, each of which has many modes of operation. To claim general high reliability of the system based on user experience, it is necessary to show the experience with all modes of operation of all software modules. This requires information about all installations of the system.

Another aspect is the configurator, i.e. the program which is used to generate the application program and include the proprietary software modules (like compiler, configurator etc.). These are used only once per installation. To get a broad user experience with these programs it is necessary to have many installations. Information about the number of installations is therefore important for the reliability assessment of the configurator.

The number of versions of the proprietary software which are released is also relevant information. A new version implies changes in the system, and changes may have influence on its reliability. It is therefore relevant to know which changes have been made, or at least where the changes are made. In an actual application one should know whether any changes have been made in the software modules which are used in the application.

3. Application of FMECA on Proprietary Software.

The design of a system with configurable software is closely related to the way conventional hardware based systems are designed, i.e. in the form of a circuit diagram with standard components. It is tempting to investigate the possibility to apply reliability analysis methods used for such systems also on a configurable software program.

A commonly used technique in this respect is Failure Mode, Effect and Criticality Analysis (FMECA). An IEC standard for FMEA and FMECA is given in [2]. The basis for an FMECA analysis is a functional description of the analysed system, in terms of its components. For each of the components in the system all potential modes of failure are identified. Then, for each failure mode one makes an evaluation with respect to:

- the *failure mode*, i.e. how the failure manifest itself.

- the *failure cause*, which includes both immediate causes and more basic causes, as e.g. design errors.
- the *failure mechanism*, i.e. the mechanism which leads from the cause to the failure.
- the *failure effect*. One can here distinguish between *local effect*, which is the effect on the component in question and its immediate surroundings (e.g. failure mode: pump stop, effect: no flow), and the *end effects*, which are the effects the failure may have at the highest system level, i.e. on the plant and its environment.
- *failure detection*, i.e. the way the failure can be detected and the likelihood it will be detected.
- *failure probability*. This can be stated in qualitative terms (e.g. high, medium, low), or quantitative as probability of occurrence per time unit or per demand.
- *mean time to repair.*
- *failure criticality, i.e.* the consequences the failure may have on the safety at the plant or potential harm in the environment. One can also here distinguish between immediate consequences (e.g. radioactive release after a tube rupture), and more indirect consequences which are consequences of the end effects.

Traditionally FMECA has been considered for hardware components where failures occur randomly during operation, although design faults also are considered. As the components considered here are realised in software, only potential design (programming) errors which results in faults in the programs are taken into account in this connection. However, such faults can result in stochastic failures during program execution, due to randomness in the input data.

One problem in the application of FMECA to proprietary software modules is the lack of detailed information. In particular one needs a more or less detailed functional specification of each module. One available source of information can however be found in the set of user manuals. These contain descriptions of how each module is working, and from this it should be possible to deduce some kind of functional specification. In addition, one has some knowledge about the general characteristics of programmable systems. Altogether this should make it possible to perform, at least partially, a FMECA on the proprietary software modules.

The following contains some general considerations on each of the points mentioned above (except mean time to repair, which is irrelevant for these modules) with respect to standard software modules.

3.1 Failure Modes.

From the specification it should be possible to identify the correct output from a module in all situations, and further to identify all potentially incorrect outputs. Most failure modes can be classified into some main types:
- incorrect response (output)
- no response when it should occur
- correct response, but outside required time limits
- correct response, but undesired side effects

Depending on the functioning of the particular module to be analysed, these general failure mode types could be divided into more specific failure modes, e.g.:

- The result of a computation can be completely wrong, or only slightly inaccurate.
- The failure can occur in all executions of the module, or only in some cases, or perhaps only in very special cases.
- The algorithm used in the module is not applicable in the particular case.

Application on examples has shown that there is a multitude of possible failure modes which should be considered.

3.2 Failure Causes

When software failures are concerned, there are two main classes of causes, inherent faults in the software or incorrect use of the module. It is the first type one thinks of in connection with reliability of proprietary software. However, the second type is just as, or even more, important.

A further step is to look for more basic causes of inherent faults. These can be defects in the specification, programming errors, incorrect corrections, incorrect modifications in new releases etc. Even if one has limited information about the software modules, one should utilise all available information to reason about likely failure causes.

The causes of the second type are different. They can be faults in the application program, or it may misunderstandings of the functional specification of the module, due to incompleteness, ambiguity or direct faults in the user manual. Experience with user manuals supports the latter assumption. Anyhow, the user manual is available information which should be studied with respect to potential causes of this kind. A third potential cause of this type is a fault in the configurator.

3.3 Failure Mechanism

The failure mechanism concerning software failures is how a programming error can lead to a software fault and how a software fault can lead to an execution failure.

For an inherent fault the failure typically occurs when an actual input hits the failure domain of the faulty program. The most common faults to look for are those which cause wrong results. As discussed above, this type of failure mode can be divided into more specific ones, and there may be different failure mechanisms which lead to different types of failure modes. The most obvious and common failure mechanism is logical or structural faults in the program, which makes clearly incorrect results.

An approximation algorithm may be too inaccurate for a certain range of input data. One should in this case assess whether there is a reason to believe that an approximation algorithm is used in the module. One should also evaluate the effect of an inaccuracy in the result, in particular whether it is important for the safety of the system.

A mechanism which can lead to failures in rare cases can occur if the module uses an algorithm which contains singularities. If the inherent program does not contain special checks for such singularities, there is a risk that the program is incorrect for data close to the singularity. These data may constitute a very small portion of the input space, and the fault may therefore be difficult to detect during testing and by field experience.

A possible failure mechanism is integer overflow. E.g. in a limit check module the input value may suddenly increase so fast that it becomes negative, and thus is below the limit. This is an example of a failure mechanism which can lead to failures with low occurrence frequency.

Another important mechanism to look for is related to timing problems. Such faults that can lead to delays of responses, or no response at all. Information about real time properties of the system is therefore necessary. This includes information about the execution time: whether it is dependent on input data, whether it is dependent upon communicating processes etc. One can hopefully obtain information about these aspects from the user manual and other documentation on the configurable software system.

A particular failure mechanism to consider is when the result from a module is dependent on the result from previous execution(s) of the module. This is typical for modules representing transfer functions computed in the time domain, or modules which computes rates of changes. A particular failure mechanism here is incorrect initiation or incorrect resetting after system outage. One should therefore investigate whether the configurable software system has a special mechanism to handle this problem, or whether it must be handled by the programmer.

Another type of failure mechanism is related to the incorrect use of the system. A typical example is of course coding errors which lead to faults in the application program. Another aspect which is relevant for the propensity to make errors in the application program is the high degree of parametrisation of the standard modules which is typical of configurable software systems. An obvious failure mechanism is to make errors in the setting of these parameters, e.g. to make a wrong transformation of engineering units to internal values.

An incorrect use of the module in the application program is related to this latter failure mechanism. Even if it there is no direct mismatch between the actual program and the specification as given by the user manual, the manual can be incomplete and ambiguous and therefore easy to misunderstand. A general impression of such manuals is that if the application program is not made by an expert on the configurable software system, it is not improbable that misunderstandings can occur. However, even if the manual is clear and understandable the module can of course be used incorrectly. Clerical errors, as e.g. interchange of parameters, may easily occur.

Other types of failure mechanisms which may potentially occur can be found by investigation of the architecture of the configurable software system. One should in particular study real-time aspects as concurrent execution of processes and sharing of resources. Deadlocks, incorrect sequencing and other timing problems may occur. Another possible failure mode is inadvertent overwriting of shared data. There might also be faults in the error detection and correction program, which can cause random hardware errors not to be corrected. These types of failures should, however, be treated in an investigation of the configurable software system as a whole, and not in the analysis of the individual modules.

3.4 Failure Effects

It is in general only possible to identify local effects based on the module itself. The end effects must be found in context with the application program. Also the local effects are difficult to see separate from their actual use in an application program, but some effects might be seen on the basis of the functional specification of a module and general knowledge about its use. If for example the failure mode is 'no response', the immediate effect is that the module cannot pass control to the next module. This failure mode will then have an end effect which might be easy to see from a graphical representation of the program.

3.5 Failure Detection

This is a point where software modules have some clear advantages compared to their conventional counterparts. Software faults can be detected and removed during V&V and testing, and therefore make no harm. Inherent faults that remains can lead to failures that are detected during execution. As the detection of a failure is important to safety, it is possible to design failure detection facilities into the software system. These are mainly designed to trap hardware errors, but facilities also exists which detect failures caused by software faults. In the analysis for failure detection, one should look for possibilities and likelihood to detect them both before implementation and during execution. Concerning the latter, the possibility for fault tolerance is also interesting.

Some types of software failure detection facilities are already inherent in some configurable software systems, as e.g. watch dog timers to trap failures of non-termination. These could be identified in the FMECA activity. Others are designed into the application program and identified in the complete analysis of the system, e.g. by a fault tree analysis.

Detection of faults during testing is substantially simplified if there exists an 'oracle' which automatically can decide whether the result of a test is correct or not. In this case one may perform a large number of tests with automatic checking to obtain high detectability of any inherent fault. This is also related to the testability of the system.

3.6 Failure Probability.

When probability of failure is discussed, one should have in mind that there is a difference between the probability that there exists a fault in the program and the probability that a failure will occur during execution. The former probability is basically a measure on the amount of information one has about a program. The other includes both the probability of a fault and the probability that the input value is in the domain of this fault.

One can also distinguish between the probability that a fault is inserted into the program during programming or modifications, and the probability that a fault remains in the program and causes a failure during execution. The former relates to the quality of the program production, and also on the complexity of the module. The second relates to the testability of the system and the testing and other V&V effort, as well as the amount of field experience one has had with the module. Fault tolerance and the existence of fault checks, as e.g. time-out checks are also relevant information for the assessment of failure probabilities.

3.7 Failure Criticality.

Software does not harm anyone, so any immediate safety consequences of failures in the modules are not expected. The safety consequences could rather be found by an analysis, e.g. fault tree analysis, of the application program and its influence on the environment.

4. Conclusions.

The objective of this paper has been to utilise the experience gained during the licensing process of a computer based protection system to formulate a framework for the assessment process. This system was implemented with a configurable software system, i.e. a program is build up by an application program and a set of standard software modules, and emphasis has been made on particular aspects related to the assessment of the proprietary software modules.

The framework is made in the form of an influence net, i.e. a directed graph where each node represents an aspect in the total assessment process. The top nodes in the graph represent the basic information sources which are used in the acceptance process, whereas the bottom node represents the final acceptance of the system. The paper discussed how the various sources of information about these modules can be utilised through the net.

One aspect which was particularly emphasised was the possibility to apply FMECA on software modules. It was shown how one should utilise different sources of available information on proprietary software modules in the application of this analysis. The work also showed that there are some similarities, but mainly differences between this analysis and a similar analysis of hardware components.

References

[1] "Software for computers in the application of industrial safety related systems." IEC- publication 880, 1986.
[2] "Analysis Techniques for Systems Reliability - Procedures for Failure Mode and Effects Analysis (FMEA)", IEC publication 812, 1985.
[3] Neil M., Littlewod B.and Fenton N.: "Applying Bayesian Belief Networks to Systems Dependability Assessment" in Proceedings of the Fourth Safety-Critical Systems Symposium, Leeds, U.K., 6-8 February 1996, pp. 71-94. Published by Springer-Verlag.
[4] Delic K, Mazzanti M. and Strigini L.: "Formalising Engineering Judgement on Software Dependability via Belief Networks". Paper submitted to DCCA'97. Garmisch-Partenkirchen, Germany March 5-7, 1997

Safe and Reliable Computer Control Systems

an Overview

Henrik Thane
Mechatronics Laboratory, The Royal Institute of Technology,
Stockholm, Sweden
30 May 97
henrikt@damek.kth.se

Abstract

In a survey of the concepts and methods regarding reliability and safety in computer based systems the author [Thane96] came to the conclusion that software engineering is still immature as a discipline. Belief in now cliché "silver bullets" is ever claimed, even though their existence have been refuted several times during the last ten years. Even in more refined circumstances where the word dependability apply belief is central. The means by which dependability is achieved is *believed* to be a combination of fault free design, fault elimination and fault tolerance. The focus on belief shows that software engineering is still a craft. Belief is not good enough — we need to know. This paper stresses some points of what yet needs to be devised.

Key words: complexity, dependability, formal methods, test, fault tolerance, metrics, hazard analysis and safe design.

1 Introduction

Software in computer based control systems is ever increasing. Computer software and hardware replace more and more of the functionality of mechanical and electromechanical system parts. If the reliability of software was greater than the hardware parts it replaced nothing would be awry. Statistics indicate however, that the number of encountered errors per kilo lines of code for 'good' software has not decreased during the last decades [Hatton95], this in spite of more elaborate programming languages, tools, methodologies and education. One explanation might be that, yes we can make better software today using modern techniques, but at the same time the size and complexity of the applications have increased greatly — therefore making it more difficult to find all the errors.

'One can only show the presence of errors not their absence' —Djikstra

Contemplating this, it is not surprising that software has gained a reputation of always being late, expensive and foremost — erroneous. The traditional engineering disciplines are founded on science and mathematics, enabling modeling and prediction of different designs' behaviors. Software engineering to the contrary is rather a craft based on trial and error.

Why is that so? The reasons are that computers and software differ from regular physical systems on two key issues: (1) They have a discontinuous behavior and (2) software lack physical restrictions (like mass, energy, size, number of components), and lack structure or function related attributes (like strength, density and form).

The sole physical entity that can be modeled and measured by software engineers is **time**. Therefore, there exists sound work and theories regarding modeling and verification of systems' temporal attributes [Puschner89, Ramamritham90, Xu90, Törngren96].

In section 2 there is a list of statements regarding the effects of (1) and (2) and the principal means by which safe and reliable software can be produced today. The means are related to the concept of dependability [Laprie92]: **Fault avoidance** – How to build the system correctly from the beginning. **Fault removal** – How to reduce, by verification, the presence of faults. **Fault tolerance** – How to provide correct function despite presence of faults. **Fault forecasting** – Includes the evaluation of the consequences of faults and is in this paper focused on safety. Some points suggesting future research is also presented.

The failure vocabulary used in this document is: **fault → error → failure** [IEC1508, Laprie92].

2 Effects and means

2.1 Complexity

Having no physical limitations, complex software designs are possible and no real effort to accomplish this complexity is needed. Complexity is a source for design faults. Design faults are often due to failure to anticipate certain interactions between a system's components. As complexity increases, design faults are more prone to occur when more interactions make it harder to identify all possible behaviors.

2.1.1 Means: Abstraction and Modularity

All problems have a certain intrinsic complexity. The most formidable weapon against complexity is abstraction, a fundamental technique for understanding and solving problems. It allows us to concentrate on the general problem and disregard low-level details. Abstraction is of utmost importance, but should not as have been believed for the last decades be based on modular decomposition [Parnas72] in absurdum. Why? Recent studies [Hatton95] have shown that, for equivalent applications, many smaller modules, instead of fewer larger ones, have a greater tendency to failure. Why is that so? It is certain that abstraction, and divide and conquer, is necessary in order to deal with the inherent complexity of problems. But, to stop decompose a problem further when a sufficient level of understanding exists. If the problem (system) is further decomposed, just because of an old doctrine: that modular decomposition is a good principle, for example, it has been believed (and taught) that if an entire module's source code can be viewed on the screen at once it is a good module.

Certainly, if you do not decompose the problem into smaller modules it will be unmanageable: you cannot see *the forest because of all the trees*— the modules are to large. But, on the other hand just because you understand how each individual small module works it is not given that you understand how all the modules interact and how their joint behavior will manifest it self. Complexity will increase if the problem (system) is decomposed further than actually needed. This will implicitly lead to more faults.

Information hiding is another holy cow, that principally Object-Oriented methodology is based on. It sure increases abstraction, maintainability and reuse, but as certainly decreases testability [Voas95], and if used too zealously it increases complexity. And, does not necessarily lead to fewer faults [Hatton95].

So when does the designer know that he/she has decomposed enough, in order to get as high a reliability as possible?

2.2 No Safety Margins

A bridge can be designed to withstand loads far greater than any it should encounter during normal use. Software on the contrary, must for example, if controlling a brain surgery robot do things exactly right. This adheres to software not being a physical entity (it is pure design) it cannot be worn-out or broken. All system failures due to errors in the software are all design-faults; built into the system from the beginning.

2.2.1 Means: Fault tolerance — Robust Designs

Robust systems are designed to cope with unexpected inputs, changed environmental conditions and errors in the model of the external system. A robust design can for example, be a servo feedback loop in a control system.

Generally, software is not designed to be robust since focus is primarily on what the system should do, and not on what it should not do; as a consequence testing (usually) does not cover abnormal inputs or outputs.

In order for a system to be robust, its state machine must satisfy the following [Leveson95,pp.373]: (1) Every state must have a behavior (transition) defined for every possible input. (2) The logical *OR* of the conditions on every transition out of any state must form a tautology. A tautology is a logically complete expression, i.e., always true. (3) Every state must have a software behavior (transition) defined in case there is no input for a given period of time (a time-out or likely in a real-time system – exception upon deadline violation).

Applying robust design to accommodate for design flaws is not satisfactory. It can be applied however: every software module has a set of pre-conditions and post-conditions to ensure that nothing *impossible* happens. The pre-conditions must be valid when entering the software module and the post-conditions must be valid at the exit of the module. If these conditions are violated the program should do something *sensible.* The problem is that if the *impossible* does happen, then the design must be deficient and a *sensible* local action might have a very suspect global effect. This is intrinsic to all interacting complex systems. A local event might have a very global effect. This method is however excellent when debugging a system trying to find residual faults.

2.2.2   Means: Fault tolerance — Redundancy

Physical parts can always succumb to manufacturing defects, wear, environmental effects or physical damage. Thus, it is a good idea to have spares handy that can replace defective components. In order for a redundant system to function properly it must by all means avoid common mode failures. For example, two parallel data communication cables were cut 1991 in Virginia, USA. The Associated Press (having learned from earlier incidents, had concluded that a spare could be a good idea) had requested two separate cables for their primary and backup circuits. Both cables were cut at the same time, because they were adjacent [Neuman95,p.16]. Design faults are *the* source for common mode failures, so fault tolerance against design faults seems futile. Adaptations of the redundancy concept have however, been applied to software, principally they are: *N*-version programming (NP) and Recovery Blocks (RB) [Kim94], and uses multiple versions of dissimilar software produced from a common specification. Utilizing NP, the *N* versions are executed in parallel and their results are voted upon. In the RB case, the different versions are executed in sequence or terminated, depending on if the previously executed version satisfied an acceptance test. Empirical studies have, unfortunately concluded that the benefit of using *N*-version programming is questionable [Knight90, Knight86]. Why? Both approaches suffer from the same major flaw: they try to compensate for design faults using diverse design. They will thus not be able to recuperate from faults in the requirements specification and are likely to be afflicted by common mode faults relating to how people think in general.

An aside. The author has held lectures on several occasions where the attendees were asked to be a part of a trivial N-version programming experiment. In total 60 people have participated. A simple problem was to be solved. They were asked to design a function that should return what kind of triangle three integers (A,B,C) formed. Where $f(A,B,C) \subseteq \{$isosceles, equilateral, scalene$\}$

They got 10 minutes to solve the problem. Then a trace commenced with numbers like (2,2,3) = isosceles, (4,5,6) = scalene, (7,7,7) = equilateral. But, when we tried (2,3,10) all but 2 out of 60 answered scalene — such triangles does not exist in Euclidean geometry. We also tried (0,0,1) and (1,3,0) and all but a few failed. The attendees then protested that this information was not included in the specification — which was exactly the whole point.

2.3 Effects on Verification and Validation

The task of considering all system behaviors and all the circumstances it might encounter during operation might be intractable. Physical systems can be tested and measured. There often exist piece-wise continuous relationships between the input and the output of a system. Only a few tests, for each continuous piece, needs to be performed. The behavior of the system intermediate to the samples can be interpolated. Thus the number of behaviors to be considered is reduced. However, it is not possible, in general, to assume that computer and software behavior is continuous: quantization[1] errors are propagated and boundaries to the representation of numbers can affect the output. Equally influential is the fact that software's execution path changes for every decision depending on whether or not a condition is true. For example, a simple sequential list of 20 if-statements may, in the *worst* case, yield 2^{20} different behaviors due to 2^{20} possible execution paths. A small change in the input can have a severe effect on which execution path is taken, which in turn may yield an enormous change in output [Rushby95b].

2.3.1 Mean: fault elimination with formal methods

Just as traditional engineers can model their designs with different kinds of continuous mathematics, formal methods attempt to supply the computer software engineers with mathematical logic and discrete mathematics as a tool.

Formal methods can be put to use in two different ways [Barroca92]: (1) They can be used as a syntax to describe the semantics of specifications which are later used as a basis for the development of systems in an ordinary way. (2) Formal specifications can be produced as stated by (1) and then used as a fundament for verification (proof) of the design (program).

If (1) and (2) are employed it is possible to prove equivalency of program and specification, i.e., to prove that the program does what it is specified to do. This stringency gives software development the same degree of certainty as a mathematical proof [Barroca92].

Unfortunately a proof (when possible) cannot guarantee correct functionality or safety. In order to perform a proof the *correct* behavior of the software must first be specified in a formal, mathematical language. The task of specifying the correct behavior can be as difficult and error-prone as writing the software [Leveson86,Leveson95]. In essence the difficulty comes from the fact that we cannot know if we have accurately modeled the "real system", so we can never be certain that the specification is complete. This distinction between model and reality attends all applications of mathematics in engineering. For example, the "correctness" of a control loop calculation for a robot depends on the fidelity of the control loop's dynamics to the real behavior of the robot, on the accuracy of the stated requirements, and on the extent to which the calculations are performed without error.

These limitations are however, minimized in engineering by empirical validation. Aeronautical engineers believe fluid dynamics accurately models the air flowing over the wing of an airplane, because it has been validated in practice many times

---

[1] Research in the field of discrete feedback control theory have however, dealt with the problem of quantization errors.

[Rushby95a,pp.284]. Validation is an empirical pursuit to test that a model accurately describes the real-world. The same dual process applies to computer science where it is better known as verification and validation (V&V). Verification and validation goes hand in hand and does not exclude one another.

Nonetheless, using formal methods to verify correspondence between specification and design does seem like a possible pursuit to gain confidence. The fact that more than half of all failures can be traced to the requirements and specifications [Leveson95, Lutz92, DeMarco78, Ell95] gives the application of formal methods some weight. Using mathematical verification of software to any great extent is however currently intractable, but will probably be feasible in the future. Formal methods, as of today, are exceedingly abstract and non intuitive, requiring extensive training of the users. There exists over 300 kinds of formal methods and notations, so there definitively is a lack of consensus in the formal methods community [Shankar96]. Most safety-critical systems are in essence multi-disciplinary, which requires all stakeholders of a project to communicate with each other. Formal methods must thus be made more easy to comprehend and use.

Further, disadvantages with current formal methods are their inability to handle timing and resource inadequacies, like violation of deadlines and overload. There are yet again, other methods that can complement formal methods with verification of timing, e.g., execution time analysis [Puschner89] and scheduling [Ramamritham90,Xu90].

Formal methods are no silver bullets. They are not *the single solution*. Formal methods in general, like other informal methods (SA/SD, OOA/OOD) does impose discipline on the users and make them think in rational and disciplined ways – helping to increase understandability, finding problems and in boosting confidence.

2.3.2   Mean: fault removal

Software does not wear out over time. It is therefore reasonable to assume that as long as faults are uncovered reliability increases for each fault that is eliminated. This notion of course relies on maintenance not introducing new faults. [Littlewood 73] elaborated on this idea and developed their reliability growth model. According to the reliability growth model the failures are distributed exponentially. Initially a system fails frequently but after faults are discovered and amended the frequency of failures decreases.

A problem with this method is that it would take years to remove a sufficient amount of errors to achieve a critical standard of reliability. For safety-critical systems where the failure rate is required to be lower than 10^{-9} failures per hour this is an intractable task [Fenton95] since testing has to be performed for at least 115 000 years.

What makes matters even worse is the fact that more than half of the errors in a system are due to ambiguous or incomplete requirement specifications. The intention of testing is often to verify that a specific input will yield a specific output, defined by the *specification*. Thus the confidence gained by testing software is limited.

Just like formal methods, testing cannot be the *sole* mean to gain assurance in a safety-critical system. When dynamic verification (testing) and static verification (e.g., formal methods) are used to augment each other, testing should focus on validation of the formal model of the system [Rushby95a,pp.284], and on timing and overload issues, which are difficult to verify with static analysis [Leveson95, pp. 495].

2.3.3 Mean: Assessment

Achieving reliability and safety is hard, but what is even tougher is assessing those qualities [Voas95].

Software which is pure design is deterministic, i.e., for specific circumstances (input, time, environment and internal state) the computer will always deliver the same output. If an error is afflicting the software it will always lead to a failure if the wrong circumstances arise. The occurrence of a circumstance is however not deterministic, but related to a stochastic process – namely the sequence of inputs and interactions with the environment. The manifestation of an error – the failure, does thus lend it self to be assigned a probability of occurrence. To say that a piece of software has a failure probability rate of maximum 10^{-9} failures per hour is to say that the probability for a specific input sequence to occur, leading to a failure is less than 10^{-9} per hour.

There are limits to the extent that experimental statistical methods allow us to gain confidence in computer based systems. The smallest failure rates that practically can be asserted are several magnitudes off the 10^{-9} that is required in safety-critical systems[Rushby95b]:

It is difficult to construct good test-profiles. Test scenarios used to evaluate reliability must be good approximations of the operational profile, i.e., the types, frequencies and distributions of inputs that a system receives during operation.

- To evaluate systems with, for example, a 10^{-9} requisite, millions of very rare scenarios that each and every one only occur once every billion times must be devised. The reason is that catastrophic failures usually happen when several very rare events occur at the same time. The mismatch between the test- and operational profiles in these remote areas can lead to an awry understanding of a system's reliability.

- The difficulty to reproduce the operational profile for rare events and the time required to perform fault-injection and "all-up" tests, limits the failure rates that can be verified empirically to about 10^{-4}.

The problem of assessing the quality of software has lead people to believe in approved processes, i.e., processes producing correct software. The problem however, is how to assess the process. It might be harder to verify that the process always produces the correct software than to verify the correctness of the process product — the software. There are mathematical proofs stating that an automata (a program) cannot decide if any arbitrarily chosen automata will ever terminate

[Turing36]. This has the implication that it is not possible to verify that a process will always produce the correct result given any problem.

2.4 Effects on Safety

Safety is a property of a system just like reliability. When estimating software reliability every failure is considered. Reliabilitywise these are equivalent: (1) A failure resulting in an 'A' on the computer screen instead of a 'B'. (2) A failure in a control system for an aircraft causes the plane to crash. Reliability only quantifies the frequency of failures, disregarding the consequences of a failure. From a safety point of view it is important to consider the consequences of failures, especially the failures that lead to hazards.

Example 1. A weapon system should destroy and kill. The property that the system destroys and kills is a reliability property. The property that the software in the weapon system does not destroy and kill friendly forces is a safety property [Voas95].

Example 2. Assume that the system properties described in previous example are valid. If a torpedo is not launched it is safe but not reliable. If a torpedo is fired, misses the foe and does a U-turn and destroys the submarine which launched it, it is reliable but not safe [Voas95].

It can be argued however, that the requirements are faulty in the examples if this is allowed to happen. Usually requirements are stated in terms of shall-criteria and not in shall-not-criteria.

The intention of testing is often to verify that a specific input will yield a specific output, defined by the *specification*. Thus the confidence gained by testing software is limited. It is not possible to disclose faulty or incomplete specifications by testing. The specification can be hazardous, when requirements regarding safety have been omitted. Preferably all safety requirements should be included in the specifications. It would then be possible to show that all accidents are failures. Safety related failures would then be a subset of all system failures. But, again the primary cause of systematic failures are wanting and ambiguous requirements. Software can be 100% correct yet still cause serious accidents.

Software by it self is not hazardous. It can be conceived that software will be hazardous when executed on a computer, but even then there exists no real danger. A computer does actually nothing else than generating electrical signals. In reality it is first when the computer and the software starts monitoring and controlling physical components that hazards can occur. *Thus safety is a system property and not a software property.*

2.4.1 Means: Hazard analysis and Safe Design

In order to design and assert that a safety-critical system is not only correct with respect to functionality but also safe, a hazard analysis ought to be undertaken. A hazard analysis determines what hazards are afflicting the system as a whole. Some methods for finding hazards are FMEA, HAZOP and checklists [Leveson95, pp. 313]. When a list of hazards has been found, a cause-effect analysis can commence. A method for finding the causal factors of hazards is Fault Tree Analysis (FTA). When a causal factor has been deemed originating in software, a Software Fault Tree Analysis (SFTA) can be employed. It verifies if the software can or cannot put the system in a hazardous state.

To design a safe system it is not sufficient to only identify the hazards in a system, the knowledge of their existence must also be taken advantage of during system design. The goal is to eliminate the existence of hazards to the lowest reasonably practical level (the ALARP principle – As Low As Reasonably Practical). When the hazards cannot be eliminated, try to reduce the impact of their existence, or when that is not possible at least try to control the hazards. There are several safety design principles that apply to computer based systems [Leveson95, pp. 395]. A virtue however, is to design safety into the system from the beginning rather than to add safety on. It will be both cheaper and more effective.

3 Conclusion

Since computer related problems, relating to safety and reliability, have just recently been of any concern for engineers, there exists no holistic engineering knowledge on how to construct a safe and reliable computer based system. There exists only bits and pieces of engineering knowledge and no silver bullets that can handle everything. Some people do nonetheless with an almost religious glee, decree that their method, principle or programming language handles or kills all werewolves (bugs). Alleged silver bullets are, e.g., formal methods, fault tolerance and testing. However, there are empirical evidence and logical arguments implying that they by themselves are not sufficient in providing the assurance level required of safety-critical systems [Hatton95, Rushby95b, Leveson95].

The next logical step would thus be to apply them in some combination, or even all at once. Then we certainly would achieve the required level of confidence!?

David Parnas has stated what should be required of safety-critical software. He calls it the tripod[Parnas95]:

1. Precise, organized, mathematical documentation and extensive systematic review.

2. Extensive testing.

   - Systematic testing – quick discovery of gross errors.

   - Random testing – discovery of shared oversights and reliability assessment.

3. Qualified people and approved process

According to Parnas the three legs are complementary, although the last one is the shortest.

One could actually stop here and say that the way to go is as Parnas and Bowen [Bowen92] proclaim: use a combination of fault avoidance, fault tolerance, fault removal and hazard analysis. Then and only then the desired level of reliability and safety will be achieved. But by doing so we lend ourselves the comfort of belief again. We do not know – at least not yet, what is the ultimate combination of approaches and methods.

This necessity of belief (not knowledge) in a concept or method shows that software engineering is unconsummated as a discipline. Software engineering is still a craft.

There are two stages in the early years of a new technology [Leveson92]: (1) the exploration of the space of possible approaches and solutions to problems, i.e., invention and (2) the evaluation of what has been learned by this trial and error process to formulate hypotheses that can be scientifically and empirically tested in order to build the scientific foundations of the technology. Most of the efforts done within the software engineering discipline have so far been emphasized on the first stage, i.e., invention.

But, we do not need yet another tool for specification of designs. What we need is to devise and validate fundamental design principles, and to understand the tradeoffs between them.

We need to establish a set of measures and metrics for software which has an empirical foundation, i.e., based not on frivolous assumptions, but on empirical data. We should try to find a measure capturing the arbitrary complexity of software and relate this complexity to reliability. We need to compare different designs' attributes and judge whether a design is better or worse than another. If this works we will be able to analyze the alleged silver bullets and perhaps refute or confirm them once and for all. And, finally relevant design principles might emerge.

Hatton [Hatton95] has given it a try and come up with some interesting results.

Summing up: If we have a theoretical foundation it can provide [Leveson92]: (1) Criteria for evaluation, (2) means of comparison, (3) theoretical limits and capabilities, (4) means of prediction, and (5) underlying rules, principles and structure.

If we can establish this foundation we will finally be able to model, compare and predict the behavior of our designs and thus transform software engineering from a craft into an engineering discipline.

4 References

[Barroca92]   L Barroca and J McDermid. Formal Methods: Use and Relevance for Development of Safety-Critical Systems. The Computer Journal, Vol. 35, No. 6, 1992.

[Bowen92]   J Bowen and V Stavridou. Safety-Critical Systems, Formal Methods and Standards. Software Engineering Journal, 1992.

[DeMarco78]   T DeMarco. Structured Analysis and System Specification. Yourdon Press 1978. ISBN 0-917072-07-3

[Ell95]   A. Ellis. Achieving Safety in Complex Control Systems. Proceedings of
               the Safety-Critical Systems Symposium. Pp. 2-14. Brighton, England,
               1995. Springer-Verlag. ISBN 3-540-19922-5

[Fen95]   N E Fenton. The Role of Measurement in Software Safety Assessment.
               12th Annual CSR Workshop, Bruges 12-15 September 1995. Proceedings,
               pp. 217-248. Springer. ISBN 3-540-76034-2.

[Hatton95]   L. Hatton. Unexpected (and sometimes unpleasant) Lessons from Data in
               Real Software Systems. 12th Annual CSR Workshop, Bruges 12-15
               September 1995. Proceedings, pp. 251-259. Springer. ISBN 3-540-76034-
               2.

[Kim94]   K.H. Kim. Design of Real-Time Fault-Tolerant Computing Stations. Real-
               Time Computing ,Edt W. Halang A. Stoyenko, Springer Verlag, Nato
               ASI series, volume 127, page 31-46.

[Knight86]   Knight J. C. and N. G. Leveson. An experimental evaluation of the
               assumptions of independence in multi-version programming. IEEE
               Transactions on Software Engineering, page 96-109, January 1986.

[Knight90]   Knight J. C. and N. G. Leveson. A reply to the criticism of the Knight and
               Leveson experiment. ACM SIGSOFT Software engineering Notes, 15, p.
               25-35, January 1990.

[Laprie92]   J.C. Laprie. Dependability: Basic Concepts and Associated Terminology.
               Dependable Computing and Fault-Tolerant Systems, vol. 5, Springer
               Verlag, 1992.

[Leveson86]   N. G. Leveson. Software safety: What, why and How. Computing surveys,
               18(2),1986

[Leveson92]   N. G. Leveson. High Pressure Steam Engines and Computer Software.
               The Int. Conference on software engineering, Melbourne, Australia, May
               1992.

[Leveson95]   N. G. Leveson. Safeware System, Safety and Computers. Addison Wesley
               1995. ISBN 0-201-11972-2.

[Littlewood73] B Littlewood et. al. A Bayesian Reliability Growth Model For Computer
               Software. Journal of the Royal Statistical Society, Series C, No. 22, p 332-
               346, 1973

[Lutz92]   R. R. Lutz. Analyzing software requirements errors in safety-critical,
               embedded systems. In software requirements conference, IEEE, January
               1992.

[Neuman95]   P G Neuman. Computer Related Risks. ACM Press, Adison-Wesley,
               1995. ISBN 0-201-55805-x.

[Parnas72]   D.L. Parnas. On the Criterion To Be Used in Decomposing Systems into
               Modules. The Communications of the ACM. Pp. 1053-1058. Vol. 15, no.
               12. 1972

[Parnas95]   D Parnas. Connecting theory with practice. Communication Research
               Laboratory, Software engineering group. McMaster University, Canada,
               November 4, 1995.

[Puschner89]   P. Puschner, C. Koza. Calculating the maximum execution time of real-
               time programs. Journal of Real-time systems 1(2), Pp. 159-176,
               September, 1989.

[Ramamritham90] K. Ramamritham. Allocation and scheduling of complex periodic tasks. In
               10th international conference on distributed computing systems. Pp. 108-
               115. 1995.

[Rushby95a]   J Rushby. Formal Specification and Verification for Critical systems: Tools, Achievements, and prospects. Advances in Ultra-Dependable Distributed Systems. IEEE Computer Society Press. 1995. ISBN 0-8186-6287-5.

[Rushby95b]   J Rushby. Formal methods and their Role in the Certification of Critical Systems. 12th Annual CSR Workshop, Bruges 12-15 September 1995. Proceedings, pp. 2-42. Springer. ISBN 3-540-76034-2.

[Shankar96]   N. Shankar. Unifying Verification Paradigms. At the 4th international symposium on Formal Techniques in Real-Time and Fault-Tolerant Systems. Uppsala, Sweden, September 1996. Lecture Notes in Computer Science, no. 1135. Springer. ISBN 3-540-61648-9

[Thane96]   H. Thane. Safe and Reliable Computer Control Systems - Concepts and Methods. Research Report TRITA-MMK 1996:13, ISSN 1400-1179, ISRN KTH/MMK/R-96/13-SE. Mechatronics Laboratory/Department of Machine Design, the Royal Institute of Technology, S-100 44 Stockholm, Sweden,1996.

[Turing36]   A. M. Turing. On Computable Numbers with an Application to the entscheidungs problem. Proceedings London Mat. Society, 2:42, pp. 23-265, 1936.

[Törngren96]   M. Törngren. Fundamentals of Implementing Real-Time Control Applications in Distributed Computer Systems. To appear in the Journal of Real-Time Systems, Kluwer,1996.

[Voas95]   J M Voas, et.al. Software Assessment: Reliability, Safety, testability. Wiley Interscience, 1995. ISBN 0-471-01009-x.

[Xu90]   J. Xu, D. Parnas. Scheduling process with release times, deadlines, precedence and exclusion relations. IEEE transactions on software engineering, vol. 16, no. 3, March 1990.

Towards Dependable Software Requirement Specifications

Stefan Scheer, Joint Research Centre of the EC - Institute for Systems, Informatics and Safety, Ispra, Italy

Thomas Maier, Daimler-Benz AG, F1M/IV, Stuttgart, Germany

ABSTRACT

Formal proof of potential software failures early in the lifecycle can both significantly enhance safety and reduce development costs. The use of appropriate structured methods will provide developers with early indications of safety related design failures. Moreover such methods will generate a superset of possible software failure behaviour to support detection of hidden faults.

The use of a functional model is proposed in order to describe functional interdependencies among software components. An analysis of what might go wrong during communication between one component and another helps to set up a list of maximal possible failure modes, their effects and possible explanations. Thus a complete input to well-established "classical" techniques as FMEA and FTA applied to software systems can be provided.

The applicability of the methodology described is demonstrated on parts of the functional specification of a robot control system.

1 Introduction

System functionality will mainly be determined in the first two phases of a software lifecycle: the capturing of user requirements and their correct analysis and interpretation in form of software requirements. Recent research strongly suggests the execution of safety-relevant development tasks and the incorporation of safety issues during these phases [1, 2]. We focus our work on the second phase where specifications usually are closer to formalisms and where first structures of the final product arise.

As in classical safety analysis (e.g. [3]) we propose to check a model of the artefact thus enhancing feedback mechanisms for requirements modifications. A structured model and a pre-established set of possible failure behaviour will be an excellent basis for a thorough search on hidden faults or potential mis-behaviour. Through [4] a well-established model of software functionality is prescribed which ideally supports such a search.

When analysing and interpreting the user requirements the ESA PSS-05 standard proposes the construction of a so-called Logical Model, or what we will term a functional model (of the software); this model is then used in order to produce a structured list of software requirements (within the software requirements document). The functional model is hierarchically layered and uses pre-defined symbols for description. The model grows by continuously splitting the system's basic functions ("Functional Decomposition"). This will be completed when its functions cover all the user-defined capabilities. Each function should fulfil a single and limited purpose described within the function description.

The functional model represents software as a set of elementary functions that communicate with each other through control and data flows. Generally, we consider each communication as an exchange of a message. A function failure manifests itself either through sending faulty or undesired messages or through a failure to send a message. Undesired and faulty messages may also be generated by correct functional behaviour if the function contains or is a consequence of a design error.

Function-related failures may have consequences in the functional model only along data and control flows, i.e., consequences only on other functions. Failures are transmitted in this model when functions themselves receive faulty messages and therefore transmit messages that are faulty. It is therefore pertinent to investigate the ways in which messages may be incorrect or faulty.

It seems that certain concepts appear steadily supposed we have a sound basis of software requirements descriptions. A methodology can be worked out which will work on a quite abstract level of description, and which will generate appropriate input for both FMEA and FTA applicable to software systems. In distinction to Leveson's pure software directed approach of SFTA (Software Fault Tree Analysis) [5] we will not investigate on program level. Our approach is - in accordance with what has been done in hardware safety analysis - to proceed on a software communication model which shows logical relationships (instead of physical ones) and which reasons upon behaviour deviations within this model.

2 The Failure Behaviour of Software Defined in the Functional Model

A software requirement specification defines software functions whose tasks can be described generally:

- reception of messages,
- checking names, origins, contents, and recipients of messages,
- transmission of incoming or newly created messages.

Additional tasks are data-oriented:

- choosing and reading of data attached to messages,
- doing calculations with data and generating new data,
- attaching newly created data to messages to be forwarded.

In the case of a real-time software system the above mentioned

- tasks are done after a certain time period, at a certain time or when a certain event has occurred; they may even be repeated with a certain frequency.

Summarising we can derive the following software-function failure categories, i.e., failure modes (FM):

> FM-1:   Communication Failure

The failure lies in non-acceptance, in faulty checking or interpretation of arriving messages, or in non-transmission of old or new messages.

> FM-2:   Data Processing Failure

The failure lies in faulty or neglecting choice, input, calculation, generation, or attachment of data.

> FM-3:   Timing Failure

The failure lies in early or late, too fast or too slow, too frequent or too infrequent execution of actions.

Categorisations of failure modes can be found in many papers; categorisations similar to those above may be found in [6, 7, 8, 9, 10].

As messages sent elsewhere may have consequences for the recipient we can also categorise the effects of sending of messages. In accordance with the above mentioned failure modes we distinguish between the following failure mode effects (FME):

> FME-1:   Missing Message

A message cannot be sent or is not sent to the recipient; consequently the recipient does not receive it.

> FME-2:   Undesired Message

A message is sent to the recipient although it should not be, or a message is sent to a wrong recipient. Consequently the recipient receives an undesired message.

> FME-3:   Faulty Message

A message which contains data is correctly sent but with incorrect data. Consequently the recipient receives a faulty message.

> FME-4:   Untimely Message

A message is sent but at the wrong time. Consequently the recipient receives the message too early or too late.

The relationship between failure mode and failure mode effect categories is represented in Table 1 (bracketed X's require a message to contain data):

	FME-1	FME-2	FME-3	FME-4
FM-1	**X**	**X**	**(X)**	
FM-2			**(X)**	
FM-3				**X**

Table 1 (relationship failure mode - failure mode effect)

In this way a communication-based failure mode can result in missing a message or in having an undesired message at the recipient; in the case that data exists even a faulty message may arrive at the recipient.

The quite straight-forward approach of looking at possible failure modes and their effects can be compared with a more transmission-oriented approach. Until now we have just considered what might go wrong within a functional specification component when it should send a message to another component. The "history" - under what circumstances one or more messages are launched - was not taken into account. The condition(s) which make valid the sending of messages can be a reinforcement of previous failures. Here we can think of condition(s) to be false although they should not be. To be exact, however, it's also possible to have condition(s) true although they should not be. A failure transmission behaviour categorisation arises as follows:

FTB-1:   Condition not fulfilled:

A necessary condition is not fulfilled because of one or more missing, undesired, faulty or untimely incoming messages. The message is not sent although it should be.

FTB-2:   Condition fulfilled:

A condition may be fulfilled due to one or more missing, undesired, faulty or untimely incoming messages. A message is sent as a consequence of faulty facts fulfilling a condition.

The effects of both possible failure transmission behaviours (FTE) are similar to the above mentioned failure modes effects. For FTB-1 only one effect can be seen: the message is not sent therefore the message is missing (FTE-1) at the recipient. For FTB-2, however, three effects are identified: the message is sent and will therefore be undesired (FTE-2), faulty (FTE-3) or untimely (FTE-4) when it arrives at the recipient.

Table 2 summarises the relationship between failure transmission behaviours and their effects; again the brackets demand the existence of data:

	FTE-1	FTE-2	FTE-3	FTE-4
FTB-1	X			
FTB-2		X	(X)	X

Table 2 (relationship between failure transmission behaviour and possible effects)

Readers familiar with FMEA and FTA techniques will see the strong relationship between FM/FME and what should be used within FMEA, and FTB/FTE and the type of information used for FTA, respectively. Failure modes and their effects can directly be taken as input to a FMEA, while failure transmission behaviour and its effects enable the construction of fault trees within a FTA.

A model of failure behaviour is derived by accomplishing the single functional descriptions (or software requirements) with their failure modes and failure transmission behaviours. If this is applied to each functional specification we will not only get a complete model of failure behaviour but also be able to approach automation of this work. The model will produce supersets of potential behaviour thus enhancing safety analysis input and contributing to product quality. With automation the elaboration of complex systems is facilitated; on the other side, however, it requires formatted software requirements as input.

3 Systematic Retrieval of Failure Behaviour

The task of a software function can be summarised as a set of messages each sent under certain conditions and each sent to other software functions or HW/SW interfaces. Thus a software requirement may be expressed by the following abstract statement:

IF $<condition_1>$ THEN send $<message(s)_1>$

ELSE IF $<condition_2>$ THEN send $<message(s)_2>$

ELSE IF ...

...

$$(1)$$

ELSE IF $<condition_{N-1}>$ THEN send $<message(s)_{N-1}>$

ELSE send $<message(s)_N>$

with $<condition_1> \neq <condition_2> \neq ... \neq <condition_{N-1}>$.

Note: The meta-condition means that each single 'condition' is semantically different from the others.

Each 'condition' is a logical combination of the results of previously executed actions and messages. For example;

a) Checking the validity of a message.

b) Calculating a value.

c) Waiting for a certain period etc.

Outgoing messages, together with their destinations, are described by the 'send message' parts with multiple messages linked with an AND.

3.1 Retrieval of Failure Modes

We can focus on single 'send IF' expressions because they are exclusive and can be treated independently during derivation of failure modes. The set of failure modes of a software requirement is the sum of failure modes of its 'send-IF' expressions.

First we start from a single 'send-IF' expression, for example

$$
\text{send} <\text{message(s)}_i> \text{ IF } <\text{condition}_i>
$$

$$
\text{with } i \in \mathbb{N} \tag{2}
$$

whose message part can - in more detail - be written as

$$
\begin{aligned}
&\text{send } m_{i1} \text{ (with } val_{i1}) \text{ to } SR_{i1} \\
&\text{AND } m_{i2} \text{ (with } val_{i2}) \text{ to } SR_{i2} \\
&\quad \ldots \\
&\text{AND } m_{ij} \text{ (with } val_{ij}) \text{ to } SR_{ij} \\
&\text{IF } <\text{condition}_i>
\end{aligned} \tag{3}
$$

with (*) $i \in \mathbb{N}$, (**) $i1, \ldots, ij, j \in \mathbb{N}$ and

(***) $\forall j,k: \in \mathbb{N}: j \neq k$ AND ($m_{ij} \neq m_{ik}$ IF $val_{ij} = val_{ik}$ AND $SR_{ij} = SR_{ik}$)

where the m_{ij}'s are outgoing messages, val_{ij}'s are optional values (data), and SR_{ij}'s are recipients (software requirement). No further investigation is done here on the condition part.

In accordance with the relationships shown in Table 1 between failure mode categories and potential effects, the following points should be considered:

1. For each m_{xj} there are two category 1 failure modes ("Communication Failures"):

   m_{xj} is sent although the necessary condition is not **fulfilled (m_{xj} (with val_{xj}) sent to SR_{xj} IF ¬<condition>)** and

   m_{xi} is not sent although the necessary condition is fulfilled (**m_{xj} (with val_{xj}) not sent to SR_{xj} IF <condition>**).

   Depending on the complexity of the underlying condition these "main" failure modes can be split into several elementary failure modes.

2. The effect of the first failure mode is m_{xj} **UNDESIRED at SR_{xj}**.

3. The effect of the second failure mode is m_{xj} (with val_{xj}) **MISSING at SR_{xj}**.

4. If there are data attached the additional effect m_{xj} with val_{xj} **FAULTY at SR_{xj}** has to be considered for both failure modes. It has to be decided whether it might be correct to send the message although it has the wrong data attached (because a certain incoming message carries wrong data). Such a decision is prevalent when regularly and continuously (i.e., without triggering condition) messages with data have to be sent and whose data vary according to the incoming messages. Example: The velocity vector of a motion component must be set to zero if an emergency stop message comes in.

5. Category 2 ("Data Processing Failures") failure modes exist only for data-transporting messages (i.e., with the keyword "with val_{xj}"). The appropriate failure mode is **failure to issue correct val_{xj}** and has the effect m_{xj} with val_{xj} **FAULTY at SR_{xj}**. The description of the software requirement then has to be checked.

6. The category 3 ("Timing Failure") failure mode **failure to send m_{xj} (with val_{xj}) to SR_{xj} when required** has the effect m_{xj} (with val_{xj}) **UNTIMELY at SR_{xj}**. The software requirement description or its context are the right sources to determine whether time-based failures may occur. The descriptions and the context have to be checked for keywords like "after", "before", "immediately", "rate", "frequency", "delay" etc.

Example:

Table 3 below illustrates the failure modes and the failure mode effects as described previously. The following software requirement consists of two message parts connected by an AND:

"send m_1 with val_1 to SR_1 AND m_2 to SR_2 IF <condition>"

Failure Modes	Failure Mode Effects
FM-1: Failure to accept check, route arriving messages, or to send messages	**FME-1 / FME-2 / (FME-3)**
1.) m_1 with val_1 sent to SR_1 IF ¬<condition>	a)* m_1 with val_1 **UNDESIRED** at SR_1 b)* m_1 with val_1 **FAULTY** at SR_1
2.) m_1 with val_1 not sent to SR_1 IF <condition>	m_1 with val_1 **MISSING** at SR_1
3.) m_2 sent to SR_2 IF ¬<condition>	m_2 **UNDESIRED** at SR_2
4.) m_2 not sent to Sr_2 IF <condition>	m_2 **MISSING** at SR_2
FM-2: Failure to select, read, process, calculate, generate data to be written, or to write data in messages.	
5.) failure to issue correct val_1	m_1 with val_1 **FAULTY** at SR_1
FM-3: Failure to send messages after a certain delay, period, time, at a certain frequency or rate	
6.) failure to send m_1 with val_1 when required	m_1 with val_1 **UNTIMELY** at SR_1
7.) failure to send m_2 when required	m_2 **UNTIMELY** at SR_2

* depending on the software requirement description it has to be decided which effect applies

Table 3 (formally derived failure modes and their effects)

3.2 Retrieval of Failure Transmission Behaviour

In order to secure the failure transmission behaviour of a software requirement the <$condition_i$> expression in (3) has to be examined in detail. It contains the logical combination of incoming messages which may trigger the sending of outgoing messages. The logical combinations of the <$condition_i$> part in (3) requires to be written in minimal cutset form; then the "send IF" expressions will be presented as:

---

send <$message(s)_i$>

IF [m_{i11} (with val_{i11}) arrived AND m_{i12} (with val_{i12}) arrived AND ...]

OR [m_{i21} (with val_{i21}) arrived AND m_{i22} (with val_{i22}) arrived AND ...]

... $\qquad\qquad$ (4)

OR [m_{ij1} (with val_{ij1}) arrived AND m_{ij2} (with val_{ij2}) arrived AND ...]

with (*) $i \in |N$, and (**) $\forall$ j, k, k' $\in |N$: k $\neq$ k' AND ($m_{ijk} \neq m_{ijk'}$ IF $val_{ijk} = val_{ijk'}$)

In accordance with Table 2 each outgoing message must be checked for missing or incorrect inputs that may be sent with wrong data, too early, too late or not at all.

Thinking of a procedure for deriving failure transmission behaviour the following steps have to be considered:

1. Messages are sent if one minimal cutset is fulfilled. i.e., if one [-bracketed expression in (4) is true. It is supposed that OR-combined incoming messages do not simultaneously appear. Single minimal cutsets may therefore be examined independently in terms of failure transmission.

2. Within one minimal cutset we have to loop over all combinations of single condition parts each time assuming that one part is m_{ij} (with val_i) MISSING (or FAULTY) or UNDESIRED or UNTIMELY and the others are m_{nm} (with val_n) ARRIVED with different m_{ij}'s and m_{nm}'s and the FAULTY part appearing only if there is also a val part.

3. Concerning the message(s)i part in (4) and in accordance with Table 2 we have to proceed for each single message part as follows: 1. m_{ij} (with val_i) sent to SR_i, 2. m_{ij} (with val_i) not sent to SR_i, again with optional val_i's. The failure transmission effects will directly follow as they are described in Table 2.

Example:

Table 4 illustrates, for a given software requirement, what the possible failure transmission effects and failure transmission behaviour should look like:

"send m_2 with val_2 to SR_2 IF m_1 with val_1 arrived AND m_3 arrived"

Failure Transmission Effects	Failure Transmission Behaviour
FTE-1:	**FTB-1**
1. m_2 with val_2 **MISSING** at SR_2	a) m_2 with val_2 **not** sent to SR_2 IF [m_1 with val_1 MISSING* OR FAULTY* OR UNTIMELY* AND m_3 arrived]
	b) m_2 with val_2 **not** sent to SR_2 IF [m_1 with val_1 arrived AND m_3 MISSING* OR UNTIMELY*]
	c) m_2 with val_2 **not** sent to SR_2 IF [m_1 with val_1 MISSING* OR FAULTY* OR UNTIMELY* AND m_3 MISSING* OR UNTIMELY*]
FTE-2 / (FTE-3) / FTE-4:	**FTB-2:**
2./3./4 m_2 with val_2 **UNDESIRED* / FAULTY* / UNTIMELY*** at SR_2	a) m_2 with val_2 sent to SR_2 IF [m_1 with val_1 UNDESIRED* OR FAULTY* OR UNTIMELY* AND m_3 arrived]

b) m_2 with val_2 sent to SR_2 IF [m_1 with val_1 arrived AND m_3 UNDESIRED* OR UNTIMELY*]
c) m_2 with val_2 sent to SR_2 IF [m_1 with val_1 UNDESIRED* OR FAULTY* OR UNTIMELY* AND m_3 UNDESIRED* OR UNTIMELY*]

* these keywords have to be edited by the user according to the semantics

Table 4 (formally derived failure transmission behaviour and effects)

3.3 Creating input for FMEA and FTA

If we generate the failure model of each software requirement in the previously described formal way, then it is possible to apply a FMEA to a software requirement specification: with the failure model the effects of failures of single software requirements may be followed up through the software until the interfaces to the physical system are reached. At this point it is determined which user requirements are either not or are badly realised by undesired or missing software outputs. In some cases, then, it may be of importance to add further functions (such as safety requirements) that may locally contribute to an increase in safety or reduce effects of possible consequences.

In practice, the failure modes and their effects must be known. In the example written down in Table 3 one can immediately see how these failure modes are produced and how their effects look like. Lists like there can therefore directly be taken as input to a FMEA on "local" basis, i.e., software requirement level.

A fault tree analysis is directed towards the safety of the total system. Starting from system failures we identify the basic malfunctions that software can have. Failed functions and software crashes of this kind are usually identified by what in classical safety analysis is called "Preliminary Hazard Analysis". It comprises the identification of major events that could contribute to a complete loss of the system or of human life. Within so-called top-level fault trees the most critical possible event (e.g., loss of life) may be explained by one or more hardware actions. Where such hardware is triggered by software actions our proposal of a software requirement FTA may be attached to the fault tree developed so far.

During this type of fault tree construction software-related basic events are identified that should later be taken into account in more detail. For further safety analysis it is crucial to find a relationship between basic events and software outputs. We achieve this by expressing the basic events as logical combinations of missing, faulty, undesired, untimely or presumably also correct data and control flows.

All this means that a basis has been created which allows invalid states of the total system (i.e., major hazards) to be followed back into and through the software. The conceptual failure model leads us in explaining incorrect data and control flows (causing the basic events). Failure transmissions (as they have been described in this paper) together with their effects represent, from a practical viewpoint, mini fault trees for a single software requirements. One will continue concatenating fault trees as long as branching is possible. In upwards direction this process will terminate when HW/SW interfaces are reached. In downwards direction one has to follow the functional model until the most detailed software requirement (i.e., the most detailed software function) has been reached.

With the methodology presented, a list can be constructed for each software requirement as it is done in Table 4 for an example. The list shows the key parts usable for a FTA: on the left side a list of failure transmission effects. They can be taken as events. Explanations for each event are listed on the right side. Again, an appropriate input structure as demanded for a FTA can be produced. In this way the means for constructing FTA parts on a software requirement level are given by the failure model output.

4 Application to a Robot Control System

The applicability of the methods has been proven in an in-house project called ROBERTINO. It's a heavy robotics facility with 4 degrees of freedom which is built for the design validation of the Remote Handling devices, tooling and procedures in Thermonuclear Fusion Reactors. The Robertino Control System (RCS) to which the methodology was applied is a kernel system responsible for the axes movements and axes control. RCS is a safety-critical system.

Not mentioning the numerous safety requirements regarding RCS, we shortly concentrate on the functional requirements "10.4: Manage DAVM (Direct Axes Velocity Mode" and "12.3: Motors Control Loop" which are somehow interconnected and whose negative effects may certainly contribute to hazards (due to an exceed of velocity, for example) [11].

Table 5a shows the first part of the methodology applied to RCS's functional requirement "FR10.4.3". The effects are derived in the same way as previously described. The command "target_cmd", for ex., carries data ("null") leading to a "null target_cmd faulty" failure mode effect. The functional requirement "FR10.4.3" consists also of a second part named "Disable_axes&CP_lamps" whose effects are calculated in a similar way.

Software Requirement	Failure Modes	Failure Mode Effects
FR10.4: Manage **DAVM**		
FR10.4.3: if a stop_motion_cmd arrives, the profile execution is stopped with a null target_cmd and the axes and Control Panel lamps are disabled	a) null target_cmd **NOT SENT IF** condition b) null target_cmd **SENT IF** not condition c) Disable_axes&CP_la mps **SENT IF** not condition d) Disable_axes&CP_la mps **NOT SENT IF** condition e) **FAILURE** to issue correct "null" f) **FAILURE** to send null target_cmd when required g) **FAILURE** to send Disable_axes&CP_la mps when required	a) target_cmd **missing** b) null target_cmd **undesired**, null target_cmd **faulty** c) Disable_axes&CP _lamps **undesired** d) Disable_axes&CP _lamps **missing** e) null target_cmd **faulty** f) null target_cmd **untimely** g) Disable_axes&CP _lamps **untimely**

Table 5a (failure modes and failure mode effects for Robertino's FR10.4.3)

In Table 5b, particularly, software requirements are expressed in a "send IF condition" format (as it could also be done for Table 5a) which helps to formulate the failure transmission behaviour and their effects. Again, functional requirement FR10.4.3 is treated.

Software Requirement expressed as "send IF condition"	Failure Transmission Behaviour	Failure Transmission Effects
FR 10.4: Manage DAVM		
FR10.4.3: send null target_cmd to FR12.3 **AND** send Disable_axes&CP_lamps **IF** stop_motion_cmd arrived	A) null target_cmd **NOT SENT** to FR12.3 **IF** stop_motion_cmd **MISSING** or **UNTIMELY** B) null target_cmd **SENT** to FR12.3 **IF** stop_motion_cmd **MISSING** or **UNTIMELY** C) Disable_axes&CP_lamps **NOT SENT** to FR12.3 **IF** stop_motion_cmd **MISSING** or **UNTIMELY** D) Disable_axes&CP_lamps **SENT** to FR12.3 **IF** stop_motion_cmd **MISSING** or **UNTIMELY**	A) null target_cmd **missing** B) null target_cmd **faulty/ undesired/ untimely** C) Disable_axes&CP_lamps **missing** D) Disable_axes&CP_lamps **undesired/ untimely**

Table 5b (failure transmission behaviour and effects for Robertino's FR10.4.3)

The results concerning 10.4.3, for ex., were then taken as input for a FTA (the tree is not shown here). Examining the FTA several weak points in the specification were found [12]: in the less critical example particularities between software and physical system have not been expressed carefully, or unclear or insufficient formulating of a software requirement was detected. The failure transmission effect "null target_cmd misssing", however, led to a serious inspection to what might happen if the (regularly sent) velocity command is not present. Then a "null target command" has to be sent. As a consequence an additional safety requirement had to be inserted into the RCS specification.

5 Conclusion and Outlook

An extension of well-approved safety analysis techniques provides a powerful mechanism to detect specifications of software requirements which might contribute to system hazards. With such an all-covering and all-explaining mechanism a great step towards a dependable software requirements specification is done. The inherent complexity of interrelated software requirements is widely overcome by using structured methods. The system developer is able to construct his safety arguments by selecting them out of a system-generated superset.

The methodology presented requires software requirements to be put in a certain format in order to facilitate formal derivation of failure models. Thus the highly formal and structured process can obviously easily be automated; relevant work is actually done and tried out on the ROBERTINO case study.

Accompanying research is also undertaken with respect to a safety-directed analysis of user requirements whose results might influence safety analysis on successive lifecycle phases.

References

1. Maier T: FMEA and FTA to Support Safe Design of Embedded Software in Safety-Critical Systems. In: Proc. of the 12th Workshop and 1st ENCRESS Conference. Brugge, 1995.

2. Ratan V, Partridge K, Reese J, Leveson: Safety Analysis Tools for Requirements Specifications. In: Proc. of the 11th Annual Conference on Computer Assurance (COMPASS'96). Gaithersburg, 1996.

3. Carpignano A, Poucet A, Scheer S: STARS Project: System Modelling and Reliability Analysis Modules, User Manual. Commission of the European Communities, Joint Research Centre. Ispra, 1992.

4. ESA Board for Software Standardisation and Control: Guide to the Software Requirements Definition Phase, PSS-05-03, Issue 1. 1991.

5. Leveson N, Harvey P: Analyzing Software Safety. IEEE Transactions on Software Engineering, SE-9, Vol. 5. 1983.

6. Chudleigh M F, Catmur J R: Safety Assessment of Computer Systems Using HAZOP and Audit Techniques. In: Proc. Safety of Computer Control Systems 1992 (SAFECOMP '92), ed.: Frey H H. Pergamon Press. 1992.

7. Fenelon P, McDermid J A: An Integrated Toolset for Software Safety Analysis. Journal of Systems and Software, Vol. 21. 1993.

8. Jackson T, McDermid J A, Wand I, Wilikens M (Editor): Dependability Measurement of Safety Critical Systems Models and Data Refinement. Technical Note I.95.43. European Commission, Joint Research Centre. Ispra. 1995.

9. Laprie J C: Dependability of Computer Systems: Concepts, Limits, Improvements. In: Proc. of the 6th Intern. Symposium on Software Reliability Engineering (ISSRE'95). Toulouse. 1995.

10. Lutz R, Woodhouse R: Experience Report: Contributions of SFMEA to Requirements Analysis. ICRE. 1996.

11. Ruiz Morales E: Software Requirements Document for the Robertino Control System. Technical Note I.94.161. European Commission, Joint Research Centre. Ispra. 1994.

12. Scheer S, Maier T: Methodology and Tools for the Specification of Safe Software Embedded in Technical Systems, Part A: Development of a Supporting Methodology. Technical Note I.96.132. European Commission, Joint Research Centre. Ispra. 1996.

Safety Cases, Management and Development

Safety Case Construction and Reuse Using Patterns

T P Kelly, J A McDermid

Rolls-Royce Systems and Software Engineering University Technology Centre
Department of Computer Science, University of York
York, UK

Abstract

This paper presents an approach to the reuse of common structures in safety case arguments through their documentation as 'Safety Case Patterns'. Problems with the existing, informal and ad-hoc approaches to safety case material reuse are highlighted. We argue that through explicit capture and documentation of reusable safety case elements as patterns, the process of safety case construction and reuse can be made more systematic. For the description of patterns a safety case pattern language and a graphical pattern notation (based on the Goal Structuring Notation) are presented. Using this framework we briefly describe a number of example argument patterns. A fully documented example pattern is included as an appendix to this paper.

1 Introduction

The purpose of a safety case is to present the argument that a system, be it physical or procedural, is acceptably safe to operate. This argument should demonstrate how the available evidence concerning the system can be reasonably and defensibly interpreted as indicating compliance with the system safety requirements. As such, each safety case will ultimately be specific to a particular system - defined by both the details of the available evidence and safety requirements. However, amongst these 'specific' safety cases, patterns of argument emerge through, for example, common approaches to addressing a standard requirement or class of requirements, typical combinations of argument and accepted interpretations of specific types of evidence.

Informal reuse of safety case material is already commonplace, especially within stable and well-understood domains, e.g. aerospace engine controllers. However, this type of uncontrolled and often ad-hoc reuse can fail to fully exploit opportunities for reuse, and can in some cases be potentially dangerous. This paper describes the problems of informal safety case reuse and introduces the concept of *Safety Case Patterns* as a means of explicitly and clearly documenting common elements found between safety cases.

2 The Problems of Informal Safety Case Material Reuse

Much of existing safety case material reuse is triggered by, and centres on, the safety engineers responsible for the production of the safety case. It is not uncommon for an engineer, having recognised a similarity, to plunder a previously developed safety case to help in the development of a safety case in a new project. In some cases, the engineer may believe certain elements of the two projects to be sufficiently similar to actually "cut-and-paste" parts of the original documentation and subject them only to minor review and modification.

The central role of people in the reuse of safety artefacts is often crucial: many existing safety cases fail to clearly present the intent and rationale of the safety arguments and safety processes. Such safety cases cannot easily be read and understood in a way that permits re-application of principles propounded. They require interpretation. To understand the intent of a safety case can take many readings. To understand the rationale behind elements of a safety case can require a form of 'reverse engineering'. Safety cases with these properties are not readily amenable to reuse. Therefore, the safety engineers who worked on a safety case form an important 'missing link' in any attempt to gain value from it in future safety case developments. However, a number of potential problems arise where people are the **principal** medium for cross-project reuse of safety case artefacts, including:

- **Artefacts being reused inappropriately**
  If the original context of a safety case artefact is not fully recognised the artefact may be applied inappropriately in another context. An argument of safety from one context that is **not** applicable in the context in which it is reused can create a false or misleading picture of a system's safety. Such reuse can carry "hidden assumptions" from the original context that are inconsistent with the application context. This danger is obviously greatest with the extreme of "cut-and-paste" reuse.

- **Reuse occurring in an ad-hoc fashion**
  Reuse is dependent entirely on an engineer's ability, firstly, to *recognise* the potential to reuse some artefact and, secondly, to *recall* the appropriate information. Consequently, reuse often occurs in a fairly random, opportunistic, fashion and is not carried out systematically. Opportunities to reuse an artefact may be wasted.

- **Loss of knowledge**
  A *total* reliance on people to achieve cross-project reuse is an admission that project documentation is insufficient to support systematic reuse. A danger is that particular people, the company 'experts', become a bottleneck on any project. Without documentation of their experience or expertise, they become a critical resource in an organisation. They effectively act as an 'index' into the organisation's existing documentation. If such people leave an organisation, disproportionately large amounts of the organisation's 'corporate memory' are lost and, as a result, less reuse is possible.

- **Lack of Consistency / Process Maturity**
  Without explicitly recognising and documenting the repeatable elements of safety case development there can be no assurance that these elements are being used consistently. If an element is not consistently applied, it is difficult to argue that the associated development process is mature. It is also difficult to argue how this process has been, and will be, improved and evolved over time.

- **Lack of traceability**
  Informal reuse is often invisible in the final safety case produced. No record is kept of reuse from existing documentation. This lack of traceability can lead to problems in maintaining the safety case. For example, if it were found that a particular *reused* safety argument was unsound (e.g. in the light of contradictory operational evidence), it would be necessary to locate all uses of that argument in order to update all appropriately. With no record of where it was reused this could be an extremely difficult task. Reuse has the potential to propagate one error many times. To deal with such situations requires adequate visibility and traceability of the reuse process.

These problems stem from the key issue of **documentation**. The process of safety case reuse must be explicitly recognised and documented in order to control and support it. This involves identifying and abstracting reusable elements from existing safety cases; documenting them with information defining their characteristic function(s), applicability, record of applications, etc. Once such things are "down on paper" they can be evaluated, exploited, evolved and traced. The following section introduces the concept of recorded patterns as a means of documenting the common elements of safety case construction.

3 Patterns

The use of patterns as a means of describing common elements (or 'themes') of complex structures was first documented in the field of building architecture. Christopher Alexander, in his book, "The Timeless Way of Building" [1], argues that "Beyond its elements each building is defined by certain patterns of relationships amongst its elements". Alexander shows how patterns can be used to abstract away from the details of particular buildings and capture something essential to the design (the principles underlying the building; the reasons why elements of the building are successful or unsuccessful) that can then be used elsewhere. In his other books, "A Pattern Language" [2], and, "The Oregon Experiment" [3], Alexander describes in more concrete terms how patterns can be documented and applied using pattern languages.

Influenced by Alexander's work, over the last five years the concept of patterns and pattern languages has received increasing interest from software designers [4,5,6]. Designers have turned to patterns as a means of capturing the repeatable and successful elements of a software design. Many have been disappointed with the unfulfilled promise of traditional component-based (compositional) reuse and believe that successful reuse lies is the ability to describe higher-level software structures [7]. These structures communicating how components are combined to achieve certain functions, the principles of interfacing components, etc. The attraction of patterns is that they offer this means of abstracting fundamental design strategies from the details of particular designs.

Analysis of the safety case domain (involving discussions with safety case practitioners, examination of a wide range of safety cases and study of the regulatory standards) suggests that patterns provide an appropriate level of abstraction to make safety case artefacts reusable without significantly reducing the benefit per application. Reuse of the specifics of safety cases (e.g. particular pieces of evidence) will largely be unsuccessful, as between different safety cases these are likely to change. However, reuse of the general principles of safety cases (i.e. the *whys* and *hows* of the construction of the safety case) is likely to be more successful as these are more constant between safety cases. Patterns can provide a means of describing these general principles, structures and processes of the safety case.

To describe safety case patterns requires a pattern language. The following section proposes a safety case pattern language, adapted from those described for software design patterns.

4   A Safety Case Pattern Language

As with the design patterns of Gamma et al. [8], safety case patterns are an attempt to capture solutions that have evolved over time. A safety case pattern should be a simple and efficient solution to a particular problem, whether it is the execution of a safety process or the construction of a particular safety argument.

In [8] a pattern format is proposed for describing design patterns. This has been adapted to provide a format suitable for safety case pattern description, see Figure 1. The principal differences between this format and the format for design patterns are firstly, the use of the **Goal Structuring Notation** (GSN) [9] rather than Rumbaugh's **Object Modelling Technique OMT** [10] to graphically describe the structural details of the pattern. Secondly, sample textual description is provided (for the eventual safety case) rather than sample source code. The use of GSN for structural pattern description is described in the next section.

A key element of the pattern format when applied to safety cases is the notion of pattern **applicability**. Applicability defines under what circumstances the pattern can be legitimately applied. For example, descriptions of applicability could indicate which standards the pattern adheres to, the level of design detail required or the assumption of system behaviour. Applicability of a safety case pattern is perhaps more closely tied to the structural description of the pattern than with design patterns. The goal structure representation of the pattern may specifically require certain elements to be present in the goal structure into which the pattern is placed (e.g. a **context** entity, **model, assumption or constraint**).

In addition to pattern rationale being documented in the *intent* and *motivation* entries of the pattern description (as with Gamma's design patterns), it is also possible to directly represent the rationale involved within a safety argument. This can be done within the structural (GSN) pattern description using the existing GSN rationale elements – *assumptions, justifications* and *strategies*.

Pattern Name and Classification	The pattern's name should convey the essence of the pattern succinctly. A good name is vital because, with use, it will become part of your design vocabulary.
Intent	A short statement that answers the following questions: What does the pattern do / represent? What is its rationale and intent? What particular safety issue / requirement / process does it address?
Also Known As	Other well known names for the pattern, if any.
Motivation	A scenario that illustrates a safety issue / process and how the elements of the goal structure solve the problem. The scenario will help you understand the more abstract description of the pattern that follows.
Applicability (Necessary Context)	What are the situations in which the safety case pattern can be applied? What information is required as context for the pattern to be successful (necessary inputs to the pattern)? How can you recognise situations in which the pattern can be applied?
Structure	A graphical representation of the pattern using the extended form of the Goal Structuring Notation. The representation can describe a product or a process style goal structure. Where the structure indicates generality or optionality it should be clear how the pattern can be instantiated.
Participants	The elements of the goal structure and their function in the pattern.
Collaborations	How the participants collaborate to carry out the function of the pattern.
Consequences	How does the pattern support its objectives? What are the trade-offs and results of using the pattern? For a product oriented pattern - what are the principal arguments put forward? For a process-oriented pattern - what are the outputs of the activities described?
Implementation	What pitfalls, hint or technique should you beware of when using the pattern? What degrees of flexibility are there in following the pattern?
Sample Text	Text fragments that illustrate how you might describe the pattern in the final safety case / safety plan.
Known Uses	Examples of the patterns application in existing safety documentation should be cited. If possible examples from two different applications should be shown.
Related Patterns	Safety Case Patterns that are related to this pattern, e.g. with the same motivation but different applicability conditions (e.g. different standards, different systems). For a process-oriented pattern, related product (argument) patterns. For a product-oriented pattern, related process patterns.

Figure 1. Elements of Safety Case Pattern Description

Safety case patterns are intended to describe **partial** solutions and will not typically describe the complete structure of a system safety argument. It is expected that a collection of patterns will therefore emerge over time – forming a 'recipe book' of safety arguments and processes, a number of which would be used together to aid in the construction of the safety case.

9 Structural Pattern Description using the Goal Structuring Notation

The Goal Structuring Notation (GSN) [9] was developed for the description of safety arguments, relating the breakdown of safety requirements to arguments based upon available evidence. Figure 2 shows an example goal structure, illustrating the key elements of the notation.

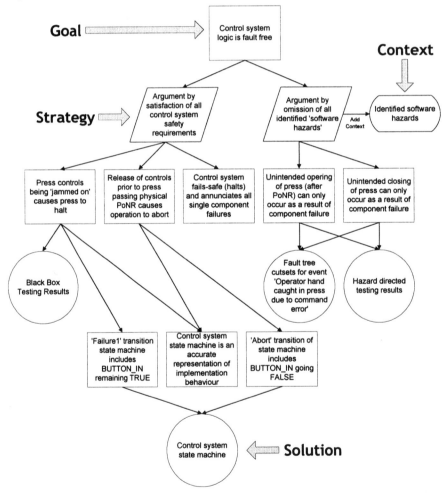

Figure 2. An Example Goal Structure

In the structure shown in Figure 2, as in most, there exist 'top level' goals – statements that the goal structure is designed to support. In this case, *"Control system logic is fault free"*, is the (singular) top level goal. Beneath the top level goal or goals, the argument is broken down into sub-goals, either directly or, as in this case, indirectly through a strategy. The two argument strategies put forward as a means of addressing the top-level goal in this structure are *"Argument by satisfaction of all control system safety requirements"*, and, *"Argument by omission of all identified software hazards"*. These strategies are then substantiated by five sub-goals. At some stage in a goal structure, a goal statement is put forward that need not be broken down and can be clearly supported by reference to some evidence. In this case, it is shown that the goal *"Unintended Opening of press after PoNR (Point of No Return) can only occur as a result of component failure"*, is supported by direct reference to the solutions, *"Fault tree cutsets ..."* and *"Hazard directed testing results"*.

In its existing form, GSN can be used to express details of a *specific* safety argument, e.g. as shown in Figure 2. However, in order to express *patterns* rather than simply *instances*, and perform the equivalent role for safety case patterns that OMT performs for design patterns, GSN must also be capable of representing generalisations of goal structures. For this reason, a number of extensions have been made to GSN to support entity and structural abstraction over the existing elements. Figure 3 shows a simple goal structure pattern that uses these extensions. (This pattern is described in the following section.)

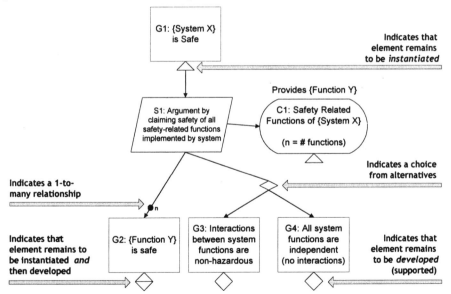

Figure 3. Extensions for Structural Abstraction

10   Example Safety Case Patterns

Patterns can emerge at many different levels in the safety argument and at varying degrees of specificity. At the highest level it is possible to identify a number of basic argument structures that are used to decompose ill-defined system safety requirements. For example, against the ultimate top level requirement …

"{System X} is safe"

… two possible argument approaches could be applied:

- **Hazard Directed Argument**
- **Functional Decomposition Argument**

Figure 4 shows the GSN pattern (without accompanying text) representing a hazard directed argument. In this pattern, the implicit definition of 'safe' is 'hazard avoidance'. The requirement G1 is addressed by arguing that all identified hazards have been addressed (S1). This strategy can only be executed in the context of some knowledge of plausible hazards, e.g. identified by Hazard Analysis. Given this information (C1), identifying n hazards, n sub-goals of the form G2 can be constructed. The argument then progresses from these 'hazard avoidance' goals.

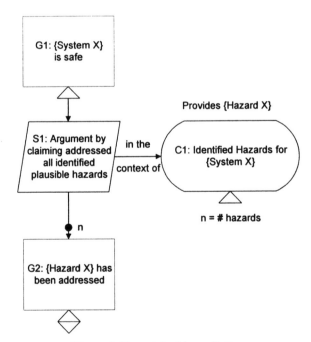

Figure 4. Hazard Avoidance Pattern

In the previous section, Figure 3 shows the GSN pattern (again, without accompanying text) representing a functional decomposition argument. In this structure, the top-level goal of system safety (G1) is re-expressed as a number of goals of functional safety (G2) as part of the strategy identified by S1. In order to support this strategy, it is necessary to have identified all system functions affecting overall safety (C1) e.g. through a Functional Hazard Analysis. In addition, it is also necessary to put forward (and develop) the claim that either all the identified functions are independent, and therefore have no interactions that could give rise to hazards (G4) or that any interactions that have been identified are non-hazardous (G3).

At lower levels in the safety case argument, patterns also emerge. For example, when arguing the safety of software it is often common to claim a level of software integrity from an appeal to having used best practice tools, techniques and methods during development and testing. Other common argument structures emerge from the use of particular techniques. For example, to support the claim that a particular software condition cannot arise, a pattern could be identified showing the typical use of either *formal verification, Software Fault Tree Analysis (SFTA),* or *black box testing* — each strand of argument having associated claims to support, e.g.:

- **Formal verification** – argument that the formal specification is an accurate representation of the final target code
- **SFTA** – argument that sequential composition has been appropriately handled
- **Testing** – argument that sufficient coverage achieved

Figure 5 shows an example pattern that could be found in the lower levels of a safety case argument.

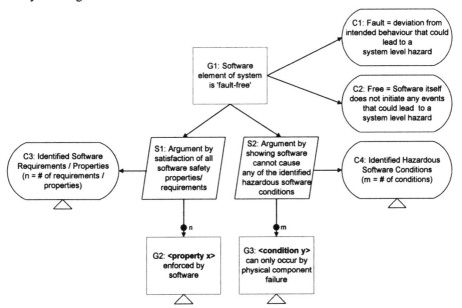

Figure 5. Fault Free Software Pattern

In this pattern, the claim that the software element in a system is 'fault free' (G1) is supported by two main strands of argument (S1 and S2). Firstly, over a list (C3) of identified hazardous software conditions (e.g. *"Controller demands speed greater than maximum safe speed"*) the *m* sub-goals of the form G3 are expressed, to argue that these hazards can only occur through physical component failures. Secondly, over a list (C4) of identified software requirements (e.g. *"Operation will not start if operator detected near machinery"*) the *n* sub-goals of the form G2 are expressed to argue that these properties are enforced in the software. In order that this pattern will be appropriately applied, the context of the pattern is made clear through the elements C1 and C2 - both defining key terms in the top-level claim.

The example patterns given here are deliberately general, as they can be readily understood and have wide applicability across technologies and regulatory contexts. However, in well understood and stable domains it is possible to identify argument patterns at a greater level of specificity. For example, in the civil aerospace sector common arguments are often developed against particular individual regulations (in Europe from the Joint Aviation Requirements) - e.g. capturing what is an acceptable approach (*'means of compliance'*) to arguing that *"Thrust Reverser will not deploy during flight"*.

An example of a pattern complete with supporting text is provided as an appendix to this paper. This pattern presents an approach to arguing satisfaction of the ALARP (As Low As Reasonably Practicable) Principle at the highest level in a safety case.

11   Using Patterns in Argument Construction

It is intended that, over time and within individual domains, collections of safety case patterns will be developed. These collections will be used as 'recipe books' for future safety case developments. When faced with particular requirements to support, engineers will then be able to retrieve and instantiate the approach as defined by the corresponding pattern. As well as potentially saving development effort, using patterns in argument construction in this way addresses many of the identified problems of informal reuse:

- **Artefacts being reused inappropriately**
  Through documentation of artefacts as patterns, including documentation of applicability and clear description of the required context (both in the text and in the structural pattern) - inappropriate use of material is made less likely.

- **Reuse occurring in an ad-hoc fashion**
  Through the development of a core 'recipe book' of patterns, opportunities for reuse can be more easily identified and exploited.

- **Loss of knowledge**
  Documentation through patterns, especially including the supporting text, helps to explicitly capture the knowledge developed within an organisation.

- **Lack of Consistency / Process Maturity**
  Through the development of a core 'recipe book' of patterns, the consistency of approach between developments can be more readily encouraged and supported.

- **Lack of traceability**
  Through the more explicit reuse of material as patterns, ease of recording traceability information (e.g. documenting those (versions of) patterns used within a new development) is improved.

12 Conclusions

There is potential for reuse of material between safety case developments. This is borne out by the levels of informal reuse instigated by safety engineers. However, there are a number of deficiencies with such an ad-hoc approach. Documentation of common safety case argument structures as patterns provides a suitable medium through which to foster systematic artefact reuse and aid in the development of new safety cases.

13 Acknowledgements

The authors would like to acknowledge the financial support given by Rolls-Royce plc for the work reported in this paper. Tim Kelly is jointly funded as a CASE (Co-operative Award in Science and Engineering) Research Student by the Engineering and Physical Sciences Research Council and Rolls-Royce and Associates Ltd.

14 References

1. Alexander C. The Timeless Way of Building, Oxford University Press, New York, 1979

2. Alexander C. A Pattern Language, Oxford University Press, New York, 1977

3. Alexander C. The Oregon Experiment, Oxford University Press, New York, 1975

4. Beck K. Patterns and Software Development, Dr. Dobbs Journal 1993 19(2):18-23

5. Booch G. Patterns, Object Magazine 1993 3(2)

6. Coad P. Object-Oriented Patterns, Communications of the ACM 1993 35(9):153-159

7. Milli H, Mili F, Mili A. Reusing software: issues and research directions, IEEE Transactions on Software Engineering 1995 21(6):528-562

8. Gamma E, Helm R, Johnson R, Vlissides J. Design Patterns: Elements of Reusable Object-Oriented Software, Addison-Wesley, Reading MA, 1995

9. Wilson S, Kirkham P, Cassano M. SAM 4 User Manual, University of York, 1997 (Available on request from authors)

10. Rumbaugh J, Blaha M, Premerlani W, Eddy F, Lorensen W. Object-Oriented Modeling and Design, Prentice-Hall, Englewood Cliffs NJ, 1991

Appendix: ALARP Pattern

ALARP (As-Low-As-Reasonably-Practicable) Pattern

Author	Tim Kelly	Created	04/02/97 10:41	Last Modified	05/02/97 09:47

Structure

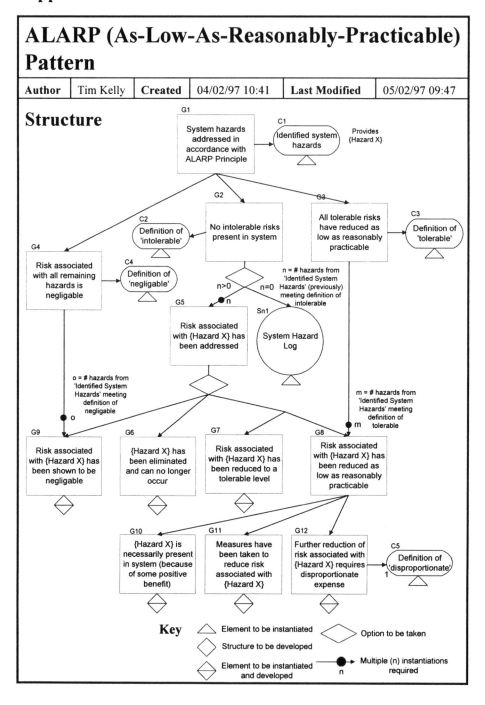

Intent		This pattern provides a framework for arguing that identified risks in a system have been sufficiently addressed in accordance with the ALARP principle.
Also Known As		• Risk Reduction Argument Pattern
Motivation		This pattern was developed for two reasons: • To argue compliance with the ALARP principle at the highest level when addressing system level hazards. • To provide a more structured approach to presenting a 'Hazard Avoidance' argument (See Hazard Avoidance Pattern) by showing differing treatment of hazards according to their associated risk.
Participants	G1	Defines the overall objective of the pattern
	G2, G3, G4	Defines targets for three classes of identified risks: negligible, tolerable, and intolerable
	Sn1	Provided at this point to support the claim that no intolerable risks have (ever) been identified with the system
	G6 or G7 and G8	Claims either that hazard has been eliminated or associated risk reduced to a tolerable level and dealt with as a tolerable risk.
	G8	Defines ALARP target for each identified tolerable risk
	G10, G11, G12	Claims required to support ALARP target: • Hazard only acceptable if positive benefit achieved • Risk reduction measures have been taken up to the point where further measures would be disproportionate to benefit gained.
	G9	Claim for each remaining hazard that associated risk shown to be negligible
	C1	A context identifying all system hazards, including indication of associated risks (e.g. Risk Category from A, B, C, D).
	C2, C3, C4	A workable definition of 'intolerable'/ 'tolerable'/ 'negligible' risks that can be used as a basis for selection from the list of hazards (e.g. Intolerable = Risk Category A, Tolerable = Risk Category B or C, Negligible = D).
	C5	The ALARP principle relies on some understanding of when it is no longer cost-effective to spend further money on risk reduction. This element, a definition of cost-effectiveness, is therefore required.

Collaborations	An important aspect of this pattern is that it divides and conquers the goal of hazard mitigation / elimination according to the level of risk associated with each hazard. There are three strands to the safety argument: one tackling intolerable risks, one tackling tolerable risk and one discounting negligible risks. To satisfactorily support the top-level goal (G1) it is important that these three strands address **all** identified risks. The definitions of tolerable, intolerable and negligible (C3, C2 and C4 respectively) should therefore be so defined to cover and classify the range of possible levels of risks.
	It should also be noted that the definitions of negligibility (C4) and disproportionate (C5) cannot be considered entirely independently. It would not make sense, for example, to force risk reduction to a level below that identified elsewhere as negligible.
	As the goal structure shows, if the means of addressing a previously identified intolerable risk is to reduce it to a tolerable level, then the remaining risk must be tackled as for all tolerable risks. If the level of risk has been reduced to a negligible level, then the hazard must be tackled as a negligible risk.
	It is important that the source of Identified System Hazards (C1) identifies the level of risk posed by a hazard in a way that permits sub-division into the classes of risk defined by C2, C3 and C4.
Applicability	This pattern is applicable in contexts where the ALARP principle is accepted as the device for reasoning about the relative importance of risks and the cost-effectiveness of risk reduction.
	In order to apply this pattern it is necessary to have access to the following contextual information:
	• **C1: Identified System Hazards** (See *Participants* section)
	• **C2, C3, C4: Definition of Intolerable / Tolerable / Negligible Risk** (See *Participants* section) These definitions are typically provided by the appropriate regulatory authority, standards or through investigations by safety engineers, including discussions with customers.
	• **C5: Definition of Disproportionate** (See *Participants* section)
Consequences	After applying this pattern, there will be a number of undeveloped goals of the form:
	• **G7: Risk associated with {Hazard X} has been reduced to a tolerable level**
	• **G9: Risk associated with {Hazard X} has been shown to be negligible**
	• **G6: {Hazard X} has been eliminated and can no longer occur**
	• **G10: {Hazard X} is necessarily present in the system**
	• **G11: Measures have been taken to reduce risk associated with {Hazard X}**
	• **G12: Further reduction of risk associated with {Hazard X} requires disproportionate expense**

Implementation	Implementation of this pattern involves first instantiating the contexts C1, C2, C3, C4. In the context of the list of hazards referenced by C1, the solutions to goals G2, G3 and G4 can be provided. If no tolerable risks were ever present in the system, then reference to the system hazard log (Sn1) is sufficient to support the claim G2. However, if any intolerable risks have been identified, it is necessary to claim (G5) that these have been resolved through complete elimination of the hazard (G6), or reduction to a tolerable (G7, G8) or negligible (G9) level.

Implementation of this pattern involves first instantiating the contexts C1, C2, C3, C4. In the context of the list of hazards referenced by C1, the solutions to goals G2, G3 and G4 can be provided. If no tolerable risks were ever present in the system, then reference to the system hazard log (Sn1) is sufficient to support the claim G2. However, if any intolerable risks have been identified, it is necessary to claim (G5) that these have been resolved through complete elimination of the hazard (G6), or reduction to a tolerable (G7, G8) or negligible (G9) level.

For each tolerable risk identified an argument must be constructed (G6, G10, G11, G12) to demonstrate that it has been addressed in accordance with the ALARP principles. Measures taken in risk reduction must be stated in support of G11. Some evidence / argument of the non cost-effectiveness of further risk reduction measures must be supplied in support of G12, in accordance with the definition given by C5.

Evidence of risk analysis (probably based upon consideration of probability of occurrence) is required in support of each claim of hazards posing negligible risk (G9).

Possible Pitfalls

- Not providing complete coverage of levels of risk through definitions C2, C3, C4

- Expressing definitions C2, C3, C4 in a way that is difficult to apply to the information provided by C1 (and vice versa)

- Not having a commonly agreed concept of when to stop attempting further risk reduction (C1) - this can result in a non-uniform approach to tackling risks where significantly different levels of effort are committed to risks at the same level.

Examples	TBD
Known Uses	See *Industrial Press Safety Argument*
Related Patterns	Safe by Hazard Mitigation Argument

A systematic approach to software safety integrity levels

Peter A. Lindsay*
Software Verification Research Centre
School of Information Technology
The University of Queensland, Australia

John A. McDermid
High Integrity Systems Engineering Group
Department of Computer Science
University of York, U.K.

Abstract

International Standards for safety-critical software typically use notions of Safety Integrity Levels (SILs) which in our experience are difficult to apply and which lack credible assessment criteria. This paper proposes risk modelling as a basis for allocation of SILs to software and illustrates its use. It also proposes software-directed evaluation criteria for SILs, to assess what level of integrity is actually achieved. We contend that the approach leads to more credible results, and more cost-effective ways of delivering software safety assurance.

1 Introduction

Software is increasingly being used in safety-critical applications. Unlike most hardware failures, software failures are "systematic" and software faults may lie hidden for a long time before being revealed.

Many standards for the development of safety-critical software and systems introduce the notion of *Safety Integrity Levels (SILs)*. Roughly, SILs represent the "degree of freedom from flaws" that is required from the system or software. The notion implicitly recognizes the fact that 100% assurance is impossible to achieve for complex systems. In essence, the standards use SILs to dictate the nature and degree of scrutiny that is applied to safety issues during development: e.g. by recommending the kinds of techniques to be applied, the degree of independence to be used in verification and validation, and the competence of staff. This could be termed a "process-oriented" view of SILs.

---

*Address for correspondence: c/o SVRC, The University of Queensland, Brisbane 4072, Australia (email: pal@it.uq.edu.au, fax: +61 7 3365 1533).

Standards which apply this kind of approach include generic standards such as IEC 1508 [1], MOD 00-56 [2] and DOD 882C [3], and industry-sector specific standards for aerospace [4],[1] railway signalling [5], and automobiles [6].

Because software does not cause harm directly, but only as part of an overall system, it is important to be able to assess the software's contribution to, and responsibility for, overall system safety. To apply the notion of SILs to software – or other components, for that matter – it is thus necessary to have a way of apportioning integrity to system components. This is the point where standards begin to differ most, and where the process-oriented view of SILs begins to reveal its shortcomings.

We contend that current approaches to SILs lack credibility because they have concentrated almost exclusively on the process and have ignored the product. They lack credibility in theory as well as in practice [7]. A short review of current approaches is given in §2 below; for each approach it is possible to identify realistic scenarios which lead to counter-intuitive results.

Another important shortcoming of current approaches is that they give little or no guidance on how to assess whether desired levels of integrity have actually been achieved, and in particular, on what forms of evidence should be required in safety cases for the different SILs. Thus, setting of SILs is often left "open loop", and the achieved levels of integrity are not verified.

A "product-oriented" view of SILs is needed, to complement the predominantly process-oriented view. This paper sets out to address this need. In §3 below we outline requirements for a more systematic approach to SILs. §4 sketches a proposal for a new basis for allocation of SILs, which generalises the current approaches and addresses many of their limitations. Finally, §5 sketches a new basis for assessment of integrity of software components, based on the notion of "depth of analysis".

2 Review of existing approaches

This section contains a brief review of some widely referenced standards, to set the context for our approach. The desire to resolve some of their various ambiguities is one of the motivations for the approach discussed below.

2.1 IEC 1508

Functional safety: safety-related systems [1]

This is a generic standard for safety-related computer-based systems. The standard attempts to be comprehensive, but is large and still in draft form in places, and so can be difficult to interpret and apply. Safety integrity is defined to be "the probability of a safety-related system satisfactorily performing the required safety functions under all the stated conditions within a stated period of time" ([1] Part 4, p.12).

In IEC 1508, safety integrity requirements for safety functions are set directly from target (maximum) failure rates. The latter are measured in two different ways: as dangerous failures per year, for continuous control systems; and as probability of failure to perform design (*sic*) function on demand, for

---

[1]SILs are called Development Assurance Levels (DALs) in DO178B.

protection systems. The guidelines for determining SILs are unclear, however. For example, Part 5 talks in terms of the amount of risk reduction achieved by adding protection mechanisms: a target probability of failure is calculated as the ratio of frequency of failure with protection against frequency of failure without protection. This fails to take account of the possibility that such additions may result in new failure modes and new risks [8]: what then is the validity of using "likelihood of failure without protection mechanisms" in calculating how much risk reduction has been achieved?

Guidance is lacking at a number of other critical junctures. For example, it is commendable to acknowledge the difference between continuous control and protection, but there is a whole spectrum of applications between these two extremes. Guidance figures in terms of dangerous failure per year are provided for SILs for continuous control systems, but there is no guidance on how to determine these, and how to allocate SILs to components.

2.2   UK MoD 00-56

Safety management requirements for defence systems containing programmable electronics [2]

This is a reasonably comprehensive standard for safety management. It is generic and requires tailoring in places: e.g. it gives recommended interpretations of probability for accidents in terms of system lifetime, then requires that a project-specific Accident Risk Classification Scheme be developed which defines levels of tolerability (i.e., it does not prescribe risk classification). In determining hazard probability targets, the user can take into account the "probability of events leading from a hazard to an accident".

In outline, the SIL assignment process is as follows: A "first function" is identified for each particular hazard, and assigned a SIL according to the severity of "worst credible accident" that could result from failure of the function (Part 1, Table 7). SILs for "second and subsequent functions" are set according to severity of outcome, combined with a failure probability for the first function. SILs for components are set according to the highest SIL of the functions they implement; rules are provided (Part 1, Table 8) that allow components of a lower SIL to implement a function of a higher SIL provided certain conditions are met.

In our experience, this process has a number of shortcomings. First, little guidance is provided on how to interpret worst credible accident. Next, it is not always clear what should be taken to be the first function. (What is the first function in an object-oriented software system, for example?) In our experience, it is quite often possible to identify and decompose functions in different ways, leading to different SIL-assignments for components under the above process.

More generally, application of the integrity decomposition rules is difficult and can lead to results which are hard to justify and/or counter-intuitive. For example, a "voter combinator" might guard against sensor faults but does not guard against common failure modes or faulty requirements; similarly, N-version programming does not guard against faults in the software requirements specification. There is a danger that SILs may be set lower than is appropriate.

On the other hand, application of the rules often results in higher than expected SILs for components which contribute only marginally to safety.

2.3 MIL-STAN 882C

System safety program requirements [3]

This US DoD standard introduces "software control categories", which are roughly a measure of the control software has over safety-critical functions. SILs are then determined directly from the control category and severity of outcome, using a risk matrix. Roughly, the more control is vested in software (rather than humans) and the worse the severity, the higher the SIL.

The software control categories are difficult to interpret – in fact, they are not even exhaustive – and little guidance is provided (however, see §2.5 below). The basis for assessing risk via such categories is highly questionable. It presumes that the risk of software fault leading to an accident is decreased by giving the human more control. This may be true for some military systems but it is certainly not true more generally: e.g. in applications calling for very short response times, or with very high operator workload.

2.4 MISRA

Motor Industry Software Reliability Association Report 2: Integrity [6]

This is an example of a sector-specific (UK) standard which is able to take advantage of its more specialised application domain – vehicle-based software – to offer tighter guidance on SILs. The standard talks in terms of controllability – roughly, likelihood that a typical driver will recover from, or tolerate, a failure without incident – and provides useful guidelines on how to determine controllability. Software SILs are then set according to software-failure implications with respect to controllability. For a combination of reasons (not least, the perception that the driver is ultimately responsible for safety of the vehicle's passengers), controllability categories have a degree of validity in this context, and seem much more convincing than the 882C software control categories.

2.5 STANAG 4404

Safety design requirements and guidelines for munition related safety critical computing systems [9]

This generic NATO software-safety standard defines safety design requirements for software, and gives guidance on how and when the requirements should be applied, verified and tested. It also has tailoring guidelines for a number of different kinds of munition-related systems. It gives "computing system control categories" for many examples, for use with sister-standard STANAG 4452 (Safety assessment requirements for munition related computing systems).

We mention STANAG 4404 here because it is one of the few examples of a combined product/process-oriented approach, whereas all of the preceding are process-oriented.

3 Requirements for an improved approach

Each of the above approaches has its problems. This section discusses requirements for a more systematic approach to SILs.

3.1 Severity

The definition of risk as a combination of severity and likelihood [10] is widely accepted and is not in dispute. When predicting or assessing system and software risk, however, the severity of a given hazard is not always clear. There may be factors outside the system's control which affect the likelihood that a system hazard leads to a mishap. Different outcomes may be possible: the "worst case" may be much rarer than the "most usual outcome" but have far greater severity.[2] The severity of an accident might be different depending on when it occurs: e.g. 00-56 allows that "distinct safety targets may be agreed for different groups of people who may be harmed" (trained operators, MOD employees, general public).

Most standards are overly simplistic in their approach to assessing severity, or give little useful guidance. An approach is required which takes into account all the outcomes in a balanced way.

3.2 Likelihood

Since software failures are "systematic" it is very difficult to predict the likelihood of a hazard occurring. In fault-tolerant design, one of the aims is to identify possible "random" failures and try to mitigate their results; in safety-critical design, systematic failures should be treated similarly. Defence-in-depth means that different layers of protection should be designed in. As a result, relatively sophisticated models of cause and effect are needed, as a basis for predicting likelihood of system failure from likelihood of component failure can be very complicated. Again, standards are overly simplistic on this point. The IEC 1508 categorisation of systems as continuous control or protection systems, and measurement of risk reduction through protection, is an example of over-simplification. The 00-56 use of first functions and subsequent functions is another example. A more sophisticated framework for likelihood prediction is required.

3.3 Hazards vs benefits

Safety analysis tends to concentrate on hazards, which means that the benefits offered by a system may be overlooked. Quantities such as "higher throughput of patients" and "faster dispatch response times" do not usually enter the safety equation since they do not directly relate to hazards of the system, although they can reduce "global" risk. Similarly, defensive systems may add to safety even if they are not highly reliable.

---

[2] For example, for an air-traffic control system, the worst outcome for a "loss of separation" hazard is many of hundreds of fatalities in a mid-air collision, but the more likely outcome is a near-miss, without loss of life or injury.

The standards' approaches to risk assessment lack a coherent basis for judging cost-benefits in such cases. The ALARP principle ("as low as reasonably practicable") is a good general principle for assessing cost-effectiveness of hazard mitigations, but the standards give little practical guidance in its application in determining SILs. For example, for defensive systems the "worst credible accident" might be associated with inaction under hostile circumstances and may have catastrophic consequences. It would clearly be unreasonable to rule out consideration of low-reliability systems where there are no alternatives. Clearly the "failure to defend" hazard is not the one to use in SIL assignment in this case, but the standards' SIL assignment processes do not cover this well.

There is thus a requirement that the framework for risk assessment be able to take into account arguments about benefits as well as about hazards.

3.4 Low integrity components

As computers become more widely used, it is increasingly difficult to argue that high integrity development techniques need to be applied to software in its entirety. For example, if a high integrity (S4) component includes a word processor for preparing reports and that word processor does not interfere with normal operation of the component, then is it really necessary to develop the word processor to level S3, as 00-56 suggests?

This argument extends to software developed to earlier, less stringent, standards and commercial off-the-shelf (COTS) software. In these cases, the SIL assignment process should enable the designer to look at the risk in the application context, rather than apply "blanket" rules. Similarly, an application developed under an S3-level process for one set of requirements should *not* automatically be considered to have S3-integrity for a different set of requirements, as the critical failure modes may be different.

A framework is required which allows components' contribution to safety to be assessed and SILs allocated accordingly.

3.5 Evaluation criteria

In existing approaches there is typically no "closing of the loop" with respect to integrity: once SILs are set they are not normally analysed, verified or tested anywhere in the rest of the development life-cycle. Knowing what process was followed in developing a system is not assurance enough on its own: evaluation criteria should be defined, and related back to integrity requirements allocation, to assess how thoroughly the process was followed and how thoroughly the product was checked.

Similarly, there are many cases where information on the development process is not available or not applicable: e.g. customization; maintenance; use of COTS; safety integrity of data (e.g. for rule-based or table-driven applications). Ideally, we would like to have ways of analysing the product and evaluation criteria which can be applied independently of knowledge about the development process.

3.6 Summary

There are a number of unsatisfactory aspects of current approaches to setting
SILs, and the absence of effective means for assessing achievement of SILs.
Taken individually, none of the difficulties are sufficient to suggest that current approaches should be abandoned, but taken together they suggest a more
systematic and defensible approach is needed.

4 Risk modelling and SILs

This section proposes what we believe to be a more effective approach to setting
and assessing SILs, together with some theoretical justification. The approach
is based on a framework for modelling risk and integrity allocation which gen-
eralizes existing approaches and addresses the requirements above.

Risk models are explained in §4.1, §4.2 indicates how SILs would be allocated, and §4.3 gives a small example. We hope to be able to provide practical
evidence of the utility of the approach in the foreseeable future.

4.1 Risk modelling using CCA

The framework adapts and refines *Cause-Consequence Analysis (CCA)* [11] as
a technique for modelling risk in computer-based systems. CCA combines the
inductive reasoning features of Event Tree Analysis (ETA) with the deductive
features of Fault Tree Analysis (FTA).

In brief, construction of a CCA *risk model* starts with the choice of a *critical
event* – typically, failure of a major component. The consequences of the event
are traced through to *outcomes* in a manner similar to ETA, by considering the
different chains of events that may arise. Branches in chains correspond, for
example, to the success or failure of protective features in the system's design.
As in ETA, probabilities are associated with branching nodes; however, as an
extension of ETA, fault trees may also be attached to nodes to explain how
the probabilities were calculated. Possible common causes are noted and taken
into account in probability calculation. Finally, another fault tree is used to
record all possible causes of the critical event in question, and to explain its
probability. A simple example of a CCA model is given in Fig. 2 below.

We have chosen CCA because it supports both causal and consequence
analysis in a single framework and it has a quantitative basis. It generalises
ETA and FTA, two of the most commonly applied quantitative approaches,[3]
and is a natural extension of CHAZOP [13].

4.2 Proposal for allocation of SILs

It is evident that, because of the huge variety of possible applications of software, a rule-based approach to allocation of SILs is inevitably of limited credibility, at least for generic standards. Rather than give rules for how SILs are
to be assigned to systems or components, we propose that system designers
be allowed to use their experience to determine SILs and then justify their
choice using risk models. The risk models would describe the system's safety

---

[3]FTA has been successfully applied at software level [12].

features and explain the allocation of integrity requirements. For the reasons given above. we believe CCA to be an appropriately general framework for risk modelling.

Following IEC 1508. we think of a SIL as a measure of "the likelihood of a safety-related system satisfactorily performing the required safety functions under all the stated conditions within a stated period of time" [1].

The integrity requirements allocation process would then proceed as follows:

1. Define risk models for the system at an appropriate level of detail.

2. Determine tolerable failure rates for each of the different possible classes of outcome.

3. Choose targets for component failure rate limits, and confirm that they lead to tolerable system failure rates using the risk models.

4. Assign SILs to components to meet all identified target failure rates, using some agreed interpretation of SILs.

A simple example is sketched in §4.3 below.

This process could be tailored to give more specific rules for setting SILs for specific application domains where, for example, the context and tolerabilities of risk are well understood. For example, the above approach would allow sector-specific regulatory authorities to define rules based on, say, worst case hazard severity, most likely hazard severity, or "average" severity as they deemed appropriate, and to have the risk analysis as the context for explaining their rules.

We believe the above to be a rational way of handling SILs which is compatible with the technically defensible aspects of the approaches reviewed above, and which avoids some of the more questionable aspects of those approaches.

4.3 A simple example

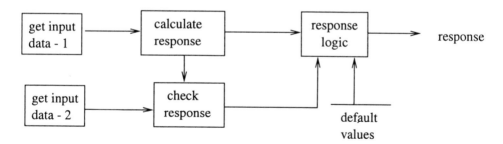

Figure 1: A simple recovery block system.

Fig. 1 shows a simple 'recovery block' strategy for checking the results of a calculation before passing them on, and substituting default values if an error is revealed. The rationale for such an architecture is that it is often simpler to check a solution than to calculate it, and default values can often be found which may be sub-optimal but which at least are safe (e.g. when calculating

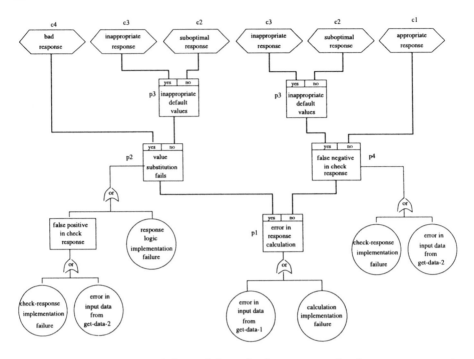

Figure 2: CCA model for failure of the 'calculate response' software component.

the setting for a control signal). We assume two independent means are used for accessing input data.

Fig. 2 shows a risk model for one of the main system failure modes: the critical event 'error in response calculation'. Note that the model makes some strong assumptions about independence of components which won't be discussed here.

Suppose the tolerable occurrence rates for the various possible outcomes are as follows:

$$c4 = 10^{-6}, \; c3 = 10^{-5}, \; c2 = 10^{-2}$$

(given as probability per operation of the system). Assuming the risk model in Fig. 2 is a reasonable model of cause and effect for the given architecture, then the designer would be justified in setting the following target component failure rates:

$$p1 = 10^{-2}, \; p2 = 10^{-4}, \; p3 = 10^{-3}, \; p4 = 10^{-2}$$

Using an interpretation of SILs as a measure of failure rates such as

SIL	$S1$	$S2$	$S3$	$S4$
failure rate †	10^{-1}	10^{-2}	10^{-3}	10^{-4}

† probability of failure upon demand

then the following assignment of SILs to software components would be consistent with the risk model: response logic ($S4$); check response ($S4$); get data-2 ($S4$); default values ($S3$); get data-1 ($S2$); calculate response ($S2$).

4.4   Observations on the example

We can briefly review the example against the requirements of §3:

1. The severity assessment takes into account all the outcomes in a balanced way, although other strategies (e.g. worst case outcome) would have been possible.

2. Likelihood is evaluated using classical, well accepted analysis techniques. Note that the possibility of new hazards (e.g. inappropriate default values substituted) is also covered.

3. Hazards and benefits are shown in one diagram, enabling benefits to be taken into account, if so desired. The CCA model includes 'appropriate response' as an outcome.

4. Software components have been isolated, enabling various integrity levels to be assigned (although this must be tempered by the ability to ensure partitioning in implementation).

5. The framework spans different technologies.

6. With each SIL is associated a range of failure probabilities for which statistical evaluation support is available (see §5 below). Note also that an integrity level has been assigned to data; in our experience this is often both necessary and helpful – although it is not fully encompassed within existing standards.

5   Software-directed evaluation criteria

As noted in §3.5 above, it is important that SIL achievement can be verified independent of assignment. As we have argued, the current process – which could be caricatured as roughly "we need this SIL so we use this process; we've used this process so we've achieved this SIL" – does not provide sufficient assurance. Ideally, standards should define what evidence is required in a safety case to show that the target SIL has been achieved.

Space does not permit a full exposition of the proposed approach here, but we give an outline, starting with three key principles:[4]

1. As far as possible, SIL probabilities (claim limits) should be statistically verifiable.[5]

2. The predominant source of problems is requirements analysis and definition, so even the lowest SIL should be based on a requirements assessment. Successively higher SILs should require deeper assessment – of detailed design, then source code, and finally object code.

3. Diverse means of assessment should be used wherever possible: e.g. static analysis and dynamic testing.

---

[4] See [14] for more discussion of these and related points.

[5] Ideally, analytic evidence of safety would be presented, in the form of software safety analysis or formal verification, for example. In many cases, however, statistical approaches may be the only alternative (e.g. with COTS).

These principles underlie the choice of failure rates ($10^{-1} \cdots 10^{-4}$ for $S1 \cdots S4$) in §4.3, since failure probabilities of 10^{-4} per demand are about the limit of what can be evaluated statistically under normal circumstances [15]. Note that by applying such stringent claim limits to SILs, we are not explicitly ruling out the use of software in higher reliability categories (i.e., with failure rates below 10^{-4}), but instead are requiring that software architectures for such applications be modelled in sufficient detail, and with sufficient justification of software component independence and fault-propagation behaviour, that the above figures can be applied.

Turning to the individual SILs, we propose the following measures to demonstrate attainment of $S1$:

- Preliminary Hazard Analysis (PHA) and traceability from requirements to PHA results and hazard log (where appropriate) to show validity of requirements;

- requirements review by an independent team to show validity (diverse check);

- design documented and reviewed;

- full traceability from requirements to code, to show all functions are implemented and no spurious functions are accessible;[6]

- black-box testing with a "life-testing" reliability probability target of 10^{-1} [15];

- testing in the integrated system, as a diverse check;

- version and configuration control [16], without which the other results are meaningless.

These measures follow the above principles and give a base level of assurance that would be required for any safety-related system: namely, that safety requirements have been identified and implemented.

For SIL $S2$ we would add:

- safety analysis of the architecture, e.g. by CHAZOP and identification of derived safety requirements, to ensure the design introduces no new hazards or intolerable risks;

- traceability extended to include derived safety requirements;

- validation of architecture by review, formal analysis or animation, as a diverse form of evidence;

- black-box testing, with reliability probability target increased to 10^{-2}.

This gives additional confidence regarding safety of the design, and thus the use of an $S2$ component has lower risk than use of $S1$ software – which is what we'd expect.

---

[6]This allows for the possibility of spurious, but inaccessible, functions in COTS software, for example.

For SIL $S3$ we would extend hazard/safety analysis down to source code and require coverage analysis (e.g. via white-box testing). At SIL $S4$, these principles would be extended to object code. At each stage, the black-box testing target would be increased by factor of 10.

Space does not allow full justification of the above, but some points are worth noting here:

1. For most software, failure probability targets of less than 10^{-4} are beyond the range of what can be established by positive testing [15]. Testing targets would still be useful, however, for negative assessment of SILs: e.g. to reject software for $S3$ or $S4$ when bugs are found when testing against a target of 10^{-4}.

2. No special case has been made for formal methods in the above. We note however that such methods become increasingly cost-effective for higher SILs: e.g. for path function analysis [17] to show source code coverage at level $S3$.

3. The degree of complexity of the software should be taken into account: the more complex the solution, the more thorough the checks applied. Consideration should also be given to the amount and nature of operating experience.

Finally, it is also worth noting that an advantage of the risk-model based approach in §4 is that it identifies the need for independence, for example in the software/hardware mapping or with respect to common-mode design faults. The analysis at each SIL can be extended to consider independence, but space does not allow discussion here.

6 Conclusions

In summary, this paper has drawn attention to some of the problems with standard approaches to software safety integrity levels and has proposed an improved approach. The proposal centres around the use of risk assessment as a technique for assigning and assessing safety integrity requirements. The paper proposes Cause-Consequence Analysis as an appropriate basis for risk assessment, and outlines an approach to evaluation criteria for assessing achievement of SILs.

We believe CCA is easier to understand and apply than current approaches to SIL allocation, and leads to more credible results. While CCA may not currently be familiar in the software safety community, and needs some adaptation and refinement for software analysis, the technique is a straightforward extension of concepts (ETA, FTA) which *are* currently widely understood and applied. We note that CHAZOP is essentially a predictive form of CCA, as it considers both causes and effects of deviations (critical events). Thus, a final benefit of our proposed approach is that it can be applied initially in association with CHAZOP and then refined in the detailed-design stages, when enough information is available to construct the CCA.

In further work we plan to validate the proposed approach by (1) showing how existing approaches map onto it, and (2) applying it to industrial case studies (albeit retrospectively).

References

[1] IEC. Functional safety: safety-related systems. Draft International Standard IEC 1508, June 1995.

[2] U.K. Ministry of Defence. Safety Management Requirements for Defence Systems Containing Programmable Electronics. Second Draft Defence Standard 00-56, August 1996.

[3] U.S. Dept of Defense. System safety program requirement. Military Standard MIL-STD 882C, January 1993.

[4] Radio Technical Commission for Aeronautics. Software considerations in airborne systems and equipment certification. RTCA DO178B, 1992.

[5] Railway Industry Association (U.K.). Safety related software for railway signalling. RIA Technical Specification No.23, 1991. Consultative Document.

[6] Motor Industry Software Research Association (U.K.). Development guidelines for vehicle based software, November 1994.

[7] B. Littlewood, M. Neil, and G. Ostrolenk. Uncertainty in software-intensive systems. *High Integrity Systems*, 1(5):407–413, 1996.

[8] N.G. Leveson. *Safeware: System Safety and Computers*. Addison Wesley, Reading, Mass, 1995.

[9] NATO. Safety design requirements and guidelines for munition related safety critical computing systems. Standardization Agreement STANAG 4404.

[10] IEC. Risk Analysis of technological systems – Application guide. International Standard IEC 300-3 Part 9, 1995.

[11] E.J. Henley and H. Kumamoto. *Probabilistic Risk Assessment: Reliability Engineering, Design and Analysis*. IEEE Press, 1992.

[12] N.G. Leveson, S.S. Cha, and T.J. Shimeall. Safety verification of Ada programs using software fault trees. *IEEE Software*, July:48–59, 1991.

[13] U.K. Ministry of Defence. A Guideline for HAZOP Studies on Systems which include a Programmable Electronic System. Draft Interim Defence Standard 00-58/1, March 1995.

[14] J. McDermid. Assurance in high-integrity software. In C.T. Sennett, editor, *High-Integrity Software*, chapter 10. Plenum Press, 1989.

[15] R.W. Butler and G.B. Finelli. The infeasibility of experimental quantification of life-critical software reliability. *ACM SigSoft*, 16(5), 1991.

[16] ISO. Quality management and assurance standards. Part 3: Guidelines for application of ISO 9001 to the development, supply and maintenance of software. International Standard ISO 9000-3, 1993.

[17] B. Carré. Program analysis and verification. In C.T. Sennett, editor, *High-Integrity Software*, chapter 8. Plenum Press, 1989.

Integration of Safety Requirements in the Initial Phases of the Project Lifecycle of Hardware/Software Systems
An Experience Report based on the application of IEC 1508

Marc Wilikens (*), Marcelo Masera(*), Davide Vallero(**)
(*)Joint Research Centre - Institute for Systems, Informatics and Safety
TP 210 - 21020 Ispra (VA) Italy
email: Marc.Wilikens@jrc.it
Tel: +39 332 789737, fax: +39 332 789576
(**)Politecnico di Torino

Abstract

This paper reports on work aimed at identifying a methodology and at defining a coherent safety life-cycle to the development of systems containing software. In particular, emphasis is placed on the initial life-cycle phases, the ones in which safety problems are generally disregarded due to limited availability of information on product characteristics and due to difficulties in treating the problem from a functional point of view. The methodology was applied to a braking system of a high speed train, and takes into account principles defined in the IEC 1508 draft standard. The methodology includes systems modelling and analysis techniques integrated in the requirements phases and organised consistent with the standard IEC 1508 in order to derive software system safety requirements. It consists in the organisation of the requirements in a structured way, functional modelling of the system, deviation analysis for hazard identification, functional Top Level Fault Tree analysis to support hazard analysis, analysis of the functional criticality and identification of safety requirements.

1. Integration of Safety in the early life-cycle phases

It is now generally acknowledged that early phases in the development life-cycle, such as requirements and specification, become extremely relevant for dependability. It is crucial to identify hazards early in the design process, then to take appropriate design measures to eliminate or control these hazards. In addition, early detection of errors significantly reduces the cost of the production process. Performing hazard analysis at various stages of the development life-cycle is now mandated by existing and emerging standards related to programmable systems. New emerging industry standards like IEC 1508 - draft [2], promote a risk based approach and introduce concepts like safety life-cycle and integrity levels as a framework for carrying out safety related activities integrated in the design activities, and considering both hardware and software components. While the enforcement of a more disciplined and structured process of critical software specification and development is certainly a must, it should also be accompanied by the development and use of tools for modelling and analysis of software requirements and design specifications, in the context of the system and the environment where the software is meant to operate.

Recent work over the last years, has lead to the utilisation of a range of specialised informal and formal analysis and verification techniques integrated in the life-cycle of the software-based system. Holistic approaches, targeted to analyse system issues, use system safety and reliability techniques, such as FMEA, FTA and HAZOP; however, their use is only recently emerging for software systems.

The HAZOP technique, a well established hazard identification technique for the petro-chemical industries, has been adapted and applied to PES by a number of organisations [1], [3]. HAZOP studies the interactions between components. It is an inductive technique for identifying consequences of deviations of interactions. At system level, these consequences can correspond to hazards. Thus models incorporating such interactions are required. In general, it is applied at mid-levels of design detail. An innovative use would be at the very high level of design abstraction (early phases), when interfaces with other systems are defined.

Safety Analysis techniques at the software requirements and specification stage have been developed in [4], [6], [9], [10]. In these works, emphasis has been placed on FMEA techniques which, usually applied at high design detail of the software, have been adapted for the earlier software development phases.

Leveson and Colleagues have been developing a series of techniques and tools to analyse safety-critical software. Safety analysis tools for a state based requirements specification have been applied to a Automated Highway System [8] and to an air transport guidance system [9].

Areas which still cause concerns with these techniques are [1], [5]: Managerial (interaction between team members, life-cycle issues, management of the information related to analysis results) and methodological (applicability to various design representations (models) of the system). Furthermore, additional problems to be dealt with when applying these analysis methods are: the choice and combination of methods, abstraction level of their application. On the other hand, emerging standards, like the draft IEC 1508 can guide the safety engineering of software based products but due to their generic nature are still difficult to apply in an industrial setting. This is the case for the initial life-cycle phases for which, apart from the information about risk levels, the IEC 1508 provides limited information on how to apply these phases.

Any safety practice integrated in the design process needs to take into account at least two more aspects:

- Support for traceability: Providing traceability through all the phases of the life-cycle, and back to the requirements phase, helps to bridge the gap between system dependability and software dependability and enables the knowledge acquired during dependability analysis to be used more effectively during design, and also for the certification procedure.
- Robustness: Safety-critical systems must strive to maintain safe behaviour even in the presence of failures of system components and when the behaviour of the environment deviates from that expected. To take these adverse circumstances into account, safety analysis must incorporate techniques that identify potential failure modes and conditions that violate basic assumptions. Additional safety requirements must be included in the software design to ensure that the software will be robust in the presence of such anomalous behaviour.

We report on the results of a realistic case study, aimed at applying from a methodological point of view, the IEC 1508 standard during the initial development phases. In practice this entails, starting from the set of system requirements at the possession of the sub-system developer, the formulation of safety requirements in terms of safety functions and their integrity level. The case study is concerned with a braking system of a high speed train. The system requirements are produced by the train integrator together with the railroad operator and expressed in natural language. This scenario corresponds with a typical one in which a sub-system supplier, designs and develops technology for a sub-system (braking system), while assuring the satisfaction of dependability requirements demanded at the system level. In figure 1, a schematic overview is given of the approach adopted. On the left hand side of the figure, the safety life-cycle phases taken into account are indicated. On the right hand side, we indicate the different modelling and analysis methods conceived and applied within each corresponding phase. These methods are part of an overall methodology that has been developed to derive software system dependability requirements consistent with the emerging IEC 1508 Standard. The method integrates a Deviation Analysis method derived from HAZOP principles applied on a functional model of the system with a Functional Top Level Fault Tree Analysis for Hazard Identification, Analysis and Dependability allocation to software functions. In the following, we explain how this methodology is integrated in the various initial life-cycle phases.

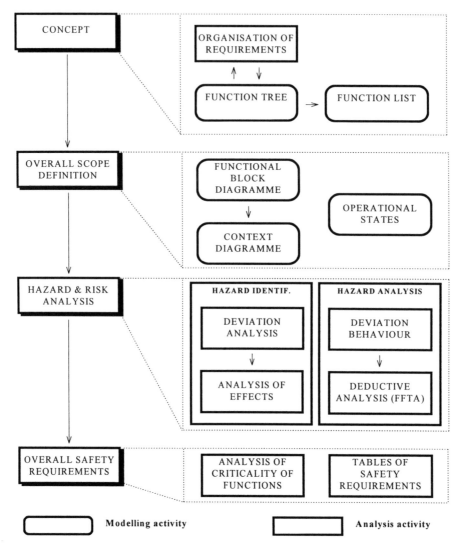

figure 1: Schematic overview of approach

2. Concept phase

The objective of this phase is to gain basic knowledge of the system under development. Starting from a narrative system requirements document, the information is uniformly organised in tabular form based on a series of attributes (figure 2). A rigid formalism based on well defined rules (structure of sentences, numbering scheme) and a requirements classification scheme allow for enhanced manageability and traceability of the requirements. The rigour with which this process is performed is fundamental for subsequent phases of the analysis. One direct result, is that the functional requirements can be separated from the other types.

		Type					Level	Flexibility	Definition	Origin
REFERENCE	**Classification of Requirements Braking system ETR 500**	FUNCTIONAL	ARCHITECTURE	PERFOMANCE	RAMS	OPERATIONAL	1 System 2 Sub-s. 3 Comp.	1 Essential 2 Negotiate 3 Suggested	1 Precise 2 Indicative 3 Generic	
1	REQUIREMENT X				X	X	1	1	2	Client
2	REQUIREMENT Y		X		X		1	1	1	Client

figure 2 : organisation of requirements: table layout

Subsequently, the functional requirements are organised in a so-called *function tree* model aimed at providing a first hierarchical view of the system in terms of functionality and at completing the functional requirements (figure 3). Starting from the principal system functions, lower level functions necessary for satisfying the parents are identified and connected by means of AND logic. At this stage it is important to note that, consistent with a functional view, the choice of AND logic precludes architectural solutions to for instance redundancy . The origin of each function in the tree must be specified in order to validate correctness of the model. As such, a function can be directly derived from a functional requirement. The need to allocate all previously identified functional requirements in the function tree is a necessary condition for its consistency. In turn, functional requirements can be specified with more precision when construction of the tree proceeds. Both processes, tree construction and functional requirements definition, occur concurrently. Cross validation and validation with the customer guarantee a minimum level of consistency with the system under development.

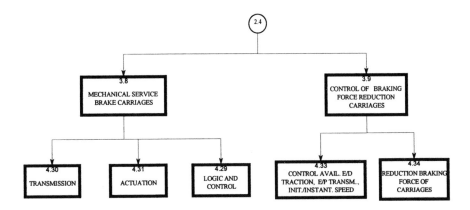

figure 3: layout of Function Tree

3.   Overall Scope definition phase

In the second phase of the safety life-cycle, one has to deepen the level of knowledge about the system. This entails defining the relationships between the various functions and the types of flows between them. In addition, the functional border of the system has to be defined in order to understand the interaction of the system with its environment. This eventually guides the process of hazard identification. We have chosen a representation based on the SADT formalism [14] as this was a design representation with which the sub-system developer had experience.

The Function Block Diagram (FBD) is a pictorial hierarchical representation of the functions and their relationship (figure 4). It uses knowledge from the function tree in such a way that with each level in the function tree corresponds one level in the FBD. In addition, it contains the flows interchanged between the functions and thus inherently knowledge about potential influences of one function on the other. We noticed that a bottom-up approach in constructing the diagram is the most effective for assuring coherence of input/output flows across the various levels.   It is important to validate the link between the block diagram and the artefacts constructed so far during the concept phase: there is a one-to-one relationship between the functions in the function tree and in the block diagram. If during construction of the diagram, some incoherence emerges in the hierarchical arrangement of a function, one has to refer back to adapt the function tree, which would in turn need a correction to the function list.

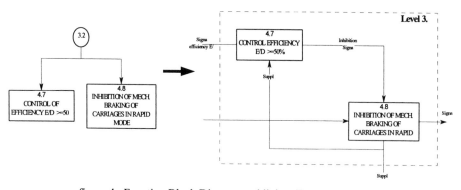

figure 4 : Function Block Diagram and link to Function Tree

The context diagram is the natural conclusion on highest level of the functional block diagram construction. It represents the top function in the context of its operational environment (figure 5). The information contained in this diagram is important because it allows to identify logical connections for the propagation of hazardous conditions from the braking system to the electro-mechanical system with which it interfaces and vice-versa.

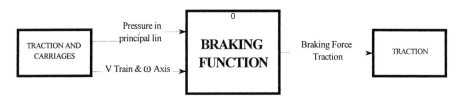

figure 5 : Part of context diagram

A type of modelling which is different but complementary from the previous ones is related to the description of the operational states of the system. The techniques developed in the subsequent hazard and risk analysis phase have indeed revealed the need for the concurrent use of such a model with the functional model. We have constructed by way of example a simplified hierarchical state model based on the Finite State Machine formalism and which is correlated with the functional groups in the function tree.

4.   Hazard and Risk analysis phase

4.1.   Hazard Identification & Risk class

In the third phase of the safety life-cycle, the results of the modelling activities prepared during the previous two phases are employed for analysis techniques aimed at identifying hazards that could jeopardise the safety of the system. Second, the objective is to, starting from a risk evaluation, give a qualitative indication of the severity classes of the hazards and a probability level of their occurrence.

In the proposed methodology applied to this case study, the hazard identification is performed by means of a systematic analysis of the flows in the functional block diagram. Indeed, a deviation analysis of the flows is appropriate at functional level, because at this stage of development, little information is available about implementation details of the functions; on the other hand, the information about flows and their types is more detailed. The analysis is performed by applying deviations to the flows in question. The possible deviations of flows can be grouped in a limited set of general classes, identified by guide words. The classes of guide words that were applied to our case study are: **Omission, Commission:, Timing (Early), Timing (Late), Value (Low)** and **Value (High)**. The application of these guide words to a specific flow will lead to a specific deviation. For our case study, a taxonomy for classifying flows has been developed which together with the appropriate guide words forms a knowledge base for supporting the deviation analysis (figure 6). A classification of flow types is useful for focusing the analysis to plausible deviations. For instance, deviations of type *Value(low)* would not be applicable to control signals of type *on/off*.

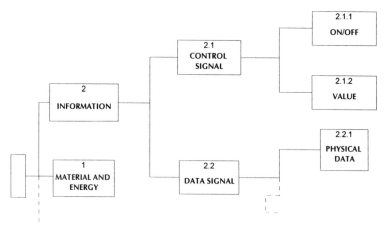

figure 6: Taxonomy of flow types

The procedure adopted for applying the deviation analysis is the following: All functions at lowest level in the Functional Block Diagram are considered and for each of them, the output flows are one by one analysed. The information this generates is compiled into appropriate tables (figure 7).

We note that the information on operational state is fundamental for at least two reasons. A particular deviation is meaningful in one or more operational states only and not in others. Moreover, a same deviation in two different states could result in different consequences possibly with different severity. The system effect represents the final effect of the deviation at low level in the model, but under the hypothesis that no other failure manifests itself concurrently. This means, typical for this type of inductive process, considering single failures in the analysis. However, for hazard identification, no information is lost in this way if one rigorously considers deviations of all the output flows of the low-level functions.

TABEL n°:			*2*	
Level in FBD:			*4.13*	
Source Function:			*5.14*	
Name of Flow:			*Signal in train cockpit*	
Type of Flow:			*2.2.2 (operational data)*	
Description:			*Signal in train cockpit of blocked axis of carriages*	

GUIDE WORD	DEVIATION	OPERATIONAL STATE	FUNCTION FAILURE	SYSTEM EFFECT
Omission	Cancellation of signal	Train in movement. Rapid braking mode. Mechanical braking mode of carriages.	Failure of 5.14: Failed to generate signal when axes blocked.	Omission of signal in cockpit. Driver not informed about axis blocking.
Commission	Inadvertent generation of signal	idem	Failure of 5.14: Generates signal with axis non-blocked.	Commission of signal in cockpit. Driver wrongly informed about blocked axis.
Timing (Late)	...	...	...	...

figure 7: Deviation analysis table

Another implicit but more serious hypothesis has to be considered more carefully. The analysis presupposes that the functions conserve their same behaviour, also when the inputs are deviated from normal values. This can not be taken for granted a priori: a function could react differently and in an unexpected way to an input which is too High than to nominal ranges of values. In the subsequent design phase, behaviours different from the one hypothesised need to be reanalysed in the light of the then available information about the real component.

In the second part of the hazard identification, the set of all *system effects* resulting from the above analysis are further analysed for identifying possible consequences for the train system, passengers, environment in terms of availability, maintainability, safety. The safety related consequences in turn give rise to the hazards. Each of them is represented according to an appropriate classification scheme (figure 8).

	Reference number:3
	Hazard: Unwanted Braking
System:	**Braking system**
Operational State:	**Train in movement. No braking.**
Hazard Description:	**Without command signal, the braking system produces a braking force on the carriages, possibly with max. force.**
Related Deviations:	**Commission** (1.1 F braking carriages)
Consequences for persons:	**In case of intense braking, possible injuries to passengers.**
Consequences for train:	**Maintenance**
Severity Category:	**2 - Marginal**
Probability Level:	**D - Remote**
Risk Class:	**Tolerable**

figure 8: Table for Hazard classification

The severity of a hazard is evaluated according to sector specific qualitative criteria and hazard severity categories, in this case the railway standard prEN 10126 [11]. Regarding the probability level, it is appropriate at this stage of development to consider this parameter as a requirement based on maximum admissible risk. Indeed, a qualitative evaluation of the risk is the best we can obtain at this stage.

	CONSEQUENCE HAZARD SEVERITY CATEGORY			
PROBABILITY LEVEL	**Catastrophic 4**	**Critical 3**	**Marginal 2**	**Insignificant 1**
A - Frequent	4A	3A	2A	1A
B - Probable	4B	3B	2B	1B
C - Occasional	4C	3C	2C	1C
D - Remote	4D	3D	2D	1D
E - Improbable	4E	3E	2E	1E
F - Incredible	4F	3F	2F	1F

figure 9: risk classes taken from (11)

4.2. Hazard Analysis

To explore the cause of a specific hazard, an effective method is a deductive analysis like for instance a Fault Tree analysis. Starting from a hazard, which is nothing more than one or a combination of deviations at system level, causes will be searched in the form of failure of functions or abnormal deviations of input flows to the braking system. The first problem in the development of a fault tree applied to a functional scheme is knowledge of the failure behaviour of the functional model i.e. how do deviated outputs relate to deviated input flows. We have developed a formalisation scheme for representing the hypothesised deviation behaviour of functions. This is useful for at least two reasons: 1) it permits construction of the fault tree with a minimum level of reproducibility possibly augmented with semi-automatic procedures; 2) a formalisation of the hypothesis made about behaviour of the functions provides to the designer a way to verify the analysis performed previously. The scheme includes a table per function (figure 10). For each plausible output deviation, the related set of input deviations and functional failure modes are compiled. These functional failure modes are described only in terms of their effects and do not indicate internal failure modes. Nevertheless, they are important for subsequent evaluation of criticality of the functions.

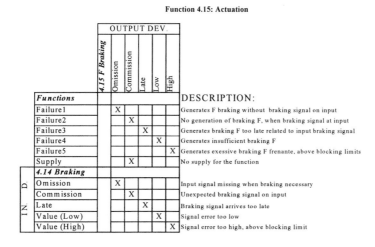

Function 4.15: Actuation

		4.15 F Braking	Omission	Commission	Late	Low	High	DESCRIPTION:
	Functions							
	Failure1		X					Generates F braking without braking signal on input
	Failure2			X				No generation of braking F, when braking signal at input
	Failure3				X			Generates braking F too late related to input braking signal
	Failure4					X		Generates insufficient braking F
	Failure5						X	Generates exessive braking F frenante, above blocking limits
	Supply			X				No supply for the function
	4.14 Braking							
IN. D	Omission		X					Input signal missing when braking necessary
	Commission			X				Unexpected braking signal on input
	Late				X			Braking signal arrives too late
	Value (Low)					X		Signal error too low
	Value (High)						X	Signal error too high, above blocking limit

figure 10: Deviation behaviour of function

The fault trees were constructed by means of ISPRA-FTA, a commercial tool developed in the JRC [12, 13]. The principal use made of the tool in this work was the determination of the minimal cut sets. On this basis, basic events (functional failure modes or input flow deviations) can be ordered according to their criticality (in the tool represented by a number between 0 and 1). The criticality of 1 corresponds with a single point failure. At this point, we note that criticality of a function is a measure for the weight of the function in the fault tree and is not yet related to the hazard severity. This is handled in the identification of safety requirements, the subject of the subsequent phase in the analysis.

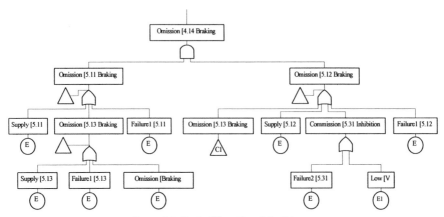

figure 11: Part of functional fault tree

5.   Overall safety requirements phase

In this phase, the results of the modelling and analysis tasks performed so far are synthesised in a set of safety requirements, which eventually have to be added to the original system requirements. The resulting requirements form the input for the successive design phases in which architectural decisions have to be taken. One of the main problems that emerges already in this initial stage of the development, is the difficulty of managing the vast amount of information generated so far and to communicate this effectively to the designers.

The mechanism proposed in the IEC 1508 consists in determining the so called *Safety Functions*. These are functions created *ex nuovo* or existing, which are in one way or another involved in the process of hazard generation and which proper functioning are on the basis of the prospected risk reduction to acceptable levels. To each of these safety functions, a Safety Integrity Level is then associated which puts requirements on the downstream development process. Such an approach permits in effect to transform in a synthetic manner all the information gathered in previous hazard analysis phases. In applying these concepts, a major problem encountered is the following. The assignment of integrity levels, according to IEC, is done quantitatively based on predefined criteria. However, the information available on the system at present is qualitative in nature. In an attempt to follow the guidelines in the standard , we used the information derived from the functional fault tree analysis for allocating the probability level of each hazard to the various basic events (functional failure modes and flow deviations) . This takes into account the criticality of the events and the cut set (single, double, ...) of which they are part. The results provided failure rates requirements which were outside reasonable range (probability of failure per hour $< 10^{-5}$) , logical consequence of the fact that there are no functional redundancies in the functional model. At this stage, it seemed more appropriate to maintain the analysis on a qualitative level and to postpone the use of integrity levels as specified in the standard to successive development phases, where more explicit knowledge about real sub-systems with their preliminary physical configuration and architecture is available. For this reason, we introduce the notion of *Criticality Index*, the corresponding but qualitative measure to integrity level.

The index is a weighted combination of the criticality of an event leading to a hazard and the associated hazard severity. A matrix (figure 12) has been created in an ad hoc manner for this purpose.

Table of functional criticality index				
Criticality / Severity	1-0,75	0,75-0,5	0,5-0,25	0,25-0
4 Catastrophic	4	4	3	3
3 Critical	4	3	3	3
2 Marginal	2	2	2	1
1 Insignificant	2	1	1	1

figure 12: Criticality Index table

Four Criticality Indices are defined, similar to the four integrity levels in IEC 1508. The analysis is furthered by ordering, for each hazard, all the events that appear in the minimal cut sets of the functional fault tree. For each event, its criticality is then combined with the hazard severity to deduce its Criticality Index.

Finally, tables which contain in a synthetic way all the information necessary for describing safety requirements have been developed (figure 13). Each table, refers to one safety function or to a critical input flow to the system. The *criticality index* associated to a function (input flow) is the maximum criticality index of the combined set of relevant events i.e failure modes (deviations) for that function (input flow) leading to the system hazards.

SAFETY FUNCTION:
4.15 - ACTUATION

Description:	**Transforms the braking command in braking power on the carriages, acting mechanically on the braking discs.**
Input flows:	• **[4.14 Braking]**
Output flows:	• **[4.15 Braking F carriages]**
Hazards associated	1. **No rapid braking carriages** 2. **Rapid braking carriages: Late** 3. **Rapid braking carriages: Insufficient**
Functional criticality index maximum	4

Functional criticality of the failure modes of the function			
Description of failure modes	Hazard n°	Criticality	
Failure1: **No braking power when braking command on input**	1	1	4
Failure 2: **Generates braking power without input signal**	3	1	3
Failure 3: **Generates braking power too late with Respect to input signal**	2	1	4
Failure 4: **Generates insufficient braking power**	1	1	4
Supply: **No supply**	3	1	3

Comments

• **The function is critical for hazard severities 3 and 4**
• **The function alone can lead to hazard numbers 1, 2 and 3 (single point Failure)**

figure 13: safety requirement

6. Conclusions

In this work, we have presented a methodological process, based on the draft IEC 1508 safety life-cycle, for integrating safety aspects into the initial phases of the system life-cycle. The main objective is by means of an adapted hazard analysis process, to identify critical functions. By translating these in safety requirements, we gave an added value to the initial system requirements provided by the customer. A representation scheme for hazards as well as safety requirements have been proposed. Such schemes form the backbone for the vast amount of information generated during the analysis and allow for traceability during subsequent design and eventual safety case production. Difficulties were found in applying the numerical criteria of IEC's integrity levels. We have opted for a quantitative approach, by means of criticality indices, for remedying this problem at the requirements phase. Another difficulty in applying the IEC standard was found in the treatment of normal functional system requirements as safety functions, independent from the introduction of specific protection functions.

7.   References

1.   A guideline for HAZOP studies on Systems which include Programmable Electronic Systems. M.F. Chudleigh, J.R.Catmur, F.Redmill. In Proceedings of the 14th International Conference on Computer Safety, Reliability and Security (SAFECOMP 95). Belgirate, Italy, 11-13 October 1995.Springer, edited by Gerhard Rabe.

2.   IEC 1508, Functional Safety- Safety related systems. International Electrotechnical Commission. 1995.

3.   A Development of Hazard Analysis to aid Software Design. J.A.McDermid, D.Pumfrey. In proceedings of the ninth annual conference on Computer Assurance (COMPASS '94). Gaithersburg, MD, July 1994. Pp. 17-25.

4.   A systematic approach for the analysis of safety requirements for process control systems. R. De Lemos, A. Saeed, T. Anderson. Second year report of PDCS2, Predictably Dependable Computing Systems.

5.   Experience with the application of HAZOP to Computer-Based Systems. J.A.McDermid, M.Nicholson, D.Pumfrey. In proceedings of the tenth annual conference on Computer Assurance (COMPASS '95). Gaithersburg, MD, June 1995. Pp. 37-48.

6.   FMEA and FTA to support safe design of embedded software in safety-critical systems. T. Maier. In proceeding of 12 th CSR workshop and 1 st ENCRESS conference, Bruges, September 1995.

7.   Safety Analysis Tools for Requirements Specifications. Vivek Ratan, Kurt Partridge, Jon Reese, Nancy Leveson. In proceedings of the eleventh annual conference on Computer Assurance (COMPASS '96). Gaithersburg, MD, June 1996.

8.   Integrated Safety Analysis of Requirements Specifications. F. Modugno, N. Leveson, J.D. Reese, K. Partridge, S.D. Sandys. Integrated Safety Analysis of Requirements Specifications. University of Washington Report, May 1996.

9.   Analyzing Software Requirements Errors in Safety-Critical Embedded Systems. Lutz R.: IEEE Proceedings of the International Symposium on Requirements Engineering, 1993.

10.   Lutz R., Woodhouse R.: *Experience Report: Contributions of SFMEA to Requirements Analysis*, ICRE, 1996.

11.   CEN prEN50126 Railway applications - The specification and demonstration of dependability - Reliability, Availability, Maintainability and Safety (RAMS), Draft 1.0, August 1995.

12.   Contini S.: ISPRA-FTA. Interactive Software Package for Reliability analysis. Fault Tree analysis tool for personal computers. Methodological aspects and User Interface description. EUR Report 13997 EN 1992, JRC Ispra 1992.

13.   Contini S. : A new hybrid method for fault tree analysis. Reliability Engineering and Systems Safety, vol 49, 1, 1995.

14.   Ross D.T., Applications and extensions of SADT. IEEE Computer, April 1985.

Managing the Safety Argument using a Memory Prosthesis

David Jenkins, Brian Lees, Daniel Livingstone and Andrew Reglinski
University of Paisley, Paisley, Scotland

Abstract

The production of the safety argument is presented as a design task and the difficulties which it faces are discussed. The nature of the design process inherently presents difficulties for the orderly presentation of its outcome, the finished design. The current and the ideal situation regarding the management of the safety argument is considered. The development of the Online Design Journal and the Designer's Assistant, which together act as a domain free *memory prothesis*, within the Safety Critical Integrated Design Support DTI-EPSRC project is presented and the way in which they can be used to support the construction of the safety case and safety argument is explained. The role of intelligent agents in the augmentation of the functionality provided is considered. Other complementary directions of exploitation of the Designer's Assistant are briefly considered and conclusions drawn.

1 Introduction

This paper discusses the way in which the Online Design Journal (ODJ) and Designer's Assistant [1] will work together to support the post hoc reconstruction of arguments. By taking account of recent reviews of what constitutes a 'Safety Case' and a 'Safety Argument', the degree of assistance which could be expected to be given to the construction of such from the normal operation of the ODJ and Designer's Assistant working together, and with normal safety engineering tools, is discussed and some tentative conclusions reached.

2 The DRG approach to design research

The work of the Design Research Group (DRG) at Paisley owes its genesis to work undertaken by Mr. J Bebbington and the first author at the Engineering Design Research Centre in Glasgow in which two prototypes of a Design History Editor (DHE) were developed to the extent that the basis ideas could be demonstrated. (This work involved Sun EWS and remote use of DB2 on an IBM mainframe in conjunction with CATIA.) Two specific insights were proposed by Mr. Bebbington and found general agreement in the literature, and reported in [2], which was also the basis for much of the DUCK proposal (see below).

The first insight was the clear distinction between how a design is arrived at and how it is finally presented. In [2] the failure of 'top down programming' as a paradigm for beginning students was discussed, maintaining that while a design may be presented in such a tidy fashion, this tidy hierarchy did not represent the actual development of the design, which was described as 'a guddle', with elements of 'bottom-up', 'top-down', 'outside-in', and 'inside-out'.

The second insight, and not unrelated, point is that the designer must not be constrained by the tool she is using by being required to decompose the problem top down (in this case). Bebbington considered that where a designer is constrained by a method, then she will work outside the tool on scraps of paper and then input the final design according to the method. This would have the result that the significant episodes of the design would still be uncaptured with loss of protocol and indexing information.

These points have implications for the implementation of support tools for the process of design. First, implementation systems which impose hierarchy, such as Hypercard, must be avoided, and the adoption of a structured model for the development of the design idea, as in [3], avoided. This conviction led to the original DHE (at least ideally) being implemented as a *free hand sketcher* with text input (labels, annotation) into the drawing a possibility.

3 Impact of work in the DUCK project

The Designers Using Cooperative Knowledge DUCK consortium comprised MARI Computer Systems, BA°SEMA, and the DRG of the University of Paisley. The project looked at the provision of support for shared design (particularly in the early design phase) via standard groupware solutions, using bespoke tools relevant to specific organisational needs, and more widely considers general issues including the creation of a new culture of collaborative and distributed working. Rather than try to restrict expression to a uniform set of notations, the philosophy is to provide an electronic analogue to the designer's day-book, a pad in which design ideas can be noted and developed, supported by other applications -spreadsheets, CAD tools, paintboxes, &c. By essentially changing only the medium, the process of design is no more constrained than before, but the advantage is gained that the design protocol can be captured, and a design history that can be more widely inspected and critiqued.

An on-line design journal has been implemented by MARI [4][5]. It emulates the pages of a journal, shared by groups working on specific projects, and with access rights given to others as required. Use of standard software is monitored invisibly by an associated Protocol Manager while utilities to support self management and reflective working summarise and report on activities using the data captured by the protocol manager. 'On the fly' recording of everyday working coupled with intelligent appraisal of processes is one of the generic benefits of the DUCK toolset.

SCIDS differed from DUCK in being originally focused on the Safety Critical domain and on support for the individual via the use of intelligent agents, but moved towards DUCK as a fuller appreciation of the role of team based activities in the construction of the safety argument developed. Its Online Design Journal retains the sketch facility discarded in DUCK since the final BAᶜSEMA software engineering users only carried out design as individuals. SCIDS developed the Protocol Manager (PM) beyond that developed in DUCK by adding the extraction and recording of the words typed by the designer. By discarding words in a default stoplist, a set of keywords remains. A Lotus Notes database contains documents describing known issues. An agent enquires of the designer when the current issue does not match any of these sufficiently well. Higher level tools assist the designer to review activities and group them in terms of these issues, to support formal reviews, e.g. safety arguments. The Online Design Journal and the Protocol manager together act as a memory prosthesis [6].

The greatest impact upon SCIDS has been from the scoping, user requirement elicitation and piloting work of DUCK. User requirement work in DUCK showed that much of the work to be captured was pure text. This resulted in the even handed treatment of annotated sketches (Bebbington's vision) and of bulk text via the provision of two panes, the LHS being a sketcher and the RHS being a notepad. The final removal of the sketcher was made for the second pilot in BAeSEMA continued this trend because this final pilot did not involve anyone who used sketching. Essentially, however, Bebbington's view of the nature of the DHE did not take any domain aspects into consideration. Thus it is not surprising that in DUCK where MARI's focus was on the user aspects arising within a specific domain that the ODJ differed so markedly. However, as the role of the ODJ and Designer's Assistant in the construction of e.g. safety arguments is considered, it is necessary to continue to distinguish between what is true of early design (the original focus), design concerned with safety aspects, and the construction of the safety argument.

The demands of piloting revealed that the appropriate tactic for requirements elicitation was to provide a minimum appropriate functionality which allowed users to gain an appreciation of the possible thus enabled them to reveal their true requirements in terms of future functionality. Equally dependability of the installed software emerged as of paramount importance, for an undependable application is not used, and this vitiates the strategy just outlined. This, in turn, necessitated a radical change in the way software was produced within the Paisley team. A small 'software cottage' was established and supported using groupware [7] and developed the Protocol Manager (DUCK & SCIDS), a series of reporting applications (DUCK), and the Design Assistant (SCIDS) over a period of thirteen months. Further the user requirement for the Design Assistant arose from the user group in the second pilot, not from the research team (although the architecture had been developed to permit its ready implementation).

4 The Safety Lifecycle

The safety lifecycle may be sketched as follows: This is not based on anyone's actual practice. It is however based on attendance at a vacation school and various safety events by the authors, as well as study of the literature, see, for example, [8], [9], [10] and, in particular, has been confirmed by [11].

Once the brief is received, safety engineers will conduct a top-level hazard analysis where the major risks will be identified. Also, a safety plan is drawn up showing how the project is going to address the task of achieving, and proving that it has achieved, the level of reliability in its safety critical parts that is required in terms of the risk analysis. FMEA and FTA conducted at this level are more concerned with dividing the contribution to overall reliability and the mitigation of risks between functional sub-units. The design of mitigation involves the introduction of safety-critical sub-systems whose only functionality is to mitigate risk, by taking action that will restore the system to a safe state if an event occurs that is being mitigated, i.e. an identified hazard. As the design develops, further hazard analyses are carried out and result in lists of hazards that must be mitigated. The designer must respond to each of these in the course of design. The output of each hazard analysis is a checklist of issues that must be addressed, each such issue being described by the appropriate content of the hazard analysis. Thus a specific set of non-functional requirements is designed to, in addition to the functional requirements. Basically, safety concerns, then merely complicate the design process, they do not alter it (at least, from the perspective of the design researcher). Thus facilities provided to support functional design will also support non-functional design. In any event, the distinction is blurred in the design of safety critical sub-systems, whose raison d'être is to assure safety by mitigating risk.

The safety critical systems added to mitigate hazards at the top (or upper) layers of design will be designed and then elaborated after their own hazard analysis to attain the reliability required to bring the risk within limits. FMEA and FTA figure highly here.

The safety plan will have included provision for the writing of the safety argument. This is seen as a reasoned (but not long-winded) argument that collects together all the evidence that particular risks have been mitigated to an acceptable level, and that, overall, the original risk has been equalled or bettered.

Practically, the safety argument can be written in two ways, either as issues are addressed in the planned way, or post hoc, by pulling together episodes of work as the top-down safety argument is developed. By comparison with earlier remarks, it will be seen that the position taken is that the former is not achievable in practice, unless, in safety engineering, the plan and its tactics are *entirely* known from the outset. Even if this is sought-after, the nature of human affairs is that some 'guddle' will creep in, and there will always be some element of *post hoc* fixing up to do. So the latter is taken as the general case, and the problem addressed is that of bringing together fragments of work in a connected way.

If the domain specific safety issues are abstracted away, then this activity is just the conduct of a design review, and the construction of a safety argument is a specialisation of the task of design documentation. Both conventional journals and the original DHE do not contain the rationale of design. The ODJ and Designer's Assistant were conceived as acting as a memory prosthesis to aid recall of rationale, or to enable its reconstruction by the observer, by finding past work and replaying its design protocol.

Gathering together safety rationale and design rationale are seen as similar tasks, differing only in their legal status and foci. Clearly, establishment of traceability from the later work back into the early work, and *vice versa*, will have considerable value here, avoiding any introduction of the 'over the wall' model which has failed mechanical engineering so dramatically in terms of response to market, &c. This lack of traceability can be argued to have contributed to the *Challenger* disaster, and to those Airbus accidents in which the (flawed) twin mode display of 'rate-of-descent setting' has been identified as a causative factor. In both causes, feedback from the review process, &c, was 'buried'.

5 Understanding design decisions - the elicitation of rationale

Interestingly, at least one author in [11] sees the responsibility for the construction of the Safety Case and its constituent Safety Arguments as belonging to the complete management team. Thus the need for team working emerges strongly from the requirement to build a 'safety culture' throughout both the operational and the design teams. The early work of the management members provides the full brief for the design work.

Understanding a problem is a necessary pre-requisite for an understanding of decisions about the problem. The former is seen as arising from discourse. Thus it is likely that the correct place to look for an explicit expression of rationale is in the project meeting in which major design decisions are taken. In Streveler's approach [12], design alternatives responding to problems (or issues) are debated and selected between the team members. Thus CSCW for team meetings (even if collocated) seems a prerequisite for the capture of rationale. How then do we obtain solutions to problems? One answer here is that we have a stock of approximately correct solutions gained from experience and one of these is selected and tried 'for fit'. This process is fairly obviously going to be helped by the matching of the current issue to previous issues described by its keywords; some will match more closely than others. Such will give guidance on the sub-division problem, and may even suggest a complete solution strategy. We replay solutions to recognised problems without thought. Only in encountering the new, is real thought engaged in. It would thus appear that, often, we must seek in the past the occasion on which a design problem appeared for the first time for an understanding of the decision, the rationale. Here a memory prosthesis is valuable. This is exactly what the Online Design Journal and Designer's Assistant combination can be, provided they has been in use for a sufficiently long time.

The alternative approach is to query the individual designer. From [13] it would appear that the reasons given by designer's in response to intrusive questioning are shaped more by a desire to minimize the interruption and less by a desire to reveal true rationale. The point has just been made that the designer may have so completely internalised the constraints, or prelearned the responses to stock situations, so that it becomes impossible for her to explain the choice, at least, without considerable thought. This would deflect her from the fluent course of the design and result in a different design process than would have occurred without such interruption. The solution adopted has been to minimize intrusion into the design process, a point heavily emphasised by users in the DUCK second pilot. This contrasts with the approach adopted by many workers [14] in design rationale, but their efforts are somewhat more focussed on the capture of rationale from team meetings. In any event tools such as gIBIS may be used in conjunction with the Designer's Asistant.

At the top of the tree, early in the design process, documents describing the 'to be achieved' contain statements about functional and non-functional requirements. For each functional requirement a list of documents appears as the design progresses by sub-division, &c. Early in the list are documents describing the functional requirement in relation to other requirements. Later, documents appear which describe how functional requirements are to be achieved by sub-systems or components, and, still later, each of these is described via further decomposition or by detailing.

6 Roles of the ODJ and of the Designer's Assistant & Protocol Manager

The original view of the DHE and then of the ODJ was that it would provide a "rich" interface by which all the tools used in the design process would be accessed. Also, at the outset, it was the idea that a set of these tools would be provided using a meta CASE tool within the X11 Windows environment so that design rationale could be captured throughout the design lifecycle. With the move to Microsoft Windows as the operating system (in response to technology push and user pull within both DUCK and SCIDS) the emphasis changed to the use of existing tools, with the idea that work, hopefully minimal, would have to be done to install tools "within" the system. In both these cases, the availability of tools would be restricted by resource constraints.

With the development of the Protocol Manager within DUCK and SCIDS, the splitting of responsibilities between the ODJ and the Protocol Manager, which had begun in May 1994, was complete. The ODJ was then seen as "just another design tool" suited to CSCW for the early conceptual stages of design especially, with no role in the Designer's Assistant activity. This final architectural change, more importantly, made it possible for any "Wintel" based design or safety engineering tool to be used in conjunction with the ODJ and removed the resource constraint from the applicability of tools with the Protocol Manager and the Designer's Assistant.

Now, recently, the pendulum has swung in the other direction with the realisation that the ODJ has a key role to play throughout the design lifecycle to support the informal achievement of design rationale capture through its use by the designer to record comments about what is going on which would not be appropriate in the formal design deliverables but which she would like to record in passing. The ODJ would thus be always open and be used as a scratch pad or "stick-it" type note over the current tool in use.

The Designer's Assistant would record in a database the activities and keyword in the ODJ with the same or similar time stamp as the record made of work carried out in the design tool proper. Thus both sets of information would be available to guide the designer. The ODJ set would enable the Designer's Assistant to present a list of pages from the past which referred to work addressing the same focus of interest as that currently in process. This would enable the date stamp information in turn to be used to select episodes of work whose use of tools and documents could be retrieved.

7 The implemented system and its use

As indicated above, the DRG developed an On-Line Design Journal; a shared network based notebook, to support informal collaborative work and record Design History. Collaborative working is supported in two ways. First, all the pages of the notebook are available in a system wide Lotus Notes database. Second, comments and questions, observations and criticisms can be made on overlays over the original page, which is available only in read-only mode once it has been filed by its originator to guarantee the validity of past design history. The overlay allows 'inking' over the LHS (the sketcher) and the placing of notes on the RHS (the text page), which are represented by hotspots which can be either hovered over or clicked on to reveal the comment. A number of overlays is permitted on each page and the reader can select which overlays to view. Overlays are distinguished by colour at this point. They page) in the Notes database.

The Protocol Manager is an independent persistent 'user agent' which operates unobtrusively on each designer's machine to capture Designer Protocol by acting as a 'layer' between the user and the ODJ or other tool. The Protocol Manager characterises work 'episodes' by the attributes: *user, tools, files, duration, pages, time, keywords...* and assembles a Record of Work. In this way, the Protocol Manager collects evidence of the work (as work item records) done by the designer. This evidence is stored in a Lotus Notes database (the *Record of Work*) from which the evidence can be reviewed using the proprietary facilities of Lotus Notes. An individual record characterises a thread of work undertaken that day with all the time spent on a particular file gathered together.

This functionality is augmented and enriched by the use of the Designer Assistant agent alongside the Protocol Manager. This agent (which can be thought of as an additional layer) associates work 'episodes' with related design *Concerns & Decisions* and augments the episode's record with that information. In this way, the two in combination build a record of work consisting of episodes of work, labelled with concern information in which key Decisions & Concerns act as crucial punctuation. The system's Record of Work database is effectively an index into the History of Design stored by the ODJ and other tools since designers can find past work by free text query and browsing of the Notes database to form an effective aid in the recovery, recall and hence reuse of past work.

The Designer's Assistant rather than the Protocol Manager is responsible for classification of work items by design concern. Unless the option has been taken of pre-loading the concerns database with concern data, the Designer's Assistant at first will have no data on concerns. In this case it asks the designer via a small status bar to state the subject concern. If the designer responds with information, then the concern is recorded and the Designer's Assistant associates the features of the active work item with this concern (for use in the longer term in identifying future work items) to maintain a register of concerns. The designer may use the status bar to define the concern in more detail. This is done by the edit/revise option as shown.

A Lotus Notes form is launched. (Alternatively these forms can be completed before work starts, perhaps as a result of a team meeting in which concerns or issues have been allocated to this designer.) The Designer's Assistant maintains a list of identified concerns in an order which reflects their recent use. If the guess about the current concern is wrong then the user can select the correct one via the status bar.

The Register of Concerns is a Lotus Notes Database as shown. A view can be constructed to show Work Items by Concern. Thus access to a history of Design BY Concern can be provided . If the ODJ is involved throughout the life cycle then ideas, concepts and meta level design can be assembled as a means of integrating the concurrent work done with other tools.

8 The use of intelligent agents

The notion of 'agency' is implicit in the preceding description of the operation and interaction of the ODJ, DA and PM. However, there are various interpretations and definitions of what constitutes an agent; the view in the current research is that an agent is an autonomous (software) entity that fulfills some clearly defined task, unobtrusively, and which has the capability of communicating with other agents (and also with the designer, when necessary).The Protocol Manager and the Designer's Assistant, as noted earlier, are themselves agents.

But the usefulness of an agent may be increased by endowing it with some "intelligence", so that it then becomes an intelligent agent. Such intelligent agents [15] form the basis of an exciting and rapidly developing area of computer-based problem solving: distributed artificial intelligence. Here, an intelligent agent is considered to be an agent which incorporates some artificial intelligence (AI) problem solving capability; for example, heuristic search, constraint satisfaction etc. In recent years there has been much interest in the application of AI to design; see, for example [16]; [17]. The further development to include intelligent agents would appear to offer much potential benefit, in design support in general [18], and also to the particular approach described here in providing a memory prosthesis for the designer. The purpose of the agents would be to advise, rather than to direct the designer.

Whilst not wishing to delegate full responsibility to an automated component, it is appropriate to associate each design oriented task with a design "critic", the function of which may be implemented in the form of one (or possibly more than one) intelligent agent. Critics operate at the level of design problem solving; intelligent agents, on the other hand, operate at the level of AI problem solving. The particular AI method employed by an agent is chosen to match the design task of its associated critic. For example, a critic whose task is to ensure compliance with certain design standards or customer requirements may be implemented in the form of a constraint satisfaction agent; the task of recognising a particular pattern in the protocol could be effected by an artificial neural network agent; opportunities for design reuse may appropriately be handled by a case-based reasoning (CBR) agent.

The use of this last mentioned AI method, case-based reasoning, is of particular relevance to design. Previous research by one of the authors in investigating the application of knowledge-based techniques to provide quality advice in engineering design [19] revealed that the practising designers consulted were much happier in adapting a previously successful design to meet new requirements, rather than to attempt to develop a new design from scratch. Such a strategy, put into a computational context, is essentially that which forms the basis of CBR; i.e. by adapting a previous successful problem solution to meet the requirements of a new situation. As well as the reuse of previous designs [20], CBR may also make use of previous design processes. It is believed this approach may also provide potential support in the construction of a safety argument, by matching the decisions and design processes of the current design situation against those of previous designs, for which exemplar safety cases are recorded.

The enhancement of the features of Designer's Assistant through the incorporation of design critics in the form of a collection of intelligent agents is an exciting possibility. The agent-based approach has the advantage of supporting incremental extension of the design environment's capability: additional agents may be added, as and when considered appropriate. The immediate task is to provide a set of critics within such a framework that may assist the designer in simple design tasks and checks, before extending the architecture to include intelligent agents to provide additional functionality. In the context of this paper, the particular extension would have to do with tasks in Safety Argument management, but, in line with our strategy for requirement elicitation these will only emerge after a period of use by safety engineers of the system as described here.

9 Concluding remarks

In the foregoing we have discussed the philosophical background to the Online Design Journal and the Designer's Asistant and sketched they way in which they work together to act as a memory prosthesis tailored to the needs of the engineering designer. Since they are domain, method, and tool independent, thay are available to the safety engineer to provide assistance in the task of assembling the safety case, and of making plain to a reviewer the rationale for a particular design decision, whether it be one arising from the past or argued through fully in the present.

T architecture is open and (as has been discussed) the possibility is being explored of adding more specific safety related functionality (or agency) via one or more additional intelligent agents or 'critics' [21], [22]. At the time of writing (January 1997) the software is still a prototype in alpha release and consideration is being given to its re-engineering, possibly in Java.

It is believed that the Online Design Journal and (particularly) the Designer's Assistant of value in the Safety Critical domain where construction of the Safety Case is a necessity yet are usable 'in the great majority of engineering design environments. The need for such will increase as the impact of liability and or regulatory EU legislation (e.g EMC legislation) requires that conformance &c be demonstrated in an argued way by th manufacturer before the CEC mark be affixed to the product. In short, the range of applicability will be limited solely by the ingenuity of the user population.

References

[1]   A. Reglinski, D. Jenkins, and D. Livingstone, The Designer's Assistant, presented at Autonomous Agents '97, Marina del Rey, California, 1997.

[2]   D. Jenkins, Adapting a Design History Editor to deal with concurrent engineering, in Design Issues in Computer-Supported Co-operative Work (CSCW), D. Rosenberg and C. S. Hutchison, Eds. Berlin: Springer Verlag, 1994.

[3]   T. C. Ormerod and H. Bloomfield, Delivering the GOODS : A System For Supporting Generic Design, PPIG Newsletter, pp. 12 - 14, 1991.

[4]   P. Turner, S. Turner, S. Green, and P. Mayne, Collaborative Notebooks for the Virtual Workplace, in Technology for the Virtual Workplace, M. Igbaria and M. Tan, Eds.: Idea Press, 1997.

[5]   P. Turner and S. Turner, Supporting cooperative working using shared notebooks, presented at ECSCW'97, Lancaster, England, 1997.

[6]   M. Lamming, P. Brown, K. Carter, M. Eldridge, M. Flynn, G. Lolie, P. Robinson, and A. Sellen, The Design of a Human Memory Prosthesis, The Computer Journal, vol. 37, pp. 153-163, 1994.

[7]   D. Jenkins and A. Reglinski, Groupware for Research Teams, presented at Technology for Organisational Effectiveness, DTI, London, 1996.

[8]   J. Bowen and V. Stavridou, Safety-critical systems, formal methods and standards, Software Engineering Journal, vol. July, pp. 189-209, 1993.

[9]   S. Wilson, J. McDermid, P. Fenelon, and P. Kirkham, No More Spineless Safety Cases, in A Structured Method and Comprehensive Tool Support for the Production of Safety Cases, 1995.

[10]   R. Whitty, Quality attributes in critical systems: report on a talk given at the IEE by Mario Barbacci, in Safety Systems: The Safety-Critical Systems Club Newsletter. London, 1996, pp. 7-9.

[11]   R. Shaw, Safety and Reliability of Software Based Systems, in Annual CSR Workshop, vol. 1, 1 ed. London: Springer, 1995, pp. 460.

[12]   D. J. Streveler, " Designing by Committee Works" - - Sometimes, Datamation, pp. 117-120, 1978.

[13] D. G. Ullman, T. G. Dietterich, and L. A. Stauffer, Preliminary results on an experimental study of mechanical design, presented at Workshop on design theory and methodology, New York, 1987.

[14] J. Conklin and R. Young, Organisational Memory and Knowledge Management, presented at Team IT/BCS meeting, May, 1996.

[15] M. J. Wooldridge and N. R. Jennings, Agent Theories, Architectures, and Languages: A Survey, : Dept. of Computing, Manchester Metropolitain University, Chester Street M1 5GD, 1994.

[16] J. R. Dixon, Knowledge-based systems for design, Transactions of the ASME, vol. 117, pp. 11-16, 1995.

[17] M. X. Tang, A knowledge-based design architecture for intelligent design support, The Knowledge Engineering Review, 1997.

[18] B. Lees and D. G. Jenkins, Supporting software quality in an integrated safety-critical systems development environment, Software Quality Journal, vol. 5, pp. 117-125, 1996.

[19] B. Lees and C. Irgens, Knowledge-based support fpr quality in engineering design., presented at 11th International Conference on Expert Systems and their Applications, Avignon, 1991.

[20] T. Bardasz and I. Zeid, DEJAVU: case-based reasoning for mechanical design, AI EDAM, vol. 7, pp. 111-124, 1993.

[21] A. Fischer, T. Lemke, Mastaglio, and A. Morch., Using Critics to Empower Users, presented at CHI'90, 1990.

[22] D. Jenkins and J. Gammack, Supporting Design Reuse in Concurrent Engineering, Virtual Prototyping, vol. 1, 1996.

Security and Human Factors

Safety and Security Requirements for an Advanced Train Control System

Jens Braband
Siemens AG Transportation Systems Group
D-38023 Braunschweig[◊]

Abstract

We discuss safety and security aspects of a safety-critical railway application: a future harmonised European train control system, which shall utilise public networks for safety-critical train control data transmission. We mainly focus on the derivation of (quantitative) safety and security requirements, in particular for the data transmission.

1   Introduction

The creation of a common European market has increased the need for efficient cross border transportation services. The railways too must respond to this European challenge but have to overcome obstacles which are inherited from railway history:

- As railways were built when a common future for Europe was unthinkable, every national railway developed its own particular operation procedures.
- The absence of international standards (starting from power supply to signalling) restricts the interoperability of trains.

As a result today thirteen different non compatible train control systems are in operation throughout Europe. Unification and harmonisation is the solution to this challenge. For this reason the European Commission (EC) has established a programme for the development of a European Rail Traffic Management System (ERTMS). The first step towards this goal is the definition of a new European Train Control System (ETCS). In the long run ETCS shall substitute or at least overlay the national train control systems. In order to achieve this goal four bodies are working closely together:

- The European Commission is supporting the specification work financially and promotes the acceptance of ETCS as an European standard.
- The international railway union UIC, in particular through its European Railway Research Institute (ERRI), has developed the requirement specifications and the global operation concepts for ETCS.

[◊] Author's E-Mail address: Jens.Braband@BWG1.ERL1.SIEMENS.NET.
This work was partly funded by EC DG VII-A4 under the ERTMS-EUROSIG contract. The author thanks the safety managers from the other EUROSIG companies and the ERTMS Users Group for their co-operation and valuable discussions.

- EUROSIG, an industry consortium of nine signalling companies, is working out the detailed and subsystem specifications.
- an ERTMS Users Group (consisting of the French, Italian and German national railways) has been formed in order to customise and harmonise the system and subsystem specifications.

As a first milestone towards realisation the ERTMS Users Group has issued a call for tender in December 1996 for three pilot tracks. It is expected that the first lines equipped with ETCS will be operable by 2000.

2   System definition

The main task of a train driver is to operate the train safely and according to the schedule. In order to assist the driver with this task two general types of protection systems have been developed:

- Automatic Train Protection (ATP) systems complement the trackside signals, which the driver should obey. Only if he does not obey the signals (e. g. over-speeding) then the ATP overrides him (e. g. braking the train).
- Automatic Train Control (ATC) systems do directly display the allowed speed limit inside the driver's cab. The driver can either choose the speed within the limits given by ATC or let the train be driven automatically by an Automatic Train Operation (ATO) system.

On high-speed tracks ATC is vital, because the driver cannot rely on the observation of the trackside signals anymore. In this case also the braking distance (e. g. more than 4 km for a high-speed train travelling at 250 km/h) becomes much longer than the observable track section.

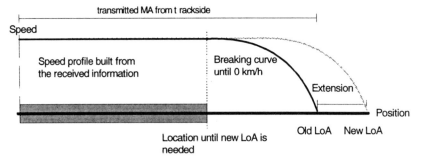

Figure 1: The Movement Authority (MA) Concept

In ATC systems a train is only allowed to move after reception of a valid movement authority from the interlocking. A movement authority is either limited in space (giving a target point and speed) or limited in space and time. In either case it must be guaranteed that the track is safely allocated to not more than one train at a time. A train is allowed to move until its limit of authority (LoA) or until its time limit (if any) has expired. Usually a train is required to be able to come to complete standstill at its LoA. The interlocking is responsible for safe allocation of MA to all trains under its control.

ETCS is planned to operate on three different levels (depending on the existing signalling infrastructure and the desired line performance):

- Level 1 is an ATP system with continuous speed control, which can be upgraded into an ATC system with partially continuous data transmission.
- Level 2 is an ATC system with continuous radio data transmission, where the location and integrity (i. e. completeness) of trains is controlled by the trackside centre.
- Level 3 defines an advanced ATC system with continuous radio data transmission without any trackside signalling. Trains have to guarantee their integrity.

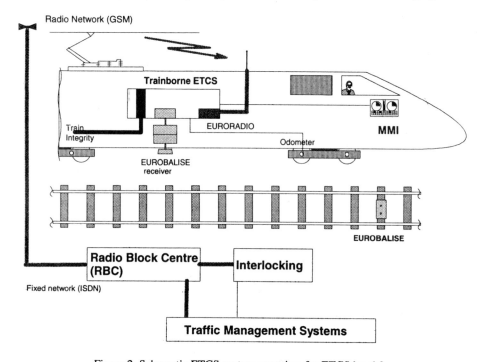

Figure 2: Schematic ETCS system overview for ETCS level 3

The basic functions, which are all highly safety-critical, in all three levels are:

1. The trackside control centre determines and transmits route maps and movement authorities to the train (based on location and speed information received from all trains and trackside equipment in its area)
2. The train determines the maximum permissible speed profile for the track section covered by its movement authority and the braking curve onto its LoA.

3. The train continuously monitors its location (and integrity in level 3) and supervises the permissible speed profile. If the speed limit is exceeded the ATC triggers the necessary braking action.
4. The train transmits information about its speed and location to the control centre.

In this paper we restrict ourselves to level 3, where ETCS shall be composed of the following standardised modules and interfaces:

- EUROBALISE: a intermittent transmission system operating at a data rate of 565 kbps, which is used in level 3 as an absolute location reference (electronic milestone)
- EURORADIO: a continuous transmission system utilising standardised networks like GSM and ISDN
- EUROCAB: The onboard part of ETCS including a vital computer for speed control and the Man-Machine Interface (MMI)

We will focus in this paper mainly on system and EURORADIO safety aspects because of the novel safety and security problems involved: For the first time safety-critical train control data are transmitted via a commercial network involving standard components, possibly not even owned by railways.

3 Railway safety standards

Up to now no commonly agreed international railway signalling standards exist, but for the interoperability and acceptance of ETCS at least a common European standard is necessary, because a unique and high level of safety is demanded. It has been decided early in the specification of ETCS to rely on the emerging CENELEC standards, which have been worked out in parallel to the work on ETCS. These standards seek to harmonise and balance the different safety cultures and traditions of European railways. They cover the main areas of safety concern in railway signalling: system aspects [C26], safety-critical software [C28] and hardware [C29] development, transmission of safety-critical data via closed [C591] and open [C592] transmission networks. They are expected to become normative in 1997/98.

CENELEC has defined five safety integrity levels, ranging from 0 to 4, for elementary signalling system elements (e. g. a balise), which are different to the levels proposed by IEC 1508, because the IEC levels apply to complete control systems and the CENELEC levels to subsystems.

4 ETCS safety targets

The harmonisation of safety targets and the derivation of a unique (quantitative) level of safety for ETCS throughout Europe is a tremendous task because of the diverse safety culture and tradition in the different European countries. The „greatest common divisor" agreed by all railway authorities was that ETCS shall be at least as safe as the train control systems used today. Fortunately up to now no accidents caused by train control systems have been observed on the European high speed lines. Thus the safety targets have to be derived by a hypothetical apportionment from overall railway safety targets, but the targets defined and statistics sampled throughout Europe are not unique and often hardly comparable. Some examples of published (average) performance figures:

a) Deutsche Bundesbahn (1991) reports less than 0.1 train accidents (i.e. derailments and collisions) per million train kilometre
b) UIC (1993) sampled 0.43 casualties per billion passenger kilometres
c) Railtrack approved a probability of 10^{-5} per year for a passenger to die in a railway accident (1995 benchmark)

As a basis for their work the following individual safety target was agreed inside the ERTMS Users Group:

The risk for a passenger to die in a railway accident shall be less than 10^{-8} per hour of travel.

This target would make railways by a factor of 50 safer than aviation. It has to be understood as an average value, which has been derived and can only be checked based on average values from railway statistics. It can be justified to be at least in a reasonable order of magnitude, if we multiply a), b) and c) by overall average figures for speed (70 km/h), railway accident casualties (less than 1:100) and frequency of travel (much less than 1000 hours per passenger per year), respectively. Nevertheless the question remains how this safety target for passengers can be related to a safety target for a particular ETCS component. The units in the target above are deaths per passenger hour ($D/(P{\times}h)$), while a meaningful technical system safety target should be defined by accidents per train hour ($A/(T{\times}h)$). In order to connect both targets in a meaningful way, we have to consider the basic sequence of events in train accidents from an individual (tagged) passenger's point of view: First a train has to be caught in an accident, as a consequence from this accident the tagged passenger may die or survive. If X denotes the tolerable train accident rate (to be determined) and R the (conditional) risk of the tagged passenger to die after an accident, then

$$X{\times}R \leq 10^{-8} \ D/(P{\times}h) \tag{1}$$

shall hold. The risk R depends on various factors such as type of accident (e. g. derailment, collision) or severity of accident (e. g. speed of train). These factors cannot be assessed in detail but the railways have accident criticality statistics. It is reasonable to assume that the mean risk is given by the ratio of the average criticality (deaths per accident) C and the average occupancy O (number of passengers) per train: $R=C/O$.

Figures from Deutsche Bahn AG for 1995 state that $O{\approx}100$ P/T. The ERTMS Users Group has determined an average criticality of train accidents $C=1/10$ D/A. Substituting these figures in (1) we arrive at

$$X < 10^{-5} \text{ A/(T} \times \text{h}). \tag{2}$$

As our derivation was based on average figures, we choose to include a factor of 10 as a safety margin for more severe conditions. We give below a reasonable apportionment methodology starting from this safety target.

Description	Factor	Target	Remarks	Justification
Tolerable train accident risk	1/10	10^{-6} A/(T×h)	Safety margin	From (2)
Tolerable train hazard rate	10 H/A	10^{-5} H/(T×h)	One out of ten hazards (near misses) actually causes an accident	Railway statistics
Tolerable hazards due to technical causes for railway transport	1/100 H_{TC}/H	10^{-7} $H_{TC}/(T×h)$	One out of hundred hazards is due to technical causes	Estimation
Tolerable hazards due to ETCS	1/100 H_{ETCS}/H_{TC}	10^{-9} $H_{ETCS}/(T×h)$	One out of hundred hazards due to technical failure may be caused by ETCS equipment	Estimation

Table 1: Derivation of the ETCS global safety target (random failure integrity)

The main result of table 1 is that the derived quantitative ETCS safety requirements are in the same order of magnitude as for a comparable safety-critical system used in aviation, although the consequences of failure are generally much more severe in aviation than in railway transport. This matches with the railways' target to be much safer than aviation.

It should be noticed that according to CENELEC safety integrity is composed of systematic failure integrity and random failure integrity. According to CENELEC philosophy systematic failures cannot be quantified but can only be avoided by appropriate qualitative countermeasures and defences. As a result the figures from table 1 can only be related to random failures.

5 Safety-critical train control data transmission

5.1 Hazard identification and analysis

prEN 50159-2 [C592] defines an open transmission system as a *transmission system with an unknown number of participants, having unknown, variable and non-trusted properties, used for unknown telecommunication services, and having a non-negligible risk of unauthorised access.* The standard sets up a framework for the safety and security aspects which should be regarded and covered in a safety case, but does not give direct guidelines which countermeasures to the threats encountered in open transmission networks should be used. prEN 50159-2 demands that a hazard identification and risk analysis shall be carried out.

As EURORADIO is a completely new system, the hazard analysis [PHA] has been carried out based on a formal system model, for which a formal safety target has been defined. For this model a complete set of basic errors, which could occur in the message stream, have been identified and assessed for their criticality. Additionally we have determined through a heuristic analysis, which threats could cause these errors, and what hazardous events could result from these threats. Figure 3 gives an overview of this process and states some examples.

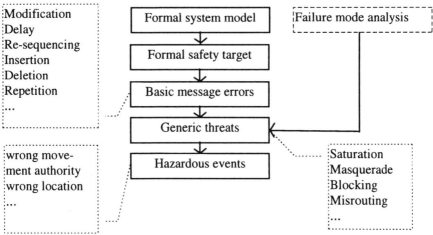

Figure 3: EURORADIO hazard analysis

The result was that the following threats are considered relevant for EURORADIO:

- Masquerade (pretension of a false identity)
- Message modification (randomly or systematically)
- Message insertion
- Message re-sequencing

Some other threats (e. g. message delay or deletion) have been identified as relevant for the ETCS system, but will be covered by countermeasures at system level (e. g. time stamps or time-out mechanisms), so that no extra precautions on EURORADIO sub-system level are necessary.

As a result of the hazard analysis the following requirements have been included in the EURORADIO requirements specification [ESRS]:

- *Any failure or inability of the transmission system to provide communications when required by the ATP/ATC system shall not result in a hazard to safety.*
- *The system shall be able to detect any errors which are introduced into transmissions as a result of the communication process including any errors which remain after any error correction performed by the radio system with a predictable probability. The safety mechanism must also guarantee that addressing information is not misinterpreted or mishandled. The ATP/ATC application has to provide protection against data obsolescence as a result of transmission delays.*
- *The system shall safeguard against malicious attacks, either within or external to the railway, attempting to use the radio system for disruptive purposes.*
- *Identification and authentication of peer entities at call set-up, message origin authentication and message integrity will be provided for safety-related communications. Any transmission of messages will only be permitted after a successful identification and authentication of the peer entity. Any authentication token (e.g. cryptographic keys) used will be protected against access, loss, misuse, duplication and forgery.*

We should be aware of the fact that the opportunity to attack railway lines is clearly given and it is unreasonable to assume measures to prevent any attempts of attacks. But the risks from these attacks shall be reduced to a level as low as reasonably practicable. It should be clear that new systems such as ETCS should not present any new promising opportunities for attacks, which are much simpler or less dangerous for the attacker to perform, e. g. anonymously from the attacker's home. It must also be clear that railways by their nature have always been very vulnerable to malicious attacks (think of sabotage) and that no railway has been able to protect its lines against attackers with practically unlimited means, e. g. big-scale organisations.

5.2 Safety targets

The target from table 1 can be further apportioned to the ETCS system components. We show in table 2 the basic allocation for EURORADIO [ESRS].

Description	Factor	Target	Remarks	Justification
ETCS safety target	-	10^{-9} $H_{ETCS}/(T \times h)$		From table 1
ETCS transmission target	0.1	10^{-10} $H_{ETCS\text{-}Transmission}/(T \times h)$	10% allocated to transmission functions	Design decision
EURORADIO safety target	0.5	5×10^{-11} $H_{EuroRadio}/(T \times h)$	50% allocated to EURORADIO, 50% to EUROBALISE	Design decision

Table 2: Derivation of the EURORADIO safety target (random failure integrity)

This random failure integrity target corresponds to a CENELEC safety integrity level 4 (safety-critical). According to CENELEC philosophy this means that methods, tools and techniques appropriate for this highest safety integrity level must be chosen in order to guarantee an adequate systematic failure integrity. We now shortly assess the impact of the safety target on the design of a safety code for EURORADIO. As a worst case we may assume

- a bi-directional data link of 9.6 kbps (maximum capacity for GSM),
- a typical telegram size of 250 bits,
- that all telegrams are (stand-alone) safety-critical, and
- that every telegram might be corrupted.

Then the target derived in table 2 results in a requirement for the undetected error probability of less than 10^{-16} per telegram. Under the usual assumptions of coding theory as applied in [C591] this hints at a necessary code lengths of much more than 50 bits of safety code in order to cope with the random errors under this scenario. Systematic errors (e. g. bit deletions or insertions) might require additional protection beyond this.

5.3   Security aspects

It was immediately clear to the EURORADIO designers that malicious attacks as identified by the hazard analysis can only be prevented with the help of cryptographic mechanisms and keys [Sch94], which authenticate the communicating entities and the transmitted messages. For EURORADIO a 64 bit Message Authentication Code (MAC, standardised by ISO/IEC 9797) based on a symmetric block cipher has been chosen as a design solution. In this section we will focus on a reasonable approach towards the assessment of the system's security.

It seems impossible to estimate the frequency of malicious attacks in a realistic way, because it may be assumed that the probability of hacking or blackmailing is too low to apply statistical analysis and because there is nearly no willingness by the respective authorities to publish figures concerning malicious attacks. Additionally the process is probably non-linear and can involve feedback, because hacking depends on the countermeasures taken against it (high security may discourage potential attackers, while low security may encourage them, or the other way around?).

Note that also the information security framework ITSEC and its predecessors and successors do not quantify security targets in terms of rates, but some, including the German predecessor, measured the strength of the mechanisms by the probability of successful attack per attempt. EUROSIG and the railways have not decided on a quantification, but have only agreed on a qualitative statement [ESRS]:

The strength of the mechanisms for authentication of peer entities at call set-up and origin authentication and integrity of messages shall be high in order to detect malicious attacks with a high probability. This means that under normal operating conditions, a successful malicious attack should be incredible and only be feasible if the attacker has an extraordinary amount of technical, financial and human resources at his disposal.

However this requirement is not sufficient for the system design, e. g. for the determination of the key length. In this section only brute-force attacks (exhaustive search of the key space) will be discussed. There are more sophisticated and subtle attacks [Sch94], but their analysis has shown that in our case they are of less importance. Based on experience from the banking sector the following criterion was proposed:

*The key length **k** shall be determined in such way that the probability that an attacker willing to spend **a** ECU could break the system within the lifetime of the key, even assuming technology advances at a rate of **t** percent per annum over the expected system lifetime, is less than **p**. It shall be further assumed that current off-the-shelf technology is used, being available at a price of **c** ECU allowing **e** block encryptions per second.*

Here it was assumed that money is the main driving force for intentional attacks and that the keys can only be broken by brute force, i. e. trying all possible combinations. There may be other motives (political or just-for-fun), but it may be assumed that these attackers will have less means than attackers with criminal motives (and monetary reward).

Taking into account additionally an inflation rate of i percent per year and a message size of b blocks per message, then in this scenario an attacker can buy equipment which may test keys with a frequency of

$$f = \frac{a}{c}(1+i)^y \times (1+t)^y \times \frac{e}{b} \qquad (3)$$

per second. Prices for equipment have assumed to remain constant. The first factor in (3) states the number of chips which can be bought with the money available, the second factor takes into consideration the speed increase over the years (y denoting the number of years from the starting point) and the last factor adjusts for the number of blocks per message. Thus for randomly selected keys the attacker has a chance of

$$P = \min\left\{ \frac{3600 \times l \times f}{2^k}, 1 \right\} \qquad (4)$$

to find (and possibly use) the correct key by exhaustive search before the lifetime of the key (assumed to be l hours) has expired.

We determine now whether the standard key length of 56 bits, which is currently used in banking transactions, would be sufficient for ETCS. We evaluate (3) and (4) for the example parameters given in table 3. Performance figures and prices are estimated for the Data Encryption Standard (DES). In figure 4 some numerical results are presented with respect to key lifetime and year. The results show that single length keys (56 bits) seem sufficient in connection with frequent key update only for the next decades but that double length keys (112 bits) would withstand attacks in our scenarios over the complete system lifetime, even if keys would not be updated at all. Based on these results the ERTMS Users Group has decided to use at least double key length without any key update. It should be noted that our results match with results for other commercial applications, e. g. [Bla96].

Parameter	Description	Proposed value
i	Inflation rate	0.05 (5 % p.a.)
t	Technology advancement rate	0.32 (32% p. a., i. e. a factor 4 in 5 years)
r	Reward of the attacker	5 MECU
a	Means of the attacker	1% of the reward
y	Year	0-50 years (system lifetime)
e	Encryptions per second (in 2000)	4,000,000
c	Cost of a single equipment (chip)	100 ECU for chip + 900 ECU overhead costs
b	Blocks per message	4 blocks (each 64 bits)
p	Tolerable success probability	10^{-3}
k	Key length	56 bits

Table 3: Example parameters

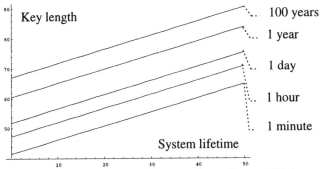

Figure 4: Necessary key length versus key and system lifetime

We have assumed that an attacker succeeds if he is able to determine a key in use with a reasonable chance and that a success probability of 1/1000 is tolerable. This figure might seem quite large, but in practice it is not true that an attacker may create a hazard or an accident by just finding the key. He must also be able to insert an apparently correct message into the message stream at the correct time and the wrong information must be accepted. We thus have additional risk reduction due to: GSM/ISDN protocols and encoding, attention of experienced train drivers and consistency checks in the ATP/ATC application. These are hard to take into account directly, but will give additional protection.

Anyhow it will finally be the responsibility of the national railways to approve these or similar scenarios. This has already been acknowledged by EUROSIG in the requirements specification [ESRS]:

The railways should define a Security Policy for EURORADIO, taking into account the European standardisation process in the Information Technology Security sector, e.g. ITSEC and ITSEM.

6 Conclusion

The approach towards the definition and derivation of safety and security requirements for ETCS as outlined in this paper is only a first, but an important step forward towards a unified approach for safety among the European railways. In particular the quantitative figures still need harmonisation between railways and industry. Next steps will include, among others, agreed approaches towards the assessment and cross-acceptance of safety cases throughout Europe.

7 References

[Bla96]   Blaze, M. et al.: Minimal key length for symmetric ciphers to provide adequate commercial security, 1996, http://www.counterpane.com/key-length.ps

[C26]   Railway applications: The specification and demonstration of dependability, reliability, availability, maintainability and safety (RAMS), Draft prEN 50126, November 1995

[C28]   Railway applications: Software for railway control and protection systems, Draft prEN 50128, November 1995

[C29]   Railway applications: Safety related electronic systems, Draft prEN 50129, January 1997

[C591]   Railway Applications: Requirements for Safety-Related Communication in Closed Transmission Systems, Draft prEN 50159-1, August 1996

[C592]   Railway Applications: Requirements for Safety-Related Communication in Open Transmission Systems, Draft prEN 50159-2, May 1997

[GO91]   Garon, G. and Outerbridge, R.: DES Watch: An examination of the sufficiency of the Data Encryption Standard for financial institution information security in the 1990's, Cryptologia, 1991, 177-193

[ESRS]   EURORADIO System Requirements Specification, version 4.0, EUROSIG, September 1995

[PHA]   EURORADIO Preliminary Hazard Analysis, version 1.0, EUROSIG, January 1996

[Sch94]   Schneier, B.: Applied Cryptography, Wiley, New York 1994

[SRS]   System Requirements Specification, version 4.0, ERTMS Users Group, December 1996

Cryptographic Protocols over Open Distributed Systems: A Taxonomy of Flaws and related Protocol Analysis Tools

S.Gritzalis [1,2], D.Spinellis [3,4]

[1] Department of Informatics, University of Athens,
TYPA Buildings, Athens GR-15771, GREECE

[2] Department of Informatics
Technological Educational Institute of Athens (T.E.I.) ofAthens,
Ag.Spiridonos St. Aegaleo GR-12210, GREECE
email: *sgritz@teia.ariadne-t.gr*

[3] Department of Mathematics, University of the Aegean,
Samos, GR-83200, GREECE
email: *dspin@aegean.gr*

[4] SENA SA
Byzantiou 2 N.Ionia GR-14234, GREECE
email: *dds@senanet.com*

Abstract

When designing and implementing cryptographic protocols one must avoid a number of possible flaws. In this paper we divide possible flaws based on the flaw pathology and the corresponding attack method, into elementary protocol flaws, password/key guessing flaws, stale message flaws, parallel session flaws, internal protocol flaws, and cryptosystem flaws. We then outline and comment on different attack construction and inference-based formal methods, protocol analysis tools, and process integration techniques and their effectiveness in aiding the cryptographic protocol design process by discovering protocol flaws with regard to the aforementioned proposed taxonomy of them.

1 Introduction

A protocol is a set of rules and conventions that define the communication framework between two or more parties. The parties are said to be communicating *(principals)* and can be end-users, processes or computing systems. In cryptographic protocols part of at least one message is encrypted.

When developing a cryptographic protocol it is desirable to uncover any flaws as soon as possible. These flaws can occur because of incomplete or erroneous specifications. However, even correct specifications do not necessarily guarantee the correctness of a given implementation. Generally we can distinguish between three categories of cryptographic protocol flaws [1] according to the flaw source:

- *functional specification flaws* occur due to a logical flaw in the protocol's high level specification,

- *implementation-dependent flaws* [2] appear when a protocol's specification can result in implementations of which at least one exhibits the flaw and at least one other does not, and

- *implementation flaws*, are those faults that occur when a correct specification is incorrectly implemented.

2 A Taxonomy of Cryptographic Protocol Faults

After a thorough study of the flaws belonging to the aforementioned general categories we propose the following more detailed taxonomy of these flaws based on the flaw pathology and the corresponding attack method:

[1]   Elementary protocol flaws
[2]   Password/key guessing flaws
[3]   Stale message flaws
[4]   Parallel session flaws
[5]   Internal protocol flaws
[6]   Cryptosystem flaws.

2.1 Elementary protocol flaws

In the elementary flaw category belong all flaws that occur in protocols providing minimal or no protection against adversary attacks.

The flaw of the protocol proposed by [3] for authentication key exchange between two communication parties belongs to this category [1]. The session key is signed by A's private key before being sent to B. The flaw in this case is that a signature is used to provide message confidentiality. Similar problems [1] [4] appear in the CCITT X.509 authentication protocol [5]. The cause behind the most important of them is that the messages are encrypted before being signed making it therefore possible for an adversary to masquerade as the sender by changing the initial signature with his own.

2.2 Password/key guessing flaws

The flaws belonging to this category occur because users often choose their passwords from a small set of common words [6] [7]. In addition, in cases where a protocol uses a pseudo-random key, it is possible that the key is constructed in a way that can be reproduced by an adversary. As a result in case of an exhaustive key search attack the adversary can use a restricted probable password key space instead of the - much larger - possible key space. For this reason attacks based on this flaw category are referred to [8] as *dictionary attacks* or as *verifiable-text attacks*.

The user-supplied passwords could be rejected if they occur in a dictionary or consist of too few characters. The smallest allowable password size P_{size} can be calculated [9] depending on the password alphabet size A_{size}, the required password life time P_{life}, the maximum rate at which passwords can be tried G_{rate} and the maximum password guessing probability G_{prob} and is given by the relationship:

$$P_{size} = log\ (P_{life} \times G_{rate} / G_{prob}) / log\ A_{size}$$

Password guessing attacks can be divided into three categories:

- *Detectable on-line password guessing attacks*: Every unsuccessful attempt is detected and logged by the authentication server S. After a specific number of unsuccessful attempts S will stop servicing the attacked password (thereby creating a denial of service vulnerability).
- *Undetectable on-line password guessing attacks*: In this attack mode [10], the attacker is trying to use a password that could be correct for an on-line transaction. The attacker gradually verifies the password's correctness from the responses elicited from S. If the guess is incorrect, then the transaction is aborted; the next guess will be tried in a new transaction. A failed attempt can not be detected and logged by S, because S can not distinguish between a genuine and a password guessing transaction.
- *Off-line password guessing attacks*: The attacker is using authentication protocol message copies, guessing the password and verifying it in an off-line environment. S is not participating and therefore the procedure can not be detected.

Authentication protocols can be strengthened by introducing two basic requirements:

- the authentication server is to respond only to fresh requests and
- the authentication server is to respond only to requests of verifiable authenticity.

These requirements are vital for dealing with detectable on-line password guessing attacks [11], but are not relevant in relation to off-line attacks [12].

A number of protocols have been proposed for dealing with on-line [13] and off-line [14] [15] [12] password guessing attacks. In addition, two tools have been proposed for helping users pick stronger passwords [16]: *password generators* and *password monitoring programs*. Password generators are programs that are made available on systems in an effort to ensure "good password choices", which means that the selected password is difficult to guess, and easy for the user to remember. These programs have to be sufficiently random in the specific method in which they select password. Password monitors are programs that accept a user's choice for a password based on how likely it is that the password could be guessed. More sophisticated password monitors may ensure the password is not a known easy-to-guess one, check that this is not in a dictionary, analyse it to see if it looks too much like a real word, and use an addition process named "password guesser", in order to try and guess this password.

2.3 Stale message flaws

Often an adversary instead of a direct attack on a security protocol will try to utilise genuine protocol message fragments that he can neither read nor legally create. For this reason a lot of effort has been put into designing protocols that are not vulnerable to replay attacks.

Studying message replay attacks [17] has proposed a taxonomy based on the *message origin* and the *message destination*.

2.3.1. Message origin attacks

In *run external attacks* message fragments from one protocol run are used in another run. An example of such an attack [18] is based on the secret key Needham-Schroeder [19] protocol where the attacker can read the third protocol message:

[1] $A \rightarrow S : A, B, N_a$

[2] $S \rightarrow A : \{N_a, B, K_{ab}, \{K_{ab}, A\}_{Kb}\}_{Ka}$

[3] $A \rightarrow B : \{K_{ab}, A\}_{Kb}$

[4] $B \rightarrow A : \{N_b\}_{Kab}$

[5] $A \rightarrow B : \{N_b-1\}_{Kab}$

and having enough time and processing power can guess the session key and use it in a next protocol run as the original communicating parties will not know that the session key has been compromised. This attack is of course only viable when there are no mechanisms for outdating session keys. This attack is a run external attack because during a protocol run a message from a previous run was used. A parallel protocol run was not needed.

A parallel protocol run can also lead to a successful attack [17]. The BAN-Yahalom [4] protocol contains the following steps:

[1] $A \rightarrow B : A, N_a$

[2] $B \rightarrow S : B, \{A, N_a\}_{Kbs}, N_b$

[3] $S \rightarrow A : \{B, N_a, K_{ab}\}_{Kas}, \{A, K_{ab}, N_b\}_{Kbs}, N_b$

[4] $A \rightarrow B : \{A, K_{ab}, N_b\}_{Kbs}, \{N_b\}_{Kab}$

When *Eve* is performing an attack masquerading as *A-Alice*, after the protocol's step 2 she starts a parallel protocol run:

[1] $A \rightarrow B : A, N_a$

[2] $B \rightarrow S : B, \{A, N_a\}_{Kbs}, N_b$

      [1'] $E_a \rightarrow B: A, (N_a, N_b)$

      [2'] $B \rightarrow E_s: B, \{A, N_a, N_b\}_{Kbs}, N'_b$

[3] ....

[4] $E_a \rightarrow B :$ $\{A, N_a (=K_{ab}), N_b\}_{Kbs}, \{N_b\}_{Kab}$

Eve is using in the second run the concatenation of N_a and N_b as a *nonce*. As soon as *Eve* receives the encrypted message from step 2 of the second run she is using it as the first encrypted part of step 4 of the first run. In the end *Eve* has masqueraded as *A-Alice* to *B-Bob* and received the session key. This attack is also a run external attack because during a protocol run a message from a previous run is used. In this case however, the attack was based on a parallel protocol run.

Run internal attacks are using message fragments from the same protocol run. Such an attack [20] on the Neuman-Stubblebine protocol [21] contains the following steps:

[1] $A \rightarrow B : A, N_a$

[2] $B \rightarrow S : B, \{A, N_a, T_b\}_{Kbs}, N_b$

[3] $S \rightarrow A : \{B, N_a, K_{ab}, T_b\}_{Kas}, \{A, K_{ab}, T_b\}_{Kbs}, N_b$

[4] $A \rightarrow B : \{A, K_{ab}, T_b\}_{Kbs}, \{N_b\}_{Kab}$

During the protocol run, the attacker *Eve*, masquerading as *A-Alice*, receives a part of message 2 and is using it to construct message 4.

[4'] $E_a \rightarrow B$: $\{A, N_a (=K_{ab}), T_b\}_{Kbs}, \{N_b\}_{Na(=Kab)}$

The new message 4 is the same as message 2, but the session key has been changed with the nonce N_a. In this way the last part of the protocol's step 4 was correctly implemented and therefore *Eve* could run a session with *B-Bob* masquerading as *A-Alice*, and make *B-Bob* accept the session key that belongs to *Eve*. This attack is a run internal attack because during a protocol run a message from the same run is used.

2.3.2 Message destination attacks

One other attack [20] on the previously discussed BAN-Yahalom protocol is the following:

[1] $A \rightarrow E_b$: A, N_a

        [1'] $E_b \rightarrow A$: B, N_a

        [2'] $A \rightarrow E_s$: $A, \{B, N_a\}_{Kas}, N'_a$

            [2''] $E_a \rightarrow S$: $A, \{B, N_a\}_{Kas}, N_a$

        [3'] $S \rightarrow E_b$: $\{A, N_a, K_{ab}\}_{Kbs}, \{B, K_{ab}, N_a\}_{Kas}, N_a$

[2] ....

[3] $E_s \rightarrow A$:$N_i, \{B, K_{ab}, N_a\}K_{as}, \{A, K_{ab}, N_a\}K_{bs}$

[4] $E_a \rightarrow B$: $\{A, K_{ab}, N_a\}_{Kbs}, \{N_i\}_{Kab}$

This attack demonstrates a *message reflection* problem, i.e. the return of a message to the original sender. *Straight replays* of message 2' to message 2", are those where the message is sent from the sender to the supposed receiver even though the message semantics are not preserved (text has been added or the message has been delayed). *Message deflection* of message 3' to message 3, occurs when protocol exchange messages are redirected to a third entity.

2.4 Parallel session flaws

Parallel session attacks (or oracle session attacks, multi-role flaws) are flaws that allow an adversary to gain the desired information by exchanging suitable protocol messages.

Participants in these protocols can be distinguished [22] either as *single role*, or as *multi-role* participants. In single role protocols there is a *one to one* relationship between a participant and his role. In a multi role protocol this relationship is a *one to many*. In both cases a participant's presence can only be interpreted as a specific *role* and not as the specific participant's *name*. Therefore a participant p can at different times act in role A and role B. It can be proven [22] that any analysis method that fails to distinguish between the possible *roles* of a participant and the participant's *name* will not yield dependable results.

In the following paragraphs we will study a parallel session single role flaw and a parallel session multi role flaw [1] using the *three-pass protocol* [23]:

[1] $A \rightarrow B : \{M\}_{Ka}$

[2] $B \rightarrow A : \{\{M\}_{Ka}\}_{Kb}$

[3] $A \rightarrow B : \{M\}_{Kb}$

The protocol can be used for transferring a secret message without the use of a trusted third party. It does however not provide authentication as A and B do not share any secrets.

The protocol utilises a cryptographic *commutative function*, which satisfies the relationship:

$$\{\{M\}_{Ka}\}_{Kb} = \{\{M\}_{Kb}\}_{Ka}.$$

2.4.1 Parallel session single role flaws

In a single role run of the protocol the following situation can occur [1]:

[1] Alice $\rightarrow$ Eve $_{Bob}$: $\{M\}_{Ka}$

[2] Eve $_{Bob}$ $\rightarrow$ Alice : $\{M\}_{Ka}$

[3] Alice $\rightarrow$ Eve $_{Bob}$: M

Participant *A-Alice*, sends a request to *B-Bob*. The message is however intercepted by *Eve* who masquerades as *Bob* and uses steps 2 and 3 for intercepting the cleartext of the secret message *M*. This attack could have been prevented if participant *A* had a way to distinguish between different message types and could therefore prevent the transmission of messages of type *unencrypted*.

2.4.2 Parallel session multi role flaws

The protocol can be used by multi role participants as follows:

[1.1]   Alice $_A$ → Eve $_{Bob\ B}$: $\{M\}_{Ka}$

[2.1]   Eve $_{Bob\ A}$ → Alice $_B$: $\{M\}_{Ka}$

[2.2]   Alice $_B$ → Eve $_{Bob\ A}$: M

[1.2]   Eve $_{Bob\ B}$ → Alice $_A$:   *any text*

[1.3]   Alice $_A$ → Eve $_{Bob\ B}$: $\{any\ text\}_{Ka}$

In this case [1], after step 1.1 *Eve* intercepts the message from *Alice*. After step 2.1 *Eve* establishes a new session masquerading as Bob_A in order to return to $Alice_B$ the message that was sent by $Alice_A$. In step 2.2 $Alice_B$ returns the message M decrypted which is of course received by *Eve*. *Eve's* mission has been accomplished since she is now in possession of a decrypted version of M. *Eve* can potentially complete the session so that *Alice* will not realise that the message has been intercepted.

2.5 Internal protocol flaws

Internal protocol flaws occur when at least one of the protocol participants fails to complete all requisite actions.

A typical example of this flaw [1] is step 3 of the three pass protocol. Before the message is sent it is desirable for the participant A to ensure that the message is encrypted. As mentioned above, this requirement should be part of the protocol specifications and implementors should always ensure that it is always satisfied.

2.6 Cryptosystem flaws

Encryption algorithms and related protocols are designed and used in order to satisfy some data confidentiality or authentication requirements. A specific implementation may satisfy all properties required by the algorithm and the protocol specification, but exhibit additional properties that compromise the confidentiality or authentication requirements. In that case *cryptosystem - related flaws* [24] [25] [1] are said to occur.

Often a poor implementation of a given cryptosystem is all that is needed in order to compromise it. [25] details a number of protocols based either on public key algorithms (e.g. the *low entropy protocol*) or on secret key algorithms (e.g. the *single key protocol*) that exhibit such flaws.

3 FORMAL CRYPTOGRAPHIC PROTOCOL ANALYSIS AND DOCUMENTATION METHODS

3.1 Introduction

In the last decade a number of methods and tools have been published and implemented that detect cryptographic protocol flaws by analysing and documenting their operation [26]. The most important methods can be divided into two categories [27] according to their operation domain:

Attack-construction tools construct probable attack sets based on the protocol's algorithms algebraic properties. These methods [28] [29] [30] [31] [32] [33] are targeted towards ensuring authentication, correctness or security properties and are not dependent on the correctness of a proposed logic. Their disadvantage lies mainly in the big number of possible events that must be examined.

Inference-construction tools are utilising either *modal logic, logic of knowledge,* or *logic of belief.* These methods [4] [34] [35] include belief logics which are potentially much faster, capable of analysing large, complicated protocols that the attack-construction tools are incapable of analysing in a reasonable time, and are widely used. A number of specific problems associated with them [27] [36] [37] [20] [38] range from their inability to analyse zero knowledge protocols or to address only authentication or to detect parallel session multi-role flaws to the difficulty of transforming messages and prepositions to idealised messages.

3.2 Flaw detection by attack construction tools

Flaw construction tools can be distinguished into three categories based on their theoretical foundation. These categories are:

3.2.1 Methods based on validation languages and tools that are not specifically developed for analysing cryptographic protocols.

These methods analyse a cryptographic protocol as any other program whose correctness they are trying to prove. This is done by specifying the protocol: as a finite-state machine [32] [33], using predicate calculus [29], or within a process algebra [39] [40].

Some researchers [32] [33] map the protocol to a finite-state machine. The analysis method proposed by [32], verifies the basic properties of a number of protocols, detects basic flaws, but can not detect flaws due to the re-use of old messages as no temporal assumptions are used. The method proposed by [33] also verifies the basic properties of a number of protocols, but exhibits a number of problems as the number of states increases. In addition, in order to deal with flaws related to the re-use of old messages the author proposes to incorporate into the analysis data from the session key message contents.

Another approach [29] is based on predicate calculus extensions. This method is using the specification language Ina Jo [41] and the Formal Development Methodology (FDM). Formal specifications written in Ina Jo specify definitions, initial conditions, transforms, axioms, and criteria. Criteria are used to specify critical requirements for a secure state. Ina Jo formal specifications can then be executed and verified by tools such as Inatest. This approach has been successful in locating both active and passive attack flaws, since in both cases the intruder is a separate entity in the model's mathematical framework.

A more recent approach [39] [40] is based on modelling the communicating principals and the intruder as CSP processes. The proposed method can be used to formalise messages, traces, intruders, and nonce challenges. The Failures Divergence's Refinement Checker (FDR) tool is a general purpose tool that can be used to determine whether an implementation refines a specification. In the case of protocol authentication, checking for refinement amounts to testing whether each trace of the implementation is also a trace of the specification.

Although these methods have been judged as an important contribution to the field, research has turned into more specialised directions. The driving force behind this turn is the desire to use cryptography domain specific reasoning knowledge.

3.2.2 Expert system, scenario based methods

The method due to [31], known as the Interrogator Model, is using a system based on a Prolog solver to guide the designer towards examining whether a specific protocol can lead to an undesirable situation, such as compromising a key. Although this method can not guarantee absolute safety, it works very well in identifying specific protocol flaws.

The method has been successfully used to find various known flaws in protocols such as the [42] [19] [43] [44] and [45]. No previously undetected vulnerabilities in well known protocols have been discovered using this method. The tool's applicability is limited by the operators it supports (conventional and public key encryption, exclusive-or and limited finite-field exponentiation).

3.2.3. Algebraic simplification theoretic model methods

Important methods in this category have been proposed by [28] [46] and [30]. Among them the NRL Protocol Analyser [30] is believed to be the most promising method of assuring correctness in cryptographic protocols. This method specifies the protocol and its analysis as a set of transition rules governing the actions of honest principals as well as rules describing possible - non intruder caused - system failures, a set of operations available to the principals, and rewrite rules obeyed by the operations.

The NRL Protocol Analyser has been successfully used to uncover known flaws of all our proposed taxonomy types, especially stale message flaws. The NRL Protocol Analyser has also been used to locate a series of previously unknown flaws in a number of protocols [45]. The current implementation's main drawback is the paucity of reduction operators which are limited to conventional and public key encryption operators. In addition, as with most rule rewrite systems, it is not clear how well the system scales as more complicated algorithms will need to be expressed using an ever increasing set of rules.

3.3 Inference based methods

Inference based methods are based on formal protocol specification modelling using the Logics of Knowledge and Trust. A representative such method, BAN Logic [4], is widely used for authentication protocol verification. BAN Logic considers authentication as a function of message freshness and integrity and is using a formal model for the authentication protocol messages based a predefined set of axioms.

BAN Logic has been successfully used to uncover a number of unknown flaws [5] [19] [47] as well as superfluous operations in widely used protocols [5] [48] [19] [49] [47]. BAN Logic can not be extended to zero knowledge protocols [20], and can not detect parallel session multiple-role flaws nor stale reflected message flaws [37], although it can detect run external attack flaws [4]. Furthermore, BAN Logic does not cover implementation-related flaws such as those included in [21] and detected in [2].

A number of other alternative logics have been proposed correcting or extending the existing framework [34] [35]. GNY Logic includes a parser that can detect whether a message has been sent in the past. However, even this extension does not completely detect stale message flaws.

The most important drawback of BAN-type logics is the lack of strict application techniques for converting messages and beliefs into idealised messages. A number of improvements have been suggested [50] [36] to deal with this problem. Despite this problem, inference based methods, and BAN Logic in particular is used in many new protocol specifications as for example in the analysis, specification and verification of Internet commercial transaction protocols [51] [52]. As BAN Logic can not prove that a protocol is secure, but can provide information about the possible occurrence of undesirable properties it can be used as a complement to the NRL Protocol Analyser [30].

3.4 Design process integration aspects

The multitude of protocol analysis approaches, methods, and tools hinders their integration into the protocol design process. Every different protocol analysis tool provides its own formal specification language; different from the message-oriented protocol descriptions that are typically published. Two approaches have been proposed in order to bridge the gap between the protocol analysis formalisms and the protocol design process.

One approach [53], proposes the use of an Interface Specification Language (ISL) in order to allow arbitrary protocol design processes to interface to the analysis tool. This approach has been used to provide a front end to the Automatic Authentication Protocol Analyser (AAPA) [54] [55] a tool that uses an extension of the GNY logic for proving protocol properties.

A second approach [56], proposes the use of a Common Protocol Specification Language (CAPSL) to bridge the gap between the typical informal presentations of protocols given in papers and the precise characterisations required to conduct formal analysis. The proposers of this approach hope that proponents of different analysis techniques will offer algorithms for compiling the CAPSL language into whatever form they require making it therefore possible to directly compare technique protocol assumptions and analysis results. This work is in progress, has not yet been completed, and it is described in a WWW site for suggestions, refinement and standardisation of the language definition.

4 Conclusions

Having examined a number of cryptographic protocol flaws we provided a possible taxonomy based on the flaw pathology and the corresponding attack method: exploitation of protocol or implementation weaknesses, password/key guessing, message re-use, or the establishment of a parallel session. The use of formal methods can definitely aid in the analysis, verification, validation, and security valuation of existing and proposed cryptographic protocols. As distributed systems and open interconnected networks are increasingly being used for transactions of commercial value, the transfer of sensitive personal data, and as society's infrastructure fabric increasingly depends on them the formal analysis of cryptographic protocols will be an important research topic.

The outlined presentation of general purpose formal analysis tools used in the cryptographic protocol domain as well as domain specific approaches presented in section 3 is an initial attempt at categorising tools and providing our view of their relative strengths and weaknesses with regard to the aforementioned proposed taxonomy of cryptographic protocols flaws. We believe that in the coming years formal method based tools will increasingly be used during cryptographic protocol design process, especially in the initial stages of the whole process.

Acknowledgements

The authors would like to thank Prof. P.Georgiadis, University of Athens, Greece, for his helpful comments.

5 References

1. Carlsen U. Cryptographic Protocol Flaws. In: *Proceedings of the 1994 IEEE Computer Security Foundations Workshop VII*. IEEE Computer Society Press, 1994, pp. 192-200

2. Carlsen U. Using Logics to Detect Implementation-Dependent Flaws. In: *Proceedings of the 9th IEEE Annual Computer Security Applications Conference.* IEEE Computer Society Press, 1993, pp. 64-73

3. Nesset D. A Critique of the BAN Logic. *ACM Operating Systems Review* 1990; 24(2) 35-38

4. Burrows M., Abadi M., Needham R. A Logic of Authentication. *ACM Transactions on Computer Systems* 1990; 8(1) 18-36

5. CCITT. *CCITT X.509: The Directory - An Authentication framework.* CCITT, 1988

6. Morris R. Password Security: A Case History. *Communications of the ACM* 1979; 22(11) 594-597

7. Klein D. Foiling the Cracker: A Survey of, and Improvements to, Password Security. In: *Proceedings of the USENIX Security Workshop II.* USENIX Association, 1990, pp. 5-14

8. Gong L. Attacks in Cryptographic Protocols. In: *Proceedings of IEEE INFOCOM '90.* IEEE Computer Security Society Press, 1990

9. Janson P., Molva R. Security in Open Networks and Distributed Systems. *Computer Networks and ISDN Systems 1991;* 22(5) 323-346

10. Ding Y., Horster P. Undetectable on-line password guessing attacks. *ACM Operating Systems Review* 1995; Vol. 29, No. 4, 77-86

11. Tsudik G., Van Herreweghen E. Some Remarks on Protecting Weak Keys and Poorly-Chosen Secrets from Guessing Attacks. In: *Proceedings of the 12th IEEE Symposium on Reliable Distributed Systems.* IEEE Computer Society Press, 1993, pp. 136-141

12. Gong L. Optimal Authentication Protocols Resistant to Password Guessing Attacks. In: *Proceedings of the 1995 IEEE Computer Security Foundations Workshop VIII.* IEEE Computer Society Press, 1995, pp. 24-29

13. Tardo J., Alagappan K. SPX: Global Authentication Using Public Key Certificates. In: *Proceedings of the 1991 IEEE Symposium on Research in Security and Privacy.* IEEE Computer Society Press, 1991, pp. 23-244

14. Bellovin S., Merritt M. Encrypted Key Exchange: Password-Based Protocols Secure against Dictionary Attacks. In: *Proceedings of the 1992 IEEE Symposium on Security and Privacy.* IEEE Computer Society Press, 1992, pp. 72-84

15. Gong L., Lomas M., Needham R. Saltzer J. Protecting Poorly Chosen Secrets from Guessing Attacks. *IEEE Journal on Selected Areas in Communications 1993;* Vol. 11, No. 5, 648-656

16. Jobusch D., Oldehoeft A. A survey of Password Mechanisms: Weaknesses and Potential Improvements. *Computers and Security 1989;* Vol. 8, No. 7, 587-603

17. Syverson P. A Taxonomy of Replay Attacks. In: *Proceedings of the 1994 IEEE Computer Security Foundations Workshop VII.* IEEE Computer Society Press, 1994, pp. 187-191

18. Denning D., Sacco G. Timestamps in Key Distribution Protocols. *Communications of the ACM 1981;* Vol. 24, No. 8, 533-536

19. Needham R., Schroeder M. Using Encryption for Authentication in large networks of computers. *Communications of the ACM 1978;* 21(12) 993-999

20. Syverson P. On Key Distribution Protocols for Repeated Authentication. *ACM Operating Systems Review 1993;* 27(4) 24-30

21. Neuman B., Stubblebine S. A Note on the Use of Timestamps as Nonces. *ACM Operating Systems Review 1993;* 27(2) 10-14

22. Snekkenes E. Roles in Cryptographic Protocols. In: *Proceedings of the 1992 IEEE Computer Security Symposium on Security and Privacy.* IEEE Computer Society Press, 1992, pp. 105-120

23. Shamir A., Rivest R., Adleman L. Mental Poker. *MIT Laboratory for Computer Science,* 1978, Report TM-125: 178-184

24. Massey J. An Introduction to Contemporary Cryptology. In: *Proceedings of the IEEE.* IEEE Computer Society Press, 1988, Vol. 76, No. 5, pp. 533-549

25. Moore J. Protocol Failures in Cryptosystems. In: *Proceedings of the IEEE.* IEEE Computer Society Press, 1988, Vol. 76, No. 5, pp. 594-602

26. Kemmerer R., Meadows C., Millen J. Three Systems for Cryptographic Protocol Analysis. *Journal of Cryprology* 1994; (7) 79-130

27. Brackin S. A HOL Extension of GNY for Automatically Analysing Cryptographic Protocols. In: *Proceedings of the 1996 IEEE Computer Security Foundations Workshop IX.* IEEE Computer Society Press, 1996, pp. 62-76

28. Dolev D., Yao A. On the Security of Public Key Protocols. *IEEE Transactions on Information Theory 1983;* 29(2) 198-208

29. Kemmerer R. Analysing encryption protocols using formal verification techniques. *IEEE Journal on Selected Areas in Communications 1989;* 7(4) 448-457

30. Meadows C. Applying Formal Methods to the Analysis of a Key-Management Protocol. *Journal of Computer Security 1992;* vol. 1, 5-35

31. Millen J. The Interrogator Model. In: *Proceedings of the 1995 IEEE Symposium on Security and Privacy.* IEEE Computer Society Press, 1995, pp. 251-260

32. Sidhu D. Authentication Protocols for Computer Networks. *Computer Networks and ISDN Systems 1986;* 11, 297-310

33. Varadharajan V. Verification of Network Security Protocols. *Computers and Security 1989;* Vol. 8, 693-708

34. Gong L., Needham R., Yahalom R. Reasoning about Belief in Cryptographic Protocols. In: *Proceedings of the 1990 IEEE Symposium on Security and Privacy.* IEEE Computer Society Press, 1990, pp. 234-248

35. Syverson P., van Oorschot P.C. On Unifying some Cryptographic Protocol Logics. In: *Proceedings of the 1994 IEEE Computer Security Foundations Workshop VII.* IEEE Computer Society Press, 1994, pp. 14-29

36. Gritzalis S. BAN logic for the analysis and verification of authentication protocols in distributed systems: A Review. In: *Proceedings of the 1st meeting of the IKAROS Human Network for the Safety, Quality, and Reliability in Information and Communication Technologies,* 1996, (in Greek)

37. Kessler V., Wedel G. AUTLOG-An advanced Logic of Authentication. In: *Proceedings of the 1994 IEEE Computer Security Foundations Workshop VII.* IEEE Computer Society Press, 1994, pp. 90-99

38. Syverson P. The Use of Logic in the Analysis of Cryptographic Protocols. In: *Proceedings of the 1991 IEEE Computer Security Symposium on Security and Privacy.* IEEE Computer Society Press, 1991, pp. 156-170

39. Roscoe, A. W. Modelling and verifying key-exchange protocols using CSP and FDR. In: *Proceedings of the 1995 IEEE Computer Security Foundations Workshop*

IIX. IEEE Computer Society Press, 1995, pp. 98-107

40. Lowe D. Breaking and Fixing the Needham-Schroeder Public-Key Protocol Using FDR. In: *Proceedings of TACAS*. Springer Verlag, 1996, pp. 147-166

41. Scheid J., Holtsberg S. *Ina Jo Specification Language Reference Manual*, System Development Group, Unisys Corporation, CA, 1988

42. Diffie W., Hellman M. New Directions in Cryptography. *IEEE Transactions on Information Theory 1976;* Vol. IT-22, No. 6, 644-654

43. Tatebayashi M., Matsuzaki N., Newman D. Key Distribution Protocol for Digital Mobile Communications Systems. In: *Advances in Cryptology, CRYPTO '89*. Springer Verlag, 1989, pp. 324-333 (Lecture Notes in Computer Science no. 435)

44. Purdy G., Simmons G., Studier J. A Software Protection Scheme. In: *Proceedings of the 1982 IEEE Symposium on Security and Privacy*. IEEE Computer Society Press, pp. 99-103

45. Simmons G. How to Selectively Broadcast a Secret. In: *Proceedings of the 1985 IEEE Symposium on Security and Privacy*. IEEE Computer Society Press, 1985

46. Syverson P. Knowledge, belief and Semantics in the Analysis of Cryptographic Protocols. *Journal of Computer Security 1992;* Vol. 1, No. 3 317-334

47. Satyanarayanan M. Integrating Security in a large distributed system. *ACM Transactions on Computer Systems 1989;* 7(3) 247-280

48. Millen J., Neuman C., Schiller J., Saltzer J. Kerberos Authentication and Authorisation system, *Project Athena Technical Plan*, Section E.2.1. M.I.T., 1987

49. Otway D., Rees O. Efficient and timely mutual authentication. *ACM Operating Systems Review 1987;* 21(1) 8-10

50. Mao W. An Augmentation of BAN-like Logics. In: *Proceedings of the 1995 IEEE Computer Security Foundations Workshop VIII*. IEEE Computer Society Press, 1995, pp. 44-56

51. Bellare M., Garay J., Hauser R., et al. iKP - a family of secure electronic payment protocols. In: *Proceedings of the First USENIX Workshop on Electronic Commerce*, USENIX Association, 1995

52. Pal G. Verification of the iKP family of secure electronic payment protocols, *http://web.mit.edu/gnpal/www/ikp/verify_ikp.html*, 1996

53. Brackin S. An Interface Specification Language for Automatically Analysing Cryptographic Protocols. In: *Proceedings of the 1997 Symposium on Network and Distributed System Security*. IEEE Computer Society Press, 1997, pp. 40-51

54. Brackin S. Automatic Formal Analyses of Cryptographic Protocols. In: *Proceedings of the 19th National Conference on Information Systems Security*, IEEE Computer Society Press, 1996

55. Brackin S. Automatic Formal Analyses of Cryptographic Protocols, updated version of [54], private communication, 1997

56. Millen J. CAPSL - Common Authentication Protocol Specification Language, work in progress: *http://www.mitre.org/research/capsl/*, 1997

Using Executable Interactor Specifications to Explore the Impact of Operator Interaction Errors

Andrew M. Dearden*and Michael D. Harrison

Department of Computer Science,
University of York, York, YO1 5DD, U.K.
Email: {andyd, mdh}@cs.york.ac.uk.

1   Introduction

In this paper, we discuss the requirements for a tool to support analysis of the impact of erroneous task performances on a system, and report on preliminary work on a prototype implementation in Prolog.

We define impact informally as:

> 'the effect that an action or sequence of actions has on the safe and successful operation of a system'

An understanding of the impact of particular sequences of interactions may help human-machine interface[1] designers to derive designs that minimise the probability that sequences with high negative impacts will occur.

In a systematic approach to impact analysis, risk analysts and interface designers are required to: identify sequences of interaction that might occur and whose impact should be considered; determine the effects of those sequences with respect to the current design; and quantify the relative impact associated with these effects. As with most risk analysis procedures, if impact analysis is to be applied to large systems, tool support will be required.

2   Impact analysis, a need, a process and a tool

Problems in human-machine interaction have been identified as a major cause of accidents in safety-critical computer systems, see e.g. Mackenzie (1994). Woods *et al.* (1994) argue that many accidents and incidents where 'operator error' (or human error, or pilot error) is given as a cause, beg the question of how the human-machine interface design might have contributed to the error's occurrence. A recent report by the US Federal Aviation Administration (FAA, 1996), gives weight to this point of view, and recommends that:

---

*Employed under EPSRC grant No. GR/J07686
[1] The term interface refers to the human-machine interface throughout this paper.

"The FAA should require evaluation in flight deck designs for suscepti-
bility to design induced flightcrew errors and the consequences of those
errors as part of the type certification process."[ibid. Recommendation
Criteria-1, page 9]

We have argued elsewhere (Dearden and Harrison, 1996a,b) that current approaches
to safety analysis for human-machine interaction do not adequately support the exploration of consequences of design induced errors during the early stages of interface
design. In particular: approaches that rely on quantifying the probability of an operator correctly executing some task, e.g. THERP (Swain and Guttman, 1983), are limited by the difficulty of constructing probabilistic accounts of human behaviour, especially when a complete, detailed description of the final system is not available; whilst
team based analysis methods, see e.g. Kirwan (1992), are likely to be too costly to
repeat whilst exploring alternative designs. Other critiques of these methods point to
an over-reliance on decomposing the work of operators into isolated tasks (Hollnagel,
1993a), overlooking wider issues that may affect safety, such as the possible migration
of task responsibilties between operators, contextual factors such as cognitive workload or competing goals, or congitive consequences arising from particular display designs.

Impact analysis aims to address some of the weaknesses of existing approaches,
and to provide support for the early stages of interface design by:

- avoiding, where possible, attempts to quantify probabilities of particular human
  errors occurring;

- focusing, instead, on the severity of consequences that would arise from particular interaction sequences; and

- providing tools that allow the interface designer to generate interaction sequences
  that they regard as 'plausible' (based on task structure, previous accident scenarios, cognitive or contextual factors, or on 'engineering judgement') and to
  explore their effects and the severity of those effects.

2.1   The process of impact analysis

One way to characterise risk analysis techniques is to classify them with regard to the
following three attributes.

- The Generator - which is used to generate a set of events or situations that need
  to be considered within the analysis.

- The Model (or set of models) - which is (are) used to explore the consequences
  of the events.

- The Evaluation Function - that is used to quantify the significance of the consequences.

For example, for failure modes and effects analysis: the generator is the set of all failure modes for any component within the system each of which must be considered as

a possible triggering event for an accident sequence; the model(s) are system diagrams and functional understandings of the system in the analyst's mind; and the evaluation function is the analyst's judgement as to the severity of different consequences. In HazOps: the generator is the set of guide words and the skill of the team facilitator; the model is the implicit understanding of the various aspects of the system brought to the meeting by the participants; and the evaluation is the severity judgement.

Following this framework, the process we envisage for impact analysis is as follows.

- **The Generator:** Design of a human-machine interface also implies an activity of designing the intended behaviour of the human within the system. A number of representational formalisms have been suggested to describe the task of the operator (Kirwan and Ainsworth, 1992). We aim to exploit these by mutating the sequences allowed by the orginal task descriptions to generate a set of erroneous interaction sequences. These mutations would correspond to 'phenotypes' of erroneous action as described by Hollnagel (1993b). The mutations should include behaviours that are plausible from the viewpoint of the interface designer or risk analyst. Some plausible mutations can be produced by automatically mutating the structure of the original task description. Others may be introduced by seeding the system with a pre-mutated task description, perhaps based on a cognitive evaluation of an interface, i.e. on 'genotypes' of error (ibid.), on previous accident scenarios, or on engineering judgement, and then applying further mutations to extend the search space covered in the analysis.

- **The model:** During early development, the state, presentation and behaviour of the interface can be represented using abstract mathematical models (Dearden and Harrison, 1996b). The 'model' for impact analysis will be based on these specifications of interface behaviour. A requirement for impact analysis is that the interface models can be made executable, and that the models include sufficient detail about system state to support the assignment of impact to state differences. Impact analysis will use these executable models to investigate the consequences associated with the mutated sequences generated above.

- **The evaluation function:** Impact analysis aims to identify sequences of interaction that would have an unacceptable impact, so that designers can seek to minimise the probability that such sequences would occur. Given this aim, it is not necessary for the evaluation function to return quantitative evaluations on a ratio scale, rather a qualitative assessment on an ordinal scale may be more appropriate. In Dearden and Harrison (1996a,b), we describe one possible evaluation function. In this paper, we discuss alternative functions that could be used.

2.2 A tool to support impact analysis

The architecture we propose for our impact analysis tool, shown in figure 1, reflects the separation of generator, model and evaluation function. The user interface permits the interface designer to input a specification of the intended behaviour of the interactive system and a description of the proposed task structure for the operator. A separate

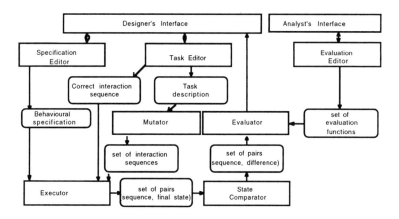

Figure 1: An architecture for the impact analysis tool

interface allows a risk analyst to declare a set of suitable evaluation functions, from which the designer may select according to the analysis that is being conducted. The task structure or scenario structure is used by the mutator to generate plausible interaction sequences, including correct interaction sequences. The interaction sequences are then executed on the behavioural specification to generate a final state for each sequence. The final states are then fed into the state comparator to identify differences between the final states of mutated sequences and the expected final state of the correct sequence(s). The state differences are then evaluated with respect to the selected evaluation function.

Where a particular scenario has been selected for evaluation, e.g. as a reflection of a previously encountered accident scenario, the tool can be seeded with a pre-mutated task description. The mutator can then be used to generate alternative versions of the scenario for analysis. By selecting specific scenarios to generate some of the plausible mutations, we prune the search space of interaction sequences considered. The sequences we aim to include in the analysis are those that involve a single mutation applied to the original task structure, or that involve a single mutation applied to a selected scenario.

3 Definitions

In what follows, we describe a prototype system designed to support impact analysis. To simplify the exposition, some definitions are useful.

Task description A description of the structure of a task that indicates a set of possible ways in which the task can be performed in a way that the designer would understand as 'correct'.

Interaction sequence A sequence of events which may be actions by the operator(s) or by the computer system.

Correct interaction sequence An interaction sequence that is permitted by a task description.

Behavioural specification A specification of a computer system's behaviour, indicating guards that must be satisfied before actions can be executed, and the relationship between the prior and posterior states of the system when an action is performed.

Expected final state The state of the system that is reached when a correct interaction sequence is executed from a given starting state. Note that we are concerned with the state of the part of the system that is modelled, rather than the achievement of some abstract goal that is expressed by a state of the world beyond the scope of the model.

Actual final state The state of the system that is reached when any interaction sequence is executed from a given starting state. For a correct interaction sequence, the actual and expected final states are the same.

4   The specification editor and executor

The tool's model of the evolving design is input using the specification editor. The executor is used to run interaction sequences over the model. Thus, the design of these two components is inseparable.

The first design decision is to select the syntax to be used for specifying the interface. In Dearden and Harrison (1996b) we use interactors as a means of specifying the behaviour of the interface to support impact analysis. An interactor is a component of a human-machine interface, that has state, behaviour, and presentation. Various syntactic styles can be used to specify interactors. Examples have been reported that are based on Modal Action Logic (Dearden and Harrison, 1996b), VDM (Fields *et al.*, 1995), Action Systems (Bramwell *et al.*, 1995), and Z (Duke and Harrison, 1994). Two criteria that we found relevant to selecting a syntax for use in the tool are listed below.

1. Initially, because we intend to measure impact by reference to differences between the actual and expected final states, a state-based (model-based) style of specification seems to be appropriate.

2. To execute the interaction sequences we need to apply actions to the model successively, updating the state as each action is applied. A language where the information needed to evaluate the effects of an action is grouped in a single syntactic structure (e.g. an action schema) is, therefore, preferable to a language where information about an action may be distributed between multiple syntactic structures (e.g. a set of axioms and invariants).

A second design decision concerns the way in which the evolving state will be recorded. In the prototype, the evolving state is maintained within Prolog's dynamic database. This reflects the spirit of Prolog's design, using the dynamic database as an evaluation space to record intermediate results.

interactor Valve   - a description of a valve

attributes

     state : {opened, closed}   - the state of the valve

actions

     open, close   - opening or closing the valve

axioms

1   state = closed
2   state = closed $\Rightarrow$ [open] state = opened
3   state = opened $\Rightarrow$ [close] state = closed

Figure 2: An example of an interactor specified using modal action logic

```
axiom(V,  close):-
itype(V, regulator),
istate(V, [(state, State)]),
State = opened,
Newstate = closed,
retractall(istate(V, _)),
assert(istate( V, [ (state, Newstate)]))).
```

Figure 3: Prolog description of axiom three of the valve interactor

4.1   Current state of implementation

Currently, the prototype violates criterion 2 above, in that the specification language, based on Modal Action Logic, describes the behaviour of an interactor using a collection of axioms. The reason for this choice is historical, following on from the work in Dearden and Harrison (1996b). Figure 2 shows a specification for a valve in this style.

To enter the specification into the tool, it is translated into a set of prolog predicates. Clauses of a relation axiom(Interactor, Action) are used to represent the axioms. Each axiom clause checks that the precondition of the axiom is satisfied and, if so, updates the dynamic database by retracting old values and asserting new state values for the interactor. For example, figure 3 shows the implementation of one axiom from the valve interactor. Invariants are handled by following each successful database update by checking a predicate axiom(Interactor, invariant).

Interaction sequences are represented as lists of (Interactor, Action) pairs. The executor reads the (Interactor, Action) pair at the head of the interaction sequence list recursively, evaluates axiom(Interactor, Action), and then checks invariants for the individual interactor, and for the plant. This handling of invariants is somewhat unsatisfactory, since the sequential implementation is not guaranteed correct relative to the formal semantics of the specification language.

5 The Task Editor and Mutator

The mutator takes a task description as input, and outputs a set of mutated interaction sequences. The intention is that the mutated sequences should represent plausible operator behaviours.

5.1 Requirements for the task description language

As with the executor and specification editor, the design of the mutator and task editor are closely interdependent. The choice of syntax for task description is a major design decision. It must be sufficiently rich to allow a wide range of possible error phenotypes to be generated. On the other hand, the richer the language, the larger the set of possible mutated sequences. Fields *et al.* (1995) consider the use of Hoare's communicating sequential processes (CSP) notation to describe the sequencing of tasks, but avoid the complexity of real time. Within the CSP framework some possible mutations are omission, repetition, or transposition of actions or subtasks, intrusion of a subtask or action from some other task in the system, or incorrect choice.

5.2 Generating plausible interaction sequences

Given a task description language of type similar to CSP, it is possible to generate mutated interaction sequences by manipulating parse trees for the correct interaction sequences. Within each parse tree, each node corresponds to the application of some binary operator combining two subtasks or actions, e.g. connecting two subtasks in sequence. Each operator is associated with a set of phenotypical mutations. By visiting each node of the parse tree, and applying the relevant mutations at that node, a set of interaction sequences, each of which includes one phenotypical error can be generated. Some automatic pruning of the search space can be achieved by identifying, from the behavioural specification, actions that are idempotent, or pairs of actions for which the order of execution is unimportant.

As well as exploring mutations of the original task description, the interface designer, or risk analyst, may want to explore the consequences of a particular interaction sequence. Sequences may be generated from cognitive analyses of the design, from study of the work context, from the engineering judgement, or from previous accident or incident scenarios. Exploring these scenarios, based on the genotypes of error, helps by pruning the search space of phenotypes that are considered in the analysis, as well as helping to avoid the limitations of other task based analysis methods, where each action or subtask is treated as somehow atomic and independent of its context (Hollnagel, 1993a).

5.3 Current state of implementation

We have chosen to begin development with a very simple task description language. In the first prototype, the task is represented by a list of lists of (Interactor, Action) pairs. Each pair represents a single action, a list of pairs represents a subtask, a list of subtasks represents a larger subtask etc. This tree structure provides a suitable representation for purely sequential tasks, but does not allow for tasks involving choices, enabling conditions, or concurrent activities involving multiple operators.

Automatic pruning of the search space is supported by manually extracting information about interdependence of actions from the specification, and representing the information explicitly.

6   Evaluation Editor and Evaluator

The analyst's input to the tool is used to indicate the relative severity that should be associated with different outcomes from a task.

6.1   Alternative evaluation functions

In Dearden and Harrison (1996a,b) we consider a measure of impact that is based on the change in hazard probability, calculated by reference to a fault tree. The fault tree expresses how, in the expected final state, spontaneous failures of components might combine to cause a hazard to occur. The probability of the hazard occuring following an erroneous interaction sequence is computed by identifying leaf nodes of the fault tree that were true, i.e. should be assigned a probability of 1, in the actual final state. The impact measure is the difference between the probability of the hazard occuring in the expected and actual final states as computed from the fault tree.

As well as calculating the impact of a single erroneous action, it may be helpful to identify where two interaction sequences lead to states where different elements of the same minimal cut set are made true. If such pairs can be detected, the designer or analyst could then actively explore whether the two errors could occur together.

For some systems, fault trees may not provide a suitable evaluation function for the severity of errors. For instance, an analysis of a pilot's interaction with an aircraft flight management system may show that some interaction sequences can lead to a state where the flight plan as represented in the flight management system takes the aircraft to a point many miles from the position given by air traffic control. Such an error cannot be evaluated using the fault tree method described above, because the hazards associated with the error do not arise as a result of spontaneous failure of components. An alternative computation of impact might be possible by defining a function based on the degree of difference between the future flight trajectory as intended and the trajectory as entered. One possible function might use a weighted sum of components reflecting the lateral, vertical and temporal differences. To discover suitable evaluation functions, we are investigating some techniques based on economic utility theory, that are designed to elicit a decision maker's views on the relative values of different options. We hope that such techniques might be applied to elicit risk analysts' understandings of relative severity.

Another possible consequence of an erroneous interaction sequence, is the introduction of a mode error into a system. A mode error may occur when the operator's expectations of system behaviour in response to inputs differs from the actual behaviour, because the system is in a mode that the operator does not expect. To define an evaluation function for mode errors, a risk analyst might be required to assign relative severities to pairs of expected and actual final modes. For instance, for the display mode used to show rate of descent in an aircraft, a confusion between flight path angle versus vertical speed of descent might be assigned a higher severity than a confusion of the way in which the aircraft is set to climb between an open climb and an altitude capture mode.

6.2 Current state of implementation

At present, the prototype system only supports the two evaluation functions based on fault trees. These fault trees are represented in Prolog clauses in two separate forms: firstly as a set of minimal cut sets, which is used to collect errors that may need to be considered together; and secondly as a set of independent event sets, which simplifies the calculation of the root probabilities. We do not expect to do further development work on the fault tree representations, instead we hope to concentrate on eliciting, and developing support for, the alternative evaluation functions discussed above.

7 Discussion and Conclusions

In this paper, we have described a process and a tool for impact analysis. Impact analysis aims to allow interface designers and risk analysts to explore possible consequences of different design decisions during the early stages of design.

The requirements for the tool indicate some of the key research questions that must influence the further development of impact analysis. The main questions that we have identified are listed below.

- What forms of interface specification or interface modelling will provide the ease of expression and (human) interpretation that the interface designer will require, whilst providing sufficient information to perform an efficient search of the space of plausible interaction sequences?

- What forms of task description language would provide the required expressiveness and readability for the interface designer? For instance, Hollnagel (1993b) considers a number of errors involving real time that are beyond the scope of untimed task descriptions, such as those expressable in CSP.

- How can constraints on a task that arise from factors that are outside the scope of the current behavioural specification be expressed. For example, constraints arising from physical properties of the system, or from devices in the larger system that are outside the scope of a particular model?

- What range of evaluation functions needs to be supported and how can these be declared by an analyst?

- How can the current framework for the behavioural specification and task description be extended to cope with real-time issues.

We hope that our future work will answer some of these questions.

References

Bramwell, C., Fields, B., and Harrison, M. D. (1995). Exploring design options rationally. In Palanque, P. and Bastide, R., editors, *DSV-IS'95: Eurographics Workshop on Design, Specification and Verification of Interactive Systems*, 134 – 148. Springer.

Dearden, A. M. and Harrison, M. D. (1996a). Impact and the design of the human-machine interface. In *Compass 96*, 161 – 170. IEEE Press.

Dearden, A. M. and Harrison, M. D. (1996b). Risk Analysis, Impact and Interaction Modelling. In Bodart, F. and Vanderdonckt, J., editors, *Proceedings of DSVIS 96*, Springer Eurographics Series. Springer.

Duke, D. J. and Harrison, M. D. (1994). *Connections from A(V) to Z*. Technical Report System Modelling/WP21, AMODEUS II project, ESPRIT Basic Research Action 7040.

FAA (1996). *The Interfaces Between Flightcrews and Modern Flightdeck Systems*. Technical report, Federal Aviation Administration.

Fields, R., Wright, P., and Harrison, M. (1995). A task centred approach to analysing human error tolerance requirements. In Zave, P., editor, *Proceedings, RE'95 The Second IEEE International Symposium on Requirements Engineering, York, UK*, 18–26. IEEE, New York.

Hollnagel, E. (1993a). *Human Reliability Assessment, Context and Control*. Academic Press.

Hollnagel, E. (1993b). The phenotype of erroneous actions. *Int. Journal of Man-Machine Studies*, 39(1):1 – 32.

Kirwan, B. (1992). Human error identification in human reliability assessment. Part I: Overview of approaches. *Applied Ergonomics*, 23(5):299 – 318.

Kirwan, B. and Ainsworth, L. K., editors (1992). *A Guide to Task Analysis*. Taylor and Francis.

Mackenzie, D. (1994). Computer related accidental death: an empirical exploration. *Science and Public Policy*, 21(4):233 – 248.

Swain, A. D. and Guttman, H. E. (1983). *Handbook of Human Reliability Analysis with Emphasis on Nuclear Power Plant Applications, Final Report*. Technical Report NUREG/CR-1278 SAND80-0200 RX, AN, U. S. Nuclear Regulatory Commission.

Woods, D. D., Johannesen, L. J., Cook, R. I., and Sarter, N. B. (1994). *Behind Human Error: Cognitive Systems, Computers, and Hindsight*. Technical report, CSE-RIAC, Ohio State University.

Design, Analysis and Implementation of a New Hash Function Based on Block Cipher

Xun Yi

National Communication Research Lab, Southeast University

Nanjing, P.R.China

Kwork-Yan Lam, Yong-Fei Han

National University of Singapore

Republic of Singapore

Abstract

In this paper, a new 2m-bit iterated hash function based on a m-bit block cipher with a 2m-bit key is firstly presented. Different from previous 2m-bit hash function based on block ciphers, the hash round function in our proposal utilizes a single underlying block cipher. Secondly, five attacks on the hash function are treated. The results show that its hash round function can completely resist target attack, collision attack and semi-free-start collision attack and the whole scheme can be expected to have ideal computational security against the five attacks when the underlying cipher is assumed to have no weakness. Finally, the implementation of the new hash function is discussed. For the underlying cipher to be easily implemented in both software and hardware, so is the new hash function because only two basic 64-bit algebraic operations are introduced in the hash round function on basis of the cipher.

1 Introduction

Cryptographic hash functions are very important for cryptographic protocols. In cryptographic applications, hash functions are used within digital signature schemes and within schemes to provide data integrity. When used with signature schemes, their role is to reduce the amount of data which must be signed and to break up any properties such as multiplicative homomorphism which might be exploited by an opponent. When used to provide data integrity, their role is to detect modification of an original message.

Block ciphers are often used to construct iterated hash function in view of their satisfying security, high speed, low expense and easy implementation. For example, DM-scheme [1] [2], PBGV-scheme [3] and QG-I-scheme [4] are such hash functions based on a m-bit block cipher with a m-bit key.

A hash function h must be an one-way function, i.e., when given x, it is easy to compute $h(x)$, but it is computationally infeasible to find an $x' \neq x$ such that $h(x') = h(x)$. In addition, the hash function must be collision free, i.e., it must be computationally infeasible to construct different messages which output the same hash value, in other words, it means that finding $x' \neq x$ with

$h(x') = h(x)$ is a hard problem. The needs for such functions to ensure data integrity, and for use with digital signature schemes are well known.

Note that we are concentrating here on publicly computable hash functions, i.e., functions that are not controlled by a secret key.

Due to the "birthday attack", about 2^{32} computations of the hash code are needed to find a collision for any hash functions of code length 64 bits. It is certainly too small in many applications. Thus, several efforts [3] [4] [5] [6] [7] [8] have been made to construct 128-bit hash functions based on block cipher of block length 64 bits. The hash round functions in these schemes use two underlying block ciphers.

In this paper, we present a new 2m-bit iterated hash function based on a m-bit block cipher with a 2m-bit key, such as IDEA [9] [10] and the block cipher in [11]. Different from the schemes mentioned above, the hash round function in our proposal utilizes a single underlying block cipher. From a practical point of view, our proposal is more efficient. The results of security analysis on the new hash function show the hash round function in our proposal is capable of completely resisting target attack, collision attack and semi-free-start collision attack and the whole scheme can be expected to have ideal computational security against five attacks when the underlying cipher is assumed to have no weakness. For the underlying cipher to be easily implemented in both software and hardware, so is the new hash function because only two basic 64-bit algebraic operations are introduced in the hash round function on basis of the cipher.

2 Overview of the new hash function

It seems to be difficult to build a 2m-bit hash function with ideal computational security that can "digest" in each round at least m bits of message by use of a m-bit block cipher with a m-bit key. However, if a m-bit block cipher with a 2m-bit key is available, there are more possibilities to construct a possibly secure 2m-bit hash round function. In the following, we construct a 2m-bit iterated hash function based on a m-bit block cipher with a 2m-bit key and that appear to be secure when the underlying cipher is assumed to have no weakness.

2.1 The new hash round function

The new hash function is an iterated hash function. The computational graph of its round function h can be illustrated in the following figure.

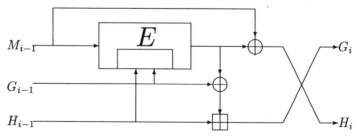

Figure 1: Computational graph for the new hash round function h

We formulate the hash round function h as follows:

$$(G_i, H_i) \quad = \quad h(G_{i-1}, H_{i-1}, M_{i-1}) \tag{1}$$

In the above equation, two m-bit values G_i and H_i are computed from the two m-bit values G_{i-1} and H_{i-1} and from the m-bit message block M_{i-1} as follows:

$$G_i \quad = \quad (E_{(G_{i-1}\|H_{i-1})}(M_{i-1})\bigoplus G_{i-1})\boxed{+}H_{i-1} \tag{2}$$

$$H_i \quad = \quad E_{(G_{i-1}\|H_{i-1})}(M_{i-1})\bigoplus M_{i-1} \tag{3}$$

In the above figure and formulae, the meanings of all symbols are explained as follows:

1. $E_K(P)$: ciphertext block responding to plaintext block P, enciphered by a m-bit block cipher E using 2m-bit key K.

2. X $\|$ Y: concatenation of m-bit block X and Y.

3. X $\bigoplus$ Y: bitwise exclusive-or of m-bit block X and Y.

4. X $\boxed{+}$ Y: addition modulo 2^m of m-bit integer X and Y.

2.2 The new hash function

We use the "meta-method" [6] to construct the new 2m-bit iterated hash function based on a m-bit block cipher with 2m-bit key.

The new hash function is a function $Hash(\cdot)$ determined by the easily computable round function $h(\cdot)$ from three m-bit values to two m-bit values in the manner that the message $M = (M_0, M_1, \cdots, M_{n-1})$, where M_i is m-bit value, is hashed to a 2m-bit hash value $(G, H) = (G_n, H_n)$ by computing (1) recursively. We write

$$(G, H) \quad = \quad Hash(G_0, H_0, M) \tag{4}$$

to show explicitly the dependence on (G_0, H_0) and M, where (G_0, H_0) is a 2m-bit specified initial value. For message data whose total length in bits is not a multiple of m, one can apply deterministic "padding" [6] to the message to be hashed by (4) to increase the total length to a multiple of m. The equation (4) shows the 2m-bit hash value (G, H) is computed from a mn-bit message $(M_0, M_1, \cdots, M_{n-1})$ and a 2m-bit initial value (G_0, H_0).

Considering the fact that a falsified message can have a length different from that of the given genuine message, Merkle [6] and Damgaard [12] independently proposed MD-strengthening of iterated hash functions to overcome this problem. In the new hash function, we take advantage of MD-strengthening, i.e., specify that the last block M_{n-1} of the message $(M_0, M_1, \cdots, M_{n-1})$ to be hashed represents the length of the "true message" in bits, i.e., the length of unpadded portion of the first $n-1$ blocks. Therefore, the hashed message must contain at least two blocks, i.e., $n \geq 2$.

The new hash function was constructed based on the following consideration:

1. Only a block cipher and two 64-bit basic algebraic operations are used in
the hash round function of our proposal in order to increase its hashing
efficiency and facilitate both hardware and software implementations.

2. It is well-known that DM-scheme with MD-strengthening is generally
considered to be secure in the sense that, if the block cipher has no
known weakness, then no attack better than the brute-force attacts is
known. The design purpose of the new scheme is to construct a 2m-bit
hash function composed of two subfunctions which are equivalent (in the
sense of security) to DM-scheme.

3. The operation "$\boxed{+}$" (addition modulo 2^m of m-bit integers) is introduced
into the new hash function so that its two subfunctions are as "different"
as possible. In addition, the two different algebraic group operations, $\oplus$
and $\boxed{+}$, are incompatible in the sense of literature [9] [10]. They do not
satisfy the associative law, i.e.,

$$(X \oplus Y) \boxed{+} Z \neq X \oplus (Y \boxed{+} Z) \tag{5}$$

This property provides the desired confusion for the new hash function
to some extent.

4. Two outputs of the new hash round function are swapped so as to balance
the number of operations which are involved in them.

5. The m bits of message M_{i-1} "digested" in the hash round function is
just the plaintext input of the underlying block cipher. Hence, hashing
the message M by using our proposal can be regarded as recursively
enciphering each message of M with variable keys.

3 Attacks on the new hash function

For iterated hash functions, there are five attacks [8] [10]. The five attacks on
the new hash function can be illustrated as follows:

1. **Target attack:** Given G_0, H_0 and M, find M' such that $M' \neq M$ but
$Hash(G_0, H_0, M') = Hash(G_0, H_0, M)$.

2. **Free-start target attack:** Given G_0, H_0 and M, find G'_0, H'_0 and M'
such that $(G_0, H_0, M) \neq (G'_0, H'_0, M')$ but $Hash(G'_0, H'_0, M') = Hash$
(G_0, H_0, M).

3. **Collision attack:** Given G_0, H_0, find M and M' such that $M' \neq M$ but
$Hash(G_0, H_0, M') = Hash(G_0, H_0, M)$.

4. **Semi-free-start collision attack:** Find G_0, H_0, M and M' such that
$M' \neq M$ but $Hash(G_0, H_0, M') = Hash(G_0, H_0, M)$.

5. **Free-start collision attack:** Find G_0, H_0, M, G'_0, H'_0 and M' such that
$(G_0, H_0, M) \neq (G'_0, H'_0, M')$ but $Hash(G'_0, H'_0, M') = Hash(G_0, H_0, M)$.

Each attack on the new hash function is treated as follows.

3.1 Target attack

A target attack on the hash round function h in our proposal reads: given G_{i-1}, H_{i-1} and M_{i-1}, find M'_{i-1} such that $M'_{i-1} \neq M_{i-1}$ but

$$h(G_{i-1}, H_{i-1}, M'_{i-1}) = h(G_{i-1}, H_{i-1}, M_{i-1}) \qquad (6)$$

Based on equations (2) and (3), the following equations can be deduced from equation (6).

$$(E_{(G_{i-1}\|H_{i-1})}(M'_{i-1}) \quad \oplus \quad G_{i-1}\boxed{+}H_{i-1}$$
$$= \quad (E_{(G_{i-1}\|H_{i-1})}(M_{i-1})\oplus G_{i-1}\boxed{+}H_{i-1} \qquad (7)$$

$$E_{(G_{i-1}\|H_{i-1})}(M'_{i-1})\oplus M'_{i-1} = E_{(G_{i-1}\|H_{i-1})}(M_{i-1})\oplus M_{i-1} \qquad (8)$$

From the above equations, we can easily obtain $M'_{i-1} = M_{i-1}$. It shows, except from M_{i-1}, no matter what value M'_{i-1} is equal to, "target" $h(G_{i-1}, H_{i-1}, M_{i-1})$ is never hit. So we can say that the hash round function can completely resist target attack.

In view of the above fact, target attack on the new hash function must attack more than two rounds of it successively. Considering that the dependent relations of hash outputs to hash inputs in more than two rounds of the new hash function are much more complex than those of one round of it, only brute-force target attack, in which one randomly chooses a M' until one hits the "target" $Hash(G_0, H_0, M)$; can be used to attack it. By carrying out brute-force target attack on it, "hitting a target" requires about 2^{2m} computations of hash values.

3.2 Collision attack

Collision attack on the hash round function in our proposal means: given G_{i-1}, H_{i-1}, find M_{i-1}, M'_{i-1} such that $M'_{i-1} \neq M_{i-1}$ but equation (6) holds.

Slightly different from the target attack on the round function, M_{i-1} is not fixed and nor is $h(G_{i-1}, H_{i-1}, M_{i-1})$. However, from equations (7) and (8), we can still obtain $M'_{i-1} = M_{i-1}$. It implies that the hash round function can completely resist collision attack and the attack on the new hash function needs attacking at least two rounds of it successively.

For more than two rounds of our proposal, the dependent relations of hash outputs to hash inputs are too complex to provide any help to collision attack on it. In order to find a "collision" of it, we have to use brute-force collision attack, in which one randomly chooses M and M' until a "collision" is sought out, i.e., equation (6) holds. Due to the usual "birthday argument", finding a "collision" with probability about 0.63 by using brute-force collision attack on the more than two rounds of our proposal requires about 2^m computations of hash values.

3.3 Semi-free-start collision attack

Semi-free-start attack on the round function in our proposal means: find G_{i-1}, $H_{i-1}, M_{i-1}, M'_{i-1}$ such that $M'_{i-1} \neq M_{i-1}$ but equation (6) holds.

Different from collision attack, G_{i-1}, H_{i-1} in semi-free-start collision attack are not fixed. But $M'_{i-1} = M_{i-1}$ can still be obtained from equations (7) and (8). So the hash round function can completely resist semi-free-start collision attack and the attack on our proposal needs attacking at least two rounds successively.

Like collision attack, since the complex dependent relations of hash outputs to hash inputs in more than two rounds of our proposal do not provide any help to semi-free-start collision attack on it, only brute-force semi-free-start collision attack, in which one randomly chooses G_0, M_0, M and M' until a "collision" $Hash(G_0, H_0, M) = Hash(G_0, H_0, M')$ is found, can be used. It requires about 2^m computations of hash values.

3.4 Free-start target attack

Free-start target attack on the hash round function in our proposal means: given G_{i-1}, H_{i-1} and M_{i-1}, find G'_{i-1}, H'_{i-1} and M'_{i-1} such that

$$(G'_{i-1}, H'_{i-1}, M'_{i-1}) \neq (G_{i-1}, H_{i-1}, M_{i-1})$$

but

$$h(G'_{i-1}, H'_{i-1}, M'_{i-1}) = h(G_{i-1}, H_{i-1}, M_{i-1}) \tag{9}$$

Based on equations (2) and (3), the following equations can be deduced from equation (9).

$$G_i = (E_{(G'_{i-1} \| H'_{i-1})}(M'_{i-1}) \oplus G'_{i-1}) \boxplus H'_{i-1} \tag{10}$$

$$H_i = E_{(G'_{i-1} \| H'_{i-1})}(M'_{i-1}) \oplus M'_{i-1} \tag{11}$$

Furthermore, from the above equations, we can obtain a necessary condition for free-start target attack on the hash round function to succeed as follows:

$$G_i = (H_i \oplus M'_{i-1} \oplus G'_{i-1}) \boxplus H'_{i-1} \tag{12}$$

In the above equation, both G_i and H_i are fixed. On basis of the necessary condition, we propose a free-start target attack on the hash round function, in which one can exhaust all possible pairs $(G'_{i-1}, H'_{i-1})(\neq (G_{i-1}, H_{i-1}))$ and determine M'_{i-1} according to equation (12), then compute $h(G'_{i-1}, H'_{i-1}, M'_{i-1})$ and make sure whether it hits the target $h(G_{i-1}, H_{i-1}, M_{i-1})$. The attack requires about 2^{2m} computations of hash values.

The hash round function in our proposal consists of two subfunctions h_1 and h_2, both of which have the same inputs. They can be illustrated as follows:

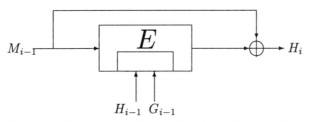

Figure 2: Computational graph for the subfunction h_1

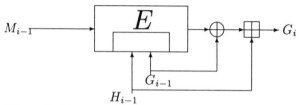

Figure 3: Computational graph for the subfunction h_2

From above figures, we can find that the subfunction h_1 is the completely same as DM-scheme. We can prove the subfunction h_2 is equivalent (in the sense of security) to DM-scheme. Thus, a free-start-target attack on the hash round function implies that one must attack two DM-schemes simultaneously.

DM-scheme with MD-strengthening is generally considered to be secure in the sense that, if the block cipher has no known weakness, then no attack better than the brute-force attacts is known, i.e., the free-start target attack on the scheme takes about 2^m computations and the free-start collision attack on the scheme takes about $2^{m/2}$ computations.

If the free-start target attack on one subfunction in the hash round function provides no help in attacking the other subfunction, we can expect that the attack on the hash round function will have complexity equal to the product of the complexities of the attack on h_1 and h_2, both of which require the same computations of hash values as the attack on DM-scheme.

Using arguments similar to those in [6][12][13], one can show the following proposition [8]:

Proposition 1. *Against a free-start (target or collision) attack, an iterated hash function with MD-strengthening has roughly the same computational security as its hash round function.*

Based on the above discussion and Proposition 1, the complexity of a free-start target attack on the new hash function is roughly equal to 2^{2m} computations of hash values if the underlying block cipher has no known weakness.

3.5 Free-start collosion attack

Free-start collision attack on the hash round function in our proposal means: find $G_{i-1}, H_{i-1}, G'_{i-1}, H'_{i-1}, M_{i-1}$ and M'_{i-1} such that $(G'_{i-1}, H'_{i-1}, M'_{i-1}) \neq (G_{i-1}, H_{i-1}, M_{i-1})$ but equation (9) holds.

Different from free-start target attack, G_i and H_i in free-start collision attack are not fixed. So we can not obtain any necessary conditions which do not consist of any variable outputs for free-start collision to succeed.

Considering that the new hash round founction is composed of two subfunctions which are equivalent to DM-schemes and free-start collision attack on one subfunction provides no help in attacking the other subfunction, we can expect that free-start collision on the hash round function have complexity equal to the product of the complexities of the attack on two DM-schemes, i.e., finding a "collision" with probability about 0.63 requires about $2^m (= 2^{m/2} \cdot 2^{m/2})$ computations of hash values.

For the whole scheme, its computational security against free-start collision attack is roughly the same as its round function on basis of Propositon 1. If the underlying block cipher has no known weakness, the complexity of a free-start collision attack on the new hash function is roughly equal to 2^m computations of hash values.

4 Implementation of the new hash function

On the basis of the underlying block cipher, the round function in our proposal only add two basic m-bit algebraic operations: bitwise exclusive-or of m-bit blocks and addition modulo 2^m of m-bit integers. Therefore, the main part in the implementation of the new hash function lies in the implementation of the underlying block cipher. For the underlying block cipher to be easily implemented in both hardware and software, so is the new hash function. In the following discussion, we will only consider the case that m is 64.

For the new hash function based on a 64-bit block cipher with 128-bit key, IDEA or the block cipher [11] (its key schedule is modified to the same as that of IDEA so as to reduce the time of key schedule run) can be adopted as the underlying block cipher because the structures of both ciphers were chosen to facilitate both hardware and software implementation.

Two software implementations of the new hash function respectively adopting IDEA and the block cipher in [11] as the underlying block ciphers were being carried out on Pentium-S100 personal computer. In the C-program of the new hash function, the operation for bitwise exclusive-or of 64-bit blocks is fulfilled by two bitwise exclusive-or of 32-bit blocks and the operation for addition modulo 2^{64} of two 64-bit integers A and B is carried out in the following way:

1. $A_0\|A_1\|A_2\|A_3 \Leftarrow A, B_0\|B_1\|B_2\|B_3 \Leftarrow B$, where $A_i, B_i (i = 0, 1, 2, 3)$ are 16-bit subblocks.

2. $i \Leftarrow 3. D \Leftarrow 0.$

3. $(D\|C_i) \Leftarrow (0\|A_i) + (0\|B_i) + (0\|D)$, where $\|$ denotes the concatenation of 16-bit subblocks and $+$ represents addition modulo 2^{32} of 32-bit integers.

4. $i \Leftarrow i - 1$. If $i >= 0$, return to step (3).

5. $C \Leftarrow C_0\|C_1\|C_2\|C_3$, where C is the result of addition modulo 2^{64} of two 64-bit integers A and B.

The perference of the new hash function heavily relies on that of its underlying block cipher. When using IDEA as the underlying block cipher, the hash data rate of the new hash function can reach about 2.5 Mbits per second on Pentium-S100 personal computer. When using the block cipher in [11], the hash data rate can reach as high as about 2.85 Mbits per second on the same computer. The above hash data rates are both almost twice as fast as those of Tandem DM and Abreast DM [8] [10] using the same underlying ciphers.

With the development of new generation of processors, the majority of systems will adopt 64-bit processor within five years or so. If a 64-bit block cipher with 128-bit key designed to implement efficiently and run quickly on 64-bit processors is available for use as the underlying block cipher in our proposal, the new hash function will "digest" the message to be hashed much faster.

5 Conclusion

A new 2m-bit iterated hash function, which is based on m-bit block cipher with 2m-bit key and designed to be both fast and secure, has been put forward above.

The hash round function in our proposal utilizes a single underlying block cipher and so our proposal is more efficient than those which use two underlying block ciphers from a practical point of view.

The security analysis of the new hash function shows:

1. The hash round function in our proposal is capable of completely resisting target attack, collision attack and semi-free-start collision attack.

2. The new hash function can be expected to have ideal computational security against five attacks when the underlying cipher is assumed to have no weakness. The computational complexities of five attacks on the new hash function can be summarized in following table.

TYPE OF ATTACKS	COMPLEXITIES
Target attack	2^{2m}
Collision attack	2^{m}
Semi-free-start collision attack	2^{m}
Free-start target attack	2^{2m}
Free-start collision attack	2^{m}

Table 1: The computational complexities of five attacks on the new hash function based on m-bit block cipher with 2m-bit key

In application where (G_0, H_0) is specified and fixed, free-start target attack, semi-free-start collision attack and free-start collision attack are not "real attacks". This is because the initial value (G_0, H_0) is then an integral part of the hash function so that a hash value computed from a different initial value will not be accepted.

So far, when the underlying block cipher is assumed to have no weakness, we have been unable to find any attacks on the new hash function better than brute-force attacks on it, in other words, the new hash function can be expected to have ideal computational complexities against five attacks (shown in Table 1).

In addition, the implementation of the new hash function is discussed. For the underlying cipher to be easily implemented in both software and hardware, so is the new hash function because only two basic 64-bit algebraic operations are introduced in the hash round function on basis of the cipher. When using IDEA as the underlying block cipher, the hash data rate of the new hash function can reach about 2.5 Mbits per second on Pentium-S100 personal computer. When using the block cipher in [11], the hash data rate can reach as high as about 2.85 Mbits per second on the same computer. The above hash data rates are both almost twice as fast as those of Tandem DM and Abreast DM [8] [10] using the same underlying ciphers.

As usual when suggesting a new cryptographic primitive, we urge people to study the strength of the new hash function. We will appreciate attacks, analysis and any other comments.

References

[1] Davies R, Price W. Digital signature–an Update. Proc. International Conference on Computer Communications, Sydney, Oct. 1984, Elsevier, North-Holland, 1985, pp 843-847.

[2] Matyas S, Meyer C, Oseas J. Generating strong one-way functions with cryptographic algorithm. IBM Technical Disclosure Bulletin, vol 27, no. 10A, 1985, pp 5658-5659.

[3] Preneel B, Bosselaers A, Govaerts R, et al. Collision-free hashfunctions based on blockcipher algorithm. Proc. 1989 International Carnahan Conference on Security Technology, 1989, pp 203-210.

[4] Quisquater J, Girault M. 2n-bit hash functions using n-bit symmetric blcok cipher algorithm. Advances in Cryptology- EUROCRYPT'89, Proceedings, Springer-Verlag, 1990, 102-109 (Lecture Notes in Computer Science no. 434).

[5] Brown L, Pieprzyk J, Seberry J. LOKI - a cryptographic primitive for authentication and secrecy applications. Advances in Cryptology-AUSCRYPT'90, Proceedings, Springer-Verlag, 1990, pp 229-236 (Lecture Notes in Computer Science no. 453).

[6] Merkle R. One way hash functions and DES. Advances in Cryptology-CRYPTO'89, Proceedings, Springer-Verlag, 1990, pp 428-446 (Lecture Notes in Computer Science no. 435).

[7] Meyer C, Schilling, M. Secure program code with modification detection code. Proc. of SECURICOM'88 SEDEP.8, Rue De la Michodies, 75002, Paris, France, 1988, pp 111-130.

[8] Lai X, Massey J. Hash functions based on block ciphers. Advances in Cryptology-EUROCRYPT'92, Proceedings, Springer-Verlag, 1993, pp 55-70(Lecture Notes in Computer Science no. 658).

[9] Lai X, Massey J. A proposal for a new block encryption standard. Advances in Cryptology-EUROCRYPT'90, Proceedings, Springer-Verlag, 1991, pp 389-404(Lecture Notes in Computer Science no. 473).

[10] Lai X. On the design and security of block cipher. ETH Series in Information Processing, vol 1, Konstanz: Hartung–Gorre Verlag, 1992.

[11] Yi X. On design and analysis of a new block cipher. Concurrency and Parallelism, Programming, Networking, and Security, Proceedins, ASIAN'96, 1996, pp 213-222(Lecture Notes in Computer Science no. 1179).

[12] Damgaard I. A design principle for hash functions. Advances in Cryptology -CRYPTO'89, Proceedings, 1990, pp 416-427(Lecture Notes in Computer Science no. 435).

[13] Naor M, Yung M. Universal one-way hash functions and their cryptographic applications. Proc. 21 Annual ACM Symposium on Theory of Computing, Seattle, Washington, May 15-17, 1989, pp. 33–43.

Biometric Techniques Applied In Security Technology

Despina Polemi

Institute of Communications and Computer Systems
National Technical University of Athens
Athens Greece

Abstract

This paper summarizes results from a study [36] carried by the author under the European Commission DGXIII (Infosec'96)[1] programme. These results are objective since they are based on the literature and not on manufacturers claims.

1 Introduction

Identification is the process whereby an identity is assigned to a specific individual, e.g. a name; and by *authentication* the process designed to verify a user's identity. Authentication procedures are based on the following approaches [14], [45]:

- *Proof by Knowledge.* The verifier known information regarding the claimed identity that can only be known or produced by a principal with that identity (e.g. password, personal identification number (PIN), questionnaire).
- *Proof by Possession.* The claimant will be authorized by possession of an object (e.g. magnetic card, smart card, optical card).
- *Proof by Property.* The claimant directly measures certain claimant properties using human characteristics.

Members of industries, hospitals, banks, airports carry ID cards, punch passwords or PINs in order to identify themselves. These are the most common means of identification since they are the easiest to remember and the easiest to confirm. However these means are the most unreliable putting all components of security at risk.

IDs can be stolen, passwords can be forgotten or cracked. Credit card fraud is rapidly increasing causing bankruptcies [8], [13]. Children have been kidnapped from day care centers after being released to strangers. Traditional technologies are not sufficient to reduce the impact of counterfeiting [35]. Additional convenient security barriers are needed as our society gets more and more computer dependent.

Biometrics, the use of biology that deals with data statistically, provides an answer to this need since the uniqueness of an individual arises from his personal or behavior characteristics with no passwords or numbers to remember. Biometric systems verify a person's identity by analyzing his physical features or behaviors. The systems record data *(template)* from the user and compares it each time the user is claimed.

---

[1] This paper represents views of the author and neither of INFOSEC nor of the European Union.

Biometrics is known for a long time. Alphouse Bertllon (France 1870) invented a system (Bertillon system) based on finger print analysis for identifying criminals. Francis Galton [18] trying to improve Bertillon system proposed various biometric indices for facial profiles and he established an Anthropometric Laboratory. We can categorize the biometric techniques into two classes: *Physiological -based techniques* and *Behavior-based techniques* which measure the physiological and behavioral characteristics respectively.

Biometric techniques can be used to secure electronic transactions [42], government and commercial environments [10], [26], [2], [39], secure public and travel documents [30], information systems and networks.

The goals of this paper are: set criteria which can be used in future independent evaluation centers in order to objectively evaluate biometric technologies (Section 2); describe physiological and behavioral biometric techniques based on the literature, outline benefits and drawbacks following some of the criteria (Section 3).

2 Criteria for evaluating Biometric techniques

In order to evaluate the biometric techniques we need to evaluate first the biometric identification methods that these techniques are based on and then the biometric systems and devices implementing these methods.

Although most of the studies and surveys concentrate on the evaluation of systems and products little has been said on the theoretical strength of the biometrics methods implemented in these products.

2.1 Criteria for evaluating Biometric methods

These methods use data compression algorithms, protocols and codes. The theoretical background of the biometric methods include three areas: statistical modeling methods, dynamic programming, and neural networks.

These tools need to be evaluated by experts on the particular fields. If algorithms implement "wrong" mathematics then the algorithms are wrong and the systems based on these algorithms are (or will be) vulnerable. If the algorithms used in the biometric methods have "leaks", or if efficient decoding algorithms can be found then the biometric methods themselves are vulnerable and thus the systems based on these methods become unsafe.

Different algorithms offer different degrees of security, it depends on how hard they are to break. The cryptographic algorithms or techniques used to implement the algorithms and protocols can be vulnerable to attacks. Attacks can also be conceived against the protocols themselves or aged standard algorithms. Some algorithms are only registered in the ISO and not checked for vulnerabilities. Thus criteria should be set for the proper evaluation of the biometric methods addressing these theoretical concerns. Such criteria should include:

1. *Correct Algorithms*: The mathematics implemented in the algorithms should be correct.

2. *Secure algorithms* Algorithms that are easy to break put any security architecture at risk however well built. The techniques used to implement the algorithms should be either unconditionally or computationally secure.

- *unconditionally secure:* no cryptanalytic techniques available for breaking the compression and other algorithms involved in the methods given infinite computing resources.

- *computationally secure:* If cryptanalytic algorithms can be found then the amount of data needed as input to a possible attack can not be stored in present and future computing systems. The time needed to compute the attack can not be performed with present or future computing resources (high time complexity). The amount of memory needed for the attack is not (will not be) available in present and future computers (high space complexity).

3. *Good choice of keys:* The choice of keys is important.

4. *Strong codes:* No efficient and rebust decoding algorithms should be available or found.

5. *Secure Data Base:* The first step in implementing a biometric system is to collect and put on file a data set (*template*) representing the biometric measurement of a user. The places where templates can be stored are: Memory of Device, Central Data Base, Tokens or Plastic Cards. The storage of the users' templates depends on the type of application that the biometric device will be used and the size of templates. The security aspect of storing templates should be carefully considered. A solution can be the establishment of a Trusted Third Party (TTP) service ensuring the safe management, transmission and storage of the templates and providing the proper data base security. Thus bodies issuing cards with biometric Pins or storing them in central data bases should be TTPs.

6. *Safe protocols:* The cryptographic algorithms used in the protocols should be secure as well as the cryptographic techniques used to implement the protocols. No cryptographic attacks could be applied to the protocols themselves so their analysis is required so no flaws can be discovered.

7. *Secure Networks and Distributed Systems:* If the templates will be transmitted over a network, the safety of the network should be evaluated.

2.2 Criteria for Biometric Systems and Devices

The reliability and acceptance of a biometric device depends on operational, technical, financial and manufacturing characteristics which set criteria for these devices.

Operational:

The devices should be *convenient* to use. For example the time required to perform its functions, such as enrollment, authentication, verification, should be minimum. In a supermarket queue or in a company's entrance (at rush hour, i.e. 9am, 5pm) where verification is to be performed, the time taken for verification is a major criterion for choosing a biometric device.

An important factor in the biometric technologies is *public acceptance.* In banking, security and public acceptance is a priority for choosing a biometric system since customers can choose another bank. *User friendliness* is important for the device to be accepted by the public. A device is user friendly if it is easy to use, it is convenient, it satisfies the user's security needs, it conforms to contemporary social standards. The device should be socially unpalatable.

A device is public acceptable if it is *not discriminatory*. Human factors such as gender, age, profession, physical and psychological condition of a person should not influence the performance of the biometric device. People with soar throat or affected by dental anesthesia might face a difficulty in being verified by certain speech verification systems.

Other operational criteria are: *uniqueness* and *exclusivity*. The outcome of the authentication process should be unique, it should not change each time the user is verified by the biometric device so no other form of identification should be necessary or used. The device should be put in a safe place so it can not be collected by anyone on any occasion.

Technical:

All technical components of the biometric device contribute to its authentication time. For example if the templates are stored in the biometric device itself, the *space of its data base* should be sufficient. The *time required to measure* human characteristics in order to create the templates and the *storing time* of the templates should be minimum. *The size of the device* should also be small. The setting of the *error tolerance* is important to the performance of these systems. Both errors should be explicitly quoted and they both need to be as low as possible. Some manufacturers quote only the best error, but this is misleading. The devices should be *simple* to use, *fast* and *precise*.

The devices should be able to perform well *independently of environmental conditions* (e.g. light, noise, heat, moist, smoke, dust). For example most hand readers can not be used in high or freezing temperatures, only in controlled indoor environments.

They should be *flexible* in adjusting threshold settings depending on the security level of the application.

Financial:

Cost is an important factor for choosing a biometric device. This might involve equipment cost, installation and training cost. Most devices are expensive and this puts a barrier to the expansion of the biometric market.

Updating the templates can be a costly process. After the templates have been extracted by the users it is very hard to classify them. Devices that can operate only in controlled environments (e.g. where the temperature is constantly 15-25 C), it is costly to physically protect them. The *cost of the software* used by these devices should also be considered. Administration support might also become a big expense.

Manufacturing:

The chosen biometric system should be *supported* by a number of manufacturers. National vendor support must be capable of accommodating national implementation. Data must be *exchangeable* from one vendor's system to another at an acceptable level of defeat.

Different criteria will be considered in different applications. Not all criteria need to be followed in all applications. For example if the potential budget of a company is big, cost will not be considered as one of the criteria for choosing a biometric system. If a company wants to solve its security problem and it is also of limited budget then the choice will be based on putting cost and security strength as its primary concerns.

3 Physiological Biometric Techniques

3.1 Fingerprint Verification

The patterns and geometry of fingerprints are different for each individual and they are unchanged with body growth. The classification of fingerprints are based on certain characteristics (arch, loop, whorl). The most distinctive characteristics are the minutiae, the forks, or endings found in the ridges [28] and the overall shape of the ridge flow. The finger print systems available for recognizing these characteristics are complex.

Benefits: Fingerprints and palm prints are extremely accurate since they rely on non modifiable physical attributes. Fingerprint devices seem to be most inexpensive than the rest of biometric devices in the market. They are very compact and they are compatible with computing equipment.

A fingerprint verifier can work with card systems such as smart cards and optical cards, to perform identity verification. It provides social welfare security by using cards such as an ID card, drivers licenses, passports, credit cards. The GAO report [19] says that "fingerprinting may be the most viable option" among the various Biometric methods investigated which were: voice verification, hand geometry, signature verification, retina scanning. The CASCADE project [11] claims that fingerprints is the best technology to reduce passenger's clearance time through customs.

Drawbacks: Fingerprint verification is associated with criminality and in many environments (e.g. medical) fingerprint technology would not be acceptable. Fingerprint systems can not be used by people with missing fingers. People with injured or swollen fingers might have a problem in being verified by these systems. In working environments where workers need to wear gloves (e.g. power plans, medical or chemistry laboratories) this method of identification will not be appropriate. Age, gender, occupation, race and environmental factors influence the validity of the fingerprint systems.

Some finger recognition systems concentrate only on the location and identification of small areas of details whether or not such areas are identical.

Applications: It is shown that fingerprint holds the largest share in the global market [6] in the following application areas: Public Services and Banking.

In particular in the public services sector there are applications in immigration and welfare. Biometric technologies are used to provide security to:

- *Passport Control*: Verify passengers through automatic passport control. The project INSPASS provide guidelines for this application.
- *Passage of people and good* between countries where visas are not required. The project CANPASS [46], [22], [32] involving USA and Canada is the most important project in this area. *Borders of Countries* where *illegal aliens* enter them holding false visas, and copied documents, monitoring illegal aliens in asylums.
- *Benefit Payments:* verifying the legal recipients of social security, unemployment, food stamps and pension benefits. An important project in this area is TASS [9], [46], [41], [44]. A future application can be the use of biometrics for home deliverable benefits.

In the banking sector application include:

- *Automated Teller Machines* (ATM): Securing the "front" of ATMs e.g. payment wages, transactions made in ATMs. Securing the "back" from fraud made by people with inside information.
- *Home Banking:* Secure transactions/payments made through telephone using voice verification technologies.
- *Credit Card:* ensuring the security of credit cards from stealing them. Fingerprint was the preferred choice.
- *Point of Sale*: transactions made in the branches.
- *Other applications* are: Dual access to bank vaults, security of bank safety boxes, Verification of bank personnel, customers and access control, authentication for transaction processing, automatic call-up of customer data of bank branches.

3.2 Iris Analysis

Ophthalmologists originally proposed that the iris of the eye might be used as a kind of optical fingerprint for personal identification [1], [38], [31], [15]. Their proposal was based on clinical results that every iris is unique and it remains unchanged in clinical photographs.

The iris consists of trabecular meshwork of connective tissue, collageneous stromal fibres, ciliary processes, contraction furrows, rings, coloration. All these constitute a distinctive fingerprint that can be seen at a distance from the person. The iris trabecular meshwork ensures that a statistical test of independence in two different eyes always pass. This test becomes a rapid visual recognition method [13]. The properties of the iris that enhance its suitability for use in automatic identification include:

- protected from the external environment.
- impossibility of surgically modifying without the risk of vision.
- physiological response to light which provides a natural test.
- ease of registering its image at some distance from the subject without a physical contact.

In [13] it is mathematically proven that they are sufficient degrees of freedoms in the iris among individuals to impart to it the same singularity as a conventional fingerprint. Efficient algorithms are developed in [13] to extract a detailed iris description reliably from a live video image to generate a compact code for the iris and render a decision about individual identity with high statistical confidence.

Benefits: The retinal blood vessels highly characterize an individual so accuracy is one of the advantages of this method of identification.

Drawbacks: The iris recognition systems had public acceptability problems in the past because of the use of a beam. The recent systems register the iris image easy at a distance from the user but users are still skeptical of this technology. Blind people or people with severe damaged eyes (diabetics) will not be able to use this Biometric method.

Duplicate artificial eyes are useless since they do not respond to light. However medical research has shown recently that retinal patterns are not as stable as it was thought. They show critical variations when there is an organ dysfunction or disease.

Applications: This technology can be applied in sectors where public acceptance is not a priority (e.g. military environments, correction facilities, department of motor vehicle).

3.3 Facial Analysis

The premise of this approach is that face characteristics (e.g. size of nose, shape of eyes, chin, eyebrows, mouth) are unique revealing individuals identity. This now increasingly developed method is expensive since it is using neural network methodologies. They use cameras to extract unique facial feature data which is stored on a chip card or a magnetic stripe card. The person swipes his card to a small camera to take an image. The software application on site compares the data with the person's stored data.

In the existing facial recognition systems certain restrictions are imposed by the user e.g. he/she should be looking straight in the camera with certain light in order for the system to analyze and identify the person. However various new graph matching techniques will enhance the quality of picture decreasing the constraints [27].

Benefits: Users find it very naturally to be identified by their face since this is the most traditional way of identification which makes this method highly acceptable.

Drawbacks: The system will not be able to analyze people with imposed physical characteristics such as beard, hair style or with certain facial expressions.

Facial recognition systems are unable to cope with angles or facial expressions which are a little different from those used during the encoding process. The templates should be updated since changes occur in the facial skeleton during the human aging process.

Applications: This technology is used in sectors where public acceptance is a priority, e.g. banking, hospitals. Recently this technology is tested in U.S.A. to secure the Internet and in particular for electronic banking.

3.4 Hand Geometry

This Biometric method is based on the distinct characteristics of the hands, these include external contour, internal lines, geometry of hand, length and size of fingers, palm and fingerprints, blood vessel pattern in the back of the hand [4]. They work by comparing the image of the hand with the previously enrolled sample. The user enters his identification number on a keypad and place his hand on a platter. A camera captures the image of the hand and then a software analyzes it. Other systems use cards where the enrollees hand is recorded [3]. This technology is mostly used in physical access control, law and order areas.

Benefits: Hand geometry systems are reasonably fast. They require little data storage space and the smallest template. They have short verification time. Sandia testing [23] conclude that hand geometry system was overall the user's favorite compared with fingerprint, signature, voice print and retinal.

INSPASS project [46], [22] claims that hand geometry is the most suitable technology for verifying travelers at passport control. Testing in various US airports occurred under this project that justified these claims.

Drawbacks: A technical problem that needs enhancement is caused by the rotation of the hand where it is placed on the plate. The performance of these systems might be influenced if people wear big rings, have swollen fingers or no fingers. The reconstruction of the bone structure of an authorized user's hand may be a reason for circumvention [40]. In those systems that are based on three dimensional hand geometry where the three dimensions length, width, thickness are measured, although they are more secure there is still a chance of defeat.

Most of the hand readers are designed to be used indoors in controlled template environment since below freezing temperatures and temperatures over 110 F cause problems. The direction of the sunlight towards the platen might influence the hand picture.

Sophisticated bone structure models of the authorized users may deceive the hand systems. Paralyzed people or people with Parkinson's disease will not be able to use this Biometric method.

Applications: Hand geometry holds the global market in Law and Order and Physical Access Control sectors [6]. Applications in the Law & Order sector include:

- *Prisons:* ensure that the persons leave the prisons are privileged visitors and stuff and not the prisoners. FBI's Integrated Automated Fingerprint [9] will replace the manual fingerprint system in order to reduce response time.
- *Patrol cars* will have the capability to capture fingerprints and relay the information to local state by the fall of 1999 [9].
- *Bureau of printing* and engraving will use biometrics to prevent any loss of currency [9].
- *Voting:* Ensuring that the person has not voted twice, he/she is a citizen of that country in the right age. The Colombian Legislature uses hand geometry to secure the voting process.
- *Identification of Missing Children:* When children's identity has been changed a Biometric verifier can identify the child by comparing the fingerprints against a national data base of children's fingerprints ([6] Nov. 1996, p.3).
- *Safe guns:* built a "safe gun" which it can fire only after verifying that the person holding it is allowed to hold it.

Specific applications in the physical access sector include: building safety, aircraft safety, securing medical records, day care centers.

Various systems have been developed for obtaining vein patterns in the back of the hand which use various vein pattern matching strategies [12]. These systems developed in VEINCHECK project [37].

3.5 DNA Pattern

This method takes advantage of the different biological pattern of the DNA molecule between individuals. Unique differences in the banding pattern of the DNA fragments occur.

The molecular structure of DNA can be imagined as a zipper with each tooth represented by one of the letters: A (Adeline), C (Cytosine), G (Guanine), T (Thymine) and with opposite teeth forming one of two pairs, either A-T or G-C. The information in DNA is determined by the sequence of letters along the zipper [5]. Unlike fingerprint that occurs only on the fingertips, DNA print is the same for every cell or tissues of the body.

This method is widely used in identifying criminals. DNA pattern recognition is a laboratory procedure that follows the next steps [5]: Isolation of DNA, Cutting, sizing and sorting, Transfer of DNA to nylon, Probing.

Benefit: It is a very accurate method.

Drawbacks: The basic concerns against this methods is the ethical and practical acceptability from the user. Time consumption for verifying an individual is also a big concern since DNA testing is neither real time nor unintrusive.

It is an expensive method and involves the provision of tissue or specimens which many people find demeaning.

Applications: The area of application is criminal justice.

3.6 Ear Recognition.

The shape, size of the ears are unique characteristics of an individual. This technique is used in police in order to identify criminals.

3.7 Sweat Pore Analysis

The distribution of the pores in the area of the finger is distinct for each individual. Based on this observation sweat pores analyzers have been developed which analyze the sweat pores on the tip of the finger. When the finger is placed on the sensor, the software records the pores as stars and stores their position relative to the area of the finger. A system under development is: PCMCIA (Personal Biometric Encoders, U.K.)

4 Behavioral Biometric Techniques

4.1 Speech Analysis

There are various characteristics of the sounds, phonetics, and vocals that an individual can be identified by. Vocal characteristics such as mouth, nasal cavities, vocal tract make the production of speech different for each individual. Although humans can use these characteristics naturally for identifying someone, it is hard for a computer system to analyze the voice characteristics.

The person speaks over the telephone or into a microphone attached system, then the system analyses the voice characteristics of that sample. Usually Fourier based methods is applied to extract a set of Biometric features associated with the voice. These are coded into a data set or template. Finally the system compares it to the voice characteristics of a prerecorded sample.

Some systems are based on a new technology called TESPAR (Time Encoded Signal Processing and Recognition) which is a simplified digital language for coding speech [20], [43], [25]. It provides a simple way of generating a computer "signature" that defines any sound. It works by analyzing "snapshots" of a sound wave against time without calculating frequencies (something different than the classical Fourier analysis).

Benefits: It is public acceptable since speech is the most natural form of identification [34]. It is a suitable technology for environments where "hands free" is a requirement. In the European project CAVE speaker verification techniques are used in telephone banking, home shopping and information services.

Drawbacks: Some systems are not (or will not be) mathematically capable of differentiating between real and prerecorded voices as digital recording systems get enhanced.

Speech verification is not as accurate as Biometric verification based on physical characteristics such as fingerprint, palmprint, retina scans.

Illness, fatigue, and stress are some of the factors that cause problems in the speaker verification systems available. The individuals' voice are changed over the years which make them hard to be verified [16]. Thus updating of the templates have to occur. This is costly since after the templates have been extracted by the users it is very hard to classify them. The techniques used (which are very complex) suffer from a number of limitations [33].

However it is less vulnerable to unauthorized access than key cards that can be lost and passwords and PINS that can be stolen [33].

Women have more complex voice frequencies which makes them harder to be identified. People with soar throat or unable to speak will not be able to use such systems. People affected by alcohol, by dental anesthesia, by oral obstruction might face a difficulty in being verified by speech verification systems.

Applications: Voice holds the biggest share in the global market ([6], vol.7, n.7). Applications in this area include: Computer terminals (they can get protected for securing sensitive data e.g. governmental documents, medical data), telephone companies (enhance calling cards, access to company telephone system), communication network and mobile phones. This technology is used to access modem pool from remote telephones, voice mail systems, long distance telephone lines, conference calls.

4.2 Handwritten Signature Verification

This Biometric method is based on the fact that signing is a reflex action, not influenced by deliberate muscular control, with certain characteristics (rhythms, successively touches the writing surface, number of contracts, velocity, acceleration). The systems developed based on this Biometric method fall into two categories:

1) Pen based systems are using special pens to capture the information.

2) Tablet based systems use special surfaces to collect the data.

In the first class the pen is the measuring device which captures the information where in the second class, the tablet contains the measuring device.

Some of the above systems use statistics in verifying a signature and some use event sequential methods. The items used in a statistical analysis include: total time of writing a signature, measurements of spacing number of horizontal turning points, number of times and duration the pen touches the tablet. In the event sequential methods the system divides the signature into independent events, and examines each piece separately. A number of signatures (depending on the system) are required for the enrollment process. At the time of verification the user is asked to sign. The system compares various aspects of its signature on a hierarchical manner. If a good match is not found between the signatures characteristics (shape, sequence of events, local characteristics) and the template then the template is rejected.

Benefits: The use of artificial neural networks make these systems more accurate and cheaper [21]. Since signature is a familiar way in identifying individuals, hand written signature verification systems are highly acceptable. In a survey performed by a branch of a UK Post Office a signature verification system was preferred over the fingerprint system.

Drawbacks: People with Parkinson's disease will not be able to use such system. In countries where the illiteracy rate is very high this technology can not be used. Some systems have difficulties with people that change their signature very radically. Other systems can not distinguish the pen from the palm pressure. High cost of acquisition and processing hardware is required in these systems.

Applications: This technology is used in welfare and banking sectors.

4.3 Keystroke Analysis

This method which is under development is based on the typing characteristics of the individuals such as keystroke duration, inter-keystroke times, typing error frequency, force keystrokes etc.

Two kinds of systems are getting developed based upon static and dynamic verification techniques [17], [28]. Static verifier uses a neural network approach while the dynamic verifier is using statistics. The static approach is where the system analyzes the way a username or password was typed using neural network for pattern recognition [7]. Dynamic approach is where the system verifies the person continuously with any arbitrary text input.

Benefits: This is a method that can be offered as supplement to some secure authentication mechanism.

Drawbacks: The performance of the method is affected by various circumstances of the human users, such as a hand injury or fatigue of the legitimate user. The systems developed for this Biometric method are costly since they use neurological methods and dedicated terminals.

Applications: It can be applied in banking (ATM) machines.

Conclusions: Biometrics provide additional security barriers and can be used in applications where high level of security is necessary. Experts need to evaluate the biometric methods and systems independently in evaluative centers following criteria as the ones in Section 2 in order for these techniques to gain confidence and acceptance. The only available information on accuracy, level of security, False acceptance and False Rejection rates of these techniques comes from the manufacturers. The important project BIOTEST in ESPRIT programme, which is still in progress, aims to establish independent evaluation centers where biometric technologies will be tested. Only then biometric technologies will be evaluated objectively. Standards need to be set for these techniques in order to promote them and in order to expand and stimulate the biometric market.

Acknowledgments
The author would like to thank INFOSEC (DGXIII) for supporting the original study and also Mrs. Emma Newman for providing the author with useful information.

References

1. Adlrer F.H. "Physiology of the Eye: Clinical Application, 4th ed., London: The C.V. Msoby Company , 1965

2. Anon. (ed.) "Colloquium on Electronic Images and Image Processing in Security and Forensic Science" IEE Colloquium (Digest), n. 087, 1990

3. Ashbourn J. "Practical Implementation of biometrics based on hand geometry " IEE Colloquium (Digest) n. 100, 1994

4. Baltscheffsky P, Anderson P. "Palmprint Project: Automatic Identity Verification by Hand Geometry" Proceedings 1986 International Carnaham Conference on Security Technology: Electronic Crime Countermeasures, 1986

5. Betch D. "DNA Fingerprinting in Human Health and Society" Biotechnology Information Series (Bio-6)

6. Biometric Technology Today, SJB Services, Somerset, England (http://www.sjb.co.uk)

7. Bleha S., Slivinsky C., Hussien B. "Computer Access Security Systems using keystroke dynamics" IEEE Transactions on Pattern Analysis and Machine Intelligence, 1990; 12:1217-1222

8. Bright R. "Smartcards: Principles, Practice, Applications" New York: Ellis Horwood, Ltd, 1988

9. Campbell J, Alyea L., Dunn J. "Biometric Security: Government Applications and Operations" http://www.vitro.bloomington.in.us:8080/~BC/

10. Carback R. " Reducing Manpower intensive tasks through automation of security technologies" IEEE Annual International Carnahan Conference on Security Technology, Proceedings 1995, pp.331-339

11. Chip Architecture for Smart Cards and Secure Portable Devices (CASCADE) Esprit Project EP8670, Data Sheet 1995

12. Cross J.M., Smith C.L. "Thermographic imaging of the subcutaneous vascular network of the back of the hand for biometric identification" IEEE Annual International Carnahan Conference on Security Technology, Proceedings of the 29th Annual 1995 International Carnahan Conference on Security Technology, pp. 20-35

13. Daugman J. "High confidence visual recognition of persons by a test of statistical independence" IEEE Transactions on Pattern Analysis and Machine Intelligence 1993; 15:.1148-1161

14. Davies D.W., Price W.L. "Security for Computer Networks" John Wiley & Sons, 1984

15. Davson H. "Davson Physiology of the Eye" 5th ed. London, Macmillan, 1990

16. Feustel T., Velius G. " Speaker identity verification over telephone line: where we are and where we are going" Proc. 1989 Int. Carnaham Conf. Secur. Publ. by IEEE, pp.181-182

17. Furnell S.M., Morrissey J.P., Sanders P.W., Stockel C.T. "Applications of keystroke analysis for improved login security and continues user authentication" Proceedings of Information Systems Security (edited by S. Katsikas, D. Gritzalis), pp.283--294, 1996

18. Galton G. "Personal Identification and Description " Nature 1988; 173-177

19. General Accounting Office "Electronic Benefits Transfer, Use of Biometrics to Deter Fraud in the Nationwide EBT program", USA, 1995

20. George M.H., King R.A. " Robust speaker verification biometric" IEEE Annual International Carnahan Conference on Security Technology, Proceedings of the 29th Annual 1995 International Carnahan Conference on Security Technology, pp. 41-46

21. Hamilton D.J.,. Whelan J., McLaren A, MacIntyre I, Tizzard A " Low cost dynamic signature verification system" IEE Conference Publication 1995; 408:202-206

22. Hays R."INSPASS" Jan 1996 <http://www.vitro.bloomington.in.us

23. Holmes, J. Wright L., Maxwell, R. " A performance evaluation of Biometric identification Devices" Sandia National Laboratories, U.S.A, 1991

24. Jouce R. and Gupta G. "Identity Authentication based on keystroke Latencies" Communications of the ACM, 1990:30:168-176

25. King R.A., Gosling W. Electronics Letters , 1978; 14: 456-457

26. Klopp C "More options for physical access control" Comput. Secur, 1990; 9:.229-232

27. Konen W. "Neural information processing in real world face recognition applications" IEEE Expert, 1996; 11:, 7-8

28. Lynch M.R., Gaunt R.G. "Application of Linear Weight Neural Networks to fingerprint recognition" IEE Conference Publication, 1995; 409:.139-142

29. Markowitz J. "Speaker Verification, Who's there?" PC AI Intelligent Solutions for Desktop Computers, 1995; 9:24-26

30. Marsh P. "Biometric Behavior is smart and secure" New Electronics 1996; 9 :25-26

31. Mercer J. "Design and strategies for optobiometric identification" Proceedings of SPIE-The International Society for Optical Engineering 1996; 2659:60-66

32. Mintie D. "Biometrics in Human Services User Group Newletter" vol.1, no. 1, July 1996

33. Morgan D.P., Scofield C.L. " Neural Networks and Speech Processing" Mass., U.S.A.: Kluwer Academic Publishers 1991

34. Newham E. "The Biometric Report" SJB Services, UK 1995; 405:198-201

35. Newton J. " Reducing plastic counterfeiting " IEE Conference Publication 1995

36. Polemi D. " Review and Evaluation of Biometric Techniques for Identification and Authentication, including an appraisal of the areas where they are most applicable", Infosec (DGXIII) Programme, 1996, http://www.cordis.lu/infosec

37. Rice J. " Quality approach to biometric imaging" IEE Colloquium (Digest) n. 100, Apr. 1994

38. Rohen J. "Morphology and Pathology of the trabecular network in the structure of the eye", Smelser, Ed. N.Y.: Academic Press 1961; 335-341

39. Scott W. "Defense skills applied to biometric ID" Aviation week and Space Technology", v. 141, n. 16, p.54

40. Sidlauskas D. " A new concept in biometric identification 3-Dimensional Hand Geometry, Nucl. Mater. Manage 1987; 16:442-447

41. Spanish Government Agency Wins Outstanding Smart card Application Award at CTST'96 Awards Banquet. May 1996. CardFlash, RAM Research Group

42. Stockel A " Securing data and financial transactions " IEEE Annual International Carnahan Conference on Security Technology, Proceedings 1995; 397-401

43. Timms S.R., King R.A. "Speaker verification utilising artificial neural network and biometric functions derived from time encoded speech (TES) Data" ICCS/ISITA Singapore 1992;447-449

44. Unisys Personal Identification Technology will be used to give Spaniers Access to Personal Information in Spain's Healthcare Databases. March 1996. UNISYS WORLD Editorial Index. Publications & communications Inc

45. Wood H.M."The use of passwords for controlled access to computer resources" National Bureau of Standards Special Publication 500-9, US Dept. of Commerce/NBS

46. Zunkel R. "Biometrics and Border Control" Security Technology & Design 1996; 22-27

Guidelines, Standards and Certification

High Integrity Ada

B A Wichmann,

National Physical Laboratory,

Teddington, Middlesex, TW11 0LW, UK

Abstract

This paper describes the approach being taken by an ISO group to produce Guidelines for the use of Ada when developing high integrity applications.

1 Introduction

As a society, we are increasingly reliant upon high integrity systems: for safety
systems (such as fly-by-wire aircraft), for security systems (to protect digital
information) or for financial systems (cash dispensers). As the complexity
of these systems grow, so do the demands for improved techniques for their
production.

Hence there is a need to ensure critical systems have the properties required,
and this can only be achieved by analysis of the software in addition to conventional dynamic testing. Unfortunately, analysis of software written using
low-level languages is prohibitively expensive, since it is necessary to analyse
every instruction in the program merely to ensure the integrity of the data or
control flow. On the other hand, the strong typing in the Ada language facilitates such analysis by reducing the potential means by which data can be
overwritten or the control flow changed. Hence not only are high integrity systems important, but Ada has appropriate attributes to provide the assurance
needed in their design.

Given that Ada is being used for a high integrity application, then further
confidence can be gained by providing guidance on the use of the language.
This guidance material identifies those features of Ada for which additional
verification steps should be performed to ensure that their use is appropriately
controlled. Following such guidance should provide all the assurance that the
high integrity application requires.

The use of Ada to produce high integrity applications is recommended on
the grounds that:

1. The semantics of Ada programs are well-defined, even in error situations.

2. The strong typing within the language can be used to reduce the scope
   (and cost) of analysis to verify key properties.

3. The Ada language has been successfully used on many high integrity
   applications. This demonstrates that validated Ada compilers have the
   quality required for such applications.

4. Guidance can be provided to facilitate the use of the language and to
   encourage the development of tools for further verification.

Annex H of the Ada 95 standard has been developed to ensure, as far as a language standard can, that the special requirements for high integrity applications can be met. The primary areas in which such additional assurance is needed are for safety and security.

In the UK, Ada is the language of choice in the Defence and Aerospace sector for high integrity applications. For an analysis of this sector, see the Foresight report on High Integrity Real Time Software [12].

These proposed Guidelines are being considered by the HRG group which operates under the auspices of the ISO Ada group (ISO/JTC1/SC22/WG9).

2   Ada Guidelines

The proposed Guidelines we are developing are specific to Ada 95 [17], the current ISO Ada standard. The desire is to effectively complete the technical work on the Guidelines in 1997 so that newer high integrity Ada systems can use the language with confidence. Indeed, since Annex H of the Ada 95 standard has specific facilities to aid the development of such applications, we conclude that very high confidence can be gained by suitable use of the language. The Guidelines would be a separate ISO document in addition to the Ada standard.

The context within which the Guidelines would be used must be carefully considered. The consensus of the approach that the ISO group wishes to adopt is summarised in the following points:

- The Guidelines must be appropriate for the development of software which is required to meet specific safety and security standards, such as: DO-178B [32], IEC 880 [18], IEC 1508 (Part 3) [15], ITSEC [31], IEC 601-1-4 [16] and UK Defence Standard 00-55 [30]. In consequence, we attempt not to repeat any material in these standards (and to avoid any inconsistencies with them).

- The Guidelines assume the appropriate use of language constructs as available in the Ada Quality and Style Guide [37].

- Where possible, we reference other Software Engineering terminology and standards [25, 28], to minimise the size and complexity of the Guidelines (which also makes the main content Ada-specific).

- There is an implicit assumption that appropriate risk assessment methods have been employed (which arise from the safety and security standards listed above). General advice on risk management is readily available, see [11, 14].

- It is assumed that appropriate quality management procedures are employed consistent with ISO 9001 [19, 20] in the context of a suitable life-cycle [21].

- The Guidelines are not aimed at specific, quantified reliability targets. It is widely understood that for the highest integrity levels, it is not possible to measure the reliability, at least by testing [24].

Given this approach, we believe that there are few viable options to achieving high integrity other than the use of the Ada language. For instance, for high integrity applications it is essential to show the the program execution is *predictable*. By using static range constraints, tools can verify that array indices are in range and that similiar insecurities cannot arise. Six years ago the author recommended (with others) Pascal as well as Ada [27] as a result of an analysis of several key aspects of the semantics of programming languages. Since then, there is evidence that the reliability of Pascal compilers is inadequate for safety applications [39], while maturity and functionality of Ada now make it significantly superior to Pascal.

A major need for such Guidelines is to present a common view for suppliers, users and certifiers. For instance, major defence projects are frequently multi-national and therefore require a common resolution of methods to produce high integrity software. Also, if a certification body is unhappy about the use of a specific Ada feature, then very expensive additional verification steps could be required, or even worse, a major re-working could be required. These Guidelines should reduce the risk of such unplanned requirements.

In some cases existing (non-Ada specific) Guidelines, which have been developed for one specific industrial sector, are being used as input for our Guidelines which are Ada-specific but for any sector. Examples of such Guidelines are: US-nuclear [35], US-space [36], US-medical [13], European-railway [26] and UK-motor [29].

One specific issue has caused the group to revise the approach taken. Almost all of the safety and security standards have a number of levels to reflect to risk or integrity of the system. The initial approach was to have Guidelines with four levels to mirror those in the majority of the standards. A number of problems were noted with this approach:

1. Given that a system is being developed to a standard with four levels (like IEC 1508, say), then the assumption would be that there is a simple mapping between the two. This is unlikely to be the case.

2. In those cases in which the standard has a different number of levels (like ITSEC, with 7 levels), then the correspondence would not be clear.

3. Some requirements do not map well into the concept of levels, but are derived from the system requirements. This is in contrast to an ISO standard which provides means of determining the software integrity required from the system requirements [23]. An example of a specific requirement is for worst-case execution time which could be needed for any integrity level system.

The Guidelines nevertheless need to reflect the requirements of very different systems which we handle by means of specific **methods**. These methods are tabulated in Table 1 to reflect their heirarchical relationship.

Language issues will then be driven by the requirement (or not) to use these methods. For instance, if Formal Code Verification is a requirement, then those language features for which no appropriate formal model exist must be excluded from use within the application. In general, language features are classified in three ways:

	Group Name	Method Name
Analysis	Functional Correctness	Formal Code Verification
		Symbolic Execution
	Flow Analysis	Control Flow
		Data Flow
		Information Flow
	Stack	Stack usage
	Timing	Worst Case Execution Time
	Range Checking	Range Checking
	Other Memory Usage	Other Memory Usage
	Object Code Analysis	Object Code Analysis
Testing	Structural Coverage	MCDC
		Branch Coverage
		Structure Coverage
	Equivalence Class	Equivalence Class
	Boundary Value	Boundary Value

Table 1: Methods

Included. These features can be included since their analysis and use provides no essential difficulties, ie, have tractable and well-understood verification techniques. All the straightforward features of Ada 95 are in this category.

Allowed. These features have known, but well-understood, problems in their use. Additional verifications steps may be needed. The Guidelines will specify the problems and known approaches to their resolution. Management may specify that a specific approval process must be invoked, or that authorization be obtained.

An example of a feature in this category would be Unchecked_Conversion, since it is likely to be needed in many applications, but has known difficulties for validation. An additional validation step might be to check the object code produced by the compiler.

Excluded. These features are essentially incompatible with the method being employed. The only effective resolution is not to use the feature.

One other possible approach to producing high integrity Ada is the standardization of a subset of the language, an example of which is the SPARK subset of Ada 83 [9]. This approach was considered by ISO and rejected. The subsequent meetings for the HRG considered the development of Guidelines.

The Guidelines approach has the following advantages over a specific subset:

- A single subset could only be optimal for at most one integrity level.

- Specific control over the use of language features is already provided in Annex H of the Ada 95 standard. (Hence the user can 'design his own' subset by permitting or not around 20 specific features.)

- As validation technology improves, the optimal subset grows. In practice, subsets are enforced by tools which would then imply changes to the tools as well. (We give an example below in which at some future date one can reasonably expect the concurrency features of Ada to be approved for the high integrity systems.)

- Some low-level features of Ada are required by many applications, even if their use is very tightly controlled and is only a tiny fraction of the code. (Hence, if a subset is enforced without exception, these low-level features would have to be included, but that would give a subset having verification problems. If the subset is not strictly enforced, then can it provide the assurance needed?)

2.1 Content of the Guidelines

The main sections of the proposed Guidelines are as follows:

Verification Techniques. This section enumerates the methods in Table 1 and their relationship to the Guidelines.

Language Usage. This section catalogues the language features in terms of the **included, allowed** and **excluded** categories together with specific guidance which is related to language features (and their interaction, of course).

Compilers and Run Time Systems. These two key elements have several properties which implies that specific guidance must be given.

Extracting information about an Ada program merely from the source text is potentially very fruitful due to the strong type checking and well-controlled interfaces that the language provides. Compilers already extract such information for code generation, but in the past, most of the information has been unavailable for validation and verification. This implies that validation tools for Ada 83 have had to repeat the source text analysis undertaken by a compiler. This is now changing due to the Ada Semantic Information System (ASIS) standard [1]. This standard provides an interface for tools to extract information from the Ada library provided the compiler supports the standard.

For high integrity systems, it would appear that ASIS provides a basis for tools undertaking quite sophisticated analyses. At this stage, the Guidelines would not necessarily *require* the use of ASIS. An ASIS-based tool which lists the **excluded** and **allowed** features in an Ada program is clearly desirable. ASIS is obviously limited to the Ada source text and therefore cannot directly handle requirements involving, say, the external environment.

The ISO Ada group is fortunate in having access to a very detailed study undertaken in Canada on the application of Ada 95 for high integrity applications [2, 3, 4, 5, 6]. Although some members of the Ada group contributed to this study and commented upon it, the resulting reports are not the consensus Guidelines that we are proposing here. In consequence, the material needs to be reformulated into an agreed form for the ISO publication.

At the lowest level, the Canadian study reports on the suitability of the majority of the Ada 95 constructs for their use in high integrity applications.

Their report only considered the highest level of integrity, while ISO will take into account the analysis required and classify this by a three-way system. However, the reworking of much of this information into the **included**, **allowed** and **excluded** categories should not be too difficult.

2.2 Difficult issues

Obtaining high integrity requires careful judgement which is more difficult as the complexity of systems increases. The Ada language provides the means of controlling complexity, but there are pitfalls for the unwary which the Guidelines will enumerate. For some issues, the best approach is hardly obvious and we consider some of these below.

Research versus standardization

The research community would like to address the intellectual challenge of demonstrating the validation of the more complex features of Ada. However, it is only established methods which have already been shown to be satisfactory which can be used with confidence. Tool support is vital here, since complete reliance upon manual validation methods is not practical.

An example of a research area is concurrency, which is directly supported in Ada 95 by two mechanisms: the rendezvous and protected types. There are clear advantages in using concurrency when the external world with which the system reacts is naturally concurrent. However, race conditions, deadlock and unsynchronized update can easily occur unless extreme care is taken. A key issue here is to ensure that test cases have deterministic execution, a view which has strong support from the certification bodies.

The ISO group has not resolved this issue, but it does appear that for the highest levels of integrity, Ada protected types could be classed as **allowed**, following ideas presented in [7]. In general, it would seem that many Ada features which would currently be classified as **allowed** could at some future date when the verification technology improves as **included**.

New features of Ada 95

It would appear that the new features of Ada 95 would present a significant challenge for the developers of high integrity applications. However, Ada 95 actually simplifies many aspects due to the following:

- Ada 95 has defined the language more closely, leaving fewer aspects which can vary between implementations.

- Annex H allows the user to restrict the usage of language features in a way that is enforced by the compiler.

- Hooks are provided so that the actual object code produced by a compiler can be audited by the developer of high integrity systems. (Of course, the auditing may be aided by tools.)

- Many of the extensions in Ada 95 are not to the basic language but in the form of additional required packages. (Such packages need only be considered if actually used in an application, whereas some basic language features have an impact even if they are not used. The additional packages have defined properties, such as the numerical accuracy of the mathematical functions, which can clearly simplify program verification.)

Of course, there are some challenges for high integrity usage in new features of Ada 95, such as: protected types (mentioned above as a means of providing concurrency in a more easily validated form than the Ada 83 rendezvous), and object-oriented extensions.

The object-oriented extensions provide the basic ability to add functionality with extensions to records (tagged types) and new operations on such records. However, this is done is a manner which allows the user to control dynamic dispatching of subprogram calls, which could otherwise require significant additional validation effort. Similarly, the programmer can restrict the use of class-wide operations to ease the verification burden. This contrasts with fully object-oriented languages like Smalltalk (or Java) which is essentially dynamic and hence would be regarded as unsuitable for the highest integrity systems.

Dynamic testing versus static analysis

Static analysis and dynamic testing are complementary ways of comparing an implementation with its specification. Testing allows the most *direct* comparison between implementation and operational requirements. However, because exhaustive testing is impossible — even modified condition decision coverage (MCDC), which is usually very onerous, does not cover more than a fraction of possible execution histories — testing in general cannot show the absence of errors.

In contrast, because 'size' of a static analysis task is determined by the size of a program source text, rather than the number of its possible execution sequences, *in principle* static analysis can be complete, in showing absence of errors *of some classes*. However, static analysis is applied only to models of a program, derived from its source text using a precise definition of the programming language. Since the validity of the models must be checked, and since they may not capture all aspects of program execution (for instance of timing, or resource utilisation), a substantial amount of testing remains essential.

Currently, the cost of validation of high-integrity software, principally incurred in the dynamic testing phases, may exceed half the total project cost. Such figures are commonly reached for avionics software, for which the MCDC testing needed to meet DO-178B requirements [32] is enormously expensive. The high costs can largely be attributed to the fact that the dynamic testing reveals flaws — often of a fundamental nature, such as mis-statement or mis-interpretation of requirements specifications — very late in the development life-cycle. Their correction then is very costly, as is the subsequent repetition, usually several times over, of large parts of the MCDC process.

Solutions are being found to this problem by using a 'lean engineering' or 'correctness by construction' approach [38]. This exploits the static semantic rigour of Ada, and the possibility of performing strong static analysis checks on Ada source texts (because the language is relatively well defined), to detect errors in specification, design and coding early in the life-cycle, as the software is being constructed.

Experience indicates that this approach substantially changes the character of software development [38], involving much more interaction between programmers and designers at relatively early stages of software development. However, even where MCDC test coverage is still required, validation costs have been dramatically reduced, because testing takes on a more confirmatory role, rather than repeated late revelation of errors, with costly repair of these.

It is proposed that the Guidelines should provide some information on how Ada can be exploited in achieving correctness by construction, with particular emphasis on the following aspects:

- How Ada 95 can be exploited, in constructing verifiable designs.

- Guidance on Ada usage to assure predictable behaviour and validity of program models employed in static analysis.

- Discussion of the range of static analysis techniques applicable to Ada 95 programs in particular (from the static-semantic checks required of compilers, through data and information-flow analysis to proof of absence of run-time errors and formal code verification).

- Guidance on ways of using Ada 95 that facilitate dynamic test.

- Discussion of co-ordination/management of a correctness by construction regime for Ada 95 software development.

Exception handling

At the highest integrity level, it is accepted that code should be exception-free. This is the view taken in the Canadian study and the SPARK subset, for instance. If one can be assured that code is exception-free, then one can use the pragma Suppress, which can simplify the code generated by the compiler, thus reducing verification costs.

At lower levels of integrity, the optimal situation is not so evident. Showing the code is exception-free is often expensive so that if this step could be avoided, there would be savings. As Ada provides the ability to detect and recover from the raising of an exception, the natural approach at the lower levels would be to allow for such an eventuality. Indeed, handling an exception can protect the system against some faults. The analysis of programs in which exceptions can be raised can be complex, but facilities like ASIS should make this practical. In consequence, it appears that this language feature needs to be handled quite differently at the various integrity levels.

Timing

Resource usage is a key requirement for the validation of systems. With predominantly static storage usage, and requirements in Ada 95 for compilers to produce memory usage information, storage is not a major problem. Unfortunately, timing is getting very complex with the pipe-lining and caches in modern processing units.

This area is more hardware than language dependent. However, it is necessary to provide worse case execution times from the object code. It remains to be seen if useful bounds can be obtained for the next generation of processors.

Fixed point versus floating point

Numerical computation on physical quantities can be logically undertaken in either floating point or fixed point. The older processor chips without built-in floating point have often forced designers to use fixed point. The compiler support for fixed point is relatively complex and hence provides an additional verification burden. In contrast, the recent fault in the division operation in the Pentium processor has illustrated the dangers inherent in the complexity of the floating point hardware (even if the compiler support is then easier to validate).

For the Ada Guidelines, it would appear that both fixed point and floating point must be considered with an analysis of the validation issues in both cases.

3 Conclusions

The belief is that with approved ISO Guidelines on the application of Ada for high integrity applications, developers can produce systems with greater confidence and wider acceptability, which will meet the requirements of both the certification bodies and the users.

4 Acknowledgements

This work would not have been possible without the support of the membership of the HRG, the ISO High Integrity Ada group. Those members who have contributed to the HRG work so far are (in alphabetical order): John Barnes (UK), Praful V Bhansali (Boeing), Alan Burns (University of York), Bernard Carré (Praxis), Dan Craigen (ORA, Canada), Mike P. DeWalt (FAA), Robert Dewar (Ada Core Technologies), David Guaspari (ORA), C. Michael Holloway (NASA), Mike Kamrad (Computing Devices International), Stephen Michell (Maurya Software), Alexander Miethe (Competence Center Informatik), George Romanski (Thomson Software Products), Mark Saaltink (ORA, Canada), Michael K. Smith (Computational Logic Inc), James C. Stewart (U.S. Nuclear Regulatory Commission), Adam Tacy (UK MoD), Phil Thornley (British Aerospace Defence), David Tombs (Defence Research Agency), and Tullio Vardanega (ESTEC).

References

[1] Ada Semantic Information System. Working draft. 1st November 1996. Available on the Internet:

    public/AdaIC/work-grp/asiswg/asis/v2.0

[2] Dan Craigen, Mark Saaltink, Steve Michell. "Ada95 and Critical Systems: An Analytical Approach." In Proceedings of "Reliable Software Technologies: Ada Europe'96, Alfred Strohmeier, Editor. Lecture Notes in Computer Science, Volume 1088, Spring-Verlag, 1996.

[3] Steve Michell, Dan Craigen, Mark Saaltink. "Using Analytical Approaches for High Integrity Ada95 Systems." International Real-time Ada Workshop, Ravenscar, U.K. April 1997. To appear in Ada Letters.

[4] Dan Craigen, Mark Saaltink, Steve Michell. "Ada95 Trustworthiness Study: A Framework for Analysis." ORA Canada Technical Report TR-95-5499-02, November 1995.

[5] Mark Saaltink, Steve Michell. "Ada95 Trustworthiness Study: Analysis of Ada95 for Critical Systems." ORA Canada Technical Report TR-96-5499-03a, January 1997.

[6] Mark Saaltink, Steve Michell. "Ada95 Trustworthiness Study: Guidance on the use of Ada95 in the Development of High Integrity Systems," Version 1.0. ORA Canada Technical Report TR-96-5499-04, November 1995.

[7] A Burns and A J Wellings. Restricted Tasking Models. Ada real-time workshop. 1997.

[8] British Computer Society Specialist Group in Software Testing. Standard for Software Component Testing (Working Draft 3.0). Glossary of terms used in software testing (Working Draft 6.0). October 1995. Available free on the Internet (until copyright is assigned to BSI):

http://www.rmcs.cranfield.ac.uk/~cised/sreid/BCS_SIG/index.htm

[9] B A Carré and T J Jennings. SPARK — The SPADE Ada Kernel. University of Southampton. March 1988.

[10] J Dawes. "The VDM-SL Reference Guide". Pitman Publishing. 1991. ISBN 0-273-03151-1

[11] Guidelines on Risk Issues. The Engineering Council. February 1993. ISBN 0-9516611-7-5.

[12] Defence and Aerospace Panel: Technology Working Party report on High Integrity Real time software. Available free on the Internet:

http://www.npl.co.uk/npl/collaboration/partners/foresight/index.html

[13] ODE Guidance for the Content of Premarket Submission for Medical Devices Containing Software. Draft, 3rd September 1996.

[14] Safety-related systems — Guidance for engineers. Hazards Forum. March 1995. ISBN 0 9525103 0 8.

[15] IEC 1508: Draft. Functional safety: safety-related systems. Parts 1-7. Draft for public comment, 1995. (Part 3 is concerned with software which is the relevant part for the ISO Ada Guide.)

[16] IEC 601-1-4: 1996. Medical electrical equipment — Part 1: General requirements for safety 4: Collateral Standard: Programmable electrical medical systems.

[17] ISO/IEC 8652:1995. *Information technology — Programming Languages — Ada.*

[18] IEC 880: 1986. *Software for computers in the safety systems of nuclear power stations.*

[19] EN ISO 9001:1994, Quality systems — Model for quality assurance in production and installation.

[20] ISO/IEC 9000-3: 1991. Quality management and quality assurance standards — Part 3: Guidelines for the application of ISO 9001 to the development, supply and maintenance of software.

[21] ISO/IEC 12207: 1995. Information technology — Software life cycle processes.

[22] ISO/IEC 13817-1:1996 Information technology — Programming languages, their environments and system software interfaces — Vienna Development Method — Specification Language — Part 1: Base language.

[23] DIS ISO/IEC 15026: 1996 Information technology — System and software integrity levels.

[24] B Littlewood and L Strigini. The Risks of Software. Scientific American. November 1992.

[25] IEEE Standard Glossary of Software Engineering Terminology, IEEE Std 610.12-1990.

[26] CENELEC, Railway Applications: Software for Railway Control and Protection Systems. Draft of EN 50128:1995. November 1995.

[27] W J Cullyer, S J Goodenough and B A Wichmann, "The Choice of Computer Languages in Safety-Critical Systems", Software Engineering Journal. Vol 6, No 2, pp51-58. March 1991.

[28] J A McDermid (Editor). Software Engineer's Reference Book. Butterworth-Heinemann. Oxford. ISBN 0 750 961040 9. 1991.

[29] Development Guidelines For Vehicle Based Software. The Motor Industry Software Reliability Association. MIRA. November 1994. ISBN 0 9524156 0 7.

[30] Defence Standard 00-55, "The Procurement of Safety Critical Software in Defence Equipment", Ministry of Defence. Available free on the Internet:

http://www.mod1ndrl.demon.co.uk/0055/0055.html

[31] "Information Technology Security Evaluation Criteria", Provisional Harmonised Criteria. Version 1.2. 1991. (UK contact point: CESG Room 2/0805, Fiddlers Green Lane, Cheltenham, Glos, GL52 5AJ.)

[32] Software Considerations in Airborne Systems and Equipment Certification. Issued in the USA by the Requirements and Technical Concepts for Aviation (document RTCA SC167/DO-178B) and in Europe by the European Organization for Civil Aviation Electronics (EUROCAE document ED-12B). December 1992.

[33] J M Spivey. The Z Notation, A Reference Manual, SECOND EDITION. Prentice Hall International Series in Computer Science. 1992.

[34] B A Wichmann, A A Canning, D L Clutterbuck, L A Winsborrow, N J Ward and D W R Marsh. An Industrial Perspective on Static Analysis. Software Engineering Journal. March 1995, pp69-75.

[35] Review Guidelines on Software Languages for Use in Nuclear Power Plant Safety Systems. Nuclear Regulatory commission. NUREG/CR-6463. June 1996.

[36] NASA Guidebook for Safety Critical Software — Analysis and Development. NASA Lewis Research Center. 1996.

[37] Ada 95 Quality and Style: Guidelines for Professional Programmers. SPC-94093-CMC. Ada Joint Program Office. October 1995.

[38] J Sutton and B Carre: Tri-Ada Conference 1995.

[39] B A Wichmann. Some Remarks about Random Testing. To be published (available from the author).

Towards an Automotive 'Safer Subset' of C

P.D.Edwards and R.S.Rivett
Rover Group Ltd

G.F.McCall
Ford Motor Company Ltd

Abstract

The C programming language is becoming more and more widely used in the automotive industry for electronic control systems, some of which have safety-related aspects. This paper studies the use of the C language and the reasons for this use. Because of the safety concerns with the language, there is a need to provide guidance to the industry on its use. The paper describes the work that has been carried out under the auspices of the MISRA consortium to develop an automotive 'safer subset' of C. The rationale behind the work is presented, along with a brief description of the contents of the Guidelines produced.

1 Language Trends in the Automotive Industry

1.1 Software in the Automotive Industry

For many years automotive engineering was principally a combination of mechanical and electrical engineering activities. The basic mechanical components of the vehicle were the body, engine, gearbox, etc. The electrical components included ignition circuits, lights, and audio. The instrument cluster was a collection of mechanical dials and lights. The radio (when fitted) was of a push-button type with several transistors.

The first significant use of embedded controllers was in engine control, to meet increasingly stringent emissions legislation (initiated by 1983 Californian emissions legislation). These systems were first developed in the early 1980's, at which time the only commercial processors available were 8-bit and 16-bit CPUs. These CPUs were only supported by assembler languages. In some cases the automotive companies developed their own custom processors due to the non-availability of CPUs designed for automotive engine management needs.

Since this time, and in parallel with consumer electronics, the number of applications of CPUs on vehicles has grown significantly. Software-based electronics is now to be found in many applications, including the following:

- airbag control
- anti-lock brakes
- cruise-control
- engine control (including full-authority electronic throttle)
- gearbox control
- instrument clusters (speedometer, odometer, tachometer, fuel level, engine temperature etc.)
- radios and entertainment systems
- security systems (immobilisers, alarms, central locking)
- traction control
- trip-computer
- window, sunroof and electric seat control
- windscreen wiper control
- control of vehicle lighting

Figure 1 shows, in a qualitative way, how while the overall engineering effort required to design a vehicle has increased over time, electronics and software are becoming an increasingly significant part of the overall effort. One much quoted figure is that 30% of the value of a modern vehicle is in the electronics.

Often software is the only technology by which the complex functionality required by today's users (and sometimes by legislation) can be achieved within appropriate cost and engineering constraints. In many systems, the personality of the system has moved into the software, with the electronic components becoming little more than a box to support the CPU environment, and provide the interfaces to other components and systems.

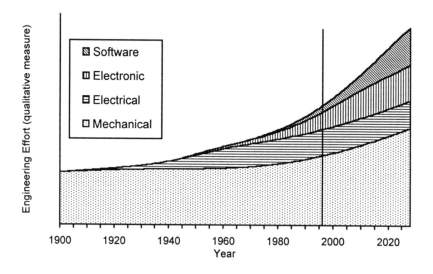

Figure 1 A qualitative view of the changing distribution of engineering
effort in automotive design

As well as understanding the widespread use of software in modern vehicles, it is important to understand where this software is written within the automotive industry. A typical vehicle will have a number of distinct electronic control units (ECUs) in it (e.g. one for engine management, one for security, one for ABS etc.). Sometimes an ECU and its software may be designed in-house by the vehicle manufacturer, but more normally each unit will be bought in from a supplier. The supplier will have written the software as part of the development of the unit, or may even have sub-contracted the software development to a second tier supplier.

As a result, much of the software on vehicles is not written by the vehicle manufacturers, but by first or second tier suppliers. Furthermore, software is often (mistakenly) seen as a simple task by these organisations. They may well assign electrical engineers to do complex software development.

It was against this background of the use of software in the automotive industry that the UK's Motor Industry Software Reliability Association (MISRA) produced its "Development Guidelines For Vehicle Based Software" in 1994 [1] (referred to in the rest of this paper as the 'MISRA Development Guidelines'). These have received widespread acceptance throughout the UK automotive industry, and also further afield.

1.2 The Move Towards C

Today's automotive applications range from 4-bit CPUs to 32-bit CPUs, with anything from a few kilobytes of code, up to 512 kilobytes of code. Historically most of the code was written in the assembly language of the processor, but increasingly the C programming language is being used. This is to obtain benefits of increased flexibility and speed of software development. Benefits exist in the improvements in testing, and portability gains of using a high-level language.

Figure 2 shows a breakdown, for a typical current vehicle project, of the programming languages used.

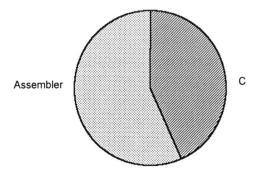

Figure 2 Programming languages used on a typical vehicle project
(measured by size of executable produced)

C has provided the automotive industry with the first really viable opportunity to move from assembler to a higher level language. Other languages have been considered, such as Ada, Pascal and Modula-2, but C is proving by far the most popular. There are various reasons for this, including the following:

- For many of the microprocessors in use, if there is any other language available besides assembler then it is usually C. In most cases other languages are simply not available for the hardware.

- C gives good support for the high-speed, low-level, i/o operations which are essential to many automotive embedded systems.

- Code size and RAM usage are very critical in the industry. With volumes of millions of units, a pound saved in hardware cost per vehicle against a more expensive and intensive software development process can be justified. Therefore moving to any environment that increases the size of the software or RAM usage (e.g. Ada) produces a significant cost increase. In addition it has been known in a few cases for Ada vendors to stipulate a per-unit run-time license fee, which makes the costs totally unacceptable.

- Some languages (e.g. Pascal) have been ruled out because of lacking modularity.

1.3 A Critique of the Use of C

Against this background of the increasing use of C in systems which may sometimes be safety-related, it is important to listen to the concerns which have been expressed about the integrity-related issues associated with the language. Some of the criticism of C is anecdotal, but some is also published.

For example Cullyer, Wichmann and Goodenough [2] rank the use of assembler as being better than that of C from the perspective of integrity. Their main concern is that in assembler, the software engineer is fully aware of the raw capability of the language. In using C, many of these problems are hidden from the software engineer. If he/she is unaware of the true implementation of many C features (due to a training in another high-level language such as Pascal), then they code under a false sense of security.

On the other hand we have to recognise the significant swing of the automotive industry towards the use of C, and acknowledge that, from an engineering point of view, this trend towards C is an improvement over assembler.

We also have to recognise that it is impossible for any individual manufacturer to prevent this industry-wide movement. This is a result of a number of factors:

- The use of C has already become so widespread and well established.

- Some writers of software are too far removed from the purchaser of the system for the purchaser to have much influence over them.

- There is no categorical evidence that the use of C is 'unsafe'.

- There is no practical evidence that the already widespread use of C in vehicles has caused any problems (safety-related or not).

- Without evidence, managers treat the 'prophets of doom' with scepticism.

Because of the above, it would be hard to convince managers across the industry (who are rarely software specialists) that C should not be used.

Rather, what we can do is to recognise that C is being used, and also that there are genuine concerns about the language, and ensure that advice exists to make the transition to using C as safe as possible.

2 What Is An Appropriate Response To These Language Trends?

2.1 A Language Subset

There is a reasonable amount of published material on the suitability of programming languages for use on safety critical systems (for example Cullyer, Wichmann and Goodenough [2]; Clutterbuck and Carré [3]; Wichmann [4]; Hayman [5]; the High Integrity Ada project [6]). These papers address the valid question of how intrinsically robust are the syntax and semantics of various programming languages. However, engineers often have to deal with the intrinsically less than perfect and so, with regard to the C programming language, the more relevant question is how safe can the use of the language be made. This question has been addressed by Hatton [7], who considers that, providing "... severe and automatically enforceable constraints ..." are imposed, the C programming language can be used to write "... software of *at least* as high intrinsic quality and consistency as with other commonly used languages".

The arguments advanced by Hatton convinced the authors that, with the identification of these issues and the use of known good practice, the C programming language could be made acceptably safe, at least for systems up to MISRA integrity level 3 (see MISRA Development Guidelines [1], section 3.2, for the definition of MISRA integrity levels). Given the seemingly unstoppable trend to use the C programming language, as described in section 1 of this paper, the professionally responsible response was to work towards getting this known good practice used throughout the industry.

Although Hatton discusses many issues, the core aspect of good practice is the language subset. This is a long established practice, even for those languages considered to be intrinsically safer than C, and is in accord with the automotive industry's MISRA Development Guidelines [1], which recommend the use of language subsets for integrity levels greater than 1. The other measures, besides subsetting, which are necessary for the best-practice use of C are mentioned in section 3.1 of this paper. The remainder of this section will discuss the issues relating to producing a public domain industry wide language subset.

2.2 Obtaining Industry Wide Acceptance of the Subset

Both Ford and Rover decided independently that there was a need for a C programming subset. Although both parties are members of the MISRA steering group, it was only through a mutual contact that they became aware of each other's activities in this area. Since starting work on the MISRA subset they have also become aware of other automotive companies who are working on subsets of C (or other approaches to regulating the use of C), so the MISRA subset has caught the spirit of the age.

Both Ford and Rover were working on internal company-wide standards but both agreed that an industry-wide standard would be preferable, for several reasons:

- Different automotive manufacturers may use common component supplier companies, and a common standard would mean that such a supplier would not have to follow a number of different standards imposed on them by different vehicle manufacturers.

- It would be easier to convince the managers, within both the manufacturing and the supplier companies, of the need to use a standard if there was an industry wide one.

- It would be easier to seek the opinion of language and safety 'experts' on the adequacy of the standard and then obtain general acceptance both within the automotive and safety critical communities.

- It would be easier to update the standard in line with advancing knowledge and experience.

These perceived advantages of a public domain standard have been clearly demonstrated by the success of the MISRA Development Guidelines [1]. These were published in November 1994 and 1300 copies have been distributed in 7 countries. The Development Guidelines have gained general acceptance both within the automotive and safety critical communities.

Given the success of the MISRA Development Guidelines, Ford and Rover decided to combine their efforts and approached MISRA to see if they would be willing to publish the C Guidelines in a similar way to the Development Guidelines. This was agreed with the MISRA steering group and work has proceeded despite the lack of external funding. The advantage of MISRA publishing the Guidelines is that they can act as a management organisation which is independent of any one company and provide a single point of contact for the Guidelines. Having the Guidelines published by MISRA immediately makes them industry wide.

Although the MISRA C Subset is being put forward as an automotive Guidelines document, it is probably applicable to the development of any embedded controller. In the short term restricting it to the automotive industry is a pragmatic approach to getting it written and accepted, but in the longer term there is probably no reason why it should not be adopted by other industries who develop embedded systems.

In publishing this C subset MISRA has a number of goals:

- That by the year 2001 all new C written for automotive embedded systems fitted to European manufactured vehicles will conform to the Guidelines. (It is a longer term goal that this should also apply to vehicles manufactured in North America and the Far East.)

- That engineers and managers within the automotive industry will become much more aware of the language-choice issues.

- That there will be much greater use made of static checking tools by the developers of automotive embedded systems.

3 The 'Safer Subset'

3.1 What Constitutes a Complete Safety-Case for C?

Before the C programming language (or any language for that matter) can be used with any degree of assurance about safety, there are a number of issues which must be addressed. All of these issues contribute to a complete justification (or 'safety-case') for the use of the language. The following issues therefore all need to be addressed to justify the use of the language, and of course need to be documented.

1. *Use of language and libraries.* Restrictions on which features of the language may be used, and rules for how they should be used. This is the language 'subset', in the strictest sense of the word.

2. *Style guidelines.* Guidelines for code-layout, local programming practices and naming conventions.

3. *Code metrics to be used.* Description of code metrics which are used to impose limits on program complexity and size.

4. *Enforcement plan.* A description of how the rules in the Guidelines will be enforced, preferably by the use of tools.

5. *Deviation procedure.* The procedure for informed sign-off, to be followed when deviation from a rule is unavoidable.

6. *Justification for choice of language.* This presents a reasoned argument as to why the language chosen, subject to the policies and rules described above, is acceptably safe.

7. *Justification for choice of compiler.* This presents a reasoned argument as to why the compiler (and its configuration) were chosen, what evaluation was undertaken, compliance to standards, results of benchmarking exercises etc.

3.2 Scope of the MISRA C Guidelines

The MISRA C Guidelines only address the first of the above issues, namely the restrictions to be placed around the use of the features of the C language. They do not cover the remaining issues in any detail. They do, however, require that these other issues be addressed and appropriate documents be written, and the Guidelines give some pointers as to what needs to be included. This additional information is included in appendices to the main Guidelines.

There are a number of reasons why the MISRA C Guidelines only address the language restrictions, and do not try to cover the remaining issues.

- Some issues, such as issues of style and of code metrics, are very subjective. It would probably be hard for any group of people to agree on what was appropriate, and anyway would be inappropriate for MISRA to give definitive advice. What is important is not the exact style guidelines adopted by a user, or the particular metrics used, but that the user *does define* style guidelines and appropriate metrics and limits.

- The MISRA consortium is not in a position to recommend particular vendors or tools to enforce the restrictions adopted. The user of the Guidelines is free to choose tools, and vendors are encouraged to provide tools to enforce the Guidelines. The onus is on the user of the Guidelines to demonstrate that their tool set enforces the Guidelines adequately.

- Justifications will depend on factors which will be unique to the environment of the user, such as choice of compiler and switches, choice of support tools, other standards in use locally and the MISRA integrity level of the systems under development.

3.3 Content of the MISRA C Guidelines

At the heart of the MISRA document is a set of 'rules' for the use of the C language. Such a set of rules is often referred to as a language 'subset', although this term can be misleading in that it implies a list of features of the language which must not be used. In reality the 'rules' in the MISRA document are broader than that, and fall into various categories, for example:

- *Whole language features which are banned.* For example, unions and the dynamic heap memory allocation functions malloc(), realloc() and calloc().

- *Certain uses of language features which are banned.* This is where a language feature may not be used in particular ways, for example an expression must not contain more than one effect, and bitwise operators must not be applied to signed integral types.

- *Constraints which are placed on language features.* These are rules about how a particular feature should be used, for example every *case* clause in a *switch* statement must be terminated with a *break* (except when no statements exist between cases), and all function definitions and calls must have a visible and matching declaration (prototype).

- *Requirements for dynamic checks.* These rules specify situations in which dynamic checks must be written into the code, for example expressions which have the potential to cause numeric errors must be checked before evaluation.

3.4 Developing the MISRA C Guidelines

The list of 'rules' for the MISRA C Guidelines was developed in three main phases. Firstly a survey was conducted of available source material, secondly this information was filtered and adapted into rules, and thirdly the resulting material was subject to expert review and revision.

The initial information was collected from a variety of sources, both published and anecdotal. The aim at this stage was to collect as much information as possible on the concerns that people have with the C language and its 'danger areas'. Published sources of information included:

- The 'portability' annex (Annex G) of the ISO C standard [8]
- "Safer C" by Les Hatton [7]
- "C Traps and Pitfalls" by Andrew Koenig [9]

Standards created in-house by member companies of the MISRA consortium were also collated to provide additional information based on experience. Finally additional ideas were collected from individuals, course notes and other such sources.

This pool of gathered information provided, in some cases, direct ideas for 'rules', and in other cases issues or problems with the language or its use which had to be addressed in some way. Thus the second stage, of producing the list of 'rules' for the Guidelines, involved filtering and refining existing rules, and developing rules to address other issues which were identified.

Although there is no totally objective way of arriving at a given set of 'rules', the following principles were used to guide this stage of the process:

- Issues of style were omitted, i.e. issues which were not believed to have any significant impact on code integrity, but were more matters of preference.

- As far as practicable, rules were to be enforceable by static tools. Rules which cannot be enforced in any way are really of no greater status than guidance to the programmer. In a few cases, however, such rules were retained because the advice they give needs to be heeded by the programmer.

Additionally the resulting rules were rationalised to avoid duplication.

3.5 Presentation of the MISRA C Guidelines

What we have called, up to this point, 'rules' are actually divided within the C Guidelines into 'rules' and 'guidelines'. The distinction is that 'rules' are considered to be mandatory, and are largely statically detectable, whereas 'guidelines' are advisory, and may not be statically detectable. The 'guidelines' form only about 20% of the full set of items, and the 'rules' the remaining 80%.

The items have been presented in the order in which the relevant language features are presented in ISO 9899 [8]. For each rule (or group of rules) supporting information is given in the form of: the source of the original issue being addressed, explanations of the language issue, examples of the application of the rule or guideline, and hints to the programmer. An example of a rule is given below.

7.10.3 Memory management functions

Rule :   Dynamic heap memory allocation shall not be used.

[Uns 19; Und 91,92; Imp 69]

This precludes the use of the functions *calloc*, *malloc* and *realloc*.

There is a whole range of unspecified, undefined and implementation-defined behaviour associated with dynamic memory allocation, as well as a number of other potential pitfalls.

Figure 3 Example of the presentation of a rule

3.6 Deviations from the Guidelines

The Guidelines require that a controlled deviation process be enforced. The authors of the Guidelines recognise that there will be situations where engineering requirements prevent certain rules from being adhered to. This should obviously be avoided if at all possible, but may sometimes be necessary. It is therefore important that when a rule has to be deviated from, there is some recognised process for ensuring that the issues are fully understood and that measures are taken to protect against the issues that the original rule was intended to address.

The MISRA C Guidelines do not define a deviations procedure, but give guidance on writing one.

3.7 Enforcement and the Compliance Table

It has already been stated that as far as possible adherence to the C Guidelines should be checked and enforced by automated static checking tools. This is both common sense, and a requirement of some standards (such as IEC 1508 [10]) which strongly recommend automatic tool enforcement. The MISRA C Guidelines require that the coverage of rules by static tools be documented. One way of doing this is in a 'compliance table', which lists all the rules in the Guidelines. Against each rule the user documents the tool(s) which enforce the rule, and which error/warning messages they produce.

Any rules which cannot be statically enforced should be documented in the safety justification for the use of the language, along with measures taken to enforce the rules (e.g. manual code review).

4 Summary

We have shown how software is playing an increasingly major part in the content of the modern automotive vehicle, and how the C programming language is rapidly gaining popularity throughout the industry as the language of choice for embedded control systems. It has been suggested that this practice has become too ingrained in the industry's culture to make it possible to change completely, and anyway that there is currently little alternative.

Given the genuine concerns that there are about the use of C, we have presented what we consider to be a pragmatic way forward: that is to encourage those in the industry who are using C to do so in as safe a way as possible. This is being done under the auspices of the MISRA consortium, by publishing a so-called 'safer subset' of C. We have described how this document gives 'rules' and 'guidelines' for how the language should or should not be used, and also how other supporting documentation needs to be written by the user of the language to form a complete justification that their use of the language and supporting tools is as safe as may reasonably be expected.

It is the opinion of the authors that concerns raised about the C language are genuine and need to be heeded. Furthermore, the MISRA Development Guidelines themselves dictate that code should be written using a 'restricted subset' of the chosen language. We therefore believe that the MISRA subset, having the credibility of an industry-wide document, will enable the industry to take a responsible approach to its use of C.

References

1. *Development Guidelines For Vehicle Based Software.* Motor Industry Research Association, Nuneaton, November 1994

2. Cullyer WJ, Goodenough SJ and Wichmann BA. *The choice of computer languages for use in safety critical systems.* Software Engineering Journal, March 1991

3. Clutterbuck DL, Carré BA. *The verification of low-level code.* Software Engineering Journal, May 1988

4. Wichmann BA. *Notes on the security of programming languages.* In Libberton GP (ed), *10th Advances In Reliability Technology Symposium.* Elsevier, 1988

5. Hayman K. *An analysis of ordnance software using the MALPAS tools.* In Proc. 5th Ann. Conf. on Computer Assurance - COMPASS '90, Gaithersburg, MD, USA, June 25-28 1990. IEEE, 1990

6. York Software Engineering Limited, *High Integrity Ada* project, various project reports.

7. Hatton L. *Safer C - Developing Software for High-integrity and Safety-critical Systems*, McGraw-Hill, 1994.

8. ISO/IEC 9899 : 1990, *Programming languages - C*, ISO

9. Koenig A. *C Traps and Pitfalls*, Addison-Wesley, 1988.

10. Draft IEC 1508, *Functional safety: safety-related systems* (Ed.1), International Electrotechnical Commission, June 1995, Reference number 65A/179-185

Computer Based Support for Standards and Processes in Safety Critical Systems[1]

S P Wilson, J A McDermid, P M Kirkham
Department of Computer Science, University of York,
York, UK

C H Pygott, D J Tombs
Defence Evaluation and Research Agency
Malvern, UK

Abstract

This paper describes an approach and tool-set, the Safety Argument Manager (SAM), that can be used to support standards and processes in the area of Safety Critical Systems. We take an example standard (for military fuzing systems) and a mandated process for showing conformance to particular aspects of that standard, and demonstrate how SAM can support them. In particular SAM can help manage conformance to the standard and process, and provide detailed automated checks between the steps of the process. We argue that using such support gives increased assurance that a system has been built in a way that conforms to the planned process, and that the integrity of the system will be at the level required.

1 Introduction

Safety Critical Systems (SCS) normally need to be certified for use, and this certification is usually done on the basis of a safety case. A safety case presents a reasoned argument that a system meets its safety requirements and will be safe for use. An important part of the argument will be that the design is free from faults, i.e. has a high integrity. There are now a large number of industrial development standards whose aim is to reduce the likelihood of systematic design and construction errors, [1,2,3,4,5]. A safety case for a given system is likely to contain a claim that the relevant standards have been adhered to. There are problems in adhering to standards however:

- A standard will normally impose constraints on the process to be used to develop and assess a system. These constraints may be regarded as coarse grain rules between the steps of a process. Adhering to these rules should make for a better product, but for the actual process used, there will be **finer grain rules** between the different techniques, and unless these other rules are 'uncovered'

---

and checked, then the quality of the product is likely to be reduced (as noted in the process modelling field, [6]).

- It can be difficult to **manage** and show compliance to standards because of their **size**, e.g. Def Stan 00-55, [1], contains almost 350 occurrences of the word 'shall[2]' and there are even larger standards. Standards also usually cover the whole development process and it can be difficult to be sure that all relevant clauses are being considered at each phase.

- There is also a large **gap** between the requirements of a standard and the means by which they can be met and demonstrated to be met. Although a number of standards do have accompanying **guidance** which provides contextual information, rationale for the requirements and suggested techniques to use (e.g. particular modelling and assessment methods), the guidance will usually be non-prescriptive.

We have developed the Goal Structuring Notation (GSN) [7, 8, 9] to capture high level arguments as to why requirements have been met or standards have been conformed to, with the ability to link out to supporting evidence. The Safety Argument Manager (SAM) [10] supports the GSN and also provides the ability to define editors for building supporting evidence (models and analyses). The editors can be defined to propagate data between each other, and to support the fine grain rules outlined above. In the rest of this paper we describe how SAM has been used to support a design standard for fuzing systems and a mandated integrated process for showing conformance.

2 Goal Structuring Notation, Method Integration and the Safety Argument Manager

2.1 Overview of the Goal Structuring Notation

The GSN is a graphical notation with an underlying logical interpretation, that enables the construction of high level arguments (HLA) with links to supporting evidence (SE). A number of approaches for making arguments have been proposed such as Toulmin arguments, [11], Claim Structures [12], and the use of standard logic gates such as that illustrated in the annexes to 00-55 Part 2, [1]. The GSN has additional features, including the ability to reference contextual information and to make more precise links with supporting evidence. In this paper we only present a subset of the elements of the GSN.

A **Goal** is a requirement, a target to be met, or an activity to be performed It may come from customer requirements, clauses of a standard, code of practice or be introduced to satisfy some other goal.

A goal can be shown to be met by **decomposition** into sub-goals, whose satisfaction entails the satisfaction of the parent goal. The sub-goals can themselves be decomposed and so on, until ultimately leaf goals are left which can

---

[2] Shall designates a mandated requirement

be shown as met by direct appeal to supporting evidence (see solutions below). So for example a goal to achieve structural integrity of a reactor vessel, could be broken down into sub-goals to achieve structural integrity for each of its components. A goal to perform safety analysis of a system could be broken down into three goals for hazard identification, causal analysis and consequence analysis. The rationale for decomposition and for the inclusion of goals can be made explicit through the use of strategies and justifications – although we omit them from this paper.

Where further information is required to clarify a goal, or to enable its satisfaction, use can be made of a **Context**. Where it is possible to provide an explicit measure or means to decide if a goal has been satisfied, use can be made of **Criteria**.

A **Solution** provides the link between the HLA and the SE, it may be a reference to a model, a piece of analysis (such as Fault Tree Analysis), a specification, test results, minutes of a meeting, an audit report, and so on.

The symbols for this subset of GSN elements and their relationships appear in Figure 1.

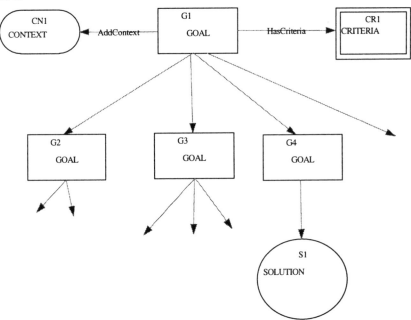

Figure 1: Important Elements of the Goal Structuring Notation and their Relationships

2.2 Integrated Modelling and Analysis

In the development and assessment of complex systems use is normally made of a number of modelling and analysis techniques. These techniques are related and so are the various models and analyses built using them. For example, a Hazards and Operability (**HAZOP**) study has to consider the effects of deviations on all of the flows in a **model**; Fault Tree Analyses (**FTAs**) have to identify the causes of all hazards identified in the HAZOP; a Failure Modes and Effects Analysis (**FMEA**) identifies the system level effects of single component faults, and where these effects can lead to a hazard they should appear in the **FTA** for that hazard. Despite the existence of such relationships, implied by the process that developers follow, the propagation of data between analyses and the rules that hold between them are not always clearly specified and checking and enforcing is handled on an ad-hoc basis. The assurance gained from following the coarse grain rules of a standard will be devalued if finer grain rules are not respected. Note that the rules vary according to the development and assessment process followed.

A first step is to specify each technique to be used in terms of the inputs that it requires to proceed (imports) and the results that it produces (exports). Pair-wise rules between techniques can then be stated unambiguously as relationships between imports and exports. This was done for a set of widely used safety analysis techniques in [13]. Nuseibeh, [14], defines a general framework for specifying notations and defining inter-notation checks, our approach is similar although he defines a special language for specifying the rules. Even after formalization such rules are tedious to check by hand, and this is exacerbated by the need to update to models and analyses during development. Therefore tool support for checking rules is essential, as we shall see in the next sub-section on SAM.

Note that the capture of rules between techniques gives no guidance as to when they should be applied in the process, and what should be done about inconsistencies that are detected. However a GSN based description of the process can be used for this, it can control the application of the checks, give direct feedback on progress, and control the generation of activities – we shall see evidence of this later.

2.3 Safety Argument Manager

SAM is a PC based tool which supports the construction, manipulation, checking, and presentation of goal structures for making arguments about system properties (product) and the process used to construct a system.

SAM is also extensible in that it is possible to specify editors for other modelling and analysis techniques, and data formats. The other editors are specified in SAM itself (as schema files). A technique is defined as a collection of entities and relationships. Entities are defined in terms of the data that they record, their graphical representation, and the user operations that they support. Relationships are defined in a similar way but with typing rules for the entities that they can link.

SAM supports the method integration discussed in section 2.2. Given the definitions of imports and exports for techniques, a data model can be designed to accommodate them. This data model can be implemented as a set of relational database tables. Within SAM it is possible to provide a mapping from the imports and exports of a notation onto a database. Once these mappings have been defined the user of an editor will be offered import, export, remove, and consistency check operations - the mechanics of which will be transparent. Where existing tools need to be integrated into the SAM framework, they can pass information via the database.

Note that the notations and data model are **NOT** hardwired into the core SAM program – on startup SAM looks in a directory to find (possibly user defined) schema files for each supported notation, and in a user specified directory for the database tables.

There are a number of commercial tools for individual techniques, a few addressing a number of analysis techniques, [15], but none that we know of supporting such integrated modelling and analysis for safety critical systems as SAM does.

3 Background to P120 and STANAG 4187

The UK MoD Ordnance Board (OB) have the task of assessing SAFUs[3] (Safety Arming and Fuzing Units) for safety. The applicable standard is STANAG 4187 *Fuzing Systems - Safety Design Requirements* [16] which specifies safety design targets for fuzes, and specifies, in broad terms, a number of development and assessment activities that have to be performed.

Assessment against STANAG 4187 involves building a large body of documentary evidence about a design and checking it complies with the standard's requirements. The OB are concerned that due to the increasing complexity of systems, the evidence that they receive may contain mistaken claims of compliance, the analysis they receive varies in quality, and there is often inconsistency between the different analyses used on a single project. To address these problems the Ordnance Board produced Pillar Proceeding P120 *Integrated Design Analysis for Fuzing System Safety* [17]. P120 defines an integrated process, the steps for which are as follows:

- **Step 0: Define a set of Frames**
  The assessment must be performed in the context of a set of frames, i.e. particular views or modelling aspects of the design. A predefined set is given as part of P120: Operating Logic, Environment, Construction, and a number of others. P120 is primarily concerned with the *Operating Logic* underlying a fuze.
- **Step 1: Develop a Basic List of Components and Functions**
  The Basic List (BL) is a list of environmental stimuli sensed by the fuze (e.g. mechanical force, acceleration), the components of the design, and the functions of those components within the overall operation of the fuze. Each component may have more than one function.
- **Step 2: Allocate Functions to Frames**
  Each component function in the BL is allocated to one or more frames identified in Step 0.

---

[3] A SAFU, or fuze, is that part of a weapon system that ensures unexpected detonation does not occur.

- **Step 3: Identify inputs to Operating Logic Functions**
  All of the Operating Logic Functions identified in Step 2 are marked as either Command or Initial. Command functions are 'commanded' by other functions or stimuli; Initial functions represent the initial state of the fuze. Command functions are allocated an identifier and have their inputs (the other functions which cause them) enumerated.
- **Step 4: Construct the Operating Logic Tree**
  A diagrammatic tree is constructed showing the sequence of Commands (from step 3) which occur during normal operation of the fuze – known as the Operating Logic Tree (OLT). This is much like a Fault Tree, but with an OLT all of the events represent the intended behaviour of a fuze.
- **Step 5: Relate design safety requirement to Frames**
  Each clause of STANAG 4187 is associated with one or more frames (from step 0). This need only be repeated if the STANAG itself is updated or the frame scheme is changed.
- **Step 6: Check conformance of OLT**
  The OLT (from step 5) is divided into zones related to major process channels, for example arming or initiation. In an acceptable design these channels will be independent, i.e. have no functions or components in common.
- **Step 7a: Perform Preliminary Hazard Analysis (PHA)**
  A PHA is to performed to identify the hazards to which the fuze is susceptible.
- **Step 7: Construct Fault Trees (FTA)**
  From the results of the PHA fault trees are constructed for the top-level hazards. The events in the fault trees may be either faults (from the FMEA, step 8), or valid commands (from the OLT, steps 3, 4).
- **Step 8: Develop Failure Modes and Effects from Basic List (FMEA)**
  Each component function (from step 1), has its potential failures modes and effects identified. A list is made for each effect of any hazards that they could lead to. Some effects will not have a hazardous effect and will be labelled "Residual". FMEA and FTA will usually be conducted in parallel, and checked for consistency in step 9.
- **Step 9: Check consistency of OLT, FTA, FMEA**
  A check is made that all fault events of FTA can be found in the FMEA, and conversely that all failure modes which can contribute to hazards occur in the appropriate FTA's. Also that all FTA command events appear in the OLT.
- **Step 10: Complete the FMEA**
  The FMEA tables are completed.

At the completion of all of these steps there will exist a large body of structured data (BL, OLT, FMEA, FTA) that one can check against specific requirements of STANAG 4187. For example, one requirement demands two safety channels, independent and isolated from each other. The presence of independent safety channels in a design can be checked on the zoned OLT (Step 6).

The purpose of Step 5 and the frames other than Operating-logic is that the STANAG can be 'filtered' for each frame, as can the BL functions. This eases the task of checking whether the environmental, constructional, etc., aspects of the STANAG have been met.

4 Support for Standard and Process

P120 has been designed as an integrated procedure where the flows and consistency rules between steps have been made explicit. For this reason it is an ideal test of the facilities claimed for SAM in section 2, and besides without tool support checking the consistency between stages is still tedious. In this section we describe integrated editors that have been built to support the detailed steps and consistency rules of P120, and how the GSN has been used to *manage* conformance to P120 and STANAG 4187.

4.1 Editors for Individual Steps

Special editing support has been built for each of the data formats and notations required to carry out P120. The editors are as follows: Frames, Basic List, Operating Logic Tree, Preliminary Hazard Analysis, Fault Tree Analysis, and Failure Modes and Effect Analysis. The support has been defined by building special SAM Schema files for each of the notations, together with a database to capture the imports and exports of each stage. SAM with these notations provided is known as SAM-P120. A screen shot of SAM-P120 during an editing session of the OLT appears in figure 2. Note the icon box on the far left, the user can drag and drop these symbols onto the drawing area in the right pane.

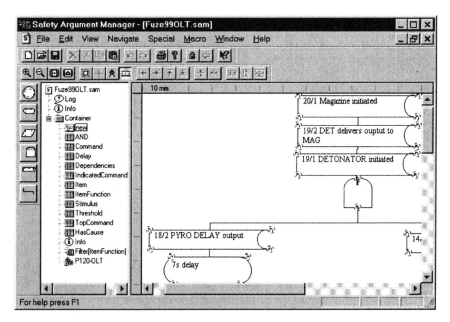

Figure 2: Specialized SAM Editor for Operating Logic Trees

Each of the editors were designed to offer internal checks to ensure that the model, analysis, or data is self-consistent and complete. For example in the Basic List editor, there is a construction check to ensure that all items have functions defined for them (**CheckConstruction**). Any errors detected are recorded in the 'Log' for that SAM document, which the user can peruse and use to navigate to the offending item. Corrections can be made and checks re-done until no more errors are reported. An example of errors that can be detected on an ill-formed OLT appears in figure 3.

Entry	Object	Description	User	Time
Notification:	-	Log Cleared	stevew	Wed Nov 13 14:25:45 1996
Action:	Container	CheckConstruction	stevew	Wed Nov 13 14:25:50 1996
ERROR:	Provides Fulcrum	Command causes nothing else	stevew	Wed Nov 13 14:25:55 1996
ERROR:	Provides Fulcrum	Command should have one input	stevew	Wed Nov 13 14:25:55 1996
ERROR:	Provides Fulcrum	Command references an initial function	stevew	Wed Nov 13 14:25:55 1996

Figure 3: A Document Log showing error reports

Editors have also been designed to offer special calculations other than normal construction checks, for example checking for any dependencies (**CheckDependencies**) between the safety features identified in step 6 of P120. The example in figure 4, below, shows the result of applying the dependency calculation to the OLT for the fuze used as a case study. It shows that Initiation and SafetyB features share common hardware items (components) and common stimuli.

Dependencies

Indicated1	Indicated2	CommonItems	CommonStimuli
Initiation	SafetyA		
Initiation	SafetyB	02 07 03	Parachute exerts retarding force
SafetyA	SafetyB		

Figure 4: Dependencies detected by the SAM Operating Logic Tree Editor

Each editor is also provided with an export operation to make its results available to other editors, and there is an associated check operation to ensure that the results in the database are consistent with the current state of the SAM document (**CheckExports**). An explicit export operation is required so that tentative changes do not have an immediate impact on individuals working on other steps. For example the Frame editor exports a list of frames, and the Basic

List Editor exports a list of components, functions (with frame allocations), and stimuli.

Each editor has an import operation to read the data that it needs, and there is an associated check operation that the imported data is up to date with the results produced by the use of other techniques. The philosophy is to allow data to be propagated to help with initial construction, and consistency checks provided to ensure consistency as changes are made. For example all of the Operating Logic functions exported by the BL editor can be imported into the OLT editor; it would be unhelpful if the user had to retype (letter perfect) the functions in the OLT editor because only consistency checks were provided. After construction, the user may wish to perform a consistency check, to verify that since the OLT was constructed there have been no changes to the BL that invalidate parts of the OLT (**CheckImports**).

Once the model, or analysis for a stage passes all checks (internal and database) then that step is deemed complete as far as SAM is concerned. The checks are comprehensive and did reveal a number of minor inconsistencies in the exemplar presented as part of P120 itself.

4.2 Managing and Controlling the Overall Process

The special editors described above provide support for each step with local consistency rules. There is still a need to manage the process, monitor progress, get some form of measure of global consistency, and be able to argue authoritatively that the process has been correctly executed so that the desired level of assurance can be deduced. It is to these ends that GSN has been applied on the P120.

A description of the P120 process has been built using GSN. The top level goal is to "Assess the System according to P120" which has sub-goals for each of the steps. The interpretation is that if all of the sub-goals are performed satisfactorily then the top level goal to assess the system will have been met. The top level of the P120 Process goal structure is shown in figure 5. The Context to the right of goal P120, indicates that the process is currently being applied to a fuze known as "Fuze99". The grey dots in the figure indicate the goals have not been solved yet, i.e. for the particular Fuze99, steps 7, 8, 9, 10 have not been completed – we will describe how SAM can deduce this later.

The sub-goals are broken down in separate figures, and the user can navigate to these figures directly from this top level view. The sub-goals on these other figures either bottom out directly to solutions or have some further sub-goals and then solutions. Solutions are the place to which the results of performing the steps are attached, i.e. there are solution nodes for the Frame list, Basic List, OLT, PHA, FMEA, and FTAs. For example the sub-goal structure for the steps to build an OLT is shown in Figure 6. Note how it is decomposed into four sub-goals, all of which contribute to the production of an OLT (the OLT appears as their solution).

To perform a given step there may be some input required from previous steps. This is represented by a Context. For example, to develop a Basic List (step 2) some representation of the design is required, and this is an example of external context since the P120 process did not produce it. As another example, note how the Basic List produced as part of step 1, appears as context to Steps 3-4 in Figure 6. Contexts representing this kind of data propagation are known as internal.

Where there are explicit checks for determining whether or not a step has been carried out successfully these can be associated with the goals as criteria. For example, Step 3a is to identify a list of operating logic functions and stimuli, the criteria for satisfaction, C7, is that they have been imported (under the assumption that the correct values were exported from the Basic List, but that is made a criterion of step 1, anyway). C7 is an example of executable criteria, since it ultimately calls one of the functions provided by the OLT editor (i.e. CheckImports). Most of the criteria for P120 are directly executable, but some will always be manual, for example to check that the Basic List accurately reflects the real fuze (in this case the user simply marks the criteria as met or not met).

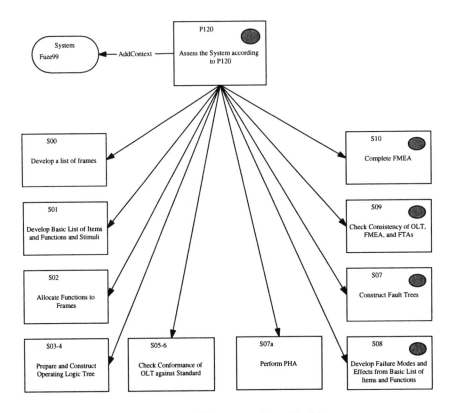

Figure 5: Steps of P120 Represented as a Goal Structure

The process goal structure can be treated as a template (for use on a number of projects) to which the actual solutions (Frame List, Basic List, OLT, etc.) can be attached. With just one function from a menu, **CheckIsSolved**, it is possible to check to see if the process has been followed. A goal is deemed to be solved if all of its sub-goals are solved and it meets its own criteria. A grey dot appears in a goal until it has been solved, and the list of failed criteria are also maintained. The user is also be warned of criteria requiring a manual check. Note that SAM and the GSN representation do not impose an ordering on the steps, P120 is deemed to be followed if all of the criteria (including rules between steps) are met.

The advantage of the check is that it immediately, and visually identifies the parts of the process which have not been successfully completed, and after a change to any of the solutions it is possible re-run the checks to get an indication of which parts of the process (at minimum) need to be repeated.

There are a number of other features of the support such as generating sub-goal structures depending upon the number of fault trees, and also checks to ensure that the goal structure is consistent with the attached solutions, e.g. that they are for the same System, in this case Fuze99, and that a goal to analyse Hazard 1, has the Fault Tree for Hazard 1 as a solution, not Hazard 2.

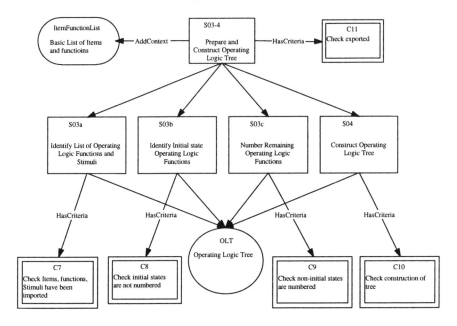

Figure 6: Goal Structure bottoming out to a Solution (OLT - Steps 3 and 4)

4.3 The Standard – STANAG 4187

A standard can be captured in goal structured form by representing the top level clauses as goals, and sub-clauses as sub-goals and so on. Figure 7 demonstrates this for Clause 9.1.a of the STANAG, and we found it useful to split the clause into smaller atomic units, since they constitute separate requirements. Note that for this particular clause, the criteria are mapped onto executable checks on the OLT which ultimately appears as the evidence for satisfaction. For example, Crit2 makes a call to CheckDependencies, described in section 4.1. Note that as a general rule failure to meet the criteria of a process goal structure means that there are errors in the models and analyses built, whereas failure to meet criteria in a product goal structure, such as this, means that there are possibly errors in the fuze itself (or at least its design).

The goal structured form of the standard, like the goal structured form of the process, provides a template which can be reused for different projects assessing different fuzing systems. It can be used to manage and check conformance, i.e. for a given system the user attaches arguments and evidence to the leaf goals of the standard, and can call the CheckIsSolved function to get a measure of global satisfaction of the standard.

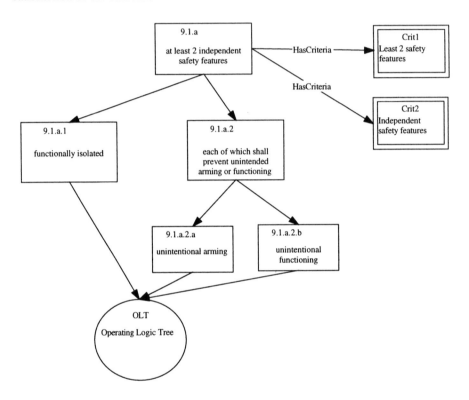

Figure 7: Goal Structured Form of Clause 9.1.a of STANAG 4187

5 Conclusions

We have shown how the detailed consistency rules between techniques can be supported in the SAM tool, and how the results of these checks can be used to control and monitor the performance of a real process. Tool support relieves a great deal of tedium from development and assessment (with the aim of reducing time and cost), and will give a higher degree of confidence in the integrity of the final product. We are currently applying a similar approach to a standard with a wider scope, 00-55, [1], the initial results seem promising even though 00-55 is much less prescriptive than STANAG 4187 and P120.

6 Acknowledgments

The authors acknowledge the important contributions of the originators of P120 (Chris Sennett, and Jack Crawford), the other developers of the GSN (Tim Kelly, Jonathan Moffett, and John Murdoch), and the other developer of SAM (Michele Cassano). The work on P120 has been supported by MoD strategic research programme AS04 BP42.

7 References

1. MoD. Defence Standard 00-55, Requirements for Safety Related Software in Defence Equipment, Parts 1 and 2. Version to supersede INTERIM Def Stan 00-55.
2. MoD. Defence Standard 00-56 Safety Management Requirements for Defence Systems. UK Ministry of Defence, April 1991.
3. IEC. IEC 1508 Functional Safety: Safety-Related Systems, IEC Sub-Committee 65A: System Aspects. International Electrotechnical Commission, June 1995.
4. JAA. JAR-25, Joint Airworthiness Requirements, Part 25. Joint Aviation Authority, 1990
5. HSE. Safety Assessment Principles for Nuclear Plants. Health and Safety Executive, HMSO, ISBN 0 11 882043 5, 1992.
6. Curtis B, Kellner M I. Over J, Process Modeling. Communications of the ACM, Vol. 35 No. 9, September 1992.
7. McDermid J A. Support for Safety Cases and Safety Arguments Using SAM. Reliability Engineering and System Safety, No 43: p111-127. 1994.
8. Wilson S P, Kelly T P, McDermid J A. Safety Case Development: Current Practice, Future Prospects. In: Shaw R (ed) Safety And Reliability of Software Based Systems. Twelfth Annual CSR Workshop, pp 135-156, Bruges 12th-15th September 1995. Springer Verlag.
9. Wilson S P, McDermid J A, Pygott C H, Tombs D J. Assessing Complex Computer Based Systems using the Goal Structuring Notation. In: Proceedings of the 2nd International Conference on the Engineering of Complex Computer Systems, pp 498-505, Montreal, 21-25 October 1996.
10. Wilson S P, McDermid J A, Fenelon P , Kirkham P. The Safety Argument Manager: An Integrated Approach to the Engineering and Safety Assessment of Computer Based Systems. In: Proceedings of the 1996 IEEE Symposium and Workshop on Engineering of Computer Based systems, pp 198-205, March 11-15 1996, Friedrichshafen, Germany.
11. Toulmin S E. The Uses of Argument. Cambridge University Press. 1958.
12. Bishop P G, Bloomfield R E. The SHIP Safety Case Approach: A Combination of System and Software Methods. In: Shaw R (ed) Safety And Reliability of Software Based Systems, Twelfth Annual CSR Workshop, pp 107-121, Bruges 12th-15th September 1995. Springer Verlag.
13. Wilson S P, McDermid J A. Integrated Analysis of Complex Safety Critical Systems, The Computer Journal, Vol. 38, No 10: 765-776, 1995.
14. Nuseibeh B A. A Multi-Perspective Framework for Method Integration. PhD Thesis, Department of Computing, Imperial College, University of London, 1994.
15. Collins R, Dent J N. A Practical Case Study of the Management of Reliability, Safety and other Concurrent Engineering Information. In: Proceedings of the Safety And Reliability Conference, 1994.
16. NATO. STANAG 4187 Fuzing Systems - Safety Design Requirements. Draft Edition 2.
17. Ordnance Board. Pillar Proceeding P120(1) Integrated Design Analysis for Fuzing System Safety. March 1996.

An Assessment of the IEC 1131-3 Standard on Languages for Programmable Controllers

Konstantinos Tourlas

Laboratory for the Foundations of Computer Science
Department of Computer Science, University of Edinburgh
The King's Buildings, Edinburgh EH9 3JZ, UK
e-mail: kxt@dcs.ed.ac.uk

Abstract

Programmable Logic Controllers (PLCs) are playing an increasing role in the construction of safety critical systems. The standard IEC 1131-3 defines a number of interrelated languages for the expression of PLC programs.

Here we consider a subset of the IEC 1131-3 languages, that of function blocks, and present an assessment of the standard from the viewpoint of providing a formal semantics to that subset. In doing so, we also provide justification for our decisions in resolving ambiguities in the standard. Finally, we comment on the overall structure of the standard and, particularly, on how it relates function blocks to the other programming elements.

1   Introduction

Programmable Logic Controllers (PLCs) are simple computers which are used in industrial and other safety-critical applications. The purpose of a PLC is to control a particular process, or collection of processes, by producing electrical control signals in response to analogue process-related inputs. Thus, the main aim of PLC programs is to maintain some desired relation between their inputs and outputs.

In 1993, the International Electrotechnical Commission (IEC) published the IEC 1131 International Standard for Programmable Controllers [1], henceforth simply referred to as *the Standard*. Part 3 of this standard defines a suite of four programming languages which have become known collectively as IEC 1131-3. These consist of two textual languages: Instruction List (IL) and Structured Text (ST) and two graphical: Ladder Diagram (LD) and Function Block Diagram (FBD). Programs in these languages are constructed using the following elements:

- **Program Organisation Units**. These, in turn, consist of *functions*; *function blocks* and *programs*. Their purpose is to specify how individual outputs relate to individual inputs, with the relationship usually being dependent on the state, i.e. execution history, of the unit.

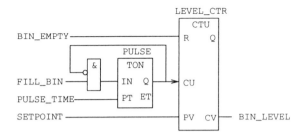

Figure 1: Example Function Block diagram.

- **Sequential Function Charts** (SFCs). These determine how the overall input-output relationship changes in response to events by specifying which program organisation units are *active* at any particular time. In other words, SFCs describe the intended relationship as a function of the *mode* of the system.

- **Configuration elements**. These provide the means for the installation of PLC programs.

Figure 1 shows an example function block in FBD[1] constructed using instances PULSE and LEVEL_CTR of standard function blocks TON and CTU, an on-timer and an up-counter respectively. The corresponding textual declaration in ST appears in Figure 2. TON has a boolean output Q triggered by a boolean input IN, where PT is the delay constant. CTU, on the other hand, counts up while the boolean input CU is high. The current count value is output at CV. Overflow relative to a specified maximum count value PV is signalled by the boolean output Q, whereas input R resets the value of CV to 0.

The aim of this article is to assess the function block subset of IEC 1131-3 based on our experience of reconstructing its essence into a small, formally defined language. Apart from serving as a vehicle for reasoning about function block programs, this formal reconstruction has raised important questions relating to the standardisation process, as well as the structure and the clarity of the Standard. Below we give a detailed analysis of those areas in [1] which have been highlighted as problematic and attempt to provide justification for our chosen solutions.

2 Motivation for a Formal Semantics

Given the use of PLCs in industrial and safety critical applications, the correctness of PLC implementations is of paramount importance. Correctness

---

[1]This example is (a slightly adapted) part of a larger program GRAVEL ([1], pp. 183–191) used to control the amount of gravel transferred from a silo into a bin before it is loaded onto a truck.

```
FUNCTION_BLOCK EXAMPLE
(** External Interface **)
  VAR_INPUT   BIN_EMPTY : BOOL; FILL_BIN   : BOOL;
              SETPOINT  : INT;  PULSE_TIME : TIME; END_VAR
  VAR_OUTPUT BIN_LEVEL : INT;                      END_VAR
  VAR         PULSE     : TON;  LEVEL_CTR  : CTU;
              LOOPVAR   : BOOL                      END_VAR
(** Body **)
  PULSE( IN := NOT LOOPVAR & FILL_BIN; PT := PULSE_TIME );
  LOOPVAR := PULSE.Q;
  LEVEL_CTR( R := BIN_EMPTY; CU := PULSE.Q; PV := SETPOINT );
  BIN_LEVEL := LEVEL_CTR.Q;
END_FUNCTION_BLOCK
```

Figure 2: Example Function Block in ST.

assurance of both PLC hardware and software is usually achieved by formal verification, testing or a mixture of the two. In all approaches, the aim is to provide *evidence* that the system in question has desirable safety and liveness properties.

Recently, there have been a number of attempts to apply formal reasoning to programs written in IEC 1131-3. Most commonly, these attempts apply standard verification techniques, such as weakest preconditions [2], Hoare triples [3] and temporal logics [4], to individual function block and SFC programs [5, 6].

A necessary pre-requisite for formal reasoning is that we have as *precise* and *implementation independent* a characterisation of the behaviour of programs as possible. Of course, one might rightly argue that a description of some program in some logic (e.g. higher-order or temporal) *is* the semantics of that program. However, this approach of applying formal methods to individual programs still leaves unaddressed the issue of how one might reason about *any* valid program in the language. This requires some kind of semantics for the entire language, yet unfortunately semantic issues in the IEC document are dealt with solely by way of example.

Due to the complexity of the Standard, giving a formal semantics to the entire IEC 1131-3 language would be both problematic and impractical. Alternatively, one could provide a formal definition to a particular *implementation* of some subset of IEC 1131-3. One such formally defined implementation conforming to IEC 1131-3 function blocks appears in [7]. Our approach, on the other hand, was to *reconstruct* the essential features of IEC 1131-3 in carefully chosen, representative core languages.

3 A Rational Reconstruction of Function Blocks

Standardisation aims at achieving agreement amongst various (perhaps competing) organisations. One strategy to arrive at such an agreement is to achieve consensus around a text [8]. This appears to be the way IEC 1131-3 was constructed, the result being a rather permissive 'superset' of most approaches to PLC programming. Yet, IEC 1131-3 does appear to have a small conceptual core consisting in the distinction between the computed input-output relation (function block level); the mode of the system (SFC level) and the allocation of resources (configuration level). Each level has its own underlying model. In earlier work [9] we have attempted to identify the conceptual core of function blocks and SFCs. Here we review the Standard against that core, emphasising function blocks and their rational reconstruction, which this section briefly outlines.

3.1 Textual Notation

Programs in our language are *function block terms* which may be either *atomic* or *combinations* of other function block terms. The syntax of such terms, notably different from IEC 1131-3 syntax, is inspired by the notation of CCS [10]. The full definition of our language appears in [9].

The language possesses a strong and sound type system. Program behaviour is also formally defined by means of a timed operational semantics. The primitive semantic relations are *evaluation*, $\rightarrow$, and *time passage*, $\leadsto$. Thus, $\langle f, I \rangle \rightarrow \langle f', O \rangle$ stands for the evaluation of f with input I producing output O. Similarly, $f \stackrel{t}{\leadsto} f'$ denotes f evolving into f' after time t has passed.

3.2 Diagrams

A formal reconstruction of FBD and its relation to the above textual language appears in [11]. Informally, a function block diagram is a graph consisting of a set of nodes, each labelled with a function block term and possessing a set of ports. Ports may then be connected by means of diagram combinators corresponding to those in the textual notation.

4 Problems Identified in IEC 1131-3

4.1 Unclear Model of Computation

The behaviour of function blocks (as well as that of SFCs) is often described by the Standard in terms of how the state of the program changes from one execution to the next[2]. However, nowhere in the Standard appears a statement

---

[2] A good example is the definition of the rising edge detector R_TRIG appearing on page 72 of [1].

of what the terms *current execution* and *next execution* mean, nor is there any specification of how the latter relates to the former. PLC programs are modular and hierarchically composed, yet any account of execution in the Standard is local to each level and irrespective of overall structure. In particular, considerable leniency is allowed as to how the evaluation of a composite function block is interpreted in terms of the evaluation of its components. Different models of execution appear to be suggested by different parts of the Standard, a situation we deem to be most confusing.

Here we are concerned with the execution model suggested by FBD and how it relates to the corresponding model suggested by definitions in ST. Consider Clause 4.1.3 defining the evaluation (i.e. execution) of graphic networks (i.e. diagrams):

> "..., it is not necessary that all networks be evaluated before the evaluation of a given network can be repeated."

What does the above statement really mean? Obviously, it does not mean that the evaluation of a network can be repeated *before* all evaluations of its subnetworks are complete. However, can a given subnetwork be multiply executed during a *single* execution of the enclosing network? Alternatively, does it simply mean that the time taken by a network or subnetwork to evaluate is *independent* of the time taken by any other network in the system? These interpretations reflect two radically different views of evaluation:

- The *circuit* view. Each subnetwork (component) of a network (program) is executed *as fast as possible* to best approximate the continuous behaviour of the corresponding electrical circuit. Thus, each component is thought of as being independently clocked, the frequency of its evaluation represents the propagation delay of the corresponding circuit and its outputs change in response to asynchronous changes in the inputs as soon as this delay allows. This model is mostly suggested in Clause 4 defining the graphical subset of IEC 1131-3.

- The *discrete time simulation*, or *program* view. In this view, there is a single clock for the entire system and all events (changes in inputs and outputs) happen in synchrony with the rising edges of the clock. Each component is evaluated *once only* during a single evaluation of the complete program. In the Standard, such a discrete model pervades the treatment of ST function blocks in Clause 2.5.2.

Now consider Figure 1 along with the body of block CTU expressed in ST:

```
IF R THEN CV := 0; ELSEIF CU THEN CV := CV + 1; END_IF;
Q := (CV >= PV);
```

The subnetwork feeding input CU is intended to generate a short pulse every PULSE_TIME units of time. Under the circuit view and assuming that the evaluation delay for CTU is shorter than the value of PULSE_TIME, one may have

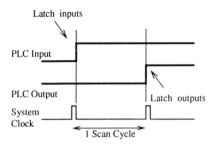

Figure 3: PLC program scan cycle.

a situation in which the value of BIN_LEVEL advances more than once during a single evaluation of the complete network. This is because LEVEL_CTR will be evaluated a number of times during a single evaluation of PULSE. Thus, if output Q of PULSE happens to be high, it will be multiply counted, as suggested by the above definition of CTU in ST. Under the program view, however, both PULSE and LEVEL_CTR are executed only once. Consequently, as the body of Fig. 2 suggests, the value of BIN_LEVEL advances at most once during a single evaluation of EXAMPLE. Thus, the circuit and program views diverge.

Having been misled by the prominence of FBD in the Standard, we first attempted to give semantics to our reconstruction of function blocks by adopting the circuit view. This, however, was soon found to contradict evidence suggested by descriptions of real PLC implementations [5, 6, 12, 13].

According to these descriptions, the execution of PLC programs proceeds in a sequence of *scan cycles*. A graphical illustration of a single scan cycle is given in Fig. 3, showing how the inputs and outputs of the program relate to the timing for the cycle. At the beginning, the input values supplied to the PLC are latched. Each active function block in the program is then executed once to produce a set of outputs. These outputs, along with those of all other active blocks, do not become available until the end of the cycle, at which point the outputs are also latched. The latching mechanism is thus a sample-and-hold operation ensuring that all changes happen in synchrony with the clock of the PLC system.

The current semantics of our language [9] models the above behaviour correctly by combining the evaluation and time passage relations into a single relation called the *step* relation:

$$\langle f, I \rangle \stackrel{t}{\Rightarrow} \langle f', O \rangle \text{ iff } \langle f, I \rangle \rightarrow \langle f'', O \rangle \text{ and } f'' \stackrel{t}{\leadsto} f' .$$

This corresponds to a single scan cycle of period t, with I and O respectively the latched inputs and outputs for the cycle.

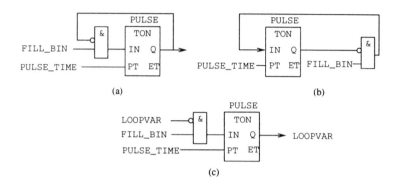

Figure 4: Examples of loops in FBD.

4.2 Translation of FBD into ST

Closely related to the underlying computation model is the issue of translating between the different languages of IEC 1131-3. The Standard mandates that a program written in any of the four languages should be convertible to an equivalent in any of the others, yet no algorithm or translation scheme is documented.

The use of diagrammatic notation, in particular, is appealing because it is derived from earlier design practice. Diagrams must be translated into textual programs before they can be compiled. Specifically for FBD, this raises an important question: which programs in ST make up the corresponding equivalence classes? In general, such a class will consist of more than one program. Thus, an obligation is placed on the language designers to establish that all methods of building the same diagram are interpreted identically. In [11] we fulfil this obligation for our reconstruction of function blocks. Unfortunately, the treatment of semantic issues in IEC 1131-3 was found inadequate to support a similar claim. The definition of evaluation order in FBD presents an illuminating example:

4.2.1 Order of Evaluation in FBD

Clause 4.3.3 of the Standard defines the order of network (i.e. diagram) evaluation for FBD. As Krämer and Völker correctly point out, "the evaluation order of function blocks within a cycle does not matter as long as casual dependencies between function blocks are respected" [6]. Consequently, different diagrammatic layouts of the same function block should admit the same evaluation order as they depict the same dependencies among the components.

The Standard uses a notion of *precedence* to describe such dependencies, although this notion is not precisely defined. It appears that precedence is implicitly related to the layout of a diagram in a way that captures the engineer's convention of reading such diagrams in a top-to-bottom, left-to-right fashion.

The problem associated with this layout-sensitive view is exemplified in Fig. 4 showing a subnetwork of Fig. 1. Part (a) shows how the two components depend upon each other. Part (b) presents a different layout in which the order of components is reversed. Assuming left-to-right precedence, as implied in the Standard, these diagrams will translate into two different ST programs since the translation process 'breaks' the loop at different points in each case. The Standard acknowledges this ambiguous situation by mandating that "the user *should* be able to define an order of evaluation by selection of feedback variables to form an *implicit* loop." Such an implicit loop appears in Fig. 4(c), where the feedback variable is LOOPVAR. Nevertheless, in the absence of a user-specified order a default order is assumed, the details of which are not specified.

Of course, one might argue that the Standard's style of definition fits the engineer's conceptual model and thus presents little problem to the *user*. This is less true, however, for an *implementor* of the language who, like us, might not share the same perspective. An implementor also has to consider the reverse translation from ST to FBD. In this case, implicit loops suggest themselves in that they preserve the ordering of components evident in the textual representation. [Compare the first couple of lines in the body of block EXAMPLE in Fig. 2 with Fig. 4(c).] In fact, the use of implicit loops becomes *necessary* whenever a feedback variable is to be initialised with a non-default constant.

Inspired by the idea of implicit loops, our reconstruction of FBD [11] requires that all feedback connections in diagrams are *decorated*. This is done by "tagging" the input ports associated with loops with their initialising constants. Such a convention completely dispenses of layout-sensitive diagrams, a particularly appealing view from a programming perspective, and facilitates the proof of the equivalence of the diagrammatic and textual notations. For instance, it becomes possible to prove that the translations into ST of parts (a) and (b) of Fig. 4 will only be equivalent if they contain the same set of decorated connections.

5   General Comments

In this article we only address the subset of the Standard defining function blocks. We are currently working on the formalisation of SFCs based upon the same idea of timed operational semantics. Preliminary investigations revealed the SFC subset to contain more and harder-to-resolve ambiguities than any other subset of IEC 1131-3. However, even the formalisation of function blocks alone was enough to raise some points about the overall structure:

- The definition of the overall state of a PLC program is heavily distributed across the different levels of the IEC 1131-3 hierarchy. Although care was taken to constrain the use of global variables, it is not clear how a variable declared at a higher level (e.g. configuration elements) is used by a program at some lower level (e.g. function blocks). Instead, our rationalisation of function blocks employs a completely functional model which records state changes as *evolutions* of the term being evaluated:

$\langle f, I \rangle \rightarrow \langle f', O \rangle$, where f' is the evolved term representing the new state of f.

- The vehicle for communication between components in IEC 1131-3 is shared memory. In other words, communication is "hidden" in the global state and thus is difficult to trace. This difficulty of relating events to the passage of time explains the confusion regarding evaluation which we analysed in Section 4. In our rationalisation, communication lies closer to an event-driven model such as the one underpinning CCS. The presence of two semantic relations, $\rightarrow$ and $\rightsquigarrow$, reflects a clear separation of the effects that evaluation and time passage have on programs.

- Finally, the IEC document poorly distinguishes implementation dependent features from those portable across implementations. For instance, storage requirements for the various types as well as directly representable variables could be neatly constrained to the configuration level with all other levels being defined independently of such details.

Our feeling is that the Standard was constructed in a 'bottom-up' fashion, hence its size and complexity. As a result, any attempt to give semantics to the original IEC 1131-3 languages would produce poorly structured and complicated definitions of little practical use in verification.

We believe that a functional/algebraic model of computation would suit PLC programming better than the imperative paradigm of IEC 1131-3. The Standard mandates, by restricting certain imperative features, that programs observe desirable behavioural constraints, e.g. that all loops terminate. It is therefore possible to describe program behaviour within a simple, tractable algebraic framework comprising a few equational laws. Equations are particularly appealing for specifying PLC programs, however, the simplicity of equational reasoning is completely obstructed by the imperative nature of IEC 1131-3.

6 Conclusion

The application of computing in other disciplines necessarily brings together expertise from all domains involved. In the specific case of PLC programming, knowledge of electrical engineering, process control and programming languages was merged in the production of the IEC 1131-3 standard.

We presented a critical assessment of the Standard from the point of view of programming language theory, concentrating upon issues such as clarity of semantic definitions, structure and correspondence of the semantics to the user's intuition. Thinking in terms of program semantics, we emphasised points of potential misinterpretation which would probably not manifest themselves in a purely user-oriented view of the language. Since the latter appears to be the view which dominated the production of IEC 1131-3, we hope to have offered positive and constructive feedback to the standardisation committee. We ourselves have gained a good appreciation of the difficulties involved in this major standardisation effort.

The approach we have taken in reviewing the Standard suggests an alternative model of standardisation where the focus is on a small, well-understood core. This could then be realised in a wide range of different implementations and act as a *lingua franca* across different PLC environments.

Acknowledgements

We wish to acknowledge the contribution of Stuart Anderson through many useful discussions and to thank Steven Haeck for his most helpful comments.

References

[1] IEC. International Standard 1131-3, Programmable Controllers, Part 3, Programming Languages, 1993

[2] Dijkstra E. A Discipline of Programming. Series in Automatic Computation, Prentice Hall, Englewood Cliffs, NJ, 1976

[3] Hoare C. A. R. An Axiomatic Basis for Computer Programming. Communications of the ACM, 12(10), pp. 576-580, 1969

[4] Manna Z, Pnueli A. The Temporal Logic of Reactive and Concurrent Systems, Volume 1, Specification. Springer Verlang, 1992

[5] Halang W, Jung S, Krämer B, Scheepstra J. A Safety Licensable Computing Architecture. World Scientific, 1993

[6] B. Krämer, N. Völker. A Highly Dependable Computing Architecture for Safety-Critical Control Applications. Real-Time Systems Journal, 1996

[7] Egger G, Fett A, Pepper P. Formal Specification of a Safe PLC Language and Its Compiler. Proceedings of SafeComp'94, ISA, 1994

[8] Bloomfield R, Bowers J, Emmet L, Viller S. PERE: Evaluation and Improvement of Dependable Processes. Proceedings of SafeComp'96, 1996

[9] Tourlas K. Semantic Analysis and Design of Languages for PLCs. M.Sc. thesis, The University of Edinburgh, 1997

[10] Milner R. Communication and Concurrency. Prentice Hall, 1989

[11] Anderson S, Tourlas K. Diagrams and Programming Languages for Programmable Controllers. To appear in the Proceedings of Formal Methods Europe, 1997

[12] Parr E. Programmable Controllers, An Engineer's Guide. Newnes, 1993

[13] Swainston F. A Systems Approach to Programmable Controllers. Newnes, 1991

Formal Methods and Models

Refinement and Safety Analysis

K. Lano

Dept. of Computing, Imperial College, 180 Queens Gate,
London SW7 2BZ. kcl@doc.ic.ac.uk

Abstract

This paper discusses the extent to which the validity of the results of safety analyses such as FTA and FMEA can be preserved through the refinement process, and to what extent it is possible to avoid repeating these analyses at later development stages.

1 Introduction

In contrast to functional properties, the safety properties of a system are not necessarily preserved by refinement from a specification to an executable implementation [9]. This is due to:

- Additional functionality may be introduced in the implementation of a specified function, which affects components or data which was not evident or present in the specification model;

- Specification functions may be decomposed into services performed by new components introduced during design;

- The range of behaviour of an operation may be constrained in the implementation, in a way which affects the possible execution of other operations which may be executed concurrently or in sequence with it.

We will examine these situations in more detail using finite state machine models of systems at the specification and design stages, in the following sections.

The introduction of additional functionality and components can render FMEA for existing components invalid, and implies the need to additionally consider failures arising in the new components. Likewise a refinement which eliminates some cases of behaviour may thereby remove recovery routes from hazardous states to safe states.

We will make use of the concept of *safety state assignment*, which is based on the safety case models of standards such as DEF-STAN 00-55 [10]. These models express the states a system can be in (from the viewpoint of safety) and the transitions between them (Figure 1). We can relate detailed state machine models of a system to this abstract model by means of an *abstraction* function (akin to the *retrieve* functions of VDM [6]) which maps each concrete state **s** to one of the four abstract states, and each concrete transition **t** to an abstract transition **i(t)** in a consistent manner[1].

---

[1]That is, the source of **i(t)** is **i(s)** where **s** is the concrete source of **t**, etc.

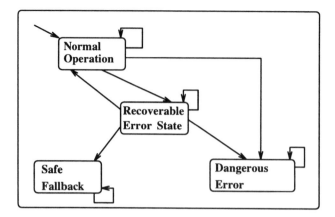

Figure 1: Safety States Model

If such an interpretation exists, we say that the system model obeys the safety model. The aim is then to remove, as far as possible, system states that map to the dangerous error state.

It is infeasible in general to analyse the functionality of a non-trivial system on the basis of its state-machine semantics, however the abstraction of this semantics which is relevant to safety may be more tractable: mappings to a safety model provide a means of such abstraction.

2   Case Studies

We will give an example of a safety-critical reactive system to illustrate the ideas presented in this paper: a controller for a milk pasteurisation process [7].

The schematic diagram of part of the pasteurisation plant is shown in Figure 2. The processing involved is that the tank, initially at the minimum fill level, exit valve closed (energised) and with the manhole closed (the manhole sensor 1.80 is in the energised state in this case), begins to be filled via pump 1.30 until a set level is reached, when the stirrer 1.40 is switched on. If the manhole is opened whilst the tank is filling, then the pump must be switched off and the exit valve opened (de-energised). The fill operation is complete once a certain maximum level is reached.

3   Statecharts and Theories

3.1   Notations

We will use the Syntropy notation and semantics for statecharts [2], as this method has appropriate models (termed the *essential* and *specification* models) for representing the required and specified behaviour of a system.

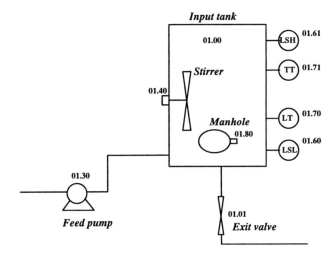

Figure 2: Schematic Plant Layout

The formalism we will use to express the semantics of statecharts is a temporal logic language termed the *object calculus* [3]. An object calculus theory consists of a set of type and constant symbols, *attribute symbols* (denoting time-varying data) *action symbols* (denoting atomic operations) and axioms describing the types of the attributes and the effects, permission constraints and other dynamic properties of the actions. The axioms are specified using linear temporal logic operators $\bigcirc$ (next), $\mathcal{U}$ (strong until), $\square$ (always in the future) and $\diamond$ (sometime in the future). There is assumed to be a first moment. The predicate **BEG** is true exactly at this time point.

$\bigcirc$ is also an expression constructor. If **e** is an expression, $\bigcirc$**e** denotes the value of **e** in the next time interval.

The version used here is that defined in [8] in order to give a semantics to VDM^{++}. In this version actions α are potentially durative and overlapping, with associated times $\rightarrow(\alpha, \mathbf{i})$, $\uparrow(\alpha, \mathbf{i})$ and $\downarrow(\alpha, \mathbf{i})$ denoting respectively the times at which the **i**-th invocation of α is requested, activates and terminates (where $\mathbf{i} \in \mathbb{N}_1$). We also define a predicate **enabled**(α) which identifies the conditions under which the system is guaranteed to respond to a request for α to be executed.

Interpretations σ from a theory $\Gamma_\mathbf{C}$ to a theory $\Gamma_\mathbf{D}$ are given by a mapping σ from the symbols of $\Gamma_\mathbf{C}$ to the symbols of $\Gamma_\mathbf{D}$: actions are interpreted by actions (basic or composed), and attributes by terms. Under this translation, every theorem φ of $\Gamma_\mathbf{C}$ must be provable from $\Gamma_\mathbf{D}$:

$$\Gamma_\mathbf{C} \vdash \varphi \implies \Gamma_\mathbf{D} \vdash \sigma(\varphi)$$

Theory interpretation can be used as the basis of a definition of refinement and subtyping: **D** is a subtype of **C** via a translation σ of attributes and actions of **C** to appropriate interpretations in **D**, if $\Gamma_\mathbf{D}$ is a theory extension of $\Gamma_\mathbf{C}$ via

σ.

A *refinement* is a particular form of subtyping in which no new external actions are introduced in **D**. In terms of the semantics of statecharts discussed in Section 3.2, this means that no new events are introduced into **D** except for internal events which are used in describing the internal reaction to an external event. Events may also be split into subcases expressed by new events.

Further restrictions and modifications of refinement will be needed in order to ensure that safety analysis results are preserved through development steps.

3.2 Formal Semantics of Statecharts

A statechart **S** can be given a logical interpretation in an object calculus theory Γ_S [1]. This theory will have a type

$$\textbf{States} = \{s_1, s_2, \ldots, s_n\}$$

where the s_i are distinct values representing the states of **S**. An attribute symbol

$$\text{states} : \textbf{States}$$

represents the currently occupied state. Action symbols α represent the events that **S** may respond to (ie, which name any transition in **S**).

The initial state s_1 has the axiom

$$\textbf{BEG} \Rightarrow \text{states} = s_1$$

A transition in **S** for an event α from state s to state t can have a number of axioms defined for it, which describe its effect, permissions for occurrence, etc. For example, a *state-transition* axiom for the effect of this transition is:

$$\text{states} = s \wedge \alpha \Rightarrow \bigcirc \text{states} = t$$

where $\bigcirc\text{states}$ is the value of states in the next time instant (α occurs in the interval between the current and next instant – the granularity of "instants" may change during refinement, as we discuss in Section 3.5). We could say that α can *only* occur if the current state is s by: $\alpha \Rightarrow \text{states} = s$ (a *permission* axiom), and that t can only be entered via α by: $\bigcirc\text{states} = t \Rightarrow \alpha$ (an *entry* axiom). An *enabling* axiom

$$\text{states} = s \Rightarrow \text{enabled}(\alpha)$$

expresses that α can be executed from state s – ie., there is a transition for α with source s.

Transitions may additionally have *preconditions* **P** which are represented axiomatically by placing them as extra assumptions in the state-transition and enabling axioms:

$$\text{states} = s \wedge \textbf{P} \wedge \alpha \Rightarrow \bigcirc\text{states} = t$$

and

$$\text{state}_S = s \ \wedge \ \mathbf{P} \ \Rightarrow \ \text{enabled}(\alpha)$$

They may also have *guards* **G** which prevent the transition occurring unless the guard holds. These are represented as extra conclusions in the permission axioms, and extra assumptions in the enabling axioms:

$$\alpha \ \Rightarrow \ \text{state}_S = s \ \wedge \ \mathbf{G}$$

and

$$\text{state}_S = s \ \wedge \ \mathbf{P} \ \wedge \ \mathbf{G} \ \Rightarrow \ \text{enabled}(\alpha)$$

Notice that if **G** holds and **P** does not, we know that α may occur from its source state, but not what its effect is going to be, or even if it is enabled – this is used in Syntropy in the same way as preconditions in the VDM or B languages [6, 7].

We will include the state-transition, enabling and permission axioms for each transition into the theory Γ_S of **S**.

However, we separate out the state-transition axioms for actions which terminate in a state classified as "dangerous error" from other axioms. Thus the semantics of a statechart will be relative to a given safety-states assignment **i** from the 4-state model, and is defined as a pair

$$\Gamma_S \ = \ (\mathbf{T_S}, \mathbf{H_S})$$

where $\mathbf{H_S}$ are the state-transition axioms for transitions with termination state **t** having i(t) = dangerous error, and $\mathbf{T_S}$ consists of the remaining axioms.

3.3 Abstraction Functions and Theory Extension

If we have 2 statecharts **A** and **C**, with an abstraction function **i** which gives, for each state **s** of **C**, a state i(s) of **A**, and for each transition **t** of **C** a corresponding transition i(t) of **A** with the same event, and with source preserved under **i**, then there is a corresponding theory interpretation σ from the theory of **A** to that of **C**, given by:

$$\sigma(\text{state}_A) \ = \ \text{i}(\text{state}_C)$$

Notice that the definition of **i** as total ensures that no new events are introduced in **C** – this condition will be relaxed to allow new *internal* events in Section 3.5 below.

Refinement of **A** by **C** will be defined as follows:

$$\Gamma_A \sqsubseteq \Gamma_C \ \equiv \ \forall \varphi \in \mathbf{T_A} \cdot \mathbf{T_C} \vdash \sigma(\varphi) \ \wedge \ \mathbf{H_C} \subseteq \sigma(\! \mathbf{H_A} \!)$$

Thus behaviour is preserved for non-hazardous transitions, but hazardous transitions can be redirected to other states.

Refinement of **A** by **C** means that the interpretation of each axiom of Γ_A is provable from those of Γ_C, apart from effect axioms for transitions into dangerous error states. For other effect axioms we need to show:

$$\sigma(\text{state}_A = s \wedge \alpha \ \Rightarrow \ \bigcirc \text{state}_A = t)$$

which is:

$$i(\text{state}_C) = s \wedge \alpha \ \Rightarrow \ i(\bigcirc \text{state}_C) = t$$

In other words, for every state s' of **C**, if $i(s') = s$, then any transition for α from s' (in **C**) leads to a state t' such that $i(t') = t$ (constraint (**C1**)).

Likewise, for a permission axiom $\alpha \ \Rightarrow \ \text{state}_A = s$, its interpretation is $\alpha \ \Rightarrow \ i(\text{state}_C) = s$, that is, α can only occur in **C** if the current state s' has $i(s') = s$ (constraint (**C2**)).

An enabling axiom $\text{state}_A = s \ \Rightarrow \ \text{enabled}(\alpha)$ has the interpretation

$$i(\text{state}_C) = s \ \Rightarrow \ \text{enabled}(\alpha)$$

In other words, there is a transition for α in **C** from any state s' that has $i(s') = s$ where there is a transition for α from s in **A**   (constraint (**C3**)).

Notice therefore, that if we have a transition α from a concrete state s into an dangerous error state t in **C**, there must also be such a transition in **A**. This means that no new hazards are introduced by this form of refinement, in a certain sense. The preservation of the permission axioms by refinement means that new transitions cannot be introduced for α except from states that correspond to abstract states which are already sources of α transitions. The preservation of enabling axioms means that existing transitions for an abstract event cannot be eliminated.

In particular, consider a situation as in Figure 3 where **C** has an abstraction function **k** to **A** which has the property (**C4**) that $k(s) = s'$ means that s is a substate of, or is equal to, s'. That is, the refinement is based on decomposing states or transitions of **A**. Let **i** and **j** be two safety-state assignment mappings to the four state model. If $k(s) = s'$, s must be assigned to a safety-state no more hazardous than s', as s is a subcase of s'.

Each of the conditions (**C1**) to (**C4**) can be mechanically checked, given the two statecharts and the proposed abstraction mapping, and a decidable language for transition conditions. We will enumerate a set of refinement transformations which lead to abstraction functions satisfying (**C1**) to (**C4**), and hence to theory extensions preserving safety properties in Section 4.

3.4 Preservation of Safety Analyses

3.4.1 Failure Modes and Effects Analysis

FMEA can be performed using statechart models of a system. For example, the filling tank [7] system has the following statecharts for the abstract design (Syntropy terms this the 'specification model') of the process of filling the feed tank (Figure 4). There are of course many other states for the controller than

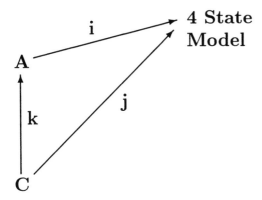

Figure 3: Refinement of Safety-state Assignment

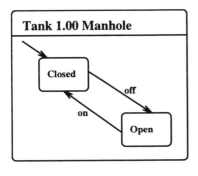

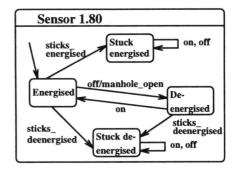

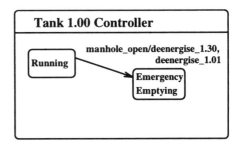

Figure 4: Statecharts of Tank Valves and Controller

the two shown here. Using these we can then examine the effect of a failure of the 1.80 sensor (which detects if the manhole in the tank is open or not) in the energised ("manhole is shut") state. This results in a transition to the stuck energised state. Consequently, subsequent **off** events are undetected by the sensor, which results in a hazardous situation (the manhole being open but no command being sent to the controller to open the exit valve 1.01 of the tank and to shut off the input pump 1.30). Table 1 shows the analysis for this failure. Rectification would require adding the generation of a **manhole_open** event

Unit	Failure Mode	Local Effects	System Effects
Sensor 1.80	Failed Energised	Manhole open undetected	Allows tank to operate whilst not sealed: damage to equipment/injury to personnel

Table 1: FMEA extract for 1.80

by the **sticks_energised** transition – and physically, by adding some means of detecting the transition to stuck energised, perhaps by periodic testing of the sensor or by comparing its output with that of a backup sensor.

Formally, an FMEA analysis maps each pair of an **event** and system state into a sequence of transitions that can lead to an error or dangerous error state. The results of such an analysis on an abstract system **A** will be preserved in a concrete system **C** which has **A** $\sqsubseteq$ **C** via an abstraction function **i** satisfying (**C**1) to (**C**4) because:

1. New external events cannot be introduced, by definition of refinement;

2. New transitions cannot be introduced for events, due to preservation of permission axioms (**C**2);

3. The effect of transitions in **C** that do not lead to a unrecoverable/dangerous error state must be compatible with their effects in **A**, due to condition (**C**1);

4. Error or dangerous error states that are the end points of a sequence of transitions in the analysis can only decrease in their criticality level in the analysis for **C**, because transitions to dangerous error states can be redirected in the refinement.

The introduction of a new chain of internal events to implement a single abstract transition will also preserve the abstract FMEA, given the change in interpretation of state-transition axioms (Section 3.5).

Thus no new hazardous consequences of existing failures can be introduced, and hazardous consequences of existing failures identified by FMEA may be removed. Introducing new components (via a parallel composition form of statechart transformation which does not obey the above constraints) will introduce new failures and potentially hazardous consequences. For example, a valve which introduces cleaning fluid into the tank could be included in the analysis – a failure of this valve in the open state can lead to a hazardous contamination of the raw product with cleaning chemicals, or unintended reactions. This is a case where there is not a refinement relationship between the concrete and abstract models which preserves safety-state assignment: the state where the new valve is stuck open but the remainder of the system is in a "normal operating" state is not categorised as a normal operating state.

3.4.2 Safety-States Assignment

For the model of Figure 4 the safety states assignment is:

(closed, energised, running) $\mapsto$ **normal operation**

(closed, stuck energised, running) $\mapsto$ **dangerous error**

(open, deenergised, running) $\mapsto$ **error**

(open, deenergised, emergency emptying) $\mapsto$ **error**

(open, stuck deenergised, emergency emptying) $\mapsto$ **dangerous error**

(closed, energised, emergency emptying) $\mapsto$ **safe fallback**

In general, any system state where the sensor is in a stuck energised or stuck deenergised state is categorised as a dangerous error state.

3.4.3 Fault Tree Analysis

FTA can be regarded as decomposing a hazardous state into conjunctions and disjunctions of more elementary states. For example, the state "manhole open whilst tank filling" can be broken down into the combinations of states where pump 1.30 is energised (operating), valve 1.01 is energised (closed), and where the sensor 1.80 is in one of the failed states or in the de-energised state (it cannot be in the energised state as the manhole opening will take it out of this state). If 1.80 is in the deenergised state then we can infer that the controller has failed to respond to the **manhole_open** command, or its reaction to this command has failed to be transmitted to the valve and pump, or that there is some failure (failed in the energised state) in one or both of the valve and pump. Figure 5 shows this in more detail. A fault tree describes a set of states (the cut sets) at each level of abstraction.

In this case the cut sets are:

{1.80 **failed deenergised**, 1.30 **failed energised**, 1.01 **failed energised**}
{1.80 **failed deenergised**, **controller not running**, 1.01 **failed energised**}
{1.80 **failed deenergised**, **communication failure** 1.80 $\rightarrow$ **controller**, 1.01 **failed energised**}
{1.80 **failed deenergised**, **communication failure controller** $\rightarrow$ **actuators**, 1.01 **failed energised**}

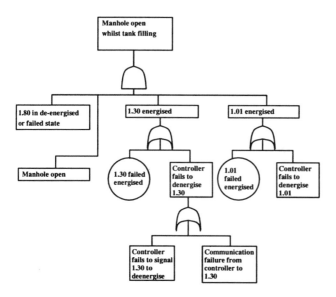

Figure 5: Fault Tree of Hazardous Filling

and similar states for the other combinations. The "manhole open" state is in each of these sets.

If there is an abstraction mapping **i** from a statechart **C** to a statechart **A** satisfying (**C4**), then the overall probability of a state **s** in the abstract statechart **A** will be the sum of the probabilities of its component states, ie, those states **s'** of **C** which have **i(s')** = **s**. Thus the fault tree analysis at the **A** level can be related directly to that at the **C** level via **i**.

Because FTA at the **C** level may decompose a fault source into a more specific substate (ie, the branches of the tree may lengthen), it follows that the probability of the top event due to the branches recognised at the **A** level can only decrease (see Section 5 for an example). However the tree may become wider or "bushier" – new alternative causes may be introduced because of new components or interactions.

3.5   Changing the Granularity of Actions

Typically during a refinement process, what was perceived at the abstract level as being a single event and state transition will be decomposed into a number of steps (internal to the software controlling the system) which together achieve the abstract state transition. In the tank example, the abstract specification could involve just the single transition **off** which goes from a Tank running state to a Responding to manhole open state. In the refined system presented above, this transition involves communication from the sensor to the controller via the **manhole_open** message, and then communication from the controller to the actuators via the **deenergise_1.30**, **deenergise_1.01** messages. Of these the **manhole_open** event is a purely internal event introduced for the design. The

deenergise_1.30 and **deenergise_1.01** events can be regarded as external.

The general pattern in such situations is that an external input event triggers a series of internal events ("microsteps") which may generate further internal events until the reaction to the event (a "macrostep") is complete (external output events may be generated at completion of this reaction). Further external input events may then be received and reactions to these initiated.

In order to express such refinements as theory extensions we need to modify the concept of "next" used in our specifications. We introduce subscripted versions $\bigcirc_S$ of the "next" operator, with $\bigcirc_S \theta$ meaning that θ holds at the earliest future activation time amongst those of any action β in the set $\mathbf{S}$.

At the specification level we now express the effect of a transition for α from state $\mathbf{s}$ to state $\mathbf{t}$ by

$$\alpha \wedge \mathbf{state} = \mathbf{s} \;\Rightarrow\; \bigcirc_{\mathbf{A}} \mathbf{state} = \mathbf{t}$$

where $\mathbf{A}$ represents the set of external events of the abstract model.

If the concrete model introduces new internal events, then these are ignored by the translation of this axiom. The translation

$$\alpha \wedge \mathbf{i(state)} = \mathbf{s} \;\Rightarrow\; \sigma(\bigcirc_{\mathbf{A}} \mathbf{state}) = \mathbf{t}$$

requires only that if α occurs in a concrete state $\mathbf{s}'$ with $\mathbf{i(s')} = \mathbf{s}$, that, after completion of the internal reaction to α, the resulting state $\mathbf{t}'$ will have $\mathbf{i(t')} = \mathbf{t}$.

As an example, consider Figure 6, which shows the refinement of the abstract model of the tank system. In the abstract model, the external event **off** moves the tank state from filling to some intermediate hazard state where the manhole is open but the emptying process has not yet started. After some interval the system can then evolve to an emergency emptying state.

At the concrete level we introduce separate sensor, controller and actuator components, and communication between them. The **off** event leads to a state where 1.80 is de-energised and the controller is in the running state. The controller then receives the generated **manhole_open** event and reacts by moving into the emergency emptying state and generating signals to de-energise the actuators. The two dashed states correspond to the abstract responding to manhole open state.

The abstract specification axiom for the effect of **off** from the 1.80 energised state is that at the next initiation time of an external event, the system will be in the responding to manhole open state. The interpretation of this axiom is valid in the refined model because at such a time the concrete system will be in the combination of the de-energised state for 1.80, the emergency emptying state of the controller, and the energised states for the actuators, which corresponds to the abstract responding to manhole open state.

The abstract state responding to manhole open has a safety states assignment to the error state abstract safety state, hence it is consistent to assign this safety state to both of the dashed states as well. Likewise, tank emergency emptying and actuators de-energised both have an assignment to the safe fallback state.

Abstract Model:

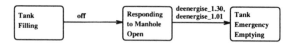

Refined Model:

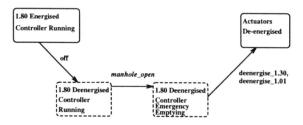

Figure 6: Refinement of Abstract Reaction

4 Refinement Transformations

In this section we give a number of transformations on statecharts which result in refinements, based on those of [2] for subtyping. We will separate out refinements which maintain the same granularity of actions (ie., which only decompose states, or which decompose transitions into alternative cases) from those which decompose transitions into sequences.

4.1 Concurrent Composition of Statecharts

The first main case is when there is no explicit modification of the abstract statechart **A**, but a new separate chart for a new component **E** is introduced. This new statechart may share transitions with the initial model but has a disjoint set of states. The resulting complete chart for the new system is the concurrent (AND) composition of the abstract statechart and the statechart of the new component.

We assume that initialisations of the two statecharts are synchronised. If an event **e** is specific to the new component **E**, then a transition for **e** leaves the original **A** state unchanged but may change the **E** state of the combined system **C**.

On the other hand, if **A** has transitions for **e** but **E** does not, then **e** may change the **A** state of **C** but not the **E** state. If **e** has transitions in both **A** and **E** then it may cause transitions in both. State-transformation axioms are preserved under a refinement derived from the projection abstraction mapping:

$$i(state_C) = a \wedge \alpha \;\Rightarrow\; \bigcirc i(state_C) = b$$

is

$$state_A = a \wedge \alpha \;\Rightarrow\; \bigcirc state_A = b$$

where $state_C$ is effectively a pair $(state_A, state_E)$ of states of the separate components. Likewise so are permission axioms. However, synchronisation between the two components can eliminate transitions that existed in **A**, and make states of **A** and **E** unreachable in **C**, thus violating the enabling axioms. To avoid this problem we make the additional constraint on concurrent composition that if there is a transition for event α from state **a** to state **b** of **A**, then in **C** there is a transition for α from every composite state (a, e) to some composite state (b, f). This ensures constraint (**C3**). It is guaranteed in the trivial case that **A** and **E** have no shared events.

Constraint (**C4**) is satisfied if the state of **E** does not negatively affect the safety state of the system. That is, new substates (a, e) of **a** are at most as hazardous as **a**.

4.2   Expanding a State

Transforming a single state in the abstract model into a state with an enclosed statechart in the concrete model will produce a theory extension of the appropriate form, ie, which meets the constraints (**C1**), (**C2**), (**C3**) and (**C4**).

This is the case since introducing nested states does not affect existing axioms, and adds new axioms for each new substate. State-transition axioms for transitions to the state are strengthened because they are now redirected to the designated initial substate of this state.

A safety-states assignment **i** for the original model is naturally extended to the refined model by interpreting $i(s)$ for each of the new substates **s** of s_0 by $i(s_0)$. This satisfies (**C4**).

An example from the tank case study above would be the refinement of the state tank filling into two states not_stirring and stirring with transitions 1.70_energised and 1.70_deenergised between them.

4.3   Weakening Transition Guards and Preconditions

This transformation (item 5 in the list of Chapter 8 of [2]) does yield a subtype in the case that just state-transition and enabling axioms are used as the semantics of a statechart. However it clearly does not yield a theory extension once permission axioms are included. It also does not preserve safety properties because it allows execution of transitions in new situations.

Strengthening permission guards yields a theory extension if enabling axioms are omitted, however this again does not preserve safety properties.

4.4   Splitting and Re-targeting Transitions

A transition **t** (but not the initialisation) can be *re-targeted* by changing its target from a state **tt** to a substate tt_i of **tt** in the new subtype model. **tt** must be an unstructured state in the original model, ie, we re-target **t** in combination with dividing **tt** into new substates. This restriction is not made explicit in [2], and is necessary because otherwise **t** could be redirected to a substate of **tt** disjoint from its original target, the designated initial substate of **tt**. Re-targeting results in a stronger theory for the new model, because the consequent of the state-transition axiom for **t** will become stronger. Permission and enabling axioms are unaffected.

Re-targeting to a state which is not a substate of the original target is clearly not a subtyping except in the case that the original target is an unrecoverable hazard state: it violates the state-transition axioms for the transition concerned.

A transition can be split either at its source or its target. Figure 7 shows a simple example of a source splitting of transition **t**. In a source splitting, the original guards, generations and postconditions must be repeated on each of the new transitions, and these can additionally define new generations and postconditions for particular cases. The guards cannot be changed. Every substate of **ss** must become a source for a split case of **t** in order that the enabling axioms are preserved.

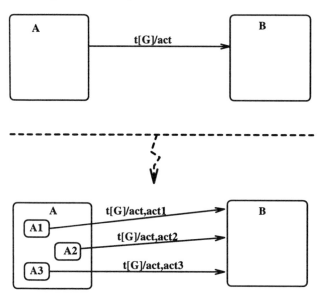

Figure 7: Source-splitting a Transition

The permission axioms for **t** are preserved by a source-splitting (and indeed, this is the case even if not every substate of the source state is maintained as a source of a split transition). Initialisation axioms are unaffected, whilst state-transition axioms for **t** are strengthened because state$_\mathbf{A}$ = **ss** implies that state$_\mathbf{C}$ = **ss**$_i$ for some substate **ss**$_i$ of **ss**; but then the theory of **C** implies that **t** from **ss**$_i$ establishes all the generations and postconditions that **t** from **ss** did in **A**. Obviously state-transition axioms would not be preserved if we allowed **t** to not be sourced from every substate of **ss**. Thus this transformation is a theory extension.

A (non-initial) transition **t** can be split at its target state **tt** by breaking the original guard into several (disjoint and exhaustive) cases, assigning these to new transitions for the same event, and giving these targets within or at the original target. New generations and post-conditions can be added to each case. Again, **tt** must be unstructured in the original model.

4.5 Redefining Generations

Contrary to item 9 in Chapter 8 of [2], we cannot allow generated events to be arbitrarily redefined in a refinement. In terms of standard concepts of subtyping such a redefinition is invalid because then the behaviour of a subtype object may not be simulatable by any supertype object. Instead, new generations can be added to any transition, including the initialisation, provided they do not introduce inconsistency due to multiple event sends to the same receiver, or infinite cycles of internal behaviour.

Likewise in the case of entry and exit generations (item 10): new generations can be added but old generations must be maintained, as must their order.

5 Examples

The introduction of new components in the specification can be illustrated on the tank example by considering the enhancement of the manhole monitoring by an additional sensor (independent of sensor 1.80) which can also trigger the emergency actions. This is shown in Figure 8. The resulting system has the states which are derived from those of the old system, by partitioning them into four substates corresponding to the states of the new sensor 1.81. We can argue that the new component does not introduce new hazard states into the system because its hazard states (1.81 stuck energised, 1.81 stuck de-energised) can only result in a system hazard if 1.80 is also in one of its hazard states at this point.

In fact we can derive the new statechart by a series of state and transition splitting transformations: splitting the Energised state for 1.80 into the five states where at least one of 1.80 and 1.81 are energised, etc (Figure 9). The **on** and **off** transitions have been split at their source and destinations (relative to the statechart of a single sensor). The Failed Energised state is interpreted by the state where both sensors are in this state. The Failed Deenergised state is interpreted by the collection of states where one or both sensors are in this state, and the other is in the Failed Energised state. It is direct to check that the safety states assignment of the abstract model can be extended to this new model via this interpretation. For example, any state in which both sensors are stuck energised or stuck deenergised must be mapped to dangerous error, and a state in which one of the sensors is deenergised and the manhole is open and the controller is running must be mapped to the error state.

The interpretation also yields a refinement in the sense of Section 3.2, since the only axioms of the abstract system not provable in the new version are state-transition axioms for the transitions of **sticks_energised**, 1.81_**sticks_energised**,

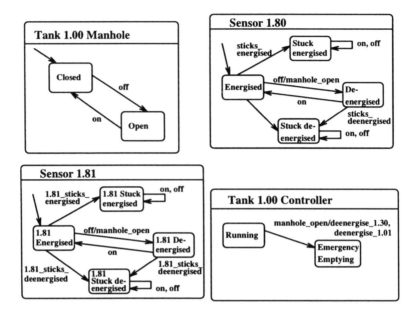

Figure 8: Revised Tank Manhole Monitor

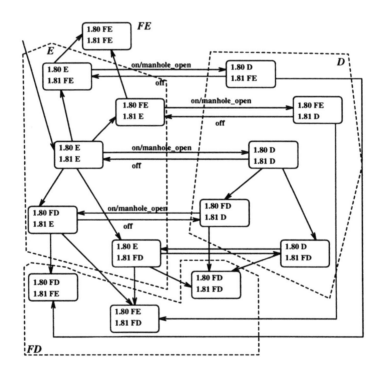

Figure 9: Expanded Statechart of New Monitor

sticks_deenergised and 1.81_**sticks_deenergised**, which have been redirected from a dangerous error state to a normal operation state. Thus the set $\mathbf{H_A}$ of hazard axioms has been reduced in size.

The FMEA sequence, in the original analysis, for the event of 1.80 failing energised, now only arises if the additional constraint that 1.81 has failed is true.

The FTA of Figure 5 retains the same structure in the new system, however the states 1.80 failed de-energised, 1.80 failed energised, etc in the left-hand branch can now be traced further to the strict sub-states (1.80 failed de-energised and 1.81 failed de-energised), (1.80 failed de-energised and 1.81 failed energised), etc.

If the probability of an individual 1.80 or 1.81 failing energised is $\alpha < 1$, then the probability of the top event due to the original branch 1.80 failed energised has been reduced from α to $\alpha * \alpha$.

6 Conclusions

We have related traditional concepts of statechart refinement to safety-state assignments and shown that constraints can be placed upon such refinements which preserve the results of some safety analysis.

The existence of an abstraction function from a statechart $\mathbf{D}$ to a statechart $\mathbf{C}$ satisfying the constraints of Section 3.3 has been shown to provide a theory extension of $\Gamma_\mathbf{C}$ by $\Gamma_\mathbf{D}$ which preserves axioms of state-transitions, permission and enabling. In turn, such a theory extension has been shown to preserve the results of FMEA, FTA and safety-states assignment. Section 4 has enumerated specific transformations which provide suitable abstraction functions.

The techniques given here are related to the concepts of *abstract interpretation* used in program analysis [4] and, at the program level, to software fault-tree analysis [9].

References

[1] Bicarregui J. C., Lano K. C. and Maibaum T. S. E. *Objects, Associations and Subsystems: a hierarchical approach to encapsulation*, ECOOP 97, to appear in LNCS, 1997.

[2] Cook S. and Daniels J. *Designing Object Systems: Object-Oriented Modelling with Syntropy.* Prentice Hall, Sept 1994.

[3] Fiadeiro J. and Maibaum T. *Temporal Theories as Modularisation Units for Concurrent System Specification*, Formal Aspects of Computing 4(3), pp. 239–272, 1992

[4] Hankin C. and Le Matayer D. *Deriving Algorithms from Type Inference Systems.* Proceedings of POPL '94, ACM Press, 1994.

[5] International Electrotechnical Commission. *Draft IEC 1508 – Functional Safety: Safety-Related Systems*, 1996.

[6] Jones C. B. *Systematic Software Construction using VDM.* Prentice Hall, 1990.

[7] Lano K. and Sanchez A. *Specification of a Chemical Process Controller in VDM^{++} and B*, ROOS project document GR/K68783-11, Dept. of Computing, Imperial College, November 1996.

[8] Lano K., Goldsack S., Bicarregui J. and Kent S. *Integrating VDM^{++} and Real-time System Design*, ZUM 97 Proceedings, LNCS, 1997.

[9] Leveson N. *Safeware: system safety and computers*, Addison-Wesley, 1995. ISBN 0-201-11972-2.

[10] Ministry of Defence, *The Procurement of Safety Critical Software in Defence Equipment*, DEF-STAN 00-55, Issue 1, Part 2. Room 5150, Kentigern House, 65 Brown St., Glasgow G2 8EX, 1997.

Automated Verification of Safety Requirements using CCS and Binary Decision Diagrams

Reiner Lichtenecker and Klaus Gotthardt

Department of Electrical Engineering, Fernuniversität-GH-Hagen,

58084-Hagen, Germany

Abstract

There is a growing interest in the application of formal methods in the software development process, especially in the area of safety critical applications. Formal verification, however, often requires a high effort. With the availability of automated methods this effort could be largely reduced and thus enable a more widespread application of formal methods. Process Calculi like CCS are a common formalism for modelling and verification of protocols and distributed applications. A major problem in computer-aided verification of CCS models is the inevitable combinatorial state space explosion. Existing verification tools mostly operate on an explicit representation of the state space in form of a labelled transition system (LTS), and often already fail in establishing this LTS. Binary Decision Diagrams (BDDs) are based on a compact, implicit representation of transition systems and state sets and therefore offer a promising alternative. In this paper we describe the implementation of such a verification tool based on BDDs. The tool accepts CCS-definitions, automatically derives suitable encodings of states and actions and creates an efficient encoding of the LTS which accounts for the structure of the modularized CCS-hierarchy. Additionally it ensures that the specification models a finite transition system. The efficiency of this method will be investigated with two examples where the first is Milners well known scheduler, which is mostly of academic relevance as a benchmark for verification tools. The second example, which is of more practical interest, considers the popular CSMA/CD-communication protocol, including propagation delays on the communication channel. As such it allows more relevant conclusions about the appropriateness of the created tool.

1 Introduction

The requirements in software development increasingly evolve towards provably correct software design, especially in safety-critical applications. A precondition for this is a systematic software development process, which guarantees adherence of the application to specified properties already during design. The objective of formal verification is to establish this proof by an abstract implementation model. A number of formalisms for system modeling and verification are known from the literature. Among these formalisms we especially consider the algebraic process calculus CCS (Calculus of Communicating Systems [1]). Process algebras describe systems as a composition of processes, synchronized by common actions. Hence, process algebras particurlarly ease a compact representation of the behaviour of concurrent, distributed systems.

Correctness is proven by establishing a bisimulation equivalence between the implementation model and a reference specification. This task can be supported by suitable software tools, such as the well known *Concurrency Workbench* (CWB) [5]. However, automated proofs often fail due to the complexity of real systems which lead to huge state spaces. This can already happen in the first step: the generation of the labelled transition system from the CCS specification. In practice one therefore often simplifies the implementation model or omits the proof of certain system properties [6].

Since their introduction by Bryant [7], Binary Decisions Diagrams (BDDs) have lead to a substantial increase of the state space size of automatically verifiable systems [8] [9], especially in the area of hardware verification. Thus, application of this technique to the verification of process algebraic specifications is an obvious idea. A basic discussion of this approach can be found in [10]. However, automatic translation from CCS models to BDDs and the application to models of realistic systems have not been investigated by now.

In this paper we describe first experiences in the design and application of a tool for automatic verification of CCS models with BDDs. After a short presentation of CCS in section 2 we present in section 3 an introduction to BDDs, the implementation of CCS operators like composition or summation and proofs by bisimulation. Following the description of the automatic translation, we consider the model of a scheduler [1] which has become a benchmark for comparing verification tools of process algebraic specifications. In section 6 we finally apply this method to a realistic model of the well known CSMA/CD-protocol.

2 The process calculus CCS

In CCS a process is described by its interaction with other processes and the environment. Its behaviour is defined as the possible sequences of atomic actions it can execute. Associated with every action α is a co-action $\bar{\alpha}$. We sometimes refer to actions α as input actions and $\bar{\alpha}$ as output actions. The operators of CCS are shown in (1). Actions are generally denoted by lower case letters while capital letters are used to identify processes. L represents a set of actions and f a relabelling function.

$$
\begin{array}{lll}
E ::= & \alpha.E & \text{prefix } \alpha.E \xrightarrow{\alpha} E \\
& 0 & \text{inactivity} \\
& E_1 + E_2 & \text{mutual exclusion} \\
& E_1 \mid E_2 & \text{parallel composition} \\
& A \stackrel{\text{def}}{=} E_i & \text{process definition} \\
& E[f] & \text{relabelling} \\
& P \backslash L & \text{restriction}
\end{array}
\tag{1}
$$

The prefix $\alpha.E$ defines a process which can execute an action α and subsequently behaves like process E. The more intuitive notation $\alpha.E \xrightarrow{\alpha} E$ is often used to denote the corresponding transition. The sum $E_1 + E_2$ defines a process which may either behave like process E_1 or E_2. The special process 0 has no behaviour, i.e. it cannot execute any actions. More complex models can be built using parallel composition $E_1 \mid E_2$. The composed process can engage in an action a, if it is enabled in either E_1 or E_2, or can execute an internal τ-action which results from a synchronization of E_1 and E_2 via some action α and its corresponding co-action $\bar{\alpha}$. In general, τ-actions are used to model internal actions of processes which cannot synchronize with any external event. We will not go further into the description of the language at this point. For a comprehensive explanation of CCS, the reader is referred to [1].

One way of verifying the desired behaviour of an implementation is to establish an equivalence between its CCS model and a CCS model of the specification. Among the many possible equivalence relations, (weak) bisimulation is probably the most useful, as it abstracts from the internal τ-actions and is still capable of detecting possible deadlocks, as opposed to the weaker trace-equivalence relation. Bisimulation equivalence of two processes P and Q is defined as follows:

A binary relation $\mathcal{S} \subseteq \mathcal{P} \times \mathcal{P}$ over processes is a *bisimulation*, if $(P, Q) \in \mathcal{S}$ implies for all actions from the action set $(\alpha \in Act)$

$$\begin{aligned} &(i) \text{ If } P \xrightarrow{\alpha} P', \text{ then, for some } Q', Q \xRightarrow{\hat{\alpha}} Q' \text{ and } (P', Q') \in \mathcal{S} \\ &(ii) \text{ If } Q \xrightarrow{\alpha} Q', \text{ then, for some } P', P \xRightarrow{\hat{\alpha}} P' \text{ und } (P', Q') \in \mathcal{S} \end{aligned} \qquad (2)$$

In the above definition, $P \xRightarrow{\hat{\alpha}} P'$ denotes an observable action α with any number of preceding or succeeding τ-actions. Intuitively, two processes P and Q are bisimulation-equivalent, if they cannot be distinguished from each other by a mere investigation of their possible, externally visible behaviour.

3 Binary Decision Diagrams (BDDs)

BDDs are a canonical representation of boolean functions. They often provide a substantially more compact representation than other canonical forms like the disjunctive or conjunctive normal form. A BDD is an acyclic, directed graph which codes a binary decision tree. The variables of the BDD are totally ordered, so that along every path from the root to the leafes the variables always occur in the same order. Fig. 1 illustrates the creation of a BDD from the decision tree of the function $(a \lor b) \land c$ for the variable ordering $a \vartriangleleft b \vartriangleleft c$.

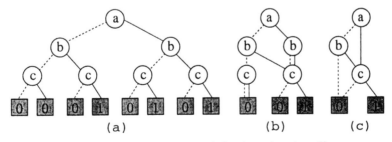

Figure 1: Building a BDD of the function $(a \lor b) \land c$

Every node of the tree is labelled by a variable and refers to two subtrees, which are called *Lo* and *Hi*. Values 0 and 1 represent the leaves of the tree. In Fig. 1, the solid edges refer to the subtree *Hi* which will be reached, if the value

1 is assigned to the variable in the represented function. Correspondingly the dashed lines lead to the subtree Lo which will be reached if 0 is assigned to the variable. An efficient representation of the function is achieved by merging identical subtrees, as shown in Fig. 1(b). Furthermore, nodes with identical subtrees Lo and Hi will be removed from the graph. By repeatedly applying these rules we finally arrive at the BDD shown in Fig. 1(c).

3.1 Operations on Binary Decision Diagrams

A basic operation on BDDs is the *restriction* $f \mid_{x=v}$, which assigns a constant value $v \in \{0, 1\}$ to variable x in function f. If function f is represented by a BDD, then restriction can be efficiently computed in the case that x is the variable of the root node of this graph, i.e. $x = \text{Var}(f)$.

$$f \mid_{x=v} \ \stackrel{\text{def}}{=} \ \begin{cases} Lo(f) & \text{if } v=0 \\ Hi(f) & \text{if } v=1 \end{cases}$$

According to the Shannon expansion for boolean functions any binary operation $\langle op \rangle$ like conjunction or disjunction on BDDs can be evaluated using the following recursive definition:

$$f \langle op \rangle g \equiv [\neg x \wedge (f \mid_{x=0} \langle op \rangle g \mid_{x=0})] \vee [x \wedge (f \mid_{x=1} \langle op \rangle g \mid_{x=1})]$$

where $x = \min(\text{Var}(f), \text{Var}(g))$. Efficient computation algorithms are given by Bryant [7]. In average the complexity of binary operations is in $O(|f| \cdot |g|)$, where $|f|$ denotes the number of nodes in BDD f. In addition to the combinatorial operators, existential quantification, universal quantification and renaming of variables will be needed later. Using the restriction operator, existential quantification $\exists x.f$ evaluates to:

$$\exists x.f = f \mid_{x=0} \vee f \mid_{x=1}$$

Correspondingly, we have for the universal quantification $\forall x.f$:

$$\forall x.f = f \mid_{x=0} \wedge f \mid_{x=1}$$

Substitution of a variable x by another variable y in a BDD f, denoted by $f[y/x]$, can be done based on existential quantification as follows:

$$f[y/x] \equiv \exists x.(x=y) \wedge f$$

Operations like restriction and existential quantification extend to vectors of binary variables in the obvious way. If $x = \{x_0, x_1, \dots x_{n-1}\}$ is such a vector and $v \in \{0, 1\}^n$ is a vector with constant elements, then we have:

$$f \mid_{x=v} \ \equiv \ f \mid_{x_0=v_0} \mid_{x_1=v_1} \mid_{x_2=v_2} \ \cdots \ \mid_{x_{n-1}=v_{n-1}}$$

$$\exists x.f \ \equiv \ \exists x_0.\exists x_1.\dots.\exists x_{n-1}.f$$

3.2 Evaluation of CCS operators

CCS specifications can always be represented as labelled transition systems. With BDDs we describe such a system as a relation $R(\alpha, x, x')$ where α represents a CCS action and the states x, x' of the transition system correspond to processes of the CCS specification. The relation R is a binary function which

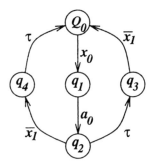

CCS representation:

$$Q_0 = x_0.a_0.(\tau.\bar{x}_1.Q_0 + \bar{x}_1.\tau.Q_0)$$

representation as transition relation:

$$\begin{aligned}
R_{Q_0}(\alpha, x, x') &= (\alpha = x_0) \wedge (x = Q_0) \wedge (x' = q_1) \\
&\vee (\alpha = a_0) \wedge (x = q_1) \wedge (x' = q_2) \\
&\vee (\alpha = \tau) \wedge (x = q_2) \wedge (x' = q_3) \\
&\vee (\alpha = \bar{x}_1) \wedge (x = q_3) \wedge (x' = Q_0) \\
&\vee \ldots
\end{aligned}$$

Figure 2: representation of a process in CCS and as transition relation

can be represented by BDDs in a straightforward way. If the transition $x \xrightarrow{\alpha} x'$ denoted by the triple (α, x, x') is an element of the relation, i.e. $R(\alpha, x, x') = 1$, then the transition system includes a state or process x which will pass over into the process x' by an action α.

Fig. 2 illustrates the relation of a CCS specification, labelled transition system and transition relation. The example describes a subprocess of Milners [1] scheduler specification which will be treated in more detail below. It should be observed that process Q_0 is not represented by the whole transition system, but rather by the initial state which is labelled Q_0. States q_i do not explicitly appear in the CCS specification. In general, they correspond to the dots between two succeeding actions, for example state q_1 in $x_0.a_0$.

To enable the evaluation of CCS operators like *restriction, composition* and *relabelling* on transition systems represented by BDDs, we first have to define an encoding of actions and states. The encoding of states in elementary transition systems, i.e. systems only described using prefix- and sum-operators in CCS, is apparent: if the system consists of M states, they will be encoded by the binary representation of the natural numbers 0 to $(M-1)$. The state vector $x = \{x_1, x_2, \ldots\}$ consists of $\lceil ld(M) \rceil$ binary valued variables. The set of all actions α occuring in the system can be represented in a similar way. However, we have to account for the fact that the τ-action and complementary actions should be easily recognizable in order to minimize the computational effort. We therefore always assign the value 0 to the τ-action. Complementary actions are distinguished by the first Bit of the vector which encodes an action α. We mark an output-action by the value $\alpha_0 = 0$ and the complementary input-action by $\alpha_0 = 1$.

3.2.1 Composition

The composition of two systems $R_1(\alpha, x_1, x_1')$ and $R_2(\alpha, x_2, x_2')$ generates a new system $R_p(\alpha, \langle x_1, x_2 \rangle, \langle x_1', x_2' \rangle)$. The transition relation of the new system consists of several subrelations. On the one hand, in a state $\langle x_1, x_2 \rangle$ system R_p can execute every transition which R_1 is able to execute in state x_1. Hence, the composition contains all possible transitions defined by the set $R_1(\alpha, x_1, x_1') \wedge (x_2' = x_2)$. Likewise, the system can perform any transition from subsystem R_2. This set is characterized by $R_2(\alpha, x_2, x_2') \wedge (x_1' = x_1)$. Finally we have to consider the set of τ-transitions resulting from a simultaneous state transition of both subsystems by complementary actions. This set of transitions is characterized by the following logical equation:

$$(\alpha = \tau) \wedge \exists \alpha . [(R_1 |_{\alpha_0 = 0} \wedge R_2 |_{\alpha_0 = 1}) \vee (R_1 |_{\alpha_0 = 1} \wedge R_2 |_{\alpha_0 = 0})]$$

Due to the chosen encoding of actions, where α_0 distinguishes complementary actions, $\exists \alpha . (R_1|_{\alpha_0=0} \wedge R_2|_{\alpha_0=1})$ specifies the set of all state transitions in which R_1 executes an output and subsystem R_2 the corresponding input. In summary, we represent the composition as follows:

$$
\begin{aligned}
R_p(\alpha, \langle x_1, x_2 \rangle, \langle x_1', x_2' \rangle) &= R_1(\alpha, x_1, x_1') \mid R_2(\alpha, x_2, x_2') \\
&= R_1(\alpha, x_1, x_1') \wedge (x_2' = x_2) \\
&\quad \vee R_2(\alpha, x_2, x_2') \wedge (x_1' = x_1) \\
&\quad \vee (\alpha = \tau) \wedge \exists \alpha . [(R_1|_{\alpha_0 = 0} \wedge R_2|_{\alpha_0 = 1}) \\
&\quad \vee (R_1|_{\alpha_0 = 1} \wedge R_2|_{\alpha_0 = 0})]
\end{aligned}
$$

3.2.2 Restriction

Restriction $R(\alpha, x, x') \backslash [a_1, a_2, \ldots]$ removes all transitions from the relation caused by actions $[a_1, a_2, \ldots]$ and co-actions $[\bar{a}_1, \bar{a}_2, \ldots]$. The set of removed actions is represented again as a BDD. It results from $[(\alpha = a_1) \vee (\alpha = a_2) \vee \ldots]$. As the new transition relation, we have:

$$R(\alpha, x, x') \backslash [a_1, a_2, \ldots] = R(\alpha, x, x') \wedge \neg \exists \alpha_0 . [(\alpha = a_1) \vee (\alpha = a_2) \vee \ldots]$$

With the existential quantification of α_0, transitions by actions $[a_1, a_2, \ldots]$ and complementary actions $[\bar{a}_1, \bar{a}_2, \ldots]$ will be removed according to the definition of restriction.

3.2.3 Relabelling

Finally, relabelling of an action in the relation $R(\alpha, x, x')[b/a]$ is represented as follows:

$$
\begin{aligned}
R(\alpha, x, x')[b/a] &= R(\alpha, x, x') \wedge (\alpha \neq a) \wedge (\alpha \neq \bar{a}) \\
&\quad \vee (\alpha = b) \wedge R(\alpha, x, x') \mid_{\alpha = a} \vee (\alpha = \bar{b}) \wedge R(\alpha, x, x') \mid_{\alpha = \bar{a}}
\end{aligned}
$$

Restriction $R(\alpha, x, x')|_{\alpha = a}$ yields the set of transitions $x \xrightarrow{a} x'$ of the system caused by an input-action a.

3.3 Bisimulation Proof

The definition of bisimulation given in equation (2) can be almost literally translated into a computation on BDDs. The transition relation $\xrightarrow{\alpha}$ corresponds to the representation of the relation $R(\alpha, x, x')$. The representation of the relation $\xRightarrow{\hat{\alpha}} = \tau^* . \alpha . \tau^*$ contains additional τ-transitions $(\alpha = \tau) \wedge (x' = x)$ connecting every state to itself as well as all transitions (a, x, x'), such that there exist intermediate states y and y' with $R(a, y, y')$ and the states x, y and y, x' are connected by zero or more τ-transitions in R.

In order to compute the representation of $\xRightarrow{\hat{\alpha}}$ we require the transitive, reflexive closure R_τ of R. A pair of states (x, x') is contained in R_τ, if the relation R contains an arbitrary sequence of τ-transitions connecting states x and x'. Thus R_τ can be computed as [1]:

$$R'(x, x') \equiv (x' = x) \vee R(\tau, x, x')$$
$$R_\tau \equiv \mu Z[R'(x, x') \vee \exists y . [R'(x, y) \wedge Z(y, x')]]$$

Using R_τ, the representation $\hat{R}$ of $\stackrel{\hat{\alpha}}{\Longrightarrow}$ is computed as:

$$\hat{R}(\alpha, x, x') \equiv (\alpha = \tau) \wedge (x' = x)$$
$$\vee \exists y_1 . \exists y_2 . [R_\tau(x, y_1) \wedge (R(\alpha, y_1, y_2) \wedge R_\tau(y_2, x'))]$$

Given two transition systems $P(\alpha, x_1, x_1')$ and $Q(\alpha, x_2, x_2')$, the bisimulation-relation $S(x_1, x_2)$ is computed as the least fixpoint of:

$$S(x_1, x_2) \equiv \nu S [\forall \alpha, x_1' . [P(\alpha, x_1, x_1') \Rightarrow \exists x_2' . [\hat{Q}(\alpha, x_2, x_2') \wedge S(x_1', x_2')]]$$
$$\wedge \forall \alpha, x_2' . [Q(\alpha, x_2, x_2') \Rightarrow \exists x_1' . [\hat{P}(\alpha, x_1, x_1') \wedge S(x_1', x_2')]]]$$

4 Automatic Translation of CCS Models to BDDs

For simplicity, we only describe the translation for the case of the parallel composition of elementary systems. During translation, suitable encodings of actions and processes are determined and representations of elementary transition systems as BDDs are computed. Operations like parallel composition, renaming and restriction are computed on the resulting BDD's, using the equations described above.

First, the description of the system is split up into a sequence of elementary CCS operations, as they appear in the definition of the grammar in (1). Next, we determine dependencies among the processes. Such a dependency results for example from a parallel composition $E = E_1 \mid E_2$. Obviously, the BDD-representations of processes E_1 and E_2 must be known before the transition system of process E can be generated. Similar dependencies arise from renaming and restriction. These dependencies define a hierarchical structure of the whole model, with the elementary processes at the bottom of the hierarchy. Figure 3 shows a simple example.

The set of transitions of an elementary system can now be determined from its CCS description using the recursive functions shown in Table 1. *Def(E)* denotes the defining equation of a process E which is either of the form $E = a.E_1$ or $E = E_1 + E_2$. Function *Trans*$(\cdot)$ computes the set of all transitions for a given definition. To determine the set of transitions for a process which is defined as a sum, we have to rename the first component E_1 of all transitions (a, E_1, E_2) of the constituing processes. This renaming is computed by function *Link*$(\cdot, \cdot)$. The notation $(a, E_1, E_2) :: l$ denotes a list of transitions consisting of a single transition $E_1 \stackrel{a}{\longrightarrow} E_2$ followed by a transition list l.

Having computed the transitions of an elementary process, the number N of its states can be determined. Since these states are encoded as natural numbers

---

[1] We use the μ-calculus notation $\mu Z[f]$ to denote the least fixpoint, i.e. the smallest solution of the equation $Z = f(Z)$, and $\nu Z[f]$ to denote the greatest fixpoint Z of a function f

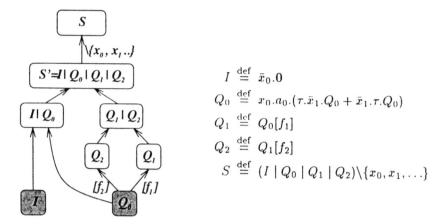

$$I \stackrel{\text{def}}{=} \bar{x}_0.0$$
$$Q_0 \stackrel{\text{def}}{=} x_0.a_0.(\tau.\bar{x}_1.Q_0 + \bar{x}_1.\tau.Q_0)$$
$$Q_1 \stackrel{\text{def}}{=} Q_0[f_1]$$
$$Q_2 \stackrel{\text{def}}{=} Q_1[f_2]$$
$$S \stackrel{\text{def}}{=} (I \mid Q_0 \mid Q_1 \mid Q_2)\backslash\{x_0, x_1, \ldots\}$$

Figure 3: Hierarchical structure of the translation of a CCS model

$$Trans(E = a.E_1) \equiv \{(a, E, E_1)\} \cup Trans(Def(E_1))$$
$$Trans(E = E_1 + E_2) \equiv Link(E, Trans(Def(E_1)) \cup Trans(Def(E_2)))$$
$$Link(E, (a, E_1, E_2) :: l) \equiv \{(a, E, E_2)\} \cup Link(E, l)$$
$$Link(E, \emptyset) \equiv \emptyset$$

Table 1: Calculation of transition sets of elementary subsystems

in the range 0 to $(N-1)$, the vector of binary variables describing the process states has dimension $\lceil ld(N) \rceil$. With this encoding of states and actions the BDD representing a process E is computed as the disjunction of its transitions:

$$R(\alpha, x, x') \equiv \bigvee_{(a,E_1,E_2)\in Trans(Def(E))} (\alpha = C(a)) \wedge (x = C(E_1)) \wedge (x' = C(E_2))$$

where function $C(\cdot)$ determines the encoding of its argument state or action.

5 Scheduler Specification in CCS

Suppose a set of processes P_i, $0 \le i \le (N-1)$ shall be controlled in such a way, that each process repeatedly executes an associated task. Additionally it is required that the processes are started sequentially, i.e. P_{i+1} may not begin execution of its task prior to P_i. A scheduler is required to control the execution of tasks. The CCS specification of the scheduler shown below consists of an initialization process I and N processes Q_i which communicate with each other via actions x_j.

$$I \stackrel{\text{def}}{=} \bar{x}_0.0$$
$$Q_0 \stackrel{\text{def}}{=} x_0.a_0.(\tau.\bar{x}_1.Q_0 + \bar{x}_1.\tau.Q_0)$$
$$\ldots$$
$$Q_{N-2} \stackrel{\text{def}}{=} x_{N-2}.a_{N-2}(\tau.\bar{x}_{N-1}.Q_{N-2} + \bar{x}_{N-1}.\tau.Q_{N-2})$$
$$Q_{N-1} \stackrel{\text{def}}{=} x_{N-1}.a_{N-1}(\tau.\bar{x}_0.Q_{N-1} + \bar{x}_0.\tau.Q_{N-1})$$

Each internal process Q_i of the scheduler awaits an initialization signal x_i and then starts the external process P_i by issuing a signal a_i. Subsequently it initializes, prior to or after an internal computation which is modelled by an externally invisible τ action, its neighbouring process Q_{i+1}. The composed scheduler for the management of N tasks is specified as:

$$S_N \stackrel{\text{def}}{=} (I \mid Q_0 \mid Q_1 \mid \ldots \mid Q_{N-1}) \backslash \{x_0, \ldots, x_{N-1}\}$$

To prove that our model of the scheduler starts the processes P_i in the required order, a reference process must be defined which exhibits the specified, externally visible behaviour. We require that the scheduler cyclically issues the sequence of signals $a_0, a_1, \ldots, a_{N-1}$. Thus its specification can be given as:

$$\text{SCHED}_N \stackrel{\text{def}}{=} a_0.a_1.a_2. \ldots .a_{N-1}.\text{SCHED}_N$$

Table 2 contains computation times in seconds for different numbers N of composed processes. Column T_{COMP} contains the times required to compute the BDD representation of the composed model, T_{REACH} the time for computation of the set of reachable states and T_{BISIM} the computation times required to determine the set of bisimulating states. For comparison, the last column of the table contains computation results determined for the CWB [5] for models of size $2, 4$ and 8. All computations were carried out on a Sparc 10 with 32MB memory. As can be seen from these results, BDDs can easily handle systems with approximately $3 \cdot 10^6$ states and $3 \cdot 10^8$ transitions. Systems of this size are clearly out of reach of conventional state space investigation techniques.

N	states	transitions	T_{BISIM}	T_{COMP}	T_{REACH}	CWB
2	13	19	0, 40	0, 06	0, 08	0, 07
4	97	241	0, 87	0, 77	0, 30	9, 41
8	3073	13825	2, 50	1, 48	2, 40	1615, 17
12	73729	479233	7, 20	1, 93	7, 27	–
16	1572865	13369345	16, 32	2, 80	18, 63	–
20	31457281	330301441	28, 50	3, 77	39, 28	–

Table 2: Verification results of the scheduler, times given in seconds

6 CSMA/CD protocol-specification in CCS

The scheduler example indicates that it is possible to handle huge state spaces efficiently with BDDs. However, this example is mostly of academic interest. Therefore, we have modelled the well known CSMA/CD protocol, including propagation delay effects. For lack of space we only give a brief overview of the model. A thorough description can be found in [12].

The general structure of the model and its specification, which is called the service specification, is shown in Figure 4. Each process accesses the transmission medium through a *medium access controller* (MAC). Events rec_i and $send_i$ model the transmission and reception of a data packet by user process i. User processes are not explicitly modelled. We assume, that send-requests occur randomly. In inorder to account for transmission delays, the model contains explicit events for the start and end of the transmission of a data packet on the

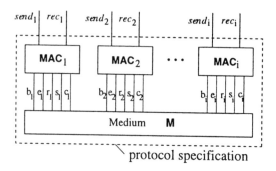

Figure 4: Structure of the protocol specification

channel. A collision occurs, if two MAC's concurrently start a transmission or a MAC starts transmission while the channel is busy. Detected collisions are signalled to each MAC through events c_i. The meanings of events occuring in the protocol model are listed below.

b_i: MAC_i starts the transmission of a packet
e_i: MAC_i ends the transmission of a packet
r_i: MAC_i receives the beginning of a packet
s_i: MAC_i receives the end of a packet
c_i: MAC_i detects a collision of transmitted packets on the medium

Different from the protocol model the service specification contains explicit connections between all processes, indicated by signals q_i and f_i. With each user process is associated a process buffer PB_i. The central buffer CB is required to account for the coordination which stems from the mutually exclusive use of a single resource i.e. the transmission medium, by different concurrent processes. As a whole, the buffers contained in the service specification reflect the storage capacities of the MAC's and the medium in the protocol model, where the capacity of the latter is due to propagation delays.

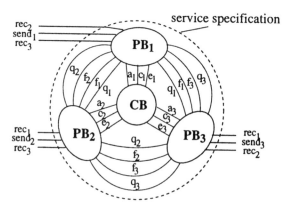

Figure 5: Structure of the service specification

6.1 Verification Results

Different from the previously described example of the scheduler, model and specification of the protocol have state spaces of almost equal size. Therefore, the following table of computation times contains separate numbers of states and transitions of both models.

process	states	transitions	T_{REACH}	T_{COMP}	T_{BISIM}	CWB
protocol	425	1122	1, 93	7,52	447,8	52,9
service	484	1229	2, 50			

As can be seen, times T_{COMP} required for the computation of the composed transition systems are again negligible. Considering the complexity of the protocol specification in comparison to the previously handled scheduler example, the number of states and transitions is surprisingly small. This results from a strong synchronization of MACs in the protocol model and PB-processes in the description of the service.

Computation of the bisimulation using BDDs is slower than the time required by the CWB by about a factor of 9. This is mainly caused by the complexity of the specification. While in the scheduler example the process describing the required behaviour contains only a few states, the protocol model and its specification have state spaces of almost identical size. This leads to large BDDs which are computed as intermediate results during the evaluation of the fixpoint equation for bisimulation and thus results in the observed computation times.

7   Conclusions

We have described the automatic translation of CCS models to a representation using BDDs and the application of BDD's to prove bisimulation equivalence for two example systems. In both cases the effort of generating a representation of the state space of the composed systems, which is often the primary bottleneck for the application of automatic verification methods, was negligible. Especially for the example of the scheduler model it could be shown that BDDs can handle state spaces which are far out of reach of conventional state space investigation techniques. Also the effort to determine bisimulation equivalence was small.

The effort to prove bisimulation equivalence in the case of the CSMA protocol, however, was much larger. This is not necessarily too surprising, because it is known from other work reported in the literature that in some cases explicit state space enumerating methods are more efficient than symbolic model checking using BDDs. The observation, that the proof of the scheduler is faster with BDDs than with the CWB, but slower for the CSMA-protocol should be further investigated. From this we expect some important ideas for the improvement of our BDD-tool. However, even with increased computation times a tool that is capable of handling huge states spaces is certainly preferable to a fast program that fails when applied to complex systems. Additionally, there are still some possibilities for improving efficiency which we have not yet investigated: for example splitting up the representation of the transition system into a set of smaller BDDs or a bisimulation preserving simplification of the model prior to bisimulation computation.

252

References

[1] R. Milner: "Communication and Concurrency", Prentice Hall International Series in Computer Science, ISBN 0-13-114984-9.

[2] H. Garavel, J. Sifakis: "Compilation and verification of lotos specifications", in L. Logrippo, R.L. Probert, H. Ural, editors, Procs. 10th International Symposium on Protocol Specification, Testing and Verification, pages 379-394, Amsterdam, June 1990, North-Holland.

[3] J.A. Manas, T. de Miguel, J. Salvachua, A. Azcorra: "Tool support to implement LOTOS formal specifications", Computer Networks and ISDN Systems, 25:815-839, 1993.

[4] R. Milner, J. Parrow, D. Walker: "A calculus of mobile processes", in Information and Computing 100, 1992, pp. 1-77.

[5] R. Cleaveland, J. Parrow, B. Steffen: "The concurrency workbench: A semantics-based tool for the verification of concurrent systems", ACM Transactions on Programming Languages and Systems, 15(1):36-72, January 1993.

[6] B. Krämer, G. Henze et al.: "Deriving ANSAware Applications from Formal Specifications", Proceedings of SDPS'95, 1995.

[7] Randal E. Bryant: "Graph-based Algorithms for Boolean function manipulation", IEEE Trans. Computers, C-35(8): 677 - 691, August 1986.

[8] J.R. Burch, E.M. Clarke, K.L. McMillan, D.L. Dill, J. Hwang: "Symbolic Model Checking: 10^{20} states and beyond". Technical Report, Carnegie Mellon University, 1989.

[9] K. L. McMillan: "Symbolic Model Checking: An approach to the State Explosion Problem.", PhD thesis, Carnegie Mellon Univeristy, 1992.

[10] R. Enders, T. Filkorn, D. Taubner: "Generating BDDs for symbolic model checking in CCS", in Distributed Computing, 1993, 6:155-164.

[11] Fernandez, Kerbrat, Mounier: "Symbolic equivalence checking", Computer Aided Verification, Proc. 5th Int. Conf., CAV'93, Elounda, Greece, June/July 1993

[12] K. Gotthardt, I. Scheler: "Formale Verifikation von Vielfach-Zugriffsprotokollen in CCS" GI-Fachtagung Softwaretechnik, Braunschweig, 1995

Consistency Checking by Type Inference and Constraint Satisfaction

Yahia LEBBAH

École des Mines de Nantes

Nantes, France

Abstract

This paper presents a method for checking the consistency of equations involving physical units, by applying techniques similar to type inference in programming languages over a formal specification of the system to check.

The checking is performed by a physical units inference system relying both on the algebraic structure of the international physical units system and a formal notation we designed to express the equations. The inference system is a three steps process: first, variables are assigned to the various expressions of the system; second, a set of equations representing the constraints of the international units system involving these variables is constructed. Finally, this set of equations is handled by a specific algorithm, which decides if the original system is consistent, and computes the physical units in a polymorphic way. We show that specializing the traditional type inference algorithms to the particular structure of the international units system boils down to solving classical linear systems symbolically.

1 Introduction

Type inference systems [8, 11] are widely used in programming languages — particularly in functional languages — to detect program inconsistencies. In this paper, we use a similar system to enforce physical units consistency in physical calculus. By physical calculus, we mean a system that can be modeled as a set of equations over physical quantities. Physical consistency is the satisfaction of the physical units constraints. For example, consider equation of voltage $U = R \times I$. It is inconsistent to have U in *milivolt*, R in *ohm* and I in *ampere* because the quantities do not have the same unit ($ohm \times ampere = volt \neq milivolt$). The detection of these inconsistencies is essential to the safety of industrial systems, particularly at EDF (Électricité de France) for which our method has been designed [6] and is now being applied.

Type inference can be described as the research of a mapping between the different parts of a program and the set of data types as {*int, string, int→ string*}. To use type inference, we must find a mapping between the set of components of the system and its specific data types. An algorithm of type inference can then be constructed using the algebraic structure of the types.

In our case, checking the physical consistency of a system is equivalent to

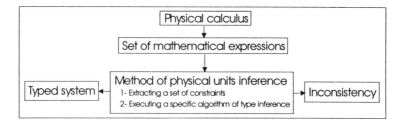

Figure 1: Consistency checking

finding a mapping between the different parts of this system and a subset of the international physical units system.

As depicted in figure 1, the physical calculus must be expressed by a mathematical notation. Our inference algorithm types the different parts of this physical calculus and checks their consistency.

We have applied our method to expressions translated from diagrams — called Function Block Diagram FBD — that are used by engineers to describe the power plants control regulation.

This paper is organized as follows: section 2 presents the problem of Function Block Diagram inconsistencies; section 2.1 describes a mathematical language to express the notion of physical calculus and define the problem of physical units inconsistency. Section 3 describes type inference systems in programming languages. Section 4 describes physical units inconsistency in terms of type inference and provides a general form to the equations produced. The algorithm of type inference is then presented in section 5.

2   Consistency in function block diagrams

FBD are graphical notations that present in a synthetic and a schematic way the principles of control and regulation. They are used by engineers to have a global view over the control, as well as designing control programs.

In practice, FBD is a network composed of elementary and standard blocks. The blocks are labeled using various kinds of operators e.g. $\{+, -, \times, \hat{}, \log, \sin\}$, or temporal operators such as {laplace transform, filtering, z transform, z corrector}. FBDs allow to express any of these expressions, and more. The nature of blocks may be glimpsed from a simplified illustration in figure 2, where:

- Op is the symbol of the block,

- $I_1, ... I_n$ are the inputs,

- $O_1, ..., O_m$ are the outputs, (some inputs are also outputs; this is a kind of feedback),

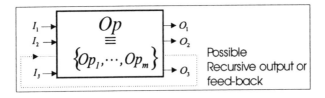

Figure 2: Representation of the different operators

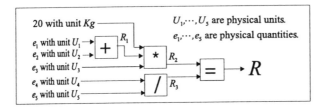

Figure 3: A simple example of a Function Block Diagram

- $Op_1, ..., Op_m$ is the decomposition of an operator Op in m sub-blocks, where $m > 1$.

We can denote every operator as $O_i = Op_i(I_1, ...I_n, O_1, ..., O_m)$. In a strict sense, we can denote every block: $y = Op_i(IO_1, ..., IO_{m+n})$, where $IO_{\{1,...,n\}} = I_{\{1,...n\}}$ and $IO_{\{n+1,...,m+n\}} = O_{\{1,...m\}}$.

The FBD expresses some physical calculus over quantities which generally represent measures coming from sensors. Figure 3 shows a simple example of an FBD.

2.1 Abstract representation of the physical calculus

An exact notation of physical calculus (or systems to check) is necessary to allow reasoning about the consistency checking. Table 1 shows a BNF notation of our language for expressing physical calculus. This notation gives a tool to the engineers to express their systems as a set of mathematical expressions. It is also straightforward to translate a FBD into this notation.

In this notation, the physical calculus is specified as a set of definitions $(id \equiv ExpAll)$ where $ExpAll$ represents any expression.

To differentiate between the two conceptual levels: the physical calculus and the expression (or conversion) over the physical units, we have added in this language the specific rule $ExpAll ::= Const.Phys$, where $Phys$ is the expression or conversion over the physical units.

For example, the specification of the calculus of the figure 3 by using this notation is: $S \equiv\!= (/(e_4.U_4, e_5.U_5), \times(20.Kg, +(e_1.U_1, e_2.U_2), e_3.U_3))$.

		⌈ Calcs: The axiom, γ: empty⌋
Calcs	::=	*Calc; Calcs* | γ
Calc	::=	*id* ≡ *ExpAll*
ExpAll	::=	*Exp* | *Const.Phys*
Exp	::=	*Op*(*ListArgs*) | *id* | *Const*
ListArgs	::=	*ListArgs, ExpAll* | *ExpAll*
		⌈ physical constants⌋
Const	::=	*id_const* | *Bool* | *Real* | ...
Bool	::=	true | false
		⌈ Operators ⌋
Op	::=	+ | × | / | ^ | if_then_else |...| pol | com | ...
		⌈ All expressions over physical units⌋
Phys	::=	m | kg | s | A | K | mol | cd | "expression of physical units"

Table 1: BNF Notation of our Language

From now on, we call the set of mathematical expressions generated by this grammar "physical expressions" to abstract our view away from particular representations used in engineering.

2.2 Consistency in physical expressions

Let us consider the expression $U = R \times I$ which is the equation of voltage. It is consistent if $Type(U) = Type(R) \times Type(I)$. For example, if this equation is specified as $U.volt = R.ohm \times I.ampere$, the equation will be consistent. Alternatively, if we have $V.volt = R.ohm \times I.miliampere$ then the equation becomes inconsistent. To preserve consistency, we must transform the latter equation to $V.volt = R.ohm \times I.(miliampere/1000)$. When the physical calculus is composed of many components, manual checking is difficult, therefore, an automatic tool would be very useful.

This problem can be tackled as follows: given a physical expression, can we assign, to the different parts of this expression, a physical unit such that the expression is consistent? We can also define this problem as finding out a mapping between the parts of the physical expression and the international units system.

This new view of physical inconsistency is equivalent to the problem of type inference in programming languages. We introduce in section 3 this domain, and discuss how ideas issued from type inference can be applied to our problem.

3 Type inference in programming languages

Type inference is used in programming languages for two main reasons [10]: safety and readability. Safety means that not all expressions in a program are thought to be correct, for example, computing the addition of a function and a text is plain nonsense, and may lead to an uncomputable expression. The readability gives a tool to express the semantics of expressions. For example, knowing that some function computes a real number from a list of integers substantially helps to understand how this function works. We obtain all the advantages when our type system admits automatic inference of types.

To find a mapping between a given program and its types, the type inference system processes in two steps. First, it extracts from the program a system of constraints expressing that the program is well-typed. Then, the constraints are solved. As we can see, the problem of finding a mapping is transformed into a constraint satisfaction problem.

Finally, the main difficulty in this process is the constraints resolution, which depends on the complexity of the mapping.

Let us take the following types generated by the Backus notation taken from [10]:

$$\underline{Types} \quad ::= \quad Int \mid Bool \mid list(\underline{Types}) \mid \underline{Types} \to \underline{Types} \mid Var$$
$$\underline{Var} \quad ::= \quad \alpha \mid \beta \mid \dots$$

Here type inference and checking is decidable, and well solved by Paterson and Wegman [9]. For example [10], $fun(g)fun(x)succ(g(x))$ can be typed, by using this system, as $(\alpha \to Int) \to (\alpha \to Int)$.

Let us now assume that we have polymorphic types, which are type expressions containing variables. For example [10]:

$$\underline{Poly} ::= \forall \ Var.\underline{Poly} \mid \underline{Types}$$

Using this kind of type expressions leads to a more complex mapping. The final consequence is that the problem of polymorphic type inference is classified as exponential (Mairson [7]).

In the next section, we shall discuss type inference in our particular set of types, which is the one of the international physical units system. We will show that finding out a particular mapping comes down to solve a linear constraints system.

4 Consistency and type inference

We first define the international physical units system. Then we explain how to extract the set of constraints over a physical expression. The resolution is discussed in section 5.

4.1 The algebraic structure of the international units

Physical quantities [1] can be included into sets, where a set contains those physical quantities which can be compared with each other. Lengths, diameters, distances, heights, wavelengths, constitute such a set. When we choose a particular quantity as quantity of reference called the unit, all other quantities can be expressed according to this unit, by the product of this unit by a number. This number is called the numeric value of the quantity expressed using this unit. Thus, every quantity can be expressed with one or several units.

For example, the wavelength of one of the spectral stripes of the sodium is $\lambda = 5.896 \times 10^{-7}.m$. Here, λ is the symbol of the physical quantity *wavelength*, m is the symbol of the length unit the *meter*; 5.896×10^{-7} is the numeric value of the wavelength expressed in meters.

We traditionally call dimension (see [1]) of a particular quantity Qu the expression $Mul \times \prod_i A_i^{\alpha_i}$, where:

- $A_i^{\alpha_i}$ indicates values of basic quantities $A_i \in^1 \{$ [length, meter, m], [mass, kilogram, kg], [time, second, s], [intensity of electric current, ampere, A] [temperature, kelvin, K], [quantity of matter, mole, mol], [light intensity, candela, cd] $\}$,

- α_i are called the dimensional powers of the quantity Qu, and Mul is a numeric coefficient.

When all dimensional powers of a quantity are zero, it will be said dimensionless; we will name it *NoDim*.

The international physical units system as defined in [1] satisfy the abstract Backus notation given bellow. The rule $(Var ::= a|b|...)$ allows the user to express variables over the international system.

$\underline{PU}$	::=	$IU \mid OU \mid \underline{PU} \times \underline{PU} \mid \underline{PU}/\underline{PU} \mid \underline{PU}^Q \mid R \times \underline{PU} \mid$ "*NoDim*" $\mid Var$
IU	::=	$m \mid kg \mid s \mid A \mid K \mid mol \mid cd$
OU	::=	"other units of the international system"
Q	::=	"syntax of the rationals"
R	::=	"syntax of the reals"
Var	::=	$\alpha \mid \beta \mid ...$

Let $\mathcal{PU}$ be the set of all expressions that can be generated by this grammar.

Proposition: $\mathcal{PU}$ satisfies:[2]
$$\forall X \in \mathcal{PU}, (\exists x_0 \in \Re, \exists [x_1, x_2, x_3, x_4, x_5, x_6, x_7] \in Q^7,$$
$$X = x_0 \times m^{x_1} \times kg^{x_2} \times s^{x_3} \times A^{x_4} \times K^{x_5} \times mol^{x_6} \times cd^{x_7})$$
$\square$

Proof: trivial, due to the fact that all units of the international system can be expressed as a function of the seven fundamental units. $\square$

The set $\mathcal{PU}$ has many properties which will be used in our physical units

---

[1] with the notation [*quantity, unit, unit symbol*].
[2] with $\Re$: the reals and Q: the rationals.

inference algorithm. The most important are :

(1)
$$\forall(a,\ b,\ c) \in \mathcal{PU}^3 : (a \times b) \times c = a \times (b \times c),$$
$$\forall a \in \mathcal{PU} : a \times NoDim = a,$$
$$\forall a \in \mathcal{PU} : a \times a^{-1} = a^{-1} \times a = NoDim,$$
$$\forall(a,b) \in \mathcal{PU}^2 : (a \times b) = (b \times a).$$

The operations have the following properties:
$$\forall(a,b) \in \mathcal{PU}^2, c \in \mathcal{Q} : (a \times b)^c = (a^c) \times (b^c),$$
$$\forall a \in \mathcal{PU} : a^1 = a,$$
$$\forall a \in \mathcal{PU}, b \in \mathcal{Q} : (a^b) \in \mathcal{PU}, a^{1/b} \in \mathcal{PU}, (a^b)^{1/b} = a,$$
$$\forall a \in \mathcal{PU} : a^0 = NoDim,$$
$$\forall a \in \mathcal{PU}, b \in \mathcal{Q} : a^{-b} = 1/(a^b),$$

So $\mathcal{PU}$ verifies all the axioms of the vectorial space.

4.2 Extraction of the constraints

Our aim is to type a physical expression in the set of the physical units $\mathcal{PU}$. To extract the constraints over $\mathcal{PU}$, we start by associating a variable to every term in the expression. A variable stands for the unknown type of a sub-expression. We use the notation $\langle expr \rangle$ to represent the physical type variable of the expression $expr$. The consistency constraints are defined by induction over the syntax of the notation table 1 and following the semantics of the operators and the properties of $\mathcal{PU}$. For example, the expression $expr_1 + expr_2$ has, in the set of the international units, the constraint $\langle expr_1 \rangle = \langle expr_2 \rangle = \langle expr_2 + expr_2 \rangle$.

Thus, we see that consistency constraints are associated with operators. Indeed, the consistency checking of an expression is equivalent to verifying the satisfiability of a set of constraints over variables of physical units.

We give bellow some constraints by induction over some rules of our notation (table 1), specially standard operators and their constraints over the physical types:

$$
\begin{aligned}
id \equiv E &\longmapsto \langle id \rangle = \langle E \rangle \\
Const &\longmapsto \langle Const \rangle = NoDim \\
Const.PhysUnit &\longmapsto \langle Const.PhysUnit \rangle = PhysUnit \\
if\ e_1\ then\ e_2\ else\ e_3\ end &\longmapsto \langle if\ e_1\ then\ e_2\ else\ e_3\ end \rangle = \\
& \qquad \langle e_2 \rangle = \langle e_3 \rangle, \langle e_1 \rangle = NoDim \\
e_1 + e_2 &\longmapsto \langle e_1 + e_2 \rangle = \langle e_1 \rangle = \langle e_2 \rangle \\
e_1 \times e_2 &\longmapsto \langle e_1 \times e_2 \rangle = \langle e_1 \rangle \times \langle e_2 \rangle \\
e_1/e_2 &\longmapsto \langle e_1/e_2 \rangle = \langle e_1 \rangle / \langle e_2 \rangle \\
e_1 = e_2 &\longmapsto \langle e_1 = e_2 \rangle = NoDim, \langle e_1 \rangle = \langle e_2 \rangle
\end{aligned}
$$

We can observe that all the concistency contraints are based over the operators $\times$, $/$, and $\char`^$. For example, the block POL commonly used in FBD is managed as depicted in figure 4.

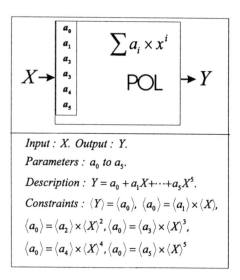

Figure 4: The functional block POL

All our constraints are expressed according to the physical type of every input/output. By using the notation of the section 2, we can state that: $\langle IO_i \rangle = FunctionOf(\langle IO_1 \rangle, ..., \langle IO_k \rangle)$, or simply $X_i = FunctionOf(X_1, ..., X_k)$.

By extracting the consistency constraints from some physical expressions, we simplify the expressions using the operators $/$ and $\char`\^{}$ as follows:

$$/ : (Mul_1 \times \prod_i A_i^{\alpha_i})/(Mul_2 \times \prod_i A_i^{\beta_i}) = (Mul_1/Mul_2) \times \prod_i A_i^{\alpha_i - \beta_i}$$
$$\char`\^{} : (Mul_1 \times \prod_i A_i^{\alpha_i})^r = (Mul_1^r) \times \prod_i A_i^{\alpha_i \times r}$$

After this simplification, the constraints will be based on the operators $\times$ and $\char`\^{}$. Thus, the constraints take the general form:

$$(X_i = coeff_j \times X_1^{R_{j1}} \times X_2^{R_{j2}} \times ... \times X_k^{R_{jk}} \times ... \times X_i^{R_{ji}} \times ... \times X_V^{R_{jV}})_j,$$
$$X_k \in The\_Set\_Of\_Variables, \ R_{jk} \in \mathcal{Q}, \ coeff_j \in \mathcal{PU},$$
$$0 \leq j \leq (E : Equations\_Number), \ 0 \leq i \leq (V : Variables\_Number)$$

By using the matrix notation:

$(X_i = coeff_j \times X^{R_j})$, or simply $X = Coeff \times X^R$
$X = [X_1, ..., X_V], \ R = [[R_{11}, ..., R_{1V}], ... [R_{E1}, ..., R_{EV}]],$
$Coeff = [Coeff_1, ... Coeff_E].$

As an example, here are consistency equations for the calculus of figure 3.

$$
\begin{aligned}
R \ &\mapsto \ \langle R \rangle = NoDim, \langle R_3 \rangle = \langle R_2 \rangle \\
R_3 \ &\mapsto \ \langle R_3 \rangle = U_4 \times U_5^{-1} \\
R_2 \ &\mapsto \ \langle R_2 \rangle = Kg \times U_3 \times \langle R_1 \rangle \\
R_1 \ &\mapsto \ \langle R_1 \rangle = U_1, U_1 = U_2
\end{aligned}
$$

For a particular physical expression, we obtain a set of E equations over V variables $\{X_i = coeff_j \times X^{R_j} \mid 1 \leq j \leq E \text{ and } 1 \leq i \leq V\}$. This set of equations is transformed in the following way:

$$X_i = b_j \times X_1^{R_{j1}} \times \ldots \times X_k^{R_{jk}} \times \ldots \times X_i^{R_{ji}} \times \ldots \times X_V^{R_{jV}}$$
$$\leadsto X_1^{M_{j1}} \times \ldots \times X_i^{M_{ji}} \times \ldots \times X_V^{M_{iV}} = coeff_j^{-1} = B_j$$
$$if \ k = i \ then \ M_{jk} = R_{ji} - 1 \ else M_{jk} = R_{jk}.$$

We can denote this set of equations as: $X^M = B$.

Where $X = [X_1, \ldots, X_V]$: the unknown vector, M: the matrix of powers $(M_{jk} \in \mathcal{Q})$, B: the vector of coefficients $(B_j \in \mathcal{PU})$.

It is now straightforward that the system is linear.

5 Resolution of the consistency equations

To solve these equations we can adapt algorithms [8, 11] of type inference used for functional languages (for example [5]). The general algorithm is not directly applicable to our system of types, because it does not take benefit of the properties of our types $\mathcal{PU}$, particularly to treat recursive equations of the form $Exp = Op(\ldots, Exp, \ldots)$. While refining the algorithm of type inference, we have identified a symbolic version of the algorithm of Gauss elimination. We present below this algorithm and some of its properties.

The standard linear systems are usually expressed using the operators $+$ and $\times$ over $\Re$. Here $\times$ and $\hat{\ }$ stand for $+$ and $\times$.

Standard linear systems are well solved by the standard Gauss algorithm. To apply this algorithm for solving equations over a particular set S with the operations $+$ and $\times$, some properties must be proved on the mathematical structure $S(+, \times)$. These properties are: $S(+)$ is an abelian group, and $S(\times)$ admits a symmetrical element. All these properties are satisfied by our structure $\mathcal{PU}$ which have been presented in the section 4.1 consisting in (1). We give bellow a set of transformations that can be used to adapt the Gauss algorithm to solve our system of symbolic equations.

$$a + b(a, b \in \Re) \implies a \times b(a, b \in \mathcal{PU})$$
$$a - b(a, b \in \Re) \implies a/b(a, b \in \mathcal{PU})$$
$$a \times b(a, b \in \Re) \implies a^b(a \in \mathcal{PU} \text{ and } b \in \mathcal{Q})$$
$$a/b(a, b \in \Re) \implies a^{1/b}(a \in \mathcal{PU} \text{ and } b \in \mathcal{Q})$$

We give in figure 5 the principle of the well-known Gauss algorithm.

This algorithm eliminates both the variables and the equations one by one $(Equ_j \mid j = 1 \ldots E)$, transforms the equation $Equ_j : X^{M_j} = B_j$ to $X_i = \beta$ and then, substitutes it in the other equations. Since we have a finite number of equations, this algorithm terminates.

At each step, one variable is eliminated. Finally, we obtain a set of substitutions where the left variables do not occur in the right part of the substitutions, this corresponds exactly to a solution.

Input: $X^M = B$, with E: number of equations, V: number of variables.
Let: $Substitutions = [\,]$, $\bar{E}=E$, $j = 1$
1. *Triangulation* of the matrix M
    while $j \le \bar{E}$ **do**
        If $M_j = (0, 0, \ldots, 0)$ and $B_j \ne NoDim$ **Then** Fail
        Else
            If $M_j \ne (0, 0, \ldots, 0)$ **Then**
                Find X_i: not eliminated variable in the equation $X^{M_j} = B_j$
                Transfom $X^{M_j} = B_j$ to $X_i = \beta$
                $Substitutions := Substitutions + (X_i = \beta)$
                Substitute $X_i = \beta$ in equations $j + 1$ to $\bar{E}$
                $j := j + 1$
            Else
                $M_j := M_{\bar{E}}$, $B_j := B_{\bar{E}}$, $\bar{E} := \bar{E} - 1$
            EndIf
        EndIf
2. *Resolution of the triangular system by simple Substitution*
    For $j = \bar{E}$ **to** 1
        Apply $Substitutions[j]$ in $Substitutions[1 \ldots (j-1)]$.
Output: Solution $= Substitutions$.

Figure 5: The Gauss algorithm

    The only difficulty in the adaptation of this algorithm is in the manipulation of the constant B_j (in $A^{M_j} = B_j$), which belongs to $\mathcal{PU}$. The operations (e.g. $\times$, $\hat{\ }$, or $/$) over $\mathcal{PU}$ are handled combining operations over $\mathcal{Q}$. The complexity of these operations depends on the number of units in the physical units expression. For example, in $((Cst_1 \times U_1^{\alpha_1} \times \ldots \times U_{nu}^{\alpha_{nu}}) \times (Cst_2 \times U_1^{\beta_1} \times \ldots \times U_{nu}^{\beta_{nu}}) = (Cst_1 \times Cst_2 \times U_1^{\alpha_1 + \beta_1} \times \ldots \times U_{nu}^{\alpha_{nu} + \beta_{nu}}))$ we have nu additions and one mutiplication. Thus, we can assert that the complexity of our physical units inference is $O(E^3/3) + O(max\_nu \times E \times (E+1)/2) \approx O(E^3/3)$, where $O(E^3/3)$ is the complexity of the gauss algorithm, $E \times (E+1)/2$ is the number of operations manipulating B in the system $X^M = B$, max_nu is the length of the longest expression B_j in B. If we use only the fundamental international units, then $max\_nu = 7 + 1$.

    The elimination algorithm (figure 5) efficiently calculates and with certainty the solution of any system $X^M = B$, since the matrix M is rational, and all calculations are then carried out in infinite-precision arithmetic.

    Consider the system $X^M = B$, the algorithm above may give a solution $\{Y_i = \beta_i | i = 1 \ldots \bar{E}\}$, where $Y \ne X$. This means that the original system admits an infinite solution. This kind of solution corresponds to the `physical polymorphism`. We present in figure 6 an example illustrating this situation.

    Remark: In the context of programming languages we can have types order superior to one, due to the presence of the type constructor $\to$. Whereas here, we have not considered construction allowing to have types order superior to

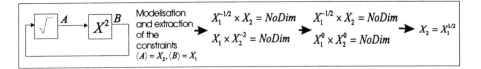

Figure 6: Example of a physical polymorphisme

one.

6 Conclusion and future work

In this article, we have presented a formalism for expressing physical calculus and a method to check the consistency — in term of physical units — of this formalism. We believe this is a first step towards a better understanding and solving of consistency problems, specially important in industrial contexts.

The first version of our system has been formally specified using the formal language *"Descartes"* [3] and is now being implemented at EDF.

We defined and specified our particular problem of physical inconsistency within the theoretical framework of type inference. We found this approach quite promising and are convinced that it can be applied to other consistency and safety problems as well.

An interesting extension of our work — asked for by ingeneers — is to simplify the task of debugging by interactively proposing a set of corrections when inconsistent equations are found.

Acknowledgment
The concepts presented in this paper were very much influenced by ongoing discussions with Jean-Luc Dormoy. Valuable comments and suggestions concerning this paper have been provided by Olivier Lhomme, Jean-Daniel Fekete, Bernard Mari, Narendra Jussien, Patrice Boizumault.

References

[1] Afnor. Grandeurs et Unités. Edition Afnor, 1985.

[2] Delcroix V. Contenu et forme des diagrammes fonctionnels analogiques. Techn. Rep. EDF; 1992.

[3] Dormoy JL, Ginoux B, Jimenez C, Laurent P, Lucas JY. The "Descartes" project, EDF; 1991-1996.

[4] Doutre JL, Keriel Y, Daffos V. Bibliothèque de blocs fonctionnels élémentaires, Techn. Rep. EDF; 1996.

[5] Field A, Harrison P: Type inference and type checking. In: Functional Programming. Addison-Wesley, 1988, pp 143-165.

[6] Lebbah Y, Dormoy JL, Mari B. Contrôle de cohérence des dimensions dans un Diagramme Fonctionnel Analogique. Tech. Rep. EDF-HI-29/96/031, 1996.

[7] Mairson H. Deciding ML typability is complete for deterministic exponential time. POPL, ACM Press, 1990;382-401.

[8] Milner R. A theory of type polymorphism in programming. Journal of computer and System Sciences, 1978;17:348-375.

[9] Paterson MS, Wegman MN. Linear unification. Journal of Computer and system science, 1978;16:158-167.

[10] Schwartzback MI. Polymorphic Type Inference. BRICS Lecture Series LS-95-3, June 1995.

[11] Wand M. A Simple algorithm and proof for type inference. Fundamentae Informaticae, 1987;10:115-122.

Safe combinations of services using B

Bruno Mermet

CRIN-CNRS URA 262

BP 239, 54506 Vandœuvre-lès-Nancy, France

Dominique Méry

Université Henri Poincaré Nancy 1 and CRIN-CNRS URA 262

BP 239, 54506 Vandœuvre-lès-Nancy, France

Abstract

The paper reports on the use of the B method and related tools to handle the feature interaction problem in telecommunications. The feature interaction problem states critical questions with respect to safety, sociological and legal aspects. Our approach proposes a new way to combine abstract machines and evaluates the resulting generation of proof obligations. The B method is a framework for specifying, refining and developing systems in a mathematical and rigorous, but simple way, and services are specified in the B method. The feature interaction problem is modelled simply as a violation of an invariant. The B method is supported by sofware that helps the specifier of services and features. We have not only modelled services within the B technology, but we have also extended possibilities of B by combining abstract machines.

1   Introduction

Feature interactions [3, 5] happen when different features of a software system interfere with each other. Within the area of telecommunications many problems are acknowledged with respect to the development of services and combinations of services. Combination of services is achieved in very different ways and requires the use of formal methods to handle questions of correctness and safety.

The specification of service is a way to solve problems for detecting, avoiding and solving interactions among services. An interaction is, within this paper, treated as an interference among processes modelling services. However, our view of interaction is still a partial approach to the general problem, since interactions may be introduced at late stages of development during design and implementation. The key idea is to describe a service using an abstract machine and to analyse the combination of services by combining abstract machines. An obvious step is to inherit invariants of abstract machines, but these can be violated since B does not allow machines to share variables. However, we obtain an extension of the B technology that is supported by the environments, namely the Atelier B [17] and the BToolkit [13], to overcome this difficulty. Our method of using B is based on the method of Owicki-Gries [16]; a proof of invariance is carried out in two steps : a first step annotates sequential processes and proves proof obligations related to pre and postconditions and a second step proves that every invariant property is not invalidated by an action of a concurrent process. The B method [1] is adequate to model services but it is limited to the expression of invariance properties. It does not address the question of fairness in services, but a lot of services can be specified and validated in B. The most interesting aspect of B is the possibility of using a tool to build, transform, refine, translate and validate abstract machines.

As no animator was provided by Atelier B[1], we had to use the BToolKit to animate specifications and several problems were discovered during the animation. However, the proof tool of Atelier B provides a very efficient way to prove the correctness of abstract machines; either it leads us to a development state where every proof obligation was proved by Atelier B, or it fails on an unproved proof obligation indicating a possible interaction between the combined services. The user has to solve the unproved proof obligation by proving it in an interactive way or by interpreting it as an interaction and resolving it. In fact, this point emphasizes the practicability of the B method in the development of safe combined services. The analysis is based on a case study relying on three services:

- the basic service providing administration operations and user operations.

- the screening list service.

- the call forwarding service.

In a first report [14], we have shown how to use the B method for modelling services and detecting feature interactions. Now, we explain the way to combine abstract machines and review the process. Others methods or languages can be used to address the question of the feature interaction and the specification of services: as LOTOS [6], SDL [11], Temporal Logic [2], Logical Approach [8], Z [15]. Our approach is in essence very simple to use by a non-specialist of algebraic framework but it is based on a very powerfull tool. However, we are limited, as with the most of the other methods, to the expression of safety properties. We have developed a study for handling fairness questions by using TLA [12] and we address the question of specifying services requiring fairness assumption.

The paper is organized as follows. Section 2 presents the B method and tools for B. Section 3 contains details on the proofs generated during services composition. Section 4 is devoted to statistics. Finally, section 5 concludes our paper.

2   The B method

This section describes the foundations of the B method, and,the environments and tools that we utilised during our case studies.

---

[1]The version 3.2 of the Atelier B provides now an animator.

2.1 The B technology

The B technology is a set of techniques and tools that implement the refinement of abstract machines into concrete machines and finally into C code. It uses the refinement of operations as a way to preserve invariance properties through the refinement process, and provides an environment that is really used in the development of safety critical systems [10, 4]. An abstract machine modifies data with operations and the B technology helps the user to define these objects in a formal and rigorous way. Abrial [1] introduces a notation to describe large systems using the B notation and there are two available tools for managing them:

- the B-Toolkit [13] is currently developed and maintained by B-Core and provides the following set of facilities : a theorem prover (namely the B Tool), a generator of proof obligations, an animator of abstract machines, and a B document processor.

- Atelier B [17] is developed and maintained by STERIA-Digilog and provides the following set of facilities : a powerful theorem prover (namely KRT), a generator of proof obligations, and a B document processor.

The two tools are complementary and we have used both. The fundamental aspect of these two tools is the power of the underlying theorem prover that aids the user. As the refinement of abstract machines is validated by proving generated proof obligations, proof process is not completely automated. However, the question of the power of a theorem prover is not within the scope of this paper; if the prover is not able to prove all the proof obligations, the user can use it in an interactive way or prove the remaining theorems (as mathematicians have been doing for centuries). The animator helps the user to visualize the specified system and it can help the customer to acknowledge the suggested expression of problem requirements. An abstract machine can be considered like a pocket calculator with buttons that allows one to execute certain actions and to activate operations over data. Furthermore, an abstract machine must satisfy proof obligations and the definition of proof obligations is expressed by the generalized substitution [1]. A B model considers that a set of data is modified by operations. The B technology provides a way to express operational semantics, in an encapsulated object-based manner. This naive view of the B underlying model can be taken when one builds a specification in B. Now, we describe the different aspects of B as operations, abstract machines,structuration mechanisms, theorem prover, and language properties. Predicates are formulae of the predicate calculus extended by set-theoretical predicates. As we will transform predicates, we need to define a notion of substitution over predicates.

Definition 1 *substitution over predicate*
A substitution [x := E]F is defined as the formula obtained by replacing all free occurences of x in F by E. It is defined by induction over the syntax of formulae F.

The B environment provides procedures to check that predicates are well defined and to manage theories required by the current specification. Properties are expressed using the language of predicates for constants. A constant is possibly a function and we need to express properties that we know and these properties are used by the prover for trying a successful processing of required proofs. Many properties can be stated in the set-theoretical framework but it is clearly difficult for the prover to derive theorems in a fully automatical way. The B book [1] contains chapters on set notations and mathematical objects that show how to use the different mechanisms provided by the B environment. The substitution is extended to express predicate transformation over predicates language, and is called the generalized substitution.

Definition 2 *generalized substitution*

A generalized substitution GSubstitution is either a substitution x := E, *or a skip, or preconditioned generalized substitution* P|GSubstitution *or a guarded generalized substitution* P $\Longrightarrow$ GSubstitution, *or a nondeterministic generalized substitution* GSubstitution$_1$ [] GSubstitution$_2$, *or a quantified generalized substitution* @ Variable GSubstitution, *or a sequential generalized substitution* GSubstitution$_1$; GSubstitution$_2$, *a parallel generalized substitution* GSubstitution$_1$ || GSubstitution$_2$, *or an applied generalized substitution* [Variable := Expression], *or a fixed-point generalized substitution* GSubstitution$^\sim$.

Definition 3 *operation*

An operation O *consists of a header and a generalized substitution* header$\hat{=}$Gsubstitution *where the header has one of the following forms :*
Id_List $\longleftarrow$ Identifier(Id_List),
Identifier(Id_List),
Id_List $\longleftarrow$ Identifier,
Identifier.

The B technology uses a concrete syntax for substitutions and operations, such as :

1. BEGIN generalized_substitution END

2. PRE precondition THEN generalized_substitution END

Now, using the above syntax, we can state what an abstract machine is in the B technology.

Definition 4 *abstract machine*

An abstract machine is a notation that describes a collection of sets, properties, constants, an initialisation statement, an invariant and a set of operations acting on data. An abstract machine has to satisfy the invariant and it may be structured with the help of other abstract machines using specific structuring clauses such as IMPORTS, INCLUDES, etc.

The properties language of B allows one to state invariance properties of abstract machines. An invariant is simply a conjunction of basic properties defined in the set-theoretical language. A B operation, namely O, is equivalent to $trm(O)|@x'.(prd_x(S) \Rightarrow x := x')$ where $trm(O)$ denotes the terminating states of S and $prd_x(S)$ is the computation relation for S. We do not want to present what is in the B book [1].

2.2 Theoretical background

The HOARE logic [9, 7] formalizes the correctness of programs with the concept of asserted programs. An asserted program is a triple $\boxed{\{ \text{ pre } \} \quad \text{P} \quad \{ \text{ post } \}}$ where *pre* is the precondition, P is a program and *post* is the postcondition. The HOARE logic provides a set of rules and axioms to infer HOARE triples. The semantics of $\boxed{\{ \text{ pre } \} \quad \text{P} \quad \{ \text{ post } \}}$ is intuitively defined as follows : *if P is executed from a current state satisfying pre and if P terminates, then the final state satisfies post*. The classical HOARE triples express the partial correctness of programs. An axiomatic system for HOARE triples allows one to derive valid HOARE triples and the system is syntax-directed. When one wants to extend the HOARE logic to deal with concurrency, one needs to take into account the possible interferences between concurrent processes. Clearly, the HOARE logic does not allow an easy way to extend its language to handle concurrent processes. We need to clearly state the problem of communication in the case of safety properties. The notation $pre \Rightarrow [P]post$ expresses the total correctness of P with respect to *pre* and *post*, if we use the generalized substitution notation of Abrial [1]. We can state invariance properties using the generalized substitution as follows:

Definition 5 *invariance property*
    An invariance property I for a set of operations $\{O_1, \ldots O_n\}$ and a generalized substitution Initialisation for initial states satisfies :
$$\begin{cases} [Initialization]I \\ \forall i \in \{1 \ldots n\} : I \wedge trm(O_i) \Rightarrow [O_i]I \end{cases}$$

We use the notation $(Init, \mathcal{O})$ for expressing the system of operations and we will use the notation $invariance(Init, \{O_1, \ldots O_n\})$ to denote the class of invariant properties for a set of operations $\{O_1, \ldots O_n\}$ and a specification of the initial states *Init*. [.] is the generalized substitution operator defined by Abrial [1] and maps every B operation to a predicate transformer. A set of proof obligations is generated from an abstract machine to ensure that the invariant is respected by the operations of the machine. An abstract machine M is made up of chapters describing different aspects of the mathematical model. We will use the notations as M.SEES, M.SETS, M.INITIALIZATION, M.INVARIANT, M.OPERATIONS to represent these chapters.

Definition 6 *proof obligations for an abstract machine*
    Let M be an abstract machine with M.I as invariant, M.INITIALISATION as specification of initial states and M.OPERATIONS as the set of operations

of M. Let $Context(M)$ be the semantical context of M (specifying domain properties, constraints, sets properties etc see pages 763-773 in [1]). $M.PO$ are proof obligations for M and defined as

$$\left\{ \begin{array}{l} Check(Context(M)) \\ Context(M) \Rightarrow [M.INITIALISATION]M.INVARIANT \\ \forall O \in M.OPERATIONS: \\ \quad Context(M) \wedge M.INVARIANT \wedge trm(O) \Rightarrow [O]M.INVARIANT \end{array} \right.$$

The expression of predicate transformers is based on the notion of generalized substitution. The proofs are attempted by the B tools and remaining proofs are done by hand. The statement of the invariance of I is combined together with the satisfaction of I by initial states. We use the expression *always true* but, as pointed out by Van Gasteren et al. [18], invariant properties are always true properties but the converse does not hold. Abstract machines can be combined into systems as is shown in figure 1. We limit the combination of abstract machines by considering only the union of a set of operations (see the figure 1).

Definition 7 *system*

A system $\mathcal{S}$ of processes $\{P_1, \ldots, P_n\}$ is modelled as a set of operations, an initial condition INITIALISATION and a set of initial conditions as follows: $\mathcal{S} = (Init, (P_1.Init, P_1.\mathcal{O}_1), \ldots, (P_n.Init, P_n.\mathcal{O}_n))$ where $Init$ specifies the initial conditions of $\mathcal{S}$, $P.Init$ is the initial condition of P and $P.\mathcal{O}$ is the set of actions executed by P.

Now, we can define proof obligations for a system. A property is an invariance property for a system if it is an invariance property for every process of the system and if the initial condition of the system strengthens initial conditions of every process of the system.

Definition 8 *invariance for a system*

An invariance property for a system $\mathcal{S}$ is a property satisfying the following requirements:

$$\left\{ \begin{array}{l} \forall P \in \mathcal{S}.Process : P.PO(I) \\ \forall P \in \mathcal{S}.Process : \mathcal{S}.Init \Rightarrow P.Init \end{array} \right.$$

The problem is that we want to combine abstract machines to model the composition of services. If a service S1 and a service S2 are developed in the B technology, we obtain an invariant for S1, $I1$, and another one for S2, namely $I2$. However, $I1 \wedge I2$ is not necessarily an invariant for the system obtained by the combination of the two abstract machines. Additional proof obligations must be proved.

Property 1 *Let $M1$ and $M2$ be two abstract machines, and $M1 \oplus M2$ the abstract machine obtained by strengthening the initial conditions and by gathering the operations of $M1$ and $M2$ in the operations part of M.*

If $[M.INITIALISATION]M1.INVARIANT \wedge M2.INVARIANT$, *and,*

$$\left\{ \begin{array}{l} M1.PO(M1.INVARIANT) \\ M2.PO(M2.INVARIANT) \\ M1.PO(M2.INVARIANT) \\ M2.PO(M1.INVARIANT) \end{array} \right. ,$$

then $M1.INVARIANT \wedge M2.INVARIANT$ *is invariant for M*

PROOF:

ASSUME: $\left\{ \begin{array}{l} [M.INITIALISATION]M1.INVARIANT \wedge M2.INVARIANT \\ M1.PO(M1.INVARIANT) \\ M2.PO(M2.INVARIANT) \\ M1.PO(M2.INVARIANT) \\ M2.PO(M1.INVARIANT) \end{array} \right.$

PROVE: $M1.INVARIANT \wedge M2.INVARIANT$ is invariant for M

⟨1⟩1. Initial conditions

PROOF:$[M.INITIALISATION]M1.INVARIANT \wedge M2.INVARIANT$ states the establishment of the invariant initially. □

⟨1⟩2. Operations conditions

PROOF:Let O be an operation of M. $M1.INVARIANT \wedge M2.INVARIANT \Rightarrow M1.INVARIANT$ and $M1.INVARIANT \wedge trm(O) \Rightarrow [O]M1.INVARIANT$ by assumption. Then $M1.INVARIANT \wedge M2.INVARIANT \wedge trm(O) \Rightarrow [O]M1.INVARIANT$. $M1.INVARIANT \wedge M2.INVARIANT \Rightarrow M2.INVARIANT$ and $M2.INVARIANT \wedge trm(O) \Rightarrow [O]M2.INVARIANT$ by assumption. Then $M1.INVARIANT \wedge M2.INVARIANT \wedge trm(O) \Rightarrow [O]M2.INVARIANT$. Hence, we can derive $M1.INVARIANT \wedge M2.INVARIANT \wedge trm(O) \Rightarrow [O](M1.INVARIANT \wedge M2.INVARIANT)$, by conjunction of the second part of implication. □

⟨1⟩3. Q.E.D.

PROOF:By ⟨1⟩1 and ⟨1⟩2, we derive that $M1.INVARIANT \wedge M2.INVARIANT$ is invariant for M. □

The main result of our observation is that the B technology is sufficient to provide tools and notations for expressing combinations of services. However, we have to take care of the new proof obligations that are generated because of the possible interferences [16]. As the B property language does not allow one to express fairness, we can not express this notion formally.

3 Modelling services in the B technology

3.1 Composition of B machines

The B method allows different kinds of composition. The most commonly used is introduced by the *IMPORTS* keyword. It allows encapsulation of data and code during the refinement process. As we do not focus on refinement in this paper, it cannot be used. An other solution to combine subsystems is to use the *INCLUDES* keyword or its variant *EXTENDS*. However, the machine *including* another one cannot, for safety reasons modify variables declared in the included

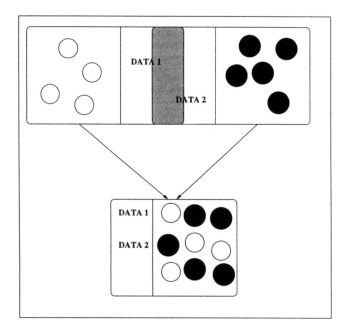

Figure 1: Combining abstract machines $M1 \oplus M2$

machine. This restriction has been chosen to avoid the generation of new proof obligations linked to the invariant of the included machine, but it is not well suited to our problems, where data may be read and written by more than one service. Finally, the last kind of composition is introduced by the word *USES*. It allows a machine A to *see* variables encapsulated in a machine B that will be later included together with A in a machine C. But once again, two machines cannot write to a shared variable. Consequently, we chose a new kind of composition, consisting in merging the different clauses of the machines we compose. However, in order to use as well as possible the existing tools, we describe a solution limiting the number of the proof obligations introduced by this step.

If we want to compose two services S_1 and S_2, we can imagine the service S_1 as the environment of S_2. So, S_2 must not break the invariant of its environment. This can be checked by proving that S_2 operations preserve the S_1 Invariant. Moreover, environment operations (S_1 operations) must not break the invariant of the S_2 service. If this is true, then, provided both invariants are established by the initialisation of the machines, they will remain true, whatever operation is executed. This is a practical point of view of the theory explained in the beginning of this paper. If we want to implement this technique with the tools that already exist, we have to proceed in two steps; we assume that S_1 and S_2 specifications are independently correct, and go on to

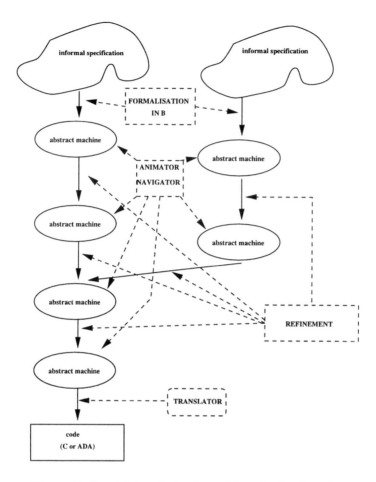

Figure 2: Combining abstract machines in the B cycle

the following :

- prove that S_2 operations preserve the invariant of S_1, by adding the invariant of S_1 to S_2;

- prove that S_1 operations preserve the invariant of the S_2, by adding the invariant of S_2 to S_1.

These two steps will also prove the compatibility of the initialisations.

However, merging the invariants is not enough : we also have to add parts of the VARIABLES, CONSTANTS, PROPERTIES, INITIALISATION, etc. clauses.

The technique of strenghtening the invariant of a machine with a given number of operations instead of adding operations to a machine with a stable invariant has been chosen because it supports a more modular strategy, with fewer proof obligations.

3.2 Composing POTS and the Screening List services

We introduce two services. The first one, called POTS[2] introduces the basic functions of a telephone system. We combine POTS with the Screening List service, a service that allows a telephone subscriber to forbid some people to call him.

We apply the theory summarized above. POTS is taken as service S_1, and Screening list is taken as service S_2.

1. Checking that Screening List operations preserve the POTS invariant :

   The specification of the Screening List feature generates, (with the Atelier B [17]) 17 POs[3] and 60 ObvPOs[4], all true.

   When we add the invariant properties of POTS that were not part of the Screening List invariant, we do not obtain any false PO.

2. Checking that POTS operations preserve the Screening List invariant

   Doing this, we obtain two false POs. Explanations are given below. A greater understanding of the following formula can be given by the B source code of the services, which can be found on the internet[5]

   - for the remove_subscriber operation :
     $$screening\_list\_subscribers \subseteq subscribers\text{-}\{subs\}\text{-}\{Null\_Subscriber\}$$

   - for the establish_communication operation :
     $$\mathbf{ran}((call\_states \lhd\!\!\!- \{com \mapsto st\})^{-1} [\{Established, Communicating\}] \lhd (called \otimes caller)) \cap screening\_list = \emptyset$$

   The first false PO corresponds to an interaction that occurs when a person stops subscribing to the POTS service, but remains as a subscriber to the Screening List. This is forbidden by the Screening List invariant, which require Screening List subscribers being POTS subscribers. The second corresponds to the fact that the **Establish_communication** operation of the POTS service can establish a communication prohibited by the Screening List service.

3.3 Adding the Call Forwarding service

The call forwarding service allows a user to forward calls to another telephone user. In order to combine the three services POTS, Screening List, and Call Forwarding, we can re-use the mixed system POTS + Screening List, that

---

[2] Plain Old Telephone System
[3] Proof Obligations
[4] Obvious Proof Obligations
[5] http://www.loria.fr/mermet/Services/index.html

becomes our new service S_1, and use the same technique, with Call Forwarding as service S_2.

1. Checking that Call Forwarding operations preserve the POTS + Screening List invariant

   We find that an interaction appears in the *initialisation* clause : in the POTS specification, we initialize the `connected_phones` variable to {`Null_Phone`}, whereas in the Call Forwarding specification, we initialize it to $\emptyset$, because we did not introduce the notion of the `Null_Phone`. So, the problem can be solved by choosing the POTS initialisation.

   This combination does not generate any false PO. So, we do not detect any kind of interaction.

2. Checking that POTS + Screening List operations preserve the Call Forwarding invariant

   This step produces 3 false POs, corresponding to the following interactions :

   - when we remove a POTS subscriber, it remains a Call Forwarding subscriber (PO associated to the `remove_subscriber` operation);

   - When we remove a POTS subscriber, it might be a Call Forwarding Target of somebody else. But the Call Forwarding specification forbid targets that are not POTS subscribers (PO associated to the `remove_subscriber` operation);

   - the `Establish` operation can establish a communication to somebody who forwarded calls to him (PO associated to the `Establish` operation).

From the case study presented above, we analyse different kinds of interactions:

- Two of the interactions produced by the `remove_subscriber` operation can be resolved by adding a new action to the operation : removing a subscriber removed from the screening_list_subscribers and call_forwarding_subscribers sets.

- The interactions produced by the `Establish` operation can be resolved by re-inforcing the precondition of this operation.

- Finally, the interaction produced by the `remove_subscriber` operation when the target of a call forwarding is removed is slightly more difficult : a solution could be to automatically cancel the call forwarding to him.

4 Practical experiments with the tools

4.1 Animating specifications

The Atelier B [17] does not yet have an animator, so, we used the animator of the B Toolkit [13]. Animating specification is useful to help other people (like clients) understanding the specification. Moreover, it helps the programmer to check that the specification is correct with respect to an informal description: it allows to check if properties not specified in the invariant (either because they cannot be expressed or because they were forgotten) are true. Here, for instance, we forgot to specify that a call with no more subscribers involved in it must be removed : in an earlier specification, if two people A and B where communicating, if we first removed A from the subscribers set, and then B, the communication between them was remaining in the current_calls set. This could have been detected if we had added the following invariant:
$caller^{-1}[Null\_Subscriber] \cap called^{-1}[Null\_subscriber] = \emptyset$

4.2 Statistics using the tool

4.2.1 Proofs of services

Proofs were made by the Atelier B [17]. We observed that the form of the specification has a great importance on the percentage of proof obligations proved. With the current specification, for example, we obtain the following results on POTS:

operation	ObvPO	PO	Unproved
initialisation	4	0	0
add_subscriber	20	4	0
remove_subscriber	7	17	10
connect	17	7	0
disconnect	4	20	8
show	18	5	0
hide	8	15	8
dial	13	11	1
establish_communication	17	6	1
Total	108	85	28

Moreover, 4 proofs can be achieved easily[6] by the *interactive prover*, a tool that helps the prover without adding, new possibly wrong, rules. So, we can say that 72% of the non-obvious proofs are achieved quite automatically (88% of all the proof obligations).

Most of the unproved POs are in fact quite similar, making the solution to one PO a great help for finding the solution to another. An interesting point is the localisation of the unproved POs : they correspond to the operations like remove_subscriber or disconnect. This can be explained by the role of these

---

[6]less than 5 minutes of reflexion for a human

operations that are permissive, but have to preserve a very strong invariant. The POs remaining could perhaps be proved by the interactive prover, but we did not try.

Services are easier to prove. Here are the results of the prover for the two services described in this paper:

service	ObvPO	PO	Unproved
screening list	60	17	0
call forwarding	57	21	1

However, once again, the Unproved PO of the call forwarding service can be easily proved with the interactive prover. Thus, our services are completely proved.

4.2.2 Proofs of compositions

When combining services, the problem becomes slightly more difficult. However, the benefit of the POs proved on each service independantly is a great help. Here is a table which summarizes the number of new POs generated. (S_L and C_F respectively mean Screening List and Call Forwarding.) The numbers given correspond to the new obvious POs, POs and Unproved POs generated.

composition	$\Delta ObvPO$	ΔPO	$\Delta Unproved$
S_L with POTS invariant	67	8	0
POTS with S_L invariant	17	22	8
C_F with S_L and POTS invariant	80	10	2
S_L and POTS with C_F invariant	29	12	8

An interesting aspect of the method is the small number of new unproved POs at each composition. When we compose POTS and the screening list, we have only eight new unproved POs. Two of them are generated by interactions. The other are true, but the prover did not succeed in the proof. When we add a new service, the Call Forwarding service, we have ten more unproved POs, three of them corresponding to interactions. The help provided by the prover and this technique is important : instead of examining by hand all the proof obligations of our composition (436 Obvious POs and 136 POs) to detect possible interactions, we focus on only 10 POs.

4.3 Limits of the method

In B, we can not express temporal properties. Thus, the fact that a particular service will happen cannot be guaranteed. Here, for instance, if we combine POTS, Screening List, and Call Forwarding services, we can imagine the following scenario :

- B subscribes to Screening List and Call Forwarding services ;

- A is on the screening list of B ;

- B has forwarded calls to him to C ;

- A calls B.

Then, either the rejecting_a_Call or the forward_call operations can be activated. But if one of them is activated, the precondition of the other becomes false. So, we have an undeterministic behaviour of our system, and this cannot be detected by the B method. The interaction of the two services could, of course, be detected if we could specify temporal properties in B machines, by saying that if the call forwarding system is on, then calls will eventually be forwarded : a rejected call would not check this property. The method lacks real structuring mechanisms. The composition is very basic and restrictive.

5   Concluding remarks

The scope of the B technology can be extended by introducing a new structuring operator of abstract machines; the new structuring operator implements the method of Owicki and Gries and introduces new proof obligations. In a preliminary paper [14], we have shown how abstract machines could model services and help in detecting interactions among services. This paper reports on practical experiments with tools showing that tools for formal methods are at a mature level. As the B technology is based on invariance properties, we have not considered the question of fairness in services. Other approaches are mainly based on formal methods for telecommunications such as LOTOS, SDL or assertional and logical methods [8]. There are two main problems with these other approaches that are partially solved by our method. A first problem is to provide a sufficiently expressive specification language and a second one is to provide a real environment for dealing with formalisms. We think that tools for B [13, 17] are realistic solutions for users that are not real specialist for formal methods, even if the prover and the environment have some limitations. It is clear that we need to extend the scope of the property language but the inclusion of a temporal semantics based TLA [12] is under development in our group. Our results are based on a simple way to combine abstract machines and the main problem is now to extend the scope of property language and the power of the prover. The development of case studies allows us to discover new possible feature interactions among classical services.

Acknowledgments

This work is partially supported by the contract n°96 1B CNET-FRANCE-TELECOM & CRIN-CNRS-URA 262 and by the Institut Universitaire de France.

References

[1] J.-R. Abrial. *The B book - Assigning Programs to Meanings*. Cambridge University Press, 1996.

[2] J. Blom, B. Jonsson, and L. Kempe. Using temporal logic for modular specification of telephone services. In L. G. Bouma and H. Velthuijsen, editors, *Feature Interactions in Telecommunications Systems*. IOS Press, 1994.

[3] L. G. Bouma and H. Velthuijsen, editors. *Feature Interactions in Telecommunications Systems*. IOS Press, 1994.

[4] M. Carnot, C. DaSilva, B. Dehbonei, and F. Mejia. Error-free sofware development for critical systems using the b technology. In *Proceedings of the Third IEEE International Conference on Software Reliability Engineering*, October 1992.

[5] K. E. Cheng and T. Ohta, editors. *Feature Interactions in Telecommunications Systems*. IOS Press, 1996.

[6] M. Faci and L. Logrippo. Formlisation of a user view of network and services for feature interaction detection. In L. G. Bouma and H. Velthuijsen, editors, *Feature Interactions in Telecommunications Systems*. IOS Press, 1994.

[7] R. W. Floyd. Assigning meanings to programs. In J. T. Schwartz, editor, *Proc. Symp. Appl. Math. 19, Mathematical Aspects of Computer Science*, pages 19 – 32. American Mathematical Society, 1967.

[8] A. Gammelgaard and J. E. Kristensen. Interaction detection, a logical approach. In L. G. Bouma and H. Velthuijsen, editors, *Feature Interactions in Telecommunications Systems*. IOS Press, 1994.

[9] C. A. R. Hoare. An axiomatic basis for computer programming. *Communications of the Association for Computing Machinery*, 12:576–580, 1969.

[10] J. Hoare, J. Dick, D. Neilson, and I. Sorensen. Applying the B technologies to CICS. In J. Woodcock, editor, *FME.96*. Springer-Verlag, March 1996. LNCS 1051.

[11] B. Kelly, M. Crowther, and J. King. Feature interaction detection using sdl models. In *GLOBECOM. Communications: The Global Bridge. Conference Record*, pages 1857–61. IEEE, 1994.

[12] L. Lamport. A temporal logic of actions. *Transactions On Programming Languages and Systems*, 16(3):872–923, May 1994.

[13] B-Core(UK) Ltd. *B-Toolkit User's Manual*, relase 3.2 edition, 1996.

[14] B. Mermet and D. Méry. Feature interaction detection in b. Internal report, Centre de Recherche en Informatique de Nancy CNRS URA262, january,15 1997.

[15] J. Nyström. A formalization of service indepedent building blocks. In *AIN'96*. Mars 25-26, 1996.

[16] S. Owicki and D. Gries. An axiomatic proof technique for parallel programs i. *Acta Informatica*, 6:319–340, 1976.

[17] GEC Alsthom Transport, DIGILOG, SNCF, INRETS, and RATP. *Atelier B, Version 3.0, Manuel de Référence du Langage B*. STERIA DIGILOG, 1996.

[18] A. J. M. van Gasteren and G. Tel. Comments on "on the proof of a distributed algorithm": always true is not invariant. *Information Processing Letters*, 35:277–279, 1990.

An Object-Based Approach to Modelling and Analysis of Failure Properties

M. Čepin[1], R. de Lemos[2], B. Mavko[1], S. Riddle[2], A. Saeed[2]

[1] Reactor Engineering Division, "Jožef Stefan" Institute,
Ljubljana, Slovenia

[2] Department of Computing Science, University of Newcastle upon Tyne,
United Kingdom

Abstract

In protection systems, when traditional technology is replaced by software, the functionality and complexity of the system is likely to increase. The quantitative evidence normally provided for safety certification of traditional systems cannot be relied upon in software-based systems. Instead there is a need to provide qualitative evidence. As a basis for the required qualitative evidence, we propose an object-based approach that allows modelling of both the application and software domains. From the object class model of a system and a formal specification of the failure properties of its components, we generate a graph of failure propagation over object classes, which is then used to generate a graph in terms of object instances in order to conduct fault tree analysis. The model is validated by comparing the resulting minimal cut sets with those obtained from the fault tree analysis of the original system. The approach is illustrated on a case study based on a protection system from the Nuclear Industry.

Keywords: safety analysis, object-oriented modelling, fault tree analysis

1 Introduction

Increasingly traditional technology (hydraulic, pneumatic, electronic) is being replaced by software in process control systems. A typical consequence is that the functionality, and hence complexity, of the software-based system tends to increase, making the system harder to certify as assurance must be provided that the overall system risk is not increased. Evidence for certification is normally provided by conducting safety analysis.

The quantitative evidence normally provided for traditional systems cannot be relied upon in software-based systems, due to the difficulty of obtaining estimates of failure rates. Instead developers will need to place greater reliance on qualitative evidence. The object-based approach we propose begins with a model of an original system implemented in conventional technology, supported by the results of traditional safety analysis. The specification is used to derive an abstract object model which is independent of the technology in which it may be implemented. Safety analysis conducted on this model provides the required qualitative evidence that risk has not increased. It also establishes criteria for assessing and certifying the software to be developed, by providing a specification which reflects the failure properties of the original system.

2 Method description

The method proposed in this paper consists of a set of techniques from the software and application domains which are used to model the structure and behaviour of the existing system, and to conduct safety analysis. The result of the method is a formalised fault tree which can be directly compared with one produced for the original system.

The starting point for the method is a functional model of the original system, and its fault tree with resultant minimal cut sets. The method then proceeds as follows:

Object class model of system structure.

The original system is analysed and, using the notation of the object view of OMT [1], an object class model is produced which represents the structure of the system.

Formal definition of class structure and behaviour.

For each object class, its behaviour and structure is formally specified using a modified form of *interactor* [2]. Instead of employing operational techniques (e.g. statecharts) to express the dynamic view of OMT, we employ an axiomatic notation [3].

Causal analysis of object class model.

From the object class model and interactor specifications, a causal model is derived for the propagation of failure behaviours through object classes. This step results in a graph of failure propagation over object classes which is termed an *impact structure* (modified from the form in which it appears in [4]).

Fault tree instantiation.

The graph of failure propagation over object classes can then be instantiated for a particular top event and used as a basis to build a fault tree over object instances.

Minimal cut sets comparison.

Comparing the minimal cut sets from the fault tree derived from the impact structure with the minimal cut sets derived from the original system, the validity of the object class model can be assessed: if any new causes are included in the cut sets then safety can be affected [5].

The techniques used in the method are established techniques employed in the fields of software engineering (OMT and first order predicate logic) and safety analysis (fault tree analysis and failure mode and effect analysis), and novel techniques for safety analysis (impact structure).

The paper illustrates the method outlined above by introducing as a case study a protection system for a Nuclear Power Plant. We begin by providing an overview of the system itself, and then go through each step in the method to perform the modelling and analysis of the case study.

3   ESFAS case study description

The case study system is the Engineered Safety Features Actuation System (ES-FAS) employed as part of the protection system in a Nuclear Power Plant [6].

The system monitors parameters in the plant and, in the event of abnormal plant conditions, activates Engineered Safety Features, for example a safety injection signal. These safety features maintain the safety of the reactor by providing core cooling, so reducing the damage to fuel and fuel cladding, and preventing the release of radioactive materials.

The ESFAS initiates a safety injection signal if the value of one or more of the parameters (pressurizer pressure, steam line pressure, containment pressure) exceeds a defined safety limit during normal plant operation. The signal can also be actuated manually.

3.1   Structure of the ESFAS

The ESFAS consists of three or four redundant analog channels to measure each of the diverse pressure parameters, and two digital trains employing solid-state logic to vote on the actuation of a safety signal in the applicable conditions.

Redundancy is employed to ensure that no single failure can prevent actuation: only two out of the four channels are needed to provide an actuation signal. This is known as 2/4 voting, or 2/3 when there are only three channels. 2/4 voting is used when the same parameter is also used for control functions. Each digital train is capable of producing independently a safety injection signal.

3.2   ESFAS Case study simplifications

The resolution of modelling is selected so that only one parameter, measured on four channels, is monitored. The system for our purposes consists of two redundant trains, four redundant channels and two manual switches. The case study system is referred to as *ESFAS_SI_Small*, the small version of the ES-FAS Safety Injection system which is fully developed in [7]. The block diagram presented in Figure 1 represents the functional model of the system.

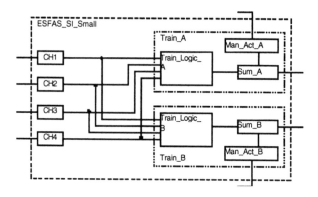

Figure 1: **ESFAS_SI_Small** Block Diagram

4 Case study application

Having provided an overview of the system we now illustrate the proposed method in more detail. We begin by forming an object class model of the structure of the system.

4.1 Object class model of system structure

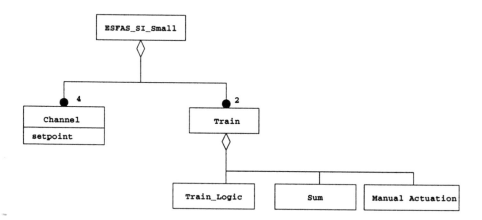

Figure 2: **ESFAS_SI_Small** Object Class Diagram

We use the notation from the object view of OMT for our object class model, which shows the objects in the system and their relationships. The object class model is formed by:

- identifying object classes - examining components of the system and abstracting common entities;

- identifying associations - examining structural and inheritance relationships between object classes, which leads to a hierarchical diagram of aggregation and specialisation of object classes.

The resulting object class model for the case study is shown in Figure 2. This model decomposes **ESFAS_SI_Small** into an aggregation (signified by a diamond) of **Channel** and **Train** classes. The numbered black circles on the arcs signify multiplicity: there are four channels and two trains. The **Channel** has an *attribute*, or state variable, which is the value of the setpoint for that channel (a constant).

4.2   Formal definition of class structure and behaviour

From the object class model we now go on to formally specify the structure and behaviour of the object classes of the system. An *interactor* [3, 2] provides a formal axiomatic representation of the structure and behaviour of an object class. It is divided into declarations and predicates in a similar way to a Z schema [8]. Table 1 is an interactor for the **ESFAS_SI_Small** class.

The declarations begin with a *composed_of* field (defining the structure) which says that the object class consists of two instances of **Train** and an indexed sequence of **Channel**s. The indexed sequence is an abstraction of an array. Constants and variables are dealt with next: each declaration gives name, type and an optional comment for variable listed. Such declarations can also include a definition, for example the state variable *high-pressure* is effectively a macro which allows us to abbreviate the expression

$$(\exists\, i, j \in \{1...4\} \bullet (i \neq j) \wedge (reading(i) > setpoint) \wedge (reading(j) > setpoint)).$$

The predicates consist of a *structure* field, defining how sub-classes communicate (via input and output variables) and how these variables relate to the inputs and outputs of the object class being specified in the interactor, and a *behaviour* field which defines the possible behaviour modes of the object class.

In terms of the variables defined in the interactor, the requirements that the system must satisfy can be summarised as follows:

1. Whenever the high pressure threshold is exceeded on at least two channels, at least one of the trains must generate a safety injection signal:

   high_pressure $\Rightarrow$ (*esfas_A* $\vee$ *esfas_B*)

2. The safety injection signal on each train can be independently actuated by a manual switch:

   (*manual_A* $\Rightarrow$ *esfas_A*) $\wedge$ (*manual_B* $\Rightarrow$ *esfas_B*)

3. The injection signal should not be activated spuriously:

   (*esfas_A* $\Rightarrow$ *high_pressure* $\vee$ *manual_A*)
   $\wedge$ (*esfas_B* $\Rightarrow$ *high_pressure* $\vee$ *manual_B*)

interactor *ESFAS_SI_Small*		
composed_of:		
$train\_A, train\_B$	*Train*	
$chann$	seq *Channel*	
constants:		
$setpoint$	$\mathbb{R}$	Pressure setpoint
variables:		
input variables:		
$reading$	seq $\mathbb{R}$	Pressure input readings
$manual\_A, manual\_B$	$\mathbb{B}$	Manual actuation inputs
output variables:		
$esfas\_A, esfas\_B$	$\mathbb{B}$	ESFAS actuation signals
state variables:		
$high\_pressure$	$\mathbb{B}$	
$high\_pressure \Leftrightarrow$		Pressure is high if and only if at
$(\exists\, i,j \in \{1...4\} \bullet$		least two channel setpoints are
$(i \neq j) \wedge (reading(i) > setpoint)$		exceeded
$\wedge\, (reading(j) > setpoint))$		
structure:		
$\forall\, i \in \{1...4\}.chann(i).reading = reading(i)\ \wedge$		
$train\_A.voters(i) = chann(i).channel\_signal\ \wedge$		
$train\_B.voters(i) = chann(i).channel\_signal$		
$esfas\_A = train\_A.vote$		
$esfas\_B = train\_B.vote$		
$manual\_A = train\_A.manual\_act$		
$manual\_B = train\_B.manual\_act$		
behaviour:		
normal:		
$((high\_pressure \vee manual\_A) \Leftrightarrow esfas\_A)$		An actuation signal is produced
$\wedge\ ((high\_pressure \vee manual\_B) \Leftrightarrow esfas\_B)$		if and only if pressure is too high, or the relevant manual actuation is present.
failure:		
$(\neg\ high\_pressure\ \wedge$		An actuation signal is produced
$((\neg\ manual\_A \wedge esfas\_A)\ \vee$		despite no automatic or manual
$(\neg\ manual\_B \wedge esfas\_B))$		signal – spurious actuation
$\vee$		
$(high\_pressure \wedge (esfas\_A \wedge \neg\ esfas\_B))$		Benign failure condition - only
$\vee (\neg\ esfas\_A \wedge esfas\_B)$		one actuation signal is produced
$\vee$		
$(high\_pressure \wedge (\neg\ esfas\_A \wedge \neg\ esfas\_B))\ \vee$		Failure to produce actuation
$(manual\_A \wedge \neg\ esfas\_A)\ \vee$		signal when needed – critical
$(manual\_B \wedge \neg\ esfas\_B)$		failure

Table 1: Interactor for object class *ESFAS_SI_Small*

Disjunction of the above requirements characterises the normal behaviour of *ESFAS_SI_Small*, specified in the interactor (Table 1) as

$$((high\_pressure \vee manual\_A) \Leftrightarrow esfas\_A)$$
$$\wedge\ ((high\_pressure \vee manual\_B) \Leftrightarrow esfas\_B).$$

A consequence of the normal behaviour is that $high\_pressure \Rightarrow (esfas\_A \wedge esfas\_B)$. The normal behaviour satisfies all the requirements.

Failure behaviours are identified either by negating the normal behaviour of the object class or by applying the FMEA technique to identify possible failure behaviours of the object class [9]. By negating the normal behaviour predicate for **ESFAS_SL_Small**, we obtain

$$(\neg\ high\_pressure \wedge (\neg\ manual\_A \wedge esfas\_A) \vee (\neg\ manual\_B \wedge esfas\_B)$$
$$\vee\ (high\_pressure \wedge (\neg\ esfas\_A \vee \neg\ esfas\_B))$$
$$\vee\ (manual\_A \wedge \neg\ esfas\_A) \vee (manual\_B \wedge \neg\ esfas\_B).$$

The first line in this predicate is related with spurious generation of an actuation signal. The remaining lines are related with a combination of critical and benign failures (benign being the case when one train fails but the requirements are still satisfied). This can be rewritten to separate out the failure modes. The benign failure is specified as

$$(high\_pressure \wedge ((esfas\_a \wedge \neg\ esfas\_b) \vee (\neg\ esfas\_a \wedge esfas\_b)))$$

and critical failure is specified as

$$(high\_pressure \wedge (\neg\ esfas\_a \wedge \neg\ esfas\_b))$$
$$\vee\ (manual\_a \wedge \neg\ esfas\_a) \vee (manual\_b \wedge \neg\ esfas\_b).$$

Each of these failure conditions is represented by a failure mode (spurious, benign or critical) in the behaviour of the interactor.

The method defines an interactor for each object class in the model (**Train, Train_Logic, Sum, Manual_Actuation, Channel**). The **Channel** is an example of a primitive object class, which is specified by the interactor in Table 2. The failure behaviour is obtained from the negation of the normal behaviour in the same way as above: in this case there is no benign failure.

4.3   Causal analysis of object class model

In this section, we describe a systematic method for the derivation of a graph of failure propagation over the modelled object classes which provides the basis for the analysis of causes and consequences of failures. The graph is known as the *impact structure* [4] and is derived from the information provided within the object class model, and the interactor specifications.

The components of an impact structure are *nodes* which represent object classes and *arrows* (connecting classes) which represent an impacts relation between classes. An *impacts relation* exists between two classes, when the behaviour of one affects the other.

There are two types of impacts relations, impacts between sub-classes of a common aggregate class (intra-impacts) and impacts between a sub-class and its aggregate class (inter-impacts).

intra-impacts For classes $A.B$ and $A.C$ an intra-impact relation exists if $A.B$ impacts $A.C$, and is depicted by a solid arrow connecting $A.B$ to $A.C$.

inter-impacts For class A and sub-class $A.B$ an inter-impact relation exists if $A.B$ impacts A, and is depicted by a broken arrow connecting $A.B$ to A.

interactor **Channel**	
constants:	
setpoint $\quad\quad$ $\mathbb{R}$	A channel has a constant set-point
variables:	
input variables:	
reading $\quad\quad$ $\mathbb{R}$	pressure value
output variables:	
channel_signal $\quad$ $\mathbb{B}$	channel output
behaviour:	
normal:	
$(reading \geq setpoint) \Leftrightarrow channel\_signal$	A signal is produced by the channel whenever the input reading exceeds the setpoint.
failure:	
$((reading \geq setpoint) \wedge \neg\, channel\_signal)$	Critical failure of the channel: no signal produced despite input reading exceeding setpoint
$\vee$	
$((reading < setpoint) \wedge channel\_signal)$	Spurious signal produced by channel when setpoint is not exceeded

Table 2: Interactor for object class **Channel**

There are three ways of composing impacts:

n-impacts For two object classes A and B, B impacts A with multiplicity n if, according to the interactor specification, at least n instances of B must fail in order to impact an instance of A. An *n-impacts* is represented by annotating the arrow with a circle containing the particular number n.

and-impacts For object classes A, B and C, instances of both B and C must fail in order to impact an instance of A. An *and-impacts* is represented by linking the arrows involved in the relation with a $\otimes$ symbol.

or-impacts For object classes A, B and C, instances of either B or C must fail in order to impact an instance of A. An *or-impacts* is represented by linking the arrows involved in the relation with a $\oplus$ symbol.

The method for generating an impact structure is a three stage process, defined as follows.

Stage 1: Determine Impacts

The impacts of an aggregate class are derived by an examination of the composition and structure fields of its interactor.

1. Intra-impacts. A solid arrow is drawn between any two object classes A, B if the behaviour of one object class can affect the other, as specified in the structure field of the interactor for the aggregate object class.

2. Inter-impacts. A broken arrow is drawn between any two object classes $A.B$ and A if A has an output defined in terms of an output of A, B.

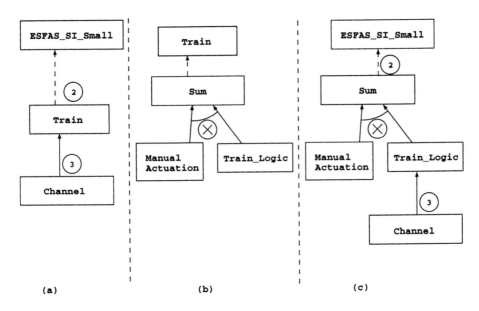

Figure 3: Impact structure for case study. (a) impact structure for the **ESFAS_SI_Small** class, (b) impact structure for **Train** subclass, (c) complete impact structure for the **ESFAS_SI_Small** class.

Stage 2: Simplification of Impacts

The impact structure obtained from Stage 1, can be simplified by the deletion of arrows and nodes. Firstly, redundant arrows are deleted by examining the transitive closure (impacts$^+$); basically if the removal of an impacts relation will not change impacts$^+$, the corresponding arrow is deleted. Secondly, nodes are deleted by substituting the impact structure of an aggregate class for the aggregate. After the substitution, those components with an impacts relation to the aggregate class will inherit the impacts of that aggregate.

Stage 3: Composition of Impacts

The composition of the impacts obtained from Stage 2, can be identified in two steps.

1. Multiple composition. When there are multiple instances of a class that impact another class, the interactor specifications are examined to determine the multiplicity.

2. Logical composition. When more than one class participates in an impact relation with another class, the interactor specifications are examined to determine if the behaviour corresponds to an *or-impacts* or an *and-impacts*.

Figure 3 shows the evolution of the impact structure for the case study. Figure 3.a illustrates the impact structure for the class *ESFAS_SI_Small*, and depicts an inter-impacts relation between the subclass *Train* and its aggregate class *ESFAS_SI_Small*, an intra-impacts relation between the subclasses *Channel* and *Train*, and a *3-impacts* composition between *Channel* and *Train*. Figure 3.b illustrates an *and-impacts* between subclasses *Manual Actuation* and *Train_Logic* and subclass *Sum*, Figure 3.c illustrates a simplified structure derived by merging figures 3.a and 3.b, deleting the subclass *Train*.

The impact structure provides a compact representation of failure propagation through object classes, thus facilitating the process for conducting a cause–consequence failure analysis of the object class model. Thereby providing an essential step to the systematic derivation of a fault tree from an object class model. This is achieved by instantiating the impact structure of the object class model, in order to obtain a structure representing failure propagation over object instances, from which a fault tree can be then generated.

4.4 Fault tree instantiation

This section presents how to derive a fault tree, for a particular failure event, from an impact structure of an object class model and the specification of interactors of the classes.

A fault tree consists of *nodes*, which represent failure events, and *gates* ("and", "or", and numerical) which represent the causal relationships between the nodes [10].

The method for generating the fault tree from the impact structure and the specifications of the interactors proceeds in two stages:

Stage 1: Generating the nodes

- Some of the nodes of the fault tree are formed by instantiating the impact structure, thus producing a node for each object instance of the classes in the impact structure.

- The nodes related to aggregate classes are split into two nodes. A node representing the failure behaviour of the object instance, which is a primitive node, and another node representing those failure behaviours which are to be refined at lower levels.

- For the particular failure event being analysed, each resulting node is annotated with the respective axiomatic specification of the behaviour from the relevant interactor, and when necessary modified to incorporate failure behaviours which are to be refined.

Stage 2: Generating the gates

- The gates of the fault tree are formed by referring to the composition of the impact (*and, or, n*) and introducing the relevant gate. An "or" gate is also used to connect two nodes that were produced by splitting the node representing an aggregate class.

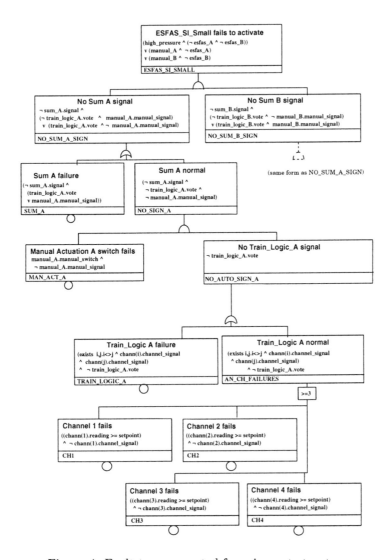

Figure 4: Fault tree generated from impact structure

Figure 4 shows the fault tree resulting from the application of this method to the **ESFAS_SI_Small** case study. The top node is annotated with the critical failure of the object class **ESFAS_SI_Small**, the failure event for this tree. The fault tree contains primitive nodes SUM_A and SUM_B representing the failure behaviours of the class **Sum**. Similarly primitive nodes are provided for the failure behaviours of **Manual_Actuation**, **Train_Logic**, and **Channel**.

The other intermediate nodes (generated from splitting an aggregate class) of the fault tree represent failure propagation from the primitive failure events to the top failure event. An example of an intermediate node is NO_SIGN_A, which represent the propagation of failures from lower levels when SUM_A exhibits normal behaviour.

There is an "and" gate joining the failure events associated with the two **Sum** instances, since the impact structure had an *2-impacts*. The **Channel**s are connected by a numerical gate "≥ 3", since there are four instances and the impact structure had a *3-impacts*.

The fault tree produced directly from the original system model is shown in Figure 5. Both fault trees have been "pruned" for reasons of space.

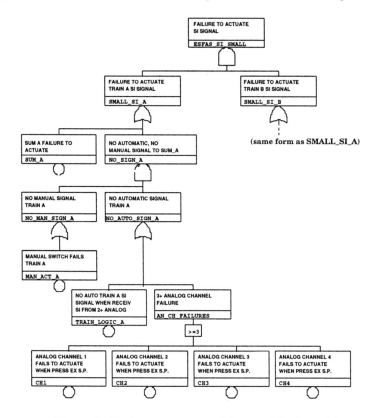

Figure 5: Fault tree generated from original model

In order to validate that the failure properties of the object class model are consistent with the original system model, the minimal cut sets of their respective fault trees are compared [5, 11]. A minimal cut set of a fault tree is a set of failures, such that if all events of the set occur the top failure event occurs. For example, one of the minimal cut sets resulting from the fault tree generated from the impact structure is: MAN_ACT_A, MAN_ACT_B,

TRAIN_LOGIC_A, TRAIN_LOGIC_B.

If the minimal cut sets are equivalent, we can conclude that the new model is valid with respect to the original system model. If not, the minimal cut sets will either be overlapping or (in the worst case) disjoint. If there is an overlap the reasons must be investigated – a new failure may have been created, or a failure from the original model may have been removed, in the case of disjoint cut sets imply totally incompatible models. For this case study, the minimal cut sets resulting from both fault trees are identical, which serves to validate the model.

5 Conclusions

The proposed method tackles the problems encountered by application domain engineers, when investigating the feasibility of replacing a traditional system with a software based system. The method provides qualitative evidence that a software based system can be developed which exhibits the same failure properties as the traditional system. Thereby, providing assurance that the software will not increase the risk posed by the system.

The method has been applied to a larger case study [7], which demonstrates the scalability of the work. Further work includes formalising causality and investigation of applicability of other safety analysis techniques.

Acknowledgements

The work reported in this paper was carried out as part of the EC Copernicus Joint Research Project ISAT (Integration of Safety Analysis Techniques for Process Control Systems).

References

[1] J Rumbaugh, M Blaha, W Premerlani, F Eddy, and W Lorenson. *Object-Oriented Modelling and Design*. Prentice-Hall International Inc., New Jersey, 1991.

[2] D Duke and MD Harrison. Abstract interaction objects. *Computer Graphics Forum*, 12(3):25–36, 1993.

[3] R de Lemos, B Fields, and A Saeed. Analysis of safety requirements in the context of system faults and human errors. In *Proc. IEEE International Workshop on Systems Engineering of Computer Based Systems*, pages 374–381, Tucson, Arizona, March 1995.

[4] A Saeed, R de Lemos, and T Anderson. Safety analysis for requirements specifications: Methods and techniques. In *Proc. 14th International Conference on Computer Safety, Reliability and Security: SAFECOMP '95*, pages 27–41, October 1995.

[5] M Čepin and A Wardziński. On integration of probabilistic and deterministic safety analysis. In *Proc. 3rd Regional Meeting: Nuclear Energy in Central Europe*, Portoroz, Slovenia, 1996. (To appear. Also Technical Report TR ISAT 96/9, Jožef Stefan Institute, Ljubljana, September 1996).

[6] M Čepin and B Mavko. Identification and preparation of case studies. Technical Report TR ISAT 96/8, Jožef Stefan Institute, Ljubljana, Slovenia, June 1996.

[7] S Riddle and M Čepin. Object modelling and safety analysis of Engineered Safety Features Actuation System. Technical Report TR ISAT 96/11, University of Newcastle upon Tyne, United Kingdom, December 1996.

[8] B Potter, J Sinclair, and D Till. *An Introduction to Formal Specification and Z*. International Series in Computer Science. Prentice-Hall International (UK) Ltd, United Kingdom, 1991.

[9] A Saeed, R de Lemos, and T Anderson. An approach for the risk analysis of safety specifications. In *Proc. 9th Annual Conference on Computer Assurance (COMPASS '94)*, pages 209–221, Gaithersburg, MD, June 1994.

[10] WE Vesely, FF Goldberg, NH Roberts, and DF Haasl. Fault tree handbook. NUREG 0492, US NRC, Washington, 1981.

[11] J Górski and A Wardziński. Formalising fault trees. In *Proc. Safety-Critical Systems Symposium*, pages 310–327, Brighton, United Kingdom, 1995.

Methodological Support for Formally Specifying Safety-Critical Software

Maritta Heisel

Technische Universität Berlin[*]

Carsten Sühl

GMD FIRST[†]

Abstract

We present the concept of an *agenda* and apply this concept to the formal specification of software for safety-critical applications. An agenda describes a list of activities to solving a task in software engineering, and validations of the results of the activities. Agendas used to support the application of formal specification techniques provide detailed guidance for specifiers, schematic expressions of the used specification language that only need to be instantiated, and application independent validation criteria. We present an agenda for a frequently used design of safety-critical systems and illustrate its usage by an example. Using agendas to systematically develop formal specifications for safety-critical software contributes to system safety because, first, the specifications are developed in a standardized way, making them better comprehensible for other persons. Secondly, using a formal language yields specifications with an unambiguous semantics as the starting point of further design and implementation. Thirdly, the recommended validation criteria draw the specifier's attention to common mistakes and thus enhance the quality of the resulting specification.

1   Introduction

Although every software-based system potentially benefits from the application of formal methods, their use is particularly advantageous in the development of safety-critical systems. The potential damage operators and developers of a safety-critical system have to envisage in case of an accident may be much greater than the additional costs of applying formal methods in system development. It is therefore worthwhile to develop formal methods tailor-made for the development of safety-critical systems.

A major drawback of formal techniques is that they are not easy to apply. Users of formal techniques need an appropriate education. They have to deal with lots of details, and often they are left alone with a mere formalism without any guidance on how to use it.

While nothing can be done about the first two points, it is definitely possible to provide guidance for the users of formal techniques. In this paper, we introduce the concept of an *agenda* that makes explicit the activities to be performed when developing an artifact in software engineering. We present a concrete agenda that supports specifiers in the development of specifications of

---

[*]Franklinstr. 28/29, Sekr. FR 5-6, 10587 Berlin, Germany, email: heisel@cs.tu-berlin.de
[†]Rudower Chaussee 5, 12489 Berlin, Germany, email: suehl@first.gmd.de

software for safety-critical applications. The agenda not only makes all steps of the specification process explicit. It also provides schematic expressions of the specification language to be used and validation criteria to check the specification for consistency and completeness.

In the following, we first describe the class of systems we consider and the specification language we will use (Section 2). We then describe the concept of an agenda in more detail in Section 3. In Section 4, we present an agenda for specifying software suitable for a common class of safety-critical systems. We illustrate the usage of this agenda in Section 5. Finally, we discuss related work in Section 6 and summarize our achievements in Section 7.

2   System Model and Specification Language

The system class we want to consider pertains to technical processes, that have to be controlled by dedicated system components being at least partially realized by software. Such a system consists of four parts: the technical process, the control component, sensors to communicate information about the current state of the technical process to the control component, and actuators that can be used by the control component to influence the behavior of the technical process.

A software-based control component affects certain process variables (*manipulated variables*) by sending commands to actuators. By evaluating the current state of certain process variables which are measured by sensors (*controlled variables*), the control component approximates the current state of the technical process to verify the effect of the commands sent to the actuators and to determine further commands to be sent. It is very important that the image of the state of the technical process that is built up in the software control component is sufficiently accurate and up-to-date. In the following, we will call this state the *internal* state, because it is internal to the software control component; the state of the technical process we will call the *external* state.

Most safety-critical systems are *reactive*. Hence, two aspects are important for the specification of software for safety-critical systems. First, it must be possible to specify behavior, i.e. how the system reacts to incoming events. Second, the structure of the system's data state and the operations that change this state must be specified. These requirements lead us to use a combination of the process algebra real-time CSP and the model-based specification language Z. Readers not familiar with these languages may consult [Dav93] and [Spi92], respectively.

In [HS96, Hei97] we have described the following principles of the combination of both languages in detail: For each system operation *Op* specified in the Z part of a specification, the CSP part is able to refer to the event *OpExecution*. For each input or output of a system operation defined in Z, there is a communication channel within the CSP part onto which an input value is written or an output value is read from. The dynamic behavior of a software component may depend on the current internal system state. To take this requirement into account, a process of the CSP part is able to refer to the current internal system state via predicates which are specified in the Z part by schemas.

3 Agendas and Reference Architectures

An agenda is a list of activities to be performed when carrying out a well-defined task in the context of some project. In this paper, we consider the application of formal specification techniques in the context of system safety. Here, agendas contain informal descriptions of the activities. They may also contain schematic expressions of the formal specification language that can be instantiated in carrying out the activity. The activities listed in an agenda may depend on each other. Usually, they will have to be repeated to achieve the goal, like in the spiral model of software engineering.

As one of the major reasons for applying formal techniques is to guarantee semantic properties of an artifact, the activities of an agenda may have validation conditions associated with them. These validation conditions state *necessary* semantic conditions that the artifact must fulfill in order to serve its purpose properly. Since the verification conditions that can be stated in an agenda are necessarily application independent, the developed artifact should be further validated with respect to application dependent needs.

Following an agenda gives no guarantee of success. Agendas cannot replace creativity, but they can tell the user what needs to be done and can help avoid omissions and inconsistencies. Their use lies in an improvement of the quality of the developed products and in the possibility for reusing the knowledge incorporated in an agenda.

In this paper, we show how agendas can be profitably employed to specify software to control safety-critical systems, as the ones described in Section 2. There are several ways to design safety-critical systems, according to the manner in which activities of the control component take place, and the manner in which system components trigger these activities. These different approaches to the design of safety-critical systems can be expressed as *reference architectures*. The architecture we consider here assumes that sensors are no passive measuring devices but can cause interrupts in the control component.

The agenda we present is tailored for this *active sensors architecture*. It describes the steps to be taken to specify a suitable software control component. It provides schematic expressions of Z or real-time CSP that only need to be instantiated, and states validation obligations that should be fulfilled. Our general approach to the specification of safety-critical software is to first decide on the architecture of the system for which a software control component must be specified, and then to follow the steps of the corresponding agenda.

The aim of this work is not to completely cover the area of specification of safety-critical systems, but to show that detailed guidance can be provided to specifiers of software systems if special contexts are considered. Consequently, other reference architectures for the design of safety-critical systems are useful, too. An example can be found in [Hei97]. Furthermore, concrete safety-critical

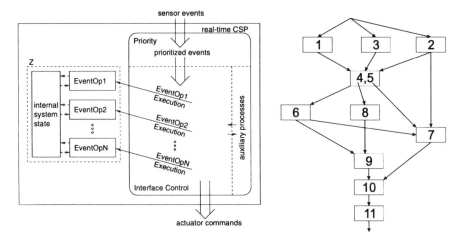

Figure 1: Software Control Component for Active Sensors Architecture

Figure 2: Dependencies of Steps

systems need not be "pure" instances of predefined architectures. When necessary, reference architectures can be combined as appropriate.

4   Agenda for the Active Sensors Architecture

An active sensor controls a certain variable of the technical process and independently reports certain changes of the controlled variable to the control component at arbitrary time instants. Such a report immediately triggers a handling operation within the control component. The active sensors architecture is applicable to systems with only active sensors. Moreover, we assume that it is appropriate to distinguish several *operational modes* of the system. Within distinct modes, which can model different environmental or internal conditions, the behavior of the system – and thus of the control component – may be totally different.

Figure 1 shows the structure of a software control component associated with the active sensors architecture. The CSP part of such a control component consists of three parallel processes. A *Priority* process receives the sensor events from the environment. If several events occur at the same time, this process defines which of these events is treated with priority. Depending on the prioritized events passed on from the *Priority* process, an *InterfaceControl* process invokes a Z operation to update the internal state of the software controller. Hence, the Z operations correspond to events that cause transitions between operational modes. The *InterfaceControl* process is also responsible for sending actuator commands to the environment. Finally, there may be auxiliary processes that interact only with the *InterfaceControl* process, not with the environment or with the *Priority* process. The active sensors architecture is suitable for systems that continuously have to react to user commands or other stimuli from the environment.

An overview of the agenda for this architecture is given in Table 1. The steps shown there need not be executed exactly in the given order. Figure 2 shows the dependencies between them. In the following, we describe the steps in more detail; their associated validation conditions are explained when necessary. For a more comprehensive presentation, see [Hei97].

Step 1 *Model the sensors and actuators as sets of CSP events or Z types.*

Sensors trigger operations of the control component. If a sensor carries a measured value, it is modeled as a Z type whose members are communicated via a communication channel. If a sensor just carries boolean information (i.e., something happens or not), it is modeled as a set of CSP events. Modeling the sensors yields a set of events *Sensor_Events*. Modeling the actuators proceeds analogously.

Step 2 *Decide on auxiliary processes.*

One can regard these auxiliary processes as subcomponents of the controller that do not need a state. Examples are timers that are controlled by the software component. The events that are used in the auxiliary processes to communicate with the rest of the control component form the set *Internal_Events*.

Step 3 *Decide on the operational modes of the system and the initial modes.*

According to different environmental conditions in which the control component has to react differently, a set of operational modes has to be defined yielding an enumeration type *MODE*. Moreover, modes must be identified in which the controller can be initialized.

Step 4 *Set up a mode transition relation, specifying which events relate which modes.*

This transition relation can be defined in Z, or it can be given as a state transition diagram. For each operational mode m and each event e (which can be internal or external), it must be decided on the successor modes that are possible when event e occurs in mode m. It should also be specified what happens when the sensors report an event that cannot normally occur in the respective mode. Hence, the mode transition relation should be made as complete as possible, and a justification should be given, if no successor mode is defined for a pair (m, e).

Step 5 *Define the internal system state and the initial states.*

The legal states of the control component as well as its initial states must be specified by means of Z schemas. Furthermore, safety constraints on the controller must be defined. These safety constraints have to be ensured by the definition of the legal states, see validation condition 5.2.

Step 6 *Specify a Z operation for each mode transition contained in the mode transition relation.*

The Z operations correspond to mode transitions caused by the occurrence of events. Different mode transitions might be associated with the same operation. The operations must be consistent with the state transition relation.

No	Step	Validation Condition
1	Model the sensors and actuators as sets of CSP events or Z types.	
2	Decide on auxiliary processes.	
3	Decide on the operational modes of the system and the initial modes.	
4	Set up a mode transition relation, specifying which events relate which modes.	4.1. All events identified in Step 1 and all modes defined in Step 3 must occur in the transition relation. 4.2. The omission of a mode-event pair from the relation must be justified. 4.3. All modes must be reachable from an initial mode.
5	Define the internal system states and the initial states.	5.1. The internal system state must be an appropriate approximation of the state of the technical process. 5.2. Each legal state must be safe. 5.3. There must exist legal initial states. 5.4. For each initial internal state, the controller must be in an initial mode.
6	Specify a Z operation for each mode transition contained in the mode transition relation.	6.1. These operations must be consistent with the mode transition relation.
7	Define the auxiliary processes identified in Step 2.	7.1. The alphabets of these processes must not contain external events or events related to the Z part of the specification.
8	Specify priorities on events (optional).	8.1. The priorities must not be cyclic.
9	Specify the interface control process.	9.1. All prioritized external events and all internal events must occur as initial events of the branches of the interface control process. 9.2. The preconditions of the invoked Z operations must be satisfied.
10	Define the overall control process.	10.1. The auxiliary processes must communicate with the interface control process.
11	Define further requirements or environmental assumptions if necessary.	

Table 1: Agenda for the Active Sensors Architecture

Step 7 *Define the auxiliary processes identified in Step 2.*

This step can be performed by defining process terms or by specifying predicates that restrict the behavior of the respective processes. The auxiliary processes should neither receive external sensor messages nor invoke Z operations or depend on the internal system state. They should exclusively interact with the *Interface Control* process, see Figure 1.

Step 8 *Specify priorities on events if necessary.*

To determine if priorities are necessary, we have to analyze the state transition diagram. If more than one event can occur at the same time when the system is in a certain operational mode, it must be decided how the system reacts when several events occur simultaneously. Usually, the event with the highest importance for safety will be treated; the other ones will be ignored.

Technically, this means to define derived events and a process *Priority* that relates the original events with the derived ones. If we have a high priority event *high* and a low priority event *low*, then the system will only react to the event *low* if *high* does not occur at the same time. Therefore, an event *excl_low* is derived that occurs at time t exactly when *low* but not *high* occurs at time t.

Step 9 *Specify the interface control process.*

The interface control process handles the prioritized events coming from the sensors. According to the internal or sensor events that occur, the interface control process triggers the execution of Z operations and sends events to actuators or auxiliary processes. The interface control process will usually contain an external choice of prioritized events. Each branch of this external choice should be robust, i.e., if the sensors send signals that contradict the internal state of the system, then the system must handle the faulty situation. Consequently, a possible form of the interface control process that is executed after the system is initialized is

$$InterfaceControl_{READY} \; \widehat{=} \; \mu X \bullet$$
$$event_1 \rightarrow \text{if} \; \langle consistency \; condition \rangle$$
$$\text{then} \; \langle execute \; event_1\text{-}Z\text{-}operation \rangle \; \langle send \; actuator \; commands \rangle;$$
$$Wait \; \epsilon; \; X$$
$$\text{else} \; \langle emergency \; shutdown \rangle \; \langle send \; actuator \; commands \rangle; \; Stop \; \text{fi}$$
$$\square \ldots \square$$
$$event_n \rightarrow \ldots$$

All branches are defined similarly. To ensure that the execution of each branch takes time, we need a *Wait* process in each of them. This form is only possible if there is a fail-safe state. Then the system can shut down when an inconsistency is detected. To express the consistency conditions, predicates on the current internal system state must be defined in Z.

According to validation condition 9.2, the preconditions of the invoked Z operations must be satisfied in the respective state. This must be guaranteed by appropriate consistency conditions guarding the invocation of the Z operations in the interface control process.

Step 10 *Define the overall control process.*

The control process combines the processes defined in Steps 7, 8, and 9. Let $Aux_1, \ldots, Aux_k$ be the auxiliary processes defined in Step 7. Then a possible form of the overall control process is

$$
\begin{aligned}
ControlComponent \;\widehat{=}\; &(InterfaceControl \parallel Aux_1 \parallel \ldots \parallel Aux_k) \\
&\setminus Internal\_Events \\
InterfaceControl \;\widehat{=}\; &Init \to (InterfaceControl_{READY} \parallel Priority) \\
&\setminus (\alpha Priority \setminus (Sensor\_Events \cup Internal\_Events))
\end{aligned}
$$

where *Init* establishes an initial internal system state. The internal events are hidden from the environment, and the prioritized events newly introduced in the alphabet of the *Priority* process are hidden from the other components of the controller (and hence from the environment).

Checking validation condition 10.1, it must be verified that the auxiliary processes communicate with the interface control process. Technically, this means that the alphabets of $(Aux_1 \parallel \ldots \parallel Aux_k)$ and *InterfaceControl* have a non-empty intersection.

Step 11 *Define further requirements or environmental assumptions if necessary.*

Usually, these will be assumptions on the environment and real-time requirements on the execution time of Z operations.

5 Example: Railroad Crossing

We illustrate the agenda by specifying a software component controlling the gates of a railroad crossing, known as the Generalized Railroad Problem, see e.g. [HM96]. We assume that there are two tracks at the crossing, one in each direction.

We begin with **Step 1** of the agenda, i.e. the definition of the sensors and actuators. For each direction, a sensor is situated in front of the crossing to report the arrival of trains. The arrival of a train is represented by the CSP events *TrainEntered*1 and *TrainEntered*2, respectively. Analogously, behind the crossing there are sensors reporting the departure of trains represented by the events *TrainLeft*1 and *TrainLeft*2.

The controller manipulates the gates of the crossing by giving the commands to close and to open the gates (events *CloseGateCmd* and *OpenGateCmd*). Sensors detect the transition of the gates into a completely closed or completely opened state.[1] These transitions are modeled by the events *GateOpened* and *GateClosed*. The interface of the controller to its environment is shown in Figure 3.

According to **Step 3** of the agenda, we define a data type *Modes* that contains the operational modes of the controller.

$$
Modes ::= OPEN \mid OPENING \mid CLOSED \mid CLOSING \mid WARNING \mid INCON
$$

---

[1] We only regard the state of the gates as a whole, i.e. the gates are regarded to be open or closed if and only if all gates are open or closed.

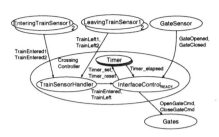

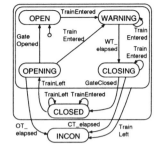

Figure 3: Controller's Architecture

Figure 4: Operational Modes

The mode *OPEN* will be the only initial mode of the controller.

To define the transitions between the operational modes, which are associated with sensor events and internal events, we have to decide on auxiliary processes (**Step 2**). The opening and closing of the gates must be finished within certain time intervals, whose lengths are expressed as constants *MaxOpeningDur* and *MaxClosingDur*, respectively. Car drivers and pedestrians are warned *WarningDur* time units before the gates are closed.

$$MaxOpeningDur, MaxClosingDur, WarningDur : \mathbb{N}_1$$

To monitor these intervals we use three timer components *WarningTimer*, *OpeningTimer*, and *ClosingTimer*, which will mark the end of these intervals by an event *Timer_elapsed*. Their alphabets, i.e. the set of events in which they can participate, is

$$Internal\_Events \,\widehat{=}\, \{\, WT\_set, \, WT\_reset, \, WT\_elapsed, \, OT\_set,$$
$$OT\_reset, \, OT\_elapsed, \, CT\_set, \, CT\_reset, \, CT\_elapsed\}$$

The operational modes and the transitions between them are depicted in Figure 4. This figure graphically defines the mode transition relation to be set up in **Step 4** of the agenda. As can be easily verified, all external and internal events are taken into account in the state transition diagram, for each mode-event pair the consequence is considered, and each mode is reachable from the initial mode *OPEN*. Hence, the validation conditions associated with Step 4 are fulfilled.

Performing **Step 5** of the agenda, we decide that the state components of the controller are the current operational mode and the number of trains currently being in the crossing area. The safety constraint for the controller is that there must not be any train in the area while the gates are open. An availability requirement is that the gates may only be closed if there are trains in the crossing area. These conditions are reflected in the state schema.

```
┌─ State ──────────────────────────────────────────────
│ mode : Modes
│ num_trains : ℕ
├──────────────────────────────────────────────────────
│ mode ∈ {OPEN, OPENING} ⇒ num_trains = 0
│
│ num_trains = 0 ⇒ mode ∈ {OPEN, OPENING, INCON}
└──────────────────────────────────────────────────────
```

While validation condition 5.1 cannot be shown formally because the notion of "appropriateness" is necessarily informal, validation condition 5.2 is satisfied by construction because the safety constraint is part of the state invariant.

When starting the controller, it is assumed that no train is in the area and that the gates are open.

$$Init \mathrel{\widehat{=}} [\, State' \mid mode' = OPEN \wedge num\_trains' = 0\,]$$

The $Init$ schema uniquely defines the initial state, whose compliance with the state invariant is straightforward to prove (validation condition 5.3). By the definition of the $Init$ schema, validation condition 5.4 is trivially fulfilled.

To carry out **Step 6**, we model the possible commands to the gates by the data type $GateCmd$.

$$GateCmd ::= CMD\_OPEN \mid CMD\_CLOSE \mid CMD\_NONE$$

The schema $Actuators$ defines how the actuator commands are derived from the operational mode of the controller.

```
┌─ Actuators ─────────────────────────────────────────
│ State'
│ gate! : GateCmd
├─────────────────────────────────────────────────────
│ gate! = CMD_OPEN ⇔ mode' = OPENING
│ gate! = CMD_CLOSE ⇔ mode' ∈ {CLOSING, INCON}
└─────────────────────────────────────────────────────
```

We can now define the operations on the abstract state. They reflect the mode transition diagram of Figure 4 and are straightforward to define.

```
┌─ TrainEntered ─────────────────         ┌─ TrainLeft ──────────────────
│ ΔState; Actuators                       │ ΔState; Actuators
├───────────────────────────────          ├──────────────────────────────
│ mode ≠ INCON                            │ mode = CLOSED
│                                         │
│ num_trains' = num_trains + 1            │ num_trains' = num_trains − 1
│ mode ∈ {OPEN, OPENING}                  │ mode' = if num_trains' = 0
│    ⇒ mode' = WARNING                    │       then OPENING
│ mode ∈ {CLOSING, CLOSED, WARNING}       │       else CLOSED
│    ⇒ mode' = mode                       │
└───────────────────────────────          └──────────────────────────────
```

$$GateOpened \mathrel{\widehat{=}} [\,\Delta State;\ Actuators \mid mode = OPENING \wedge$$
$$mode' = OPEN \wedge num\_trains' = num\_trains\,]$$

The remaining operations $GateClosed$, $WarningFin$ and $Incon$ (that enters the fail-safe state), are defined analogously.

The relationship between the modes in the pre and post state, as defined by the operation schemas, directly reflects the state transition diagram. Therefore, validation condition 6.1 can be checked successfully.

Continuing with **Step 7**, we specify the auxiliary timer subcomponents which monitor the maximal closing and opening duration of the gates as well as the warning period.

$$WarningTimer \,\hat{=}\, \mu X \bullet (WT\_set \rightarrow$$
$$(Wait \; WarningDur; \; WT\_elapsed \rightarrow X)$$
$$\triangle \; WT\_reset \rightarrow X)$$

The processes *ClosingTimer* and *OpeningTimer* are defined analogously.

Inspecting the mode transition diagram reveals that there is no need to give priority to some event in any mode. Hence, **Step 8** is omitted.

To accomplish **Step 9**, we first specify a process *TrainSensorHandler*, which serves two purposes. First, it abstracts from the concrete sensor reporting the event of a train arrival or a train departure. Second, it buffers incoming events, thus guaranteeing that no sensor report is ignored by the controller.

$$TrainSensorHandler \,\hat{=}\,$$
$$(\mu X \bullet TrainEntered1 \rightarrow TrainEntered \rightarrow X)$$
$$||| \; (\mu X \bullet TrainEntered2 \rightarrow TrainEntered \rightarrow X)$$
$$||| \; (\mu X \bullet TrainLeft1 \rightarrow TrainLeft \rightarrow X)$$
$$||| \; (\mu X \bullet TrainLeft2 \rightarrow TrainLeft \rightarrow X)$$

We can then specify the interface control process as follows.

$$InterfaceControl \,\hat{=}\, Init \rightarrow$$
$$(InterfaceControl_{READY} \; |[\; EvSet \;]| \; TrainSensorHandler) \setminus EvSet$$

$$EvSet \,\hat{=}\, \{ \, TrainEntered, TrainLeft \, \}$$

The process $InterfaceControl_{READY}$ reacts to the derived events contained in *EvSet* that are supplied by the process *TrainSensorHandler*. The derived events are hidden from the environment.

With the subprocess *ActOut*, we specify how the actuator command is derived from the respective operation output.

$$ActOut \,\hat{=}\, gate?CMD\_OPEN \rightarrow OpenGateCmd \rightarrow Skip$$
$$\square \; gate?CMD\_CLOSE \rightarrow CloseGateCmd \rightarrow Skip$$
$$\square \; gate?CMD\_NONE \rightarrow Skip$$

The process $InterfaceControl_{READY}$, specifying the reactive behavior after initialization, contains an instance of the schematic process presented in Section 4. To define it, we need some predicates on the internal state, which are defined in Z.

$IsClosed \ \widehat{=} \ [\,State \mid mode = CLOSED\,]$
$IsOpening \ \widehat{=} \ [\,State \mid mode = OPENING\,]$
$IsClosing \ \widehat{=} \ [\,State \mid mode = CLOSING\,]$
$IsWarning \ \widehat{=} \ [\,State \mid mode = WARNING\,]$
$AreaEmpty \ \widehat{=} \ [\,State \mid num\_trains = 0\,]$
$FirstTrain \ \widehat{=} \ [\,State \mid num\_trains = 1\,]$

$InterfaceControl_{READY} \ \widehat{=} \ \mu\, X \ \bullet$
    $(\,TrainEntered \rightarrow TrainEnteredExecution \rightarrow Wait\,\epsilon;\ ActOut;$
        (if $FirstTrain$ then $WT\_set \rightarrow Skip$ else $Skip$ fi); X
    $\square\ TrainLeft \rightarrow$if $IsClosed$ then $TrainLeftExecution \rightarrow Wait\,\epsilon;\ ActOut;$
            (if $AreaEmpty$ then $OT\_set \rightarrow Skip$ else $Skip$ fi); X
        else $InconExecution \rightarrow Wait\,\epsilon;\ ActOut;\ Stop$ fi
    $\square\ GateOpened \rightarrow$if $IsOpening$
        then $GateOpenedExecution \rightarrow Wait\,\epsilon;\ ActOut;\ OT\_reset \rightarrow X$
        else $InconExecution \rightarrow Wait\,\epsilon;\ ActOut;\ Stop$ fi
    $\square\ GateClosed \rightarrow$if $IsClosing$
        then $GateClosedExecution \rightarrow Wait\,\epsilon;\ ActOut;\ CT\_reset \rightarrow X$
        else $InconExecution \rightarrow Wait\,\epsilon;\ ActOut;\ Stop$ fi
    $\square\ WT\_elapsed \rightarrow$if $IsWarning$
        then $WarningFinExecution \rightarrow Wait\,\epsilon;\ ActOut;\ CT\_set \rightarrow X$
        else $InconExecution \rightarrow Wait\,\epsilon;\ ActOut;\ Stop$ fi)
  $\triangle\ (OT\_elapsed \rightarrow Skip\ \square\ CT\_elapsed \rightarrow Skip);\ InconExecution \rightarrow$
    $Wait\,\epsilon;\ ActOut;\ Stop$

The reactive behavior is recurrent which is indicated by the recursion operator μ. When an event is reported by a sensor, the controller checks whether this report is consistent with the current state. Such a consistency check is modeled by referring to the respective Z predicate. If the event is consistent with the internal state, the controller executes the system operation related to the sensor report. Afterwards, the actuator command determined by the operation is sent to the actuators. In case of an inconsistency, the controller changes to the mode *INCON* and attempts to fail safe by closing the gates.

Each branch of the external choice operator $\square$ defines the reaction to the occurrence of a certain event. All derived sensor events and internal timer events are initial events of the branches (validation condition 9.1). Moreover, the predicates guarding the branches guarantee that the preconditions of the corresponding Z operations are fulfilled (validation condition 9.2).

This "normal" behavior in front of the interrupt operator $\triangle$ can be interrupted at any time, if a timer, monitoring the gates' opening or closing duration, elapses without being reset.

Having reached **Step 10** of the agenda, we specify the overall control process according to the schematic expression given in Section 4.

$$CrossingController \; \hat{=} \; (InterfaceControl$$
$$|[\, Internal\_Events \,]|$$
$$(WarningTimer \; ||| \; OpeningTimer \; ||| \; ClosingTimer))$$
$$\backslash \; Internal\_Events$$

The auxiliary timer processes communicate with the interface control process via the events contained in the set *Internal_Events* defined in Step 2. Hence, validation condition 10.1 is fulfilled.

Finally, performing **Step 11** of the agenda, we require that, at each time instant, the actuators are able to accept the commands to open or close the gates. Furthermore, the sensors are supposed not to send contradictory events[2].

$$EnvironmentalAssumption \; \hat{=} \; \forall \, t : [0, \infty) \; \bullet$$
$$((OpenGateCmd \; \mathsf{open} \; t \wedge CloseGateCmd \; \mathsf{open} \; t) \wedge$$
$$\neg \, (GateOpened \; \mathsf{open} \; t \wedge GateClosed \; \mathsf{open} \; t))$$

This concludes the development of a specification for the controller of the railway crossing. The example shows that, following an agenda, specifications for safety-critical software can be developed in a fairly routine way. When specifiers are relieved from the task to find new ways of structuring a specification for each new application, they can better concentrate on the peculiarities of the application itself.

6 Related Work

The work presented in this paper further elaborates the results of an earlier paper [HS96]. There, we described related work presenting different formalisms for specifying safety-critical software and case studies using these formalisms. The focus of this paper, however, is on *methodological* support for applying formal techniques. Related to this aim is the work of Souquières and Lévy [SL93]. They support specification acquisition with *development operators* that reduce *tasks* to subtasks. However, they do not consider safety-related issues, and the development operators do not provide means to validate the developed specification. Chernack [Che96] uses a concept called *checklist* to support inspection processes. In contrast to agendas, checklists presuppose the existence of a software artifact and aim at detecting defects in this artifact.

7 Conclusions

With the concept of an agenda, we have introduced a means for organizing work that has to be carried out in a particular context. The purpose of agendas is to capture the knowledge used by the domain experts when carrying out their

---

[2]The predicate e open t means that the environment of a process offers event e at time t.

tasks. Agendas are specific to the task to be performed, not to the formalism to be used. Therefore, the use of agendas can be smoothly introduced into an organization. Developers essentially proceed as before, only that the steps to be taken in performing the task are made explicit. Thus, agendas contribute to making formal techniques applicable for non-experts. A further step in this direction will be tool support of the development process, where the tool — according to a specific agenda — could determine the set of steps to be possibly performed next and could derive the corresponding validation obligations automatically.

Based on a reference architecture capturing a common design of safety-critical systems, we have presented an agenda that gives detailed guidance (i) for developing specifications of software components suitable for the architecture and (ii) for validating the component specifications. An example demonstrated the practicality of the agenda.

Using agendas, specification acquisition is performed in a standardized way. This not only supports specifiers but also other persons who must understand the specification process and its results, for example, because they must change or further develop the specification.

All in all, our approach to supporting the specification of software for safety-critical applications enhances the safety of the entire technical system, because the embedded software is specified in a systematic way, the specification has an unambiguous semantics, and the specification is validated more rigorously than this would be possible with informal specifications.

Acknowledgment. We thank Thomas Santen for his comments on this work.

References

[Che96] Yuri Chernack. A statistical approach to the inspection checklist formal synthesis and improvement. *IEEE Transactions on Software Engineering*, 22(12):866–874, December 1996.

[Dav93] Jim Davies. *Specification and Proof in Real-Time CSP*. Cambridge University Press, 1993.

[Hei97] Maritta Heisel. *Improving Software Quality with Formal Methods: Methodology and Machine Support*. Habilitation Thesis, TU Berlin, 1997. submitted.

[HM96] Constance Heitmeyer and Dino Mandrioli, editors. *Formal Methods for Real-Time Computing*, chapter 1. Trends in Software. John Wiley & Sons, 1996.

[HS96] Maritta Heisel and Carsten Sühl. Formal specification of safety-critical software with Z and real-time CSP. In E. Schoitsch, editor, *Proceedings 15th International Conference on Computer Safety, Reliability and Security*, pages 31–45. Springer, 1996.

[SL93] Jeanine Souquières and Nicole Lévy. Description of specification developments. In *Proc. of Requirements Engineering '93*, pages 216–223, 1993.

[Spi92] J. M. Spivey. *The Z Notation – A Reference Manual*. Prentice Hall, 2nd edition, 1992.

Applications and Industrial Experience

Embedded Systems in Avionics and the SACRES Approach[*]

Philippe Baufreton
SNECMA - Elecma
77550 Moissy-Cramayel, FRANCE

Xavier Méhaut
TNI
29608 BREST Cedex, FRANCE

Éric Rutten
IRISA/INRIA, 35042 RENNES Cedex, FRANCE
fax: +33 2 99 84 71 71, e-mail: `Eric.Rutten@irisa.fr`

Abstract

This paper presents an industrial experiment in avionics of the programming environment SILDEX based on the synchronous model, and an approach to the design and implementation of such safety critical embedded systems, developed in the framework of the Esprit project SACRES. The goal of the project is to integrate into a complete and unified environment, around the synchronous models technology, a variety of specification tools such as STATEMATE, SILDEX, TIMING DIAGRAMS and tools for verification, code generation and validation of the code produced.

1 Motivations

The ever increasing part taken by numerical computers in the control of safety critical systems makes the methodology for their development particularly crucial. Their complexity entails risks of errors in the interpretation of the objectives, as well as in their translation in terms of specification language and design. Passing from one phase to the next in their life cycle also entails risks in the translation from one formalism to another. Their very nature as potentially dangerous controllers, or which might have disastrous consequences if disrupted, imposes a particular care in their verification.

The answer to these safety requirements are in the automation and in the capacity for analysis and proof of properties of the systems under design. Formal methods are oriented towards the satisfaction of these needs. They present the advantage of defining automatable calculi for the analysis, optimization, and transformation of specifications. The latter may be used for the generation of code and for verification. Their effect and significance in the building of the kind of systems we are interested in is, therefore, on the one hand in reducing the risk of errors in the transformations leading to final implementation and, on the other hand, in making possible certain specification property checks and implementation checks in order to validate its compliance with the objectives and working constraints of the system.

The purpose of the Esprit project SACRES (*SAfety CRitical Embedded Systems: from requirements to system architecture*) is to integrate into a unified and complete environment a variety of tools for specification, verification, code generation and validation of the code produced. Among the application domains

---

[*]The work described in the article is partly funded by the CEC as Esprit Project EP 20897 SACRES (*SAfety CRitical Embedded Systems: from requirements to system architecture*).

targeted are avionics and process control. The question of certification and validation is integrated into the environment. Member partners of the SACRES project are: British Aerospace (UK), aircraft builder; i-Logix (UK), who develop and distribute STATEMATE, the environment for designing in STATE-CHARTS; INRIA (France), a research institute where new technologies are defined and developped around the synchronous language SIGNAL [7]; OFFIS (Germany), research institute bringing verification technology; Siemens (Germany), where controllers for industrial processes are developped; SNECMA (France), builder of aircraft engines; SNI (Germany), who develop and distribute verification tools; TNI (France), who develop and distribute the SILDEX tool and the SIGNAL language; the Weizmann Institute (Israel), as regards semantic aspects and the validation of code.

2   The SACRES project

The goal of the SACRES project is to offer tools and techniques to help designers and developpers of embedded systems, in particular those involving critical safety [4]. The project involves the integration of existing tools, the development of new technologies and the experimentation of associated methodologies on effective industrial systems. The previously existing tools integrated here are STATEMATE, SILDEX, TIMING DIAGRAMS and a tool for verification. Specification languages are integrated through a System Specification Language (SSL). New technologies studied in the project are related to the generation of code, possibly distributed according to the target architecture (hardware and operating system), the validation of the code generated (using formal verification in order to automatically prove its correction with regard to the specification), and the formal verification of properties on the behaviours of the system (re-using results from the Esprit project FORMAT [3]). These functionalities are based on synchronous technology [1] and results from the EUREKA project SYNCHRON [2]. Industrial partners of the project include users who will each develop an effective system using the environment developped by SACRES; the acquired experience will help improve and validate the environment and the associated methodology for its use, prior to broader distribution.

The SACRES tool is composed of a set of elements that exchange specifications in various states of design. They exchange information through the DC+ (Declarative Code) format, within which models are represented. Among the tools available are the specification tools, designed for the construction and edition of specifications and systems design. There is also a code generation tool, offering functionalities of optimization and distribution of code, and producing ANSI C and Ada83, taking into account the restrictions related to the development of avionic systems of safety level 1. In the case of Ada, this means in particular its sub-language SPARK. A tool for the validation of the generated code formally proves the correction of the generated code with regard to the model of the specification in the exchange format DC+. A tool for verification evaluates the satisfaction of logical and temporal properties on models of the specification. The synchronous format DC+ has been defined in the framework of the Eureka project SYNCHRON [2]. Figure 1 illustrates the central position of the format between the tools of the environment, and information flows in the global architecture of SACRES. Translators to and from DC+ are devel-

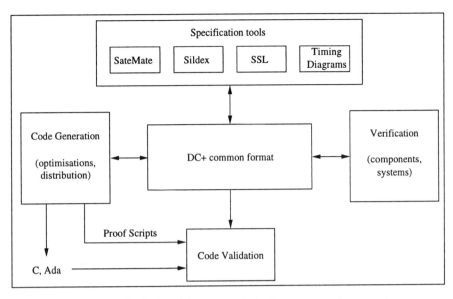

Figure 1: Global architecture of the SACRES environment.

opped in the framework of the project, and enable the connection of all the representations specific to the different tools with the common format.

STATEMATE and SILDEX are two tools well adapted to embedded systems. The former is founded on STATECHARTS, a notation of a hierarchized finite state machine type, whereas the latter supports the SIGNAL language, which is data-flow oriented, with block diagrams and equations. Their combination therefore covers the spectrum of applications from the sequencing of modes to signal processing and regulation. TIMING DIAGRAMS are a language for the specification of properties and constraints, particularly those that will have to be checked by the verification tool. SSL is the System Specification Language that enables the combination of sub-systems specified in the different languages, and to instanciate them to models that can evolve in the life cycle of the system. The way the behaviors described in these different languages are effectively composed resides in their translation into the DC+ common format.

This format supports the semantics of the different languages in presence. Therefore, it supports the integration of specifications, the construction of the models upon which verification techniques are performed, and the compilation and optimization up to code generation. Finally, it serves as a reference for the code validation technique. It consists of a data-flow graph where flows and operations are related by data dependencies and control dependencies, with synchronization information (i.e. the conditions for which the dependencies hold effectively). The format is itself structured into sub-formats, that are distinguished by their synchronization properties. Starting from DC+ in its most general form, one particularization consists of transforming events that might be used in the specification into tests on boolean conditions; another concerns the serialization of the computations in the application in order to respect data dependencies between them, and in the perspective of generating sequential code.

The tool for the verification of the specified system components is based on model-checking techniques, and re-uses results from the Esprit project FORMAT. It uses BDD techniques (Binary Decision Diagrams), and allows properties of the possible behaviors, expressed with the help of TIMING DIAGRAMS to be checked against the specification, using its modelling by a symbolic transition system [3]. The project will increase these proof capabilities by the treatment of real-time information, handling properties on durations, and with system-level verification, by facilitating the re-use of verifications of sub-systems assembled with SSL, in order to verify the system that includes them.

Code generation is considered in the broad sense as the compilation of DC+. Architecture-independent code generation will extend the functionalities of sequential code generation already featured in STATEMATE and SILDEX. It will feature the capacity to optimize computations, for instance according to the actual use of their results. It will also focus on modularity, by offering support to separate compilation. Implementation on specific target architectures (hardware and operating system), and particularly on distributed ones, will use sequential code generation to produce the distributed processes or tasks. Partitioning of the application will be effected by partitioning the DC+ graph into sub-graphs, between which the correctness of synchronizations is ensured. DC+ will also be used for the modelling of architectures. In particular, performance evaluation will be supported. Section 6 describes how the validation of this code is approached in SACRES.

One aspect of the SACRES project, additionally to the construction of a design environment integrating all these tools, is the definition of a methodology for their use. The current design processes of user members of the project are studied, so as to determine precisely the place and role of the functionalities offered by SACRES. This methodology will be experimented with a prototype version of the SACRES environment on applications by the user members: British Aerospace, Siemens et SNECMA. The goal is to establish that the tools work well on industrial-size problems, to offer an experimental feedback towards designers of the tools, and to adapt industrial development practices in order to make the most of the new functionalities offered.

3 Gas turbine engine control

Our application domain concerns civil and military aviation propulsion systems. The demands made on such systems have been constantly increasing over the last few years. Engine thermodynamic cycles have developed considerably, and consequently, so has the number of functions to be checked. In order to optimize the integration of these aspects and also meet the targets set by the users (pilots, airlines or air forces) regarding functional and operational performance, such as safety, maintenance, weight and cost, engine control systems are making increasing use of digital electronics.

Engine monitoring. The functions to be carried out in order to ensure automatic control of the engine operating point with regard to its state, its environment and the pilots demands, while integrating its operating limits, are numerous and complex. The engine state is determined directly through acquisition of parameters that characterize the thermodynamic airflow or the limitations to be taken into account. The engine environment consists primarily of the aircraft information acquired by the control system through the point-to-point digital links, such as atmospheric pressure, Mach number, angle of attack, etc. Command execution is devolved to hydromechanical components such as fuel pumps, flow controllers, actuators, etc. The engine control system architecture is of the full authority type. The electronic part of the system acts with full authority on all the control functions and interfaces with the aircraft, the sensors, the hydromechanical units, and the actuators. The digital computer provides the necessary computing power and upgrading flexibility both for development and operational service. By optimizing weight and costs, the centralization of the electronics enables the operating conditions to be improved by integrating the electronics in a suspended cooled unit, thereby isolating it from the severe vibrational and thermal environment of the engine.

Safety. To ensure protection against sudden failures of the electronics, which could jeoparde safety, and to ensure dependability, the engine manufacturers have turned to fully redundant electronics. The system architecture is of the FADEC type (Full Authority Digital Engine Control). The sensors, the computer, the electrical part of the actuators are duplicated. One channel is active and assigned to the engine controls, while the other channel monitors operation and can become active if a failure is detected on the first channel. The control system is managed entirely automatically by the engine computers. During the flight, failure detection is ensured by hardware and software tests performed on the sensors and actuators, and testing of the computer central processors and the exchanges between the two channels. The system fulfills these engine safety functions while monitoring any failures of sensors, actuators, the digital heart or the engine itself. It takes the necessary measures to prevent the propagation of these failures in order to avoid catastrophic consequences. The two engine computers have exactly the same software. Failure avoidance is ensured by implementing a strict and rigorous development methodology. Certain systems (military sector) are based on a real-time executive program of the SCEPTRE type which ensures task sequencing according to fixed priorities assigned statistically before starting the program, event and message management and task synchronization.

The techniques used. A large quantity of functions can be described by a formal system (block diagrams, GRAFCET[1]) specific to the control system. The development of servomechanisms in the design phase is based on advanced simulations including the engine and the control system. These computer-run simulations are being increasingly implemented using tools that can automatically generate source code (C in most cases). The experimental studies carried out to date have drawn widely upon the advantages of a formal technique based on the synchronous language SIGNAL, the commercial tool SILDEX and academic tools concerning the verifications and appropriateness of the algorithms for the architecture. Outside the SACRES project, experimentation on this latter aspect is currently being conducted with the INRIA on the basis of a new distributed computer architecture.

---

[1] also called Sequential Function Charts

4   The SIGNAL language and SILDEX

SILDEX is an ergonomic programming environment particularly adapted to the development of real-time applications. It covers a part of the traditional "V" development cycle from specification to implementation, including the proof of programs and validation by simulation. SILDEX is based on the SIGNAL synchronous language designed by INRIA [7]. The application domains of SILDEX can be found in general in safety-critical software. For signal processing, the data flow aspect and time manipulation of SIGNAL allow an intuitive programming style for instance in multi-timing filtering. Control systems will advantageously use SIGNAL multiple clocks and the GRAFCET. For embedded softwares, the compiler provides an efficient executable code.

Software engineering. From the point of view of software engineering, developing an application with SILDEX offers a useful and easy methodological framework. A hierarchical and compositional description of processes allows a clear description of the application to develop. The description and reuse of components libraries allow the work to be structured and development teams to capitalize knowledge; components can be generic (parameterized by type). A rigorous data typing is featured. The use of predefined libraries containing frequently used processes is possible: boolean and arithmetic operators, linear filters, signal generators... The description of processes in GRAFCET or finite state automata allows to describe the problems qualified as "imperative", with explicit sequencing. Modular compilation is provided as well. All the work phases, from specification to final code, are based on a unique programming style (no more transformation between different formalisms, no more errors), and defined in reference to the mathematical semantics of the SIGNAL language.

SILDEX **characteristics.** The SILDEX environment features a number of functionalities. A **graphical editor** allows iconic programming of complex computation models based on data flows and GRAFCET sequencers or automaton sequencers. The SILDEX **compiler** for SIGNAL, efficient and very fast, is the result of a long work of research and optimization. The **separate compilation** helps you to solve large problems. The generated executable code can be plotted with regard to the edited diagram, and directly embedded (it offers a sufficient efficiency/memory-use ratio in order to be directly compiled by a cross compiler then effectively embedded). The debugging process of a SIGNAL program is designed to handle "local" errors (syntax errors indicated at the editing, incoherent types of data, non-connected ports between processes...) and "global" errors (detection via the compiler of the program's global incoherences with a **symbolic debugger**). The rigorous semantics of Signal allows programs properties to be proved far beyond what can be conceivable with classical languages. The SIGNAL compiler is its own dynamic debugger, and the properties to be checked are specifications like the other ones which are directly translated into SIGNAL. If in a program one of the properties is not provable, then it is not compilable. The **animation** deals with the generated C code. It is possible to visualize signals by means of display views. A step-by-step mode and the break-point capability are available. It is also possible to play simulation scenarios. A specific editor allows configurable documents to be created in different formats. SILDEX is an open tool, featuring an interface with external functions to write optimized algorithms in all the classic languages, "scripts" calling the system, **code generation (C, Ada ...)** and customizable **documentation generation**.

5 Industrial experience with SIGNAL

The following experiment follows on from previous work [5] and is part of more than two years on the application of the synchronous technique to digital engine control computers. It resulted in a path that should lead to operational service on engine development programs. Internal experiments carried out since then, and those performed through the SYNCHRON EUREKA project have led to the adoption of a development methodology for the control systems of ground gas turbine engines, based as widely as possible on synchronous technology. As these developments stop at the engine test bench, they are not subject to the same safety requirements. Consequently, the constraints and requirements are less stringent than those imposed by the avionics standards. At present an internal control system development, which is scheduled for on-engine testing in 1997, is is being developed as a result of this new methodology. The choice of development methods and processes was guided by document DO-178B [8] in order to include the majority of requirements that will be imposed upon us in a true level 1 development. The major functions to be provided by SACRES are the generation of a code that is proved correct after generation and the guarantee of correct operation of the application whatever the demands made on the system (temporal verifications at strict time intervals). These verifications are particularly useful during both the dimensioning of the digital system and the subsequent development of each new software version. Our reflections after four years of experience with the SIGNAL language have led us to identify the following six major phases.

High-level functional specification. The difficulties encountered during the development of software specifications often arise from the large quantity of data and algorithms, and are aggravated by information redundancy and management of different nominal or degraded operating modes. The specifications contain both the engine control algorithms (process control) and the failure detection, redundancy management and operating mode algorithms. The basic idea first consists in globally substantiating all the control algorithms developed by the process control experts using a unique global SIGNAL model. This model is first compiled statically, then simulated. The success of the static compilation guarantees the consistency of the signals in all the operating modes and ensures that all "local" and "global" errors are eliminated. This work represented over 50 elementary SILDEX models which will be used in the detailed design phase. This model is then used in the final product acceptance tests after development of the software and integration with the target hardware. The new version simulator features finite state transition system animation which produces considerable time-saving during debugging. Moreover, this provides an excellent means of communicating with the system orderer and any newcomer to the project.

Proof of properties. The proof of properties is an extremely powerful mechanism in view of the confidence it brings. The new SILDEX version now provides proof through the difference or equality of bounded integers, which enables us to verify logical sequencing properties including timeouts (integer number of basic periods). This extension substantially increases the attraction of the verifications performed, which was already one of the strong points of the tool. Properties involving the values of counters, such as timeouts, for example, can now at least be checked in theory, because if the time scales are very different, the number of accessible states becomes prohibitive (in this case the timeout values are changed in the verification model). In the event of failure in the dynamic properties verification mode, the tool displays a scenario which invalidates the property. In the new version this scenario will be able to be replayed immediately at the simulator input, significantly reducing the debugging time and allowing a constructive dialogue with the orderer. The model of a timeout is made by a SIGNAL counter external to but interfaced with the controller. Proof of property verifications by addition of constraints are then performed on certain elementary models and on an aggregate of several of them performing a global function.

Software specification. As the modular compilation function will not be available until version V4, we have reused the terminal boxes of the Signal hierarchy (elementary models) in the software specification phase and attempted to do it in the software design phase. This approach was conducted in an iterative manner so as to match the specification functional breakdown with the object-based software design breakdown as far as possible. The problem we have encountered lies in the fact that the generation of a structured C code in a single procedure is unacceptable as regards both real-time performance levels and hardware constraints and the requirements of DO-178B. A hierarchical decomposition is made such that the sheet functions of the hierarchy contain the elementary models (calculation algorithms) of the previously single model. The sum of all the elementary models reconstructs the major part of the functional single model. Each elementary model is compiled statically with SILDEX. Some of the elementary models are then compiled with the addition of verification constraints (dynamic compilation).

Object-oriented design. This is achieved using the HOOD (Hierarchical Object Oriented Design) method. In this application, system operation is of the cyclic type (purring) and monoperiodic, that is to say that all the calculations are performed at each basic period. The target language is a subset of Ada 83 based on SMART Ada from Thomson Software Products, which does not use the Ada task management function. Furthermore, we have developed a protected subset of the language for operational developments.

Code generation. The global design phase has now been completed. The elementary SILDEX models have been interfaced with the Ada code skeletons defining the encapsulation sequencing and interfaces. The advantage is a saving in cost and time and a reduction in the development risk. The new version of the generator will considerably facilitate its integration in the new methodology. This development is not based on the use of a real-time executive program, although the decision of whether to use a real-time executive program or not must be made taking the various project constraints into account. It is interesting that SACRES can generate the multi-task code and provide points for interfacing with certain executive programs, subject to restrictions relating to the service envelope.

Testing. Although the test methodology is less stringent than a true critical software development (no code reviews), it retains the same basic principles (unit, integration and acceptance testing). It is possible to optimize at the SIGNAL coding level without this being detrimental to the imposed requirements. The development of a single high-level SIGNAL model enables us to run multiple simulation scenarios and to prepare the acceptance tests by determining the test oracles. This process also allows a verification of consistency between the specification, design and coding phases. As regards the development, which is the subject of this section, we are currently in the software/hardware integration phase. The Esprit SACRES project should facilitate the transition of synchronously developed non-critical test applications to full-scale critical applications including substantiation of the C code and protected Ada. The certification aspect is vital to obtain the possibility of using applications generated automatically with these techniques and intended for submittal to the certification authorities.

6   Solutions developped in SACRES

This section presents some activities of the SACRES project that are addressing the needs expressed in Section 5.

Assistance in the certification of safety critical systems is approached in the SACRES project in the form of the validation of the C or Ada code generated by the compilation of DC+. Indeed, the compilation of C or Ada into executable binary code depends on tools external to the SACRES project, over which it has no control. The proof of the consistency between the code generated and the DC+ model relies on formal verification techniques. This validation offers elements on the way to the certification of the system that are complementary to the necessary testing techniques.

In order to be able to evaluate and analyse the performances of the system in terms of response time, upper and lower bounds must be available for response times of each procedure and function defined, as well as other temporal constraints of the global system. The characteristics can be described in the DC+ format. The evaluation technique relies on a notion of homomorphism of a DC+ or SIGNAL program [6]. The temporal homomorphism of a program is another program, generated automatically from the former and from data modelling the system. This latter program computes the dates when outputs are produced in function of input arrival dates. It can evaluate them in function of the values received as input and those computed internally, because the computations of the program under evaluation are part of its homomorphism. It is an automated production of a simulator of functional as well as temporal aspects of the execution of a system on the chosen architecture. This tool provides assistance for dimensioning and validating implementation choices with regard to performance and the respect of response times.

Modularity is supported in version V4 of SIGNAL, which offers support for the use of external or imported objects. This functionality is also present in the DC+ format, and allows combination of sub-systems designed separately, and possibly in different specification formalisms in the SACRES environment. In particular, importation mechanisms support the specification of a design in different contexts, by configuring it each time with different views of imported sub-systems. They can be partial specifications (input-output interfaces, with the possibility of representing an abstraction of dependency relations concerning computations or control), or complete specifications, or even a property on their behaviors, assembled to be used as an hypothesis or an objective for verification tools.

7 Conclusion

This article presents an approach for the design and implementation of safety critical embedded systems, such as is proposed by the Esprit project SACRES. It is supported by the construction of a complete design environment, from specification in various formalisms (STATECHARTS, SIGNAL and TIMING DIAGRAMS), to verification (using model checking techniques), and validation of the code prpoduced, finally to implementation on possibly distributed target architectures. The tools integrated into the environment benefit from the support of formal methods, that allow for the automation and the verification of correctness of the transformations between functional specifications and their implementation. An industrial application of the SILDEX environment to the regulation of turboreactors is analysed, and the needs expressed are addressed in SACRES.

References

[1] A. Benveniste and G. Berry. The synchronous approach to reactive and real-time systems. *Proceedings of the IEEE*, 79(9):1270–1282, September 1991.

[2] A. Benveniste e.a. Synchronous technology for Real-Time Systems. In *Actes du Salon* Real-Time Systems *RTS'94*, Paris, Janvier 1994.

[3] W. Damm, B. Josko, R. Schlör. Specification and verification of VHDL-based system-level hardware designs. In E. Börger ed., *Specification and Validation Methods*, pp. 331–410. Oxford University Press, 1995.

[4] A. Grazebrook. SACRES - Formalism for Real Projects. In *Safer Systems*, ed. F. Redmill & T. Anderson, Springer Verlag, London, 1997.

[5] A. Janvier, P. Beaufreton. Expérience synchrone pour la régulation numérique de turbo-réacteurs. In *Actes du Salon* Real-Time Systems *RTS'95*, Paris, Janvier 1995. Teknéa.

[6] A. Kountouris, P. Le Guernic. Profiling of SIGNAL programs and its application in the timing evaluation of design implementations. In *Proc. of the IEE Colloq. on HW-SW Cosynthesis for Reconfigurable Systems*, Feb. 22, 1996, HP Labs., Bristol, UK, pp.6/1–6/9. 1996.

[7] P. Le Guernic, M. Le Borgne, T. Gautier, C. Le Maire. Programming real-time applications with SIGNAL. *Proceedings of the IEEE*, 79(9):1270–1282, September 1991.

[8] RTCA & EUROCA. *DO-178B,ED-12B : Software Consideration in airborne systems and equipment certification*. décembre 1992.

Towards Safer Industrial Computer Controlled Systems

P.R. Croll   C. Chambers
Department of Computer Science The University of Sheffield
Sheffield.

M. Bowell
Health and Safety Laboratory Broad Lane
Sheffield   S3 7HQ

P.W.H Chung
Department of Chemical Engineering Loughborough University of Technology
Loughborough Leicestershire

Abstract

A study of 21 incidents involving electrical, electronic and/or programmable electronic safety-related systems in small manufacturing enterprises, originally investigated by the Health and Safety Laboratory, has revealed that 40% of contributory faults are due to inadequate specification of system or safety requirements.   Consequently the HAZAPS methodology and supporting software tool is proposed as a useful step forward in producing safer industrial computer controlled systems. The tool is demonstrated using a case study and suggestions are made for its improvement.

1. Introduction

The UK government's Health and Safety Executive (HSE) helps ensure that employers reduce the risk of harm to employees and the general public to levels that are as low as is reasonably practicable. HSE is concerned that industry identifies all possible hazards that could arise from its activities and the systems it develops. Industry must find how these hazards could be caused and how they can be prevented, and this calls for tools and models to help analyse and assess those hazards. The Health and Safety Laboratory (HSL), the research agency of the HSE, offers forensic facilities to investigate the causes of reported incidents involving such systems. HSL also provides expertise on appropriate tools and models to analyse complex systems. As industry turns to computers to control its complex manufacturing processes, these same computers form part of safety-related systems that reduce any risks present to an acceptable level. In industries where safety-critical systems (also called "high integrity systems") play a prominent role, such as nuclear, aviation and defence, considerable time and effort is expended on their development. This can require the use of formal methods, especially where the aim is to demonstrate to a regulatory body that a system is "provably" safe [1, 2]. However, it would appear that less time and effort is spent looking at safety problems with systems in Small Manufacturing Enterprises (SMEs). The aim of this research is to find out both why and how incidents are caused in SMEs, and hence what industrially relevant methods can be implemented easily and effectively by safety practitioners (who are also likely to be the design engineers) in SMEs to help mitigate incident causes.

This paper is structured into five main sections. Section two reviews a study outlining causes of a number of incidents investigated by HSL [3], and analyses the results, highlighting problem areas. Section three outlines a methodology developed by researchers at Loughborough University, suitable for application to the most frequent problems discussed in section two. Section four looks at the HAZAPS tool which implements this methodology. Section five introduces a case study of a lift design which has been applied to evaluate the HAZAPS tool and hence the underlying methodology. Section six gives conclusions and suggestions for future work.

2. Incident Study

Croll et al [3] have conducted a study of 21 incidents, originally investigated by HSL, that involved Electrical and/or Electronic and/or Programmable Electronic (E/E/PE) safety-related systems. Typically, these used Programmable Logic Controllers (PLCs) to perform the safety-related functions. The aim of this study was to highlight the causes of the incidents and find common solutions to the causes. HSL staff have indicated that the range and type of these incidents are typical of those reported in the manufacturing industry.

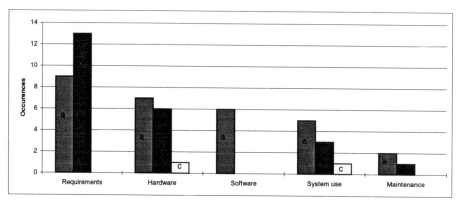

Figure 1: Number of occurrences per fault sub-category

2.1 Causes

It can be argued that all incidents involving computer controlled systems can be mitigated given the incorporation of sufficient safety features in the system design, e.g. software and hardware redundancy (fault tolerance), fail-safe design methods and independent safety features such as hard wire trips. Hence all incidents can be said to have been caused by safety requirements omissions [4]. However, in this study, only when "obvious" omissions are made are they recorded as such. Figure 1 shows the individual number of occurrences of causes in each category, including further subdivision of top level categories into subcategories (see Table 1) to aid further analysis of the results.

Category	Definition
Requirements	a Inadequate system definition
	b Inadequate safety requirements specification
Hardware	a Design
	b Random
	c Interface or communications
Software	a Design
	b Coding error
System use	a Unsafe system use and operation
	b Human error
	c Deliberate bypass of correct operating procedures
Maintenance	a Corrective maintenance
	b Adaptive maintenance
	c Perfective maintenance

Table 1: Classification of incidents

2.2 Analysis of causes

The *Requirements stage* was responsible for 40% of faults contributing to the incidents in this study. Many of the incidents were caused by a lack of understanding of the systems involved, and in several cases a total lack of safety considerations. In 13 out of the 21 incidents studied, deficiencies in the safety requirements capture stage contributed directly to the incidents. For example, in more than one incident only single channel safety systems were in place, and in several the safety systems were easily bypassed by operators, leaving them with no protection. A common deficiency encountered was an inadequate level of sensing, where for example in one incident access to a guillotine blade from the sides of the machine (rather than the front) was not detected by sensors. In another incident, it was possible for the operator to work under a protective light curtain from the front of the machine. A hazard analysis should highlight this type of potential hazard, since machines of this nature have been in regular use for some time. Independent safety-related protection systems are beneficial since they are less dependant on missing requirements knowledge.

The *hardware faults* (26% of the total faults) consisted mainly of hardware design and random faults. In the case of hardware design faults, typical causes of incidents were badly positioned guards, or sensors partially obscured by other physical components of the system. Hardware faults can be mitigated by the use of fault tolerant design methods, and software can be used to detect and warn the operator about certain common types of hardware faults or put the system into a safe state.

Software faults accounted for 11% of the total faults. For example: errors in program layout caused control variables to be updated at an incorrect time in the control cycle leading to an incorrect PLC output; there were mistakes in timing calculations and in the algorithms used to stop machines safely; and the use of PLC relay ladder logic and instruction list in combination, both poorly commented, made programs difficult to understand. Software faults can be reduced by using higher level structured programming languages (for example function block diagram, sequential function charts and structured text as described in IEC 1131-3 [5]), rather than the very common relay ladder logic and instruction list, both of which have known deficiencies [6].

The low percentage of software faults indicates that the coding of software is a comparatively minor problem for computer controlled plant. However, the amount (number of lines) of code used to control individual items of manufacturing equipment and their associated safety systems was relatively small in the cases investigated (typically less than two hundred lines of code). Small programs are considerably easier to verify compared with that needed for the Darlington nuclear generating station in Canada (2,000+ lines of code for the emergency shutdown software [7, 8, 9]).

Maintenance accounted for only 6% of faults. Cases include: a new safety guard added after equipment had been in use for some time and the correct operation of this new equipment did not match the machine it was fitted on; safety features disabled to allow easy access to equipment to carry out corrective maintenance; and the brakes on a machine mis-adjusted during corrective maintenance. Note that this category does not include faults due to insufficient maintenance; these are classified as either hardware design faults or associated with random hardware failures.

System (mis)use comprised 17% of all faults. The main problem faced here was the failure by equipment operators to follow correct or safe operating procedures, or the deliberate bypass of safety features, with the general aim of making a particular machine more productive or easier to operate.

34% of incident causes in this study are attributable to an inadequate knowledge of how the system works or how it interacts with surrounding systems. Hence there is a need for independent safety-related protection systems that do not rely on this missing knowledge. A further 26% of incident causes are categorised as hardware design or failure, which in the former case also suggests a lack of understanding of the system. Software can compensate for, or at least detect and warn the operator about, certain types of hardware failure, concentrating particularly on those failures most likely to occur. It would appear from this study that the largest area of concern, with 40% of the causes of incidents being directly connected, is the *requirements capture* stage of systems development. These results agree with similar studies [10].

The results of this study imply that SMEs need to be educated in the need for risk assessment and hazard analysis. There also needs to be a mechanism for ensuring adherence to relevant standards and guidelines. Indeed, appropriate standards and guidelines must exist in the first place. These must be sufficiently approachable in terms of size and applicability, but also sufficiently flexible to allow for continuing technological development. The international standard IEC 1508 [11], goes some way towards providing the necessary guidance, but is hampered by its generality across all industrial sectors. Application sector standards based on IEC 1508 are needed to improve the situation but are unlikely to be available in the immediate future.

3. A methodology for computer systems hazard analysis

We have shown that there is a need for industrially relevant methods with PC-based software tool support that are straightforward to use, to help developers of industrial systems obtain a more complete set of safety requirements for E/E/PE safety-related systems. Kletz et al [12] have said HAZOP type studies applied to manufacturing systems containing computers are gaining wide spread acceptance as suitable for hazard identification in E/E/PE safety-related systems. Several methods based on HAZOP already exist, but tool support is apparently not available [13]. This section describes the HAZAPS methodology which has the advantage of tool support.

Classification of incidents involving computer control systems are often made in terms of what is deemed to be the major contributory causes of those incidents; this is useful for highlighting areas of concern in the development of safety-related systems. In the incident study in section 2.1 above, incident categories are in terms of functional areas, depending on their causes. Functional areas are further subdivided into specific problem areas, and from this we are able to analyse faults and select the most appropriate method of mitigation. Any method attempting to achieve a safe system should consider how to avoid typical faults. Therefore, in attempting to achieve a safe system, we can employ *fault prevention*, *fault removal* and *fault tolerance* concepts. Laprie has defined these concepts in relation to dependable systems [14]. The view taken here is that fault prevention is a systematic methodology which can help prevent the introduction or occurrence of faults, fault removal is the application of this methodology to help remove faults, and finally, fault tolerance is the application of this methodology to help minimise the effects of any faults remaining in the system. Studies of incident reports are very useful because they are representative of the "real world", they allow us to investigate how faults occur and how these faults propagate in a system.

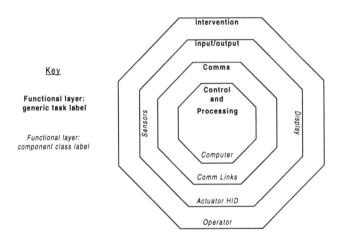

Figure 2: Model showing basic components and functional levels [15]

The HAZAPS approach [15], is different from other computer HAZOP approaches in that a generic model of an incident is proposed. This model shows the hierarchy of the functional levels (see Figure 2) and illustrates their interdependency. All components associated with the intervention level that interact with the computer must use some component at the input/output level. Similarly all components associated with the input/output level that interact with the computer, must involve some component at the communication level. The model can be used to establish "what if" scenarios. For example, if the operator inputs incorrect data, what happens if the error propagates through to the inner levels? In the worst case, the operator error causes a failure at the control and processing level. This model, in combination with a new graphical technique, the Event Time Diagram (ETD) is used to analyse each incident. The results of the analysis form the basis for a safety assessment methodology.

Elliot and Owen's pioneering work in analysing chemical plant design using an approach called *method study* [16] has evolved into the well established HAZOP technique. The basis of this is to examine a problem by asking the questions What?, Why?, How? and When?. One of the major problems with method study is the amount and complexity of the information that can be generated. In this work, the method study is constrained by asking questions related to fault prevention, fault removal and fault tolerance and by grouping the questions in a 'keyword' structure. The result is a computer HAZOP methodology with a supporting software tool called HAZAPS. The methodology was derived using a functional analysis of over 300 recorded (non-HSL) incidents involving E/E/PE safety-related systems in the process and avionics industries.

In each case the methodology asks the question *"How could this incident have been avoided?"*. The study produces a set of basic considerations (specification, implementation and protection) and a set of attributes (e.g. definition, objectives, I/O etc.), all of which are used to produce a library of questions. These are then generalised for practical use, so that when applied to a broad spectrum of industrial tasks, they identify potential causes of hazards similar to those found in the initial study. The use of the HAZAPS methodology with lessons learnt from past mistakes should improve safety in the design and development of E/E/PE safety-related systems, by forcing the design team to consider all relevant and, hopefully, possible areas of concern. The process of deriving the methodology and its application is shown in Figure 3.

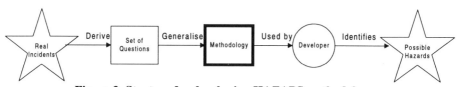

Figure 3: Strategy for developing HAZAPS methodology

The methodology consists of generating a set of safety requirements from the initial system functional requirements. Each safety requirement is decomposed into tasks which are given a type and description. An ETD may be drawn of tasks selected for further analysis showing the interrelationship between tasks with respect to time, control and data flow.

4. Overview of the HAZAPS methodology and tool

The HAZAPS tool is a prototype developed at Loughborough to run on a PC under Microsoft Windows. Each (safety) function is decomposed into tasks and each task has an associated type e.g. human, processor, sensor, display, actuator and human input device (HID). HAZOP style questions, predetermined by the associated task type and grouped into three categories (fault prevention, fault avoidance and fault tolerance), are applied to each task.

For example, below are a few typical questions from the *Sensor* category:
- Why is this task necessary ?
- What are the inputs and outputs of this task ?
- What would happen if this task failed ?
- Are there any emergency trips or alarms associated with this task ?

The HAZAPS tool consists of three basic levels, each with associated or shared tools:
1. System Level
2. Requirements Level
3. Tasks level

At the HAZAPS *System Level*, a set of safety requirements are derived using the original functional requirements, the results of an initial preliminary hazard identification stage, and a potential hazards list supplied with the tool. The *safety requirements* are entered as an ASCII text file, with a general description of the system. Next a *Process* option is selected, which reorganises the requirements ready for the next stage (Requirements Level).

At the HAZAPS *Requirements Level*, the safety requirements are decomposed into tasks, each task is given a task type from a drop down list. Figure 4 shows a Requirements Level screen shot, the requirement displayed in the upper left window is decomposed manually in to tasks which are considered one at a time. Each task is saved, giving the task one of seven types. The next step is to plot the derived tasks on to an *Event Time Diagram* (ETD), which is shown in Figure 5. The ETD is based on the functional incident model shown in Figure 2, and allows the behaviour of the tasks in terms of events, time, control and data flow to be analysed. The ETD may be viewed as a polar diagram where the angle represents time, the distance from the centre gives the functional level, and the arrows give direction of control and data flow, thus allowing decisions to be made regarding criticality with respect to time of the task under consideration.

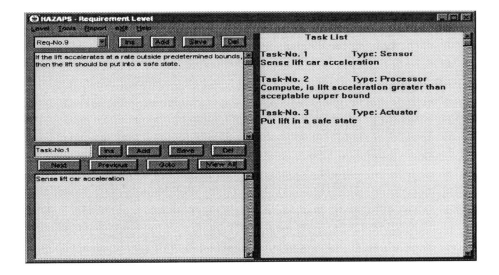

Figure 4: HAZAPS Requirements Level

In the HAZAPS *Task Level* shown in Figure 6, questions relevant to the *Task Type* and *Group* (Specification, Implementation and Protection) are asked. For each question the design team gives a response, which includes associated actions required. Only questions considered relevant need be considered, but all associated questions are recorded in the automated documentation, with a "no response" so that it is clear that a particular question has been left out. A library browser is available to view all questions and any associated information for selected groups. A library editor is also available to edit, delete or add questions.

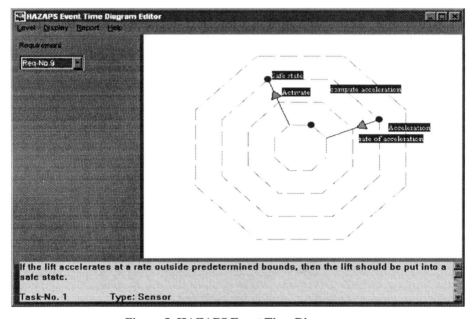

Figure 5: HAZAPS Event Time Diagram

The HAZAPS *Report* generator is available at each level, allowing the user to generate full or partial reports at any stage of the operation.

Users have found the HAZAPS tool easy to use, that moving between levels is straightforward, and the tools provided (preliminary hazard list, ETD editor, graphics viewer and library editor) are helpful in the development process.

5. Lift case study

The lift case study was chosen because it is an good example of a real-time reactive system that requires safety to be considered, with possible risks to human life.

Functional requirements were defined and from these a set of safety requirements was derived, partly from a system preliminary hazard analysis, and partly from a "potential hazards list" included in the HAZAPS tool. A total of 18 safety requirements were decomposed into 57 tasks, to which a possible 1,972 questions can be applied (although in practice not all would be!).

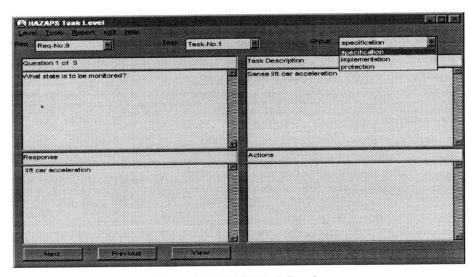

Figure 6: HAZAPS Task Level

To demonstrate the hazard assessment technique, a section of the analysis from safety requirement number 9 is detailed here. This requirement considers unsafe acceleration of the lift car, which could result in lift passengers sustaining injuries. From the ETD in Figure 5, we see that the initial task involves sensing the lift car acceleration in real-time. Taking this task as our example, we consider further the assessment produced by the HAZAPS methodology. From the associated questions it can be seen that practicalities investigated are the sensors used for this task, in terms of their specification (basic objectives and operational parameters), implementation (type, how many etc.) and protection (associated alarms, safety trips). This implies that from past experience, all aspects of sensor configuration, operation and associated interfaces require close attention. For example, from the protection category of the *sensor* task, a typical question is:

Question: How will the system know if the sensor is performing OK ?

Response: Consideration of hardware monitors, employed to detect that the sensor is still connected and giving some output.

Actions: After further consideration, diagnostic routines performed by an independent processor responsible for safety functions, with additional hardwired trips, would increase the safety level.

Like other questions for this task, this level of detail was not considered until prompted by the HAZAPS tool. As can be seen in the actions associated with this question, the initial response was that each sensor would be fitted with a 'watchdog' monitor, however upon further consideration, the concept of independent safety processing was considered. In addition, an independent hardwired trip was considered, which would apply the lift brakes in case the primary safety features suffered from common mode failure (loss of power).

6. Conclusions and Future Work

This work has considered incidents involving E/E/PE safety-related systems investigated by the Health and Safety Laboratory. Deficiencies in the requirements stage of the development process have been shown to be a significant cause of incidents. Consequently, industry is likely to benefit from the adoption of a thorough risk-based approach to systems design and development, engendered by general company-wide safety culture.

It is necessary to perform a thorough hazard analysis of computer systems, to get the safety requirements issues resolved. The hazard analysis performed should be of the whole system, including the hardware, the software, the outside world, and their interfaces. In light of this there is a need for industrially relevant PC-based software tool support that is straight-forward to use, and that would help the industrial systems developer to obtain a more complete set of safety requirements for E/E/PE safety-related systems. This could be obtained through hazard identification and assessment with the goal of facilitating the development of 'safer' systems.

The HAZAPS tool is seen as a useful step forward in meeting these requirements. It is easy to understand and use and highlights problem areas that may otherwise have been overlooked when developing E/E/PE safety-related systems. The types of hazard addressed when applying the HAZOPS-style questions are pertinent to the type of system being assessed since this method has been derived using data from over 300 (non-HSL) incidents. The HAZAPS tool produces well structured documentation, showing exactly what concerns have been raised in the requirements stage of systems development and how those concerns were dealt with. The documentation produced by the HAZAPS tool could be utilised in either quality audits, safety cases or as general evidence of conformance to safety guidelines, by showing the use of 'best practice' at the requirements stage of systems development.

The HAZAPS tool currently has the following drawbacks which could be addressed in future work.

- It is not clear how alterations in the design would be introduced into the documentation and be recorded as such, so that iterative development can be recorded.
- Although some help is provided in the form of a preliminary hazard list supplied with the tool, the identification of top level hazards is still performed by the developer who may be inexperienced.
- When applying the HAZAPS tool to the case study, the process was time consuming. Further automation would help, e.g. it is noted that one of the reasons for creating an ETD manually is that the developer is free to design the ETD from whatever viewpoint is deemed 'best' suited to the analysis being performed. However, it would be useful if a 'standard' ETD was automatically produced by the tool, perhaps when the safety requirements have been decomposed into tasks, but keeping the option to create an ETD manually.
- Past experience might not cover all possible risks unless the system and its environment remain the same, although the constant and careful update of questions used by the tool may help.

HSL does not endorse the use of the HAZAPS methodology or tool, neither of which have been used in connection with incidents or assessments by HSL. The views expressed in this paper are the opinion of the authors and not necessarily those of their respective organisations.

References

[1] Stavridou V. Boothroyed A. Boyce T. et al. Developing and Assessing Safety Critical Systems with Formal Methods: The SafeFM way, High Integrity Systems, Vol 1, pp 541-545, 1996.

[2] Brazendale J. Bell R. Safety-Related Control and Protection Systems: Standards Update, Computing & Control Engineering Journal, Vol. 5, pp. 6-12, Oct 1994.

[3] Croll P.R. Chambers C. Bowell M. A Study of Incidents Involving Electrical/Electronic/Programmable Electronic Safety-Related Systems, Proc 1st Int workshop on Human Error and System Development, Glasgow, March 20-22, 1997.

[4] Modugo F. Leveson N.G. Reese J.D. et al. Creating and Analysing Requirement Specifications of Joint Human-Computer Controllers for Safety-Critical Systems, Symposium on Human Interaction with Complex Systems, Aug 25-26, 1996.

[5] IEC, Int Standard IEC1131 Programmable Controllers - part 3: Programming Languages, Geneva, International Electrotechnical Commission. 1993.

[6] Lewis R. W. Programming industrial control systems using IEC 1131-3, IEE, 1995.

[7] Leveson N.G., Safeware; System Safety and Computers, Addison Wesley, 1995.

[8] Storey N. Safety-Critical Computer Systems, published by Addison-Wesley, 1996.

[9] Parnas D.L. Asmis G.J.K. Madey J. Assessment of Safety-Critical Software in Nuclear Power Plants, Nuclear Safety, Vol 32, pp. 189-198, 1991.

[10] UK Health and Safety Executive, Out of Control, HMSO Press, 1995.

[11] Draft Int. Standard IEC 1508, Functional Safety of Electrical/Electronic/Programmable Electronic Safety-Related Systems, Geneva, International Electrotechnical Commission. 1995.

[12] Kletz T. Chung P.W.H. Broomfield E. Chaim S. Computer Control and Human Error, IChemE, 1995.

[13] Fenelon P.N. Hebbron B.N Applying HAZOP to Software Engineering Models, Tech Report, HISE Group, University of York. 1996.

[14] Laprie J.C. Dependability: from Concepts to Limits, 12th Int. Conf on Computer Safety, Reliability and Security, London, pp 157-168, 1993.

[15] Broomfield E.J. Chung P.W.H. Using Incident Analysis to Derive a Methodology for Assessing Safety in Programmable Systems, Proc 3rd Safety-Critical Systems Symposium, pp. 223-239, Springer-Verlag, 1995.

[16] Elliot D.M. Owen J.M. Critical Examination in Process Design, The Chemical Engineer, pp 377-383, November 1968.

Safety Cases for Software-intensive Systems: an Industrial Experience Report[1].

Stephen Barker (Lloyd's Register), Ian Kendall (Jaguar Cars) and Anthony Darlison (Lloyd's Register).

Abstract

This paper describes the development of a safety case for the electronic throttle system for the recently launched Jaguar XK8 sports car. It presents the practical application of a wide range of safety assurance techniques to a significant industrial project and shows how these techniques may be used together to build up evidence supporting a sound safety argument.

The system design and safety assessment took full account of the risk-based approach to safety, and of contemporary and emerging standards such as dIEC1508 [1]. The application of best practice was found to be both feasible and beneficial. However lessons were also learnt for future developments. The paper is therefore of direct relevance to practising engineers faced with the problem of assuring the safety of computer-based systems. It is also relevant to researchers investigating how best to combine evidence to form a safety case.

1.   Introduction

1.1   Overview

The safety case for the electronic throttle for the Jaguar XK8 sports car was compiled from the results of a programme of independent safety assessments that were conducted throughout system development. The safety case was required to:

- summarise and present the results of the assessment,
- review the status of earlier findings,

Figure 1 : The Jaguar XK8

- state the safety implications of any outstanding findings,
- set out a structured argument for the safety of the throttle,
- present a definitive statement regarding the safety of the throttle.

The assessment programme commenced with system level safety analyses to identify the hazardous failure modes and single out the aspects of the design requiring further attention. The analyses evaluated the safety features of the throttle, which were designed to ensure continued safe operation, even in the presence of faults, taking due account of driver reactions to events.

Later parts of the assessment concentrated on the embedded software, examining the quality management and testing regimes at Jaguar and its Japanese supplier, and the fulfilment of specific software safety properties derived from the hazard analysis.

Formal proof techniques were used to demonstrate that the software satisfied the software safety properties. This was considered to be particularly important for the safety case because it involved taking a view of the system that was truly independent of the development process. The efficacy of this approach was demonstrated when the analysis yielded a number of potentially significant anomalies, although none of these were found to have safety implications. The safety property proofs were significant because they demonstrated the feasibility of using such techniques as a practical tool to contribute to "industrial strength" safety cases. Although the proofs represented a significant proportion of the total software assessment effort, this was in proportion to the benefits achieved.

The assessment was scoped specifically to take into account relevant standards and codes of practice. These included Jaguar's own codes of practice, ISO 9000-3 [2] and, significantly, dIEC1508 [1][2]. During the assessment, the MISRA Guidelines [3] were published. Although scoped without the benefit of these guidelines, much of the assessment is compatible with the MISRA guidance. Future assessments will take more explicit account of this key industry-specific document.

1.2 The XK8 AJ26 Electronic Throttle

The Jaguar XK8 sports car includes many advanced features, including an electronic throttle. The throttle valve, which regulates air into the engine, is controlled by the engine management computer, rather than by a more conventional simple cable. This has benefits for improved driver feel, exhaust emissions control and the integration of related functions previously requiring their own separate sensors, actuators and control (e.g. engine idle speed control).

---

[2] At the time that the assessment was scoped, this was IEC 65A(Secretariat)122 'Software for computers in the application of industrial safety-related systems'. IEC committee draft, November 1991.

The XK8 electronic throttle system is a hybrid of an electronic control[3] and a mechanical system that limits the authority of the software to a safe envelope of operation and also provides back-up in the event of electronic control system failure. Such an arrangement allows new hazards arising from software control to be mitigated by more conventional mechanical means.

Figure 2: The XK8 Electronic Throttle

The overall system design is relatively complex, and assessment activities were considered necessary for both the development process and the product design details. The resulting reports provided evidence to support a safety case that demonstrated the required confidence in overall system safety.

1.3   Requirement for Assessment

The Safety Assessment was conducted to demonstrate that the throttle was acceptably safe, according to the requirements established by Jaguar, and according to best industry practice. Jaguar prepared a risk policy document that defined specific safety targets to be achieved. This formed the main basis for the assessment.

This is not only important to meet Jaguar's customers' needs and expectations of product quality, but also is the responsible approach demanded in a climate of increasing product liability risk. Manufacturers must take all reasonable precautions to deliver defect free products, using best-practice methods during development. Additionally, publications such as the MISRA Guidelines [3] (to which Jaguar made a major contribution) recognise that assessment is a key technique contributing to the assurance of safety-related systems and software.

Jaguar also had a strategic motivation for using independent assessment. Although primary system safety does not rely on the software, due to the mechanical guard, Jaguar wished to ensure that the software used in the system took into account the requirements of emerging documents such as dIEC1508 [1] and the MISRA Guidelines [3]. The lessons learned by such an activity could play a major role in the future, as the industry moves towards full-authority systems with no mechanical guard.

Jaguar contracted Lloyd's Register to undertake the safety assessment to provide a high level of assurance that the system met its safety criteria. Lloyd's Register's independence from Jaguar was also key to securing open access to technical design

---

3 The electronic control is primarily a "programmable electronic system", although there is also a fall-back mode where the throttle is controlled by non-programmable electronics with reduced functionality.

and development details that the supplier would not have released to Jaguar, on commercial confidentiality grounds.

2.   Throttle Design

2.1   Safety Design Philosophy

The inherent safety provided by a mechanical limiter and back-up is realised in the design by a device called the "mechanical guard". This is connected to the driver's accelerator pedal by a conventional cable, and the electronic control is only allowed to move below the position of the guard. The throttle is actuated by a DC motor under the control of the Engine Control Module, and acts in conjunction with several springs on the throttle body (see Figure 3). The maximum motor torque and spring forces are chosen such that the springs closing the throttle (with the mechanical guard) can always override the motor, even if it is trying to drive the throttle open. More details of the electronic throttle design are given in [4].

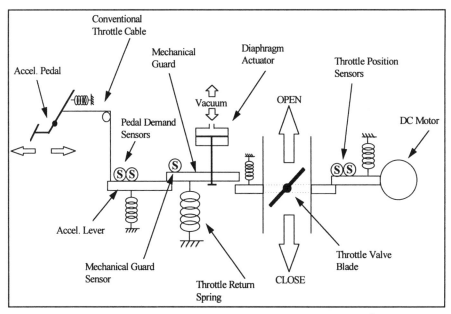

Figure 3 : XK8 Electronic Throttle Body - Main Components[4]

The system has been designed to react to all identified failure modes, resulting in one of 7 possible "default" modes that, whenever possible, provide continued safe operation in the presence of electrical, electronic and mechanical failures. The default modes have varying effects on system functionality ranging from no effect other than a warning light to complete engine shutdown (only required for

---

[4] Where appropriate, double springs are used

combinations of failures). The throttle thus achieves safety whilst maximising reliability.

The system exhibits many examples of redundancy and diversity including:

- twin CPU's in a Main-Monitor architecture with diverse software,
- redundant sensors for measuring throttle and pedal position, using both simple comparison techniques and voting,
- redundant springs where required,
- two diverse methods of cutting power to the throttle motor,
- redundant cruise control release valves.

2.2   Human Factors

During the development, great emphasis was placed on the human aspects of the design. Unlike many industries, the motor industry has to consider a wide range of driver abilities. Due regard is needed for the likely driver reaction to the way failures are mitigated by default modes and to the warnings presented.

Such aspects were considered from the outset of development, during Hazard Analysis (see section 3.1), the results of which were used to drive the design. As part of the validation of the XK8, Jaguar performed extensive real world testing to assess the behaviour of the vehicle under all identified failure conditions. Some minor changes were required to tune the performance under the default modes to ensure that an optimum response is achieved.

Warnings are presented by illuminating with a red or an amber warning light on the instrument cluster, together with a text message to provide further information on the nature of the problem. Considerable deliberation and consultation were required to settle on suitable messages, not least as the vehicle must be capable of being configured to display any of 11 languages!

3.   The Assessment

3.1   Safety Analysis

It was first necessary to determine the potential hazards associated with the throttle and to classify them. The hazard analysis evaluated the proposed system design and identified the potential failure modes of the system, and the resultant effects were classified according to probability and severity of outcome.

The automotive industry has particular difficulty with classification of hazards, because there is a range of possible outcomes from the same hazardous event. The outcome depends on several factors, including traffic density, road surface, weather, attentiveness of driver, vehicle speed, and the proximity of pedestrians, vehicles and other objects. Consequently, hazard severity was classified according to controllability (see [5] and subsequently [3]). This scheme evaluates hazards in terms of the level of control that the driver has when the hazard occurs, rather than in terms of the nature or magnitude of an adverse consequence.

Jaguar's internal risk policy set a limit on the acceptable occurrence rate for the most severe hazard categories, in terms of probability of occurrence in a vehicle lifetime. Fault Trees were therefore constructed to evaluate the probability of the hazards and, in conjunction with a Markov Analysis to model transitions between the various "default" modes in the throttle system, the resulting rates were shown to be acceptable.

Full coverage cannot be claimed for a top down approach, such as Fault Tree Analysis. A Failure Modes and Effect Analysis was therefore undertaken to ensure that no single failure resulted in an unacceptable outcome. This helped to ensure the coverage of the overall safety analysis process and demonstrated the effectiveness of the hazard mitigation techniques. Further details of the system safety analyses are given in [6], published before the software analysis was performed and before the safety case was prepared.

The safety analyses were backed up by reviews of the requirement specification and design of the throttle. These ensured that the specification for the throttle adequately addressed all aspects relevant to safety and reliability.

The Fault Trees had made some assumptions that were subsequently validated by further analysis. In particular, a working assumption was made that the software did not cause the hazards. This assumption was validated by demonstrating that the software fulfilled safety properties derived from the hazard analysis. The required behaviour to prevent the software causing the hazard was defined and reviewed with Jaguar and its supplier. The software was then shown to correctly implement the safety properties by using the most appropriate techniques, including testing and formal proof.

3.2 Process Audits

In scoping the assessment, it was assumed that good quality management is necessary but not sufficient to produce a safe system. Quality management can ensure consistency in the design process generally, but provides only indirect evidence that a product possesses a specific attribute. However, combined with other more direct evidence, it increases confidence that a sample (of test results for example) is representative of the development as a whole.

3.2.1 Jaguar

To ensure that the process by which the throttle was procured did not introduce any unnecessary risks, audits and reviews were conducted in the area of the technical interface between Jaguar and its supplier. These included reviews of the relevant procurement specifications, change control procedures, etc., and witnessing and evaluation of the safety validation tests conducted by Jaguar (naturally Jaguar also conducts extensive testing to assure vehicle performance in hostile conditions, etc.).

3.2.2 *Denso*

The throttle system and engine control module were supplied by the Denso Corporation of Japan. Although there was close technical contact on the overall throttle design, the safety management techniques and the way that the software was developed were critical to the safety of the throttle. Consequently, Lloyd's Register made several visits to Japan, to review safety management and software development procedures, to audit compliance with the procedures, and to witness testing.

The development procedures were evaluated against the requirements of Jaguar's Code of Practice for software development, and also against ISO 9000-3 [2], knowledge of best practice and the MISRA Guidelines [3] when they were published. The auditors recorded the practices identified when they complied with the requirements, and raised formal non-compliances when practices did not. All non-compliances were followed up during subsequent audits and by fax.

In searching for evidence it was necessary to keep an open mind about how requirements were fulfilled. The most obvious practice to a European auditor was not necessarily the most obvious way to the Japanese developers, so it was important to distinguish the reason for the requirement from the expected "normal" implementation of the requirement.

3.3 Software Review

3.3.1 *Analysis*

The process audits and test reviews gave highly satisfactory results and indicated Denso's considerable commitment to Jaguar's quality requirements. However, it was prudent to demonstrate that the required safety properties were satisfied by the implemented system. The safety case could not be considered complete without a rigorous validation of the working assumption in the system safety analysis, that the software did not cause the hazards. Process audits alone could not yield this degree of assurance.

The first stage was to define the required behaviour of the software (including functional and timing requirements) to avoid causing the hazards. This was developed from the hazard analysis and referred to as the *software safety properties*.

The software data dependencies were examined to extract all parts of the software that could affect the required behaviour; that is, all parts of the software involved in computing the values appearing in a safety property. All such modules or groups of modules were then modelled as *procspecs* (effectively a formalised module specification consisting of preconditions and postconditions) in MALPAS Intermediate Language (IL) by inspection of module specifications and direct inspection of source code. The whole system was modelled as control loops calling the modelled functions in an appropriate sequence. Proof obligations were then formulated from the safety properties and discharged using the MALPAS Compliance Analyser [7].

This amounts to using MALPAS as a formal proof tool, and not as a static code analyser (for which it is better known). The formal proofs verified that the functional aspects of a design (the module procspecs) satisfied formally specified safety properties5. The analysis could of course have been extended by translating the source code into MALPAS IL and proving that the resulting code model implemented the procspecs. The justification for not doing this was that it was not cost-effective considering the large quantity of other evidence that implementation could be relied upon (such as audits, unit test results, document reviews, etc.).

Some of the safety properties involved timing deadlines. The scheduling of the functions involved was examined to verify that the timing requirements would be met. It was not possible to verify by analysis that no process could cause an overrun of the scheduler; however such an overrun would cause a watchdog trip (a safe failure mode). The code was also checked for non-terminating loops. Additionally, at Lloyd's Register's request, the software was exercised to demonstrate that it was capable of functioning at engine speeds far in excess of the engine rev limit.

3.3.2   Results

The rigorous proofs described above could only be discharged if certain assumptions were made, mostly relating to calibration data and to normal events in vehicle/throttle interaction. These were all reviewed and agreed to be acceptable by Jaguar and Denso. It was recommended that the constraints on calibration data were used as a safety validation test for future calibrations.

The proofs also identified specific circumstances under which the safety properties did not hold. Jaguar and Denso reviewed these circumstances and agreed that each exception represented correct and safe behaviour, when the basic safety property should not necessarily hold.

The exceptions mostly represented cases where the software boundary (throttle demand) and the real world (vehicle speed) did not match. In a conventional throttle, a constant throttle demand does not mean constant vehicle speed. Driveability features (including cruise control) provided by the electronic throttle address these issues, and result in adjustments to throttle opening that are related to road/vehicle conditions. The software safety properties were stated in terms of throttle demand, for example that no increase in throttle demand was allowed when a certain event occurred. Analysis therefore sometimes identified that it was possible that the throttle could open under certain restricted conditions, in contradiction to the software safety property.

These circumstances were reviewed by Lloyd's Register, Jaguar and Denso and confirmed to be reasonable and not detrimental to safety. They were also checked against the original hazard analysis. This was vital to ensure that they did not contradict the circumstances envisaged in the hazard analysis.

---

5 To the best of the authors' knowledge, no formal language semantics for MALPAS IL currently exists. In this sense MALPAS cannot be considered strictly formal. However, for practical purposes the implementation of the compliance analyser imposes a semantics on IL, and MALPAS can be considered formal in all but an academic sense.

4.   The Safety Case

The final task of the assessment was to pull together the results and conclusions from all the earlier analyses and assessments, to reach an overall conclusion regarding the safety of the system. Essentially, this is the safety case for the XK8 electronic throttle.

The work involved a critical review of all previous reports to produce a reasoned and defensible argument that the system is acceptably safe, based on the *evidence* gathered and recorded. The actions taken to address all recommendations and conclusions in those reports was also evaluated to ensure that each issue had been cleared satisfactorily. The resulting report summarised the arguments that the electronic throttle met its safety targets, and that the development processes used were appropriate.

The main safety arguments were:

- the electronic throttle met the requirements of Jaguar's risk policy,
- that this was demonstrable from identified evidence,
- the throttle had no single failure modes, and/or associated effects, that would result in a hazardous state,
- all software used to perform safety functions was developed to appropriate standards,
- that Lloyd's Register had performed an in-depth assessment of the throttle design and its development process, with a satisfactory result.

In retrospect, it may have been advantageous to draft the safety case earlier in the assessment, to identify if there were any weaknesses in the safety arguments. In practice this risk was managed informally as work progressed. However, it is believed that this risk may be better controlled formally using a safety argument management tool.

An important point to note is that the safety case for the throttle was not dependent upon one particular argument, but had been assured through several complementary analysis techniques. Thus, although the number of software development audits meant that the samples taken were small, the safety argument was not unnecessarily dependent on the coverage of the audits, because there were other arguments that, taken together, strengthened the case.

Recommendations were made on issues that needed to be considered for the future. One particular issue that was addressed was to define what modifications could be made without invalidating the safety case.

A final report, including the safety case, was delivered to Jaguar and accepted. In the automotive industry, there is no 'regulator' to whom such a safety case should be submitted. However, the report, along with the supporting work, is available to demonstrate that Lloyd's Register, as an independent assessment body, has thoroughly assessed the electronic throttle and its development, and satisfied itself that:

- the throttle was developed in an appropriate and responsible manner,
- the throttle implements such measures as are required to ensure that it is acceptably safe,

- the development of the throttle conformed to relevant standards,
- the tools, techniques and methods used were appropriate for the application.

5. Lessons Learnt

Commitment from the parties affected by the assessment is important because, as an independent assessor, Lloyd's Register did not have direct authority over the development. Neither Jaguar nor Denso fully appreciated the implications of assessment at the start of the project, but soon became responsive to the needs of the assessor's role. Equally, the assessor must show sensitivity to the business environment and culture of the automotive industry, which often has a different view to other sectors more familiar with safety assessment practices.

Frequent design changes were inevitable as the throttle was being developed in parallel with several phases of mechanical prototype design. This is characteristic of the automotive and many other industries. It is therefore important to verify that changes are handled properly. However, technical analyses (e.g. design reviews, software analysis) must be conducted on stable products to avoid large amounts of rework. This dependence did sometimes cause problems for the timing of safety assessment activities, and it is important to plan for this wherever possible.

The system development and safety assessment were intended to follow best practice, and implement the philosophy and much of the detail of both [1] and [3]. The project was completed successfully and resulted in a high quality product accompanied by a reasoned, fully documented argument for its safety. This approach is therefore seen as both feasible and beneficial, and will be used on future projects.

The risk-based approach has been found to be useful, and enabled the targeting of mitigative techniques to yield the maximum risk-reduction. The controllability hazard classification scheme used in this XK8 safety assessment (similar to that in [3]) was found to be satisfactory, and overcame the problem of the multiple hazard outcomes in the automotive environment.

The XK8 throttle system contains significant amounts of software. A very thorough analysis of the software was undertaken and no software faults were discovered which could initiate hazardous failure modes, although it cannot be claimed that such an analysis is exhaustive. However, the analysis succeeded in identifying exceptions to the safety properties, and necessary assumptions for the safety properties to hold, from the implemented source code. Once all the identified exceptions and assumptions were shown to be acceptable, this gave a high degree of confidence in the rigour and findings of the analysis and, when coupled with the absence of any identified faults with safety implications, a correspondingly high degree of confidence in the software.

The use of formal methods in a real-time industrial application has been found to be a practical and cost-effective way of gaining a high level of assurance in the software. The use of the MALPAS tool to prove satisfaction of safety properties by the implemented system proved to be effective even without a formal translation of the source code into MALPAS IL. This was achieved by working with a formal model of the software, which overcame both the code translation obstacle, and the prohibitive cost of full code level analysis.

The best mixture of techniques to be used in an assessment has to be planned to provide maximum assurance within cost constraints. It is not possible to "do everything you can think of", and one aspect should not be over-assessed to the detriment of others. Too much reliance on one argument could result in severe project delays (and extra cost) if lack of rigour was discovered in the safety argument, or design problems were discovered late in development. It would therefore be advantageous to design a skeleton safety argument as an early deliverable, during planning stages. This could be created using a safety argument management tool such as that proposed by the ASAM project [8], which could then be used to manage the evidence gathered during development of the full argument, and to assist in its presentation.

Safety assessment in the motor industry is not currently a mandatory requirement, and hence its justification is subject to commercial considerations. The extensive safety and design assessment described in this paper involved significant effort at a commensurate cost to Jaguar; a cost that would be difficult to justify in terms of a direct return on investment. It is not possible to identify savings made during the development as a direct result of the independent assessment, or in reduced warrantee costs. However, the results from the assessment would undoubtedly be used as defence evidence, should Jaguar ever find itself in a product liability situation involving the electronic throttle. This evidence would be of great value due to the independent and impartial role of Lloyd's Register, coupled with its reputation for independent assessment. Real value was also found in the knowledge gained regarding the implications of approaching automotive safety-related systems in the way being promoted in emerging standards.

6. References

1 dIEC1508. Functional Safety: safety-related systems. Parts 1 to 7, 65A/179/CDV to 65A/185/CDV, draft, June 1995.

2 ISO 9000-3 : 1991(e). Guidelines for the application of ISO 9001 to the development, supply and maintenance of software.

3 The Motor Industry Software Reliability Association. Development Guidelines For Vehicle Based Software. November 1994. ISBN 0 9524156 0 7.

4 Kendall I. The safety assurance of the AJV8 electronic throttle. In: The Electrical System of the Jaguar XK8, IEE Digest 96/281, 1996. UK ISSN 0963-3308

5 DRIVE Safely (Project V1051). Towards a European Standard: The Development of Safe Road Transport Informatic Systems. Draft 2, March 1992.

6 Allen R, Ashworth A, and Hoskins W. Safety: A Modern Approach for Modern Vehicles. C498/1/178 in: IMechE Proceedings from Autotech 95, 1995.

7 Farnsworth A and Marshall H. User Guide for MALPAS Release 6.1. Report TACS/1019/N7, TA Consultancy Services Ltd, April 1996.

8 McDermid J, Wilson S, Fenelon P. ASAM-II: Concepts and Process. Report ASAM-II/REQ/95.3, Issue 2.2, University of York, 14 May 1996.

Testing, Validation and Verification

Dynamic Decision on Checkpointing by Use of Reduced Ordered Binary Decision Diagrams

Francesca Saglietti
Institute for Safety Technology (ISTec)
Forschungsgelände Garching Germany

Abstract

This article aims at supporting design for safety: it suggests a strategy in order to optimize checkpointing while processing large amounts of binary data. The approach developed allows to design a mechanism capable of taking appropriate decisions during execution on whether to interrupt the ongoing operation to check intermediate values or whether to proceed and postpone the check until a later point. In order to improve problem tractability, the use of Reduced Ordered Binary Decision Diagrams is recommended.

1 Introduction

Data processing in safety-relevant systems frequently involves a considerable loss of information: large amounts of variables (e.g. signals read by lots of redundant sensors) are commonly processed by a minor number of basic operations to yield few intermediate values. These values are meant to reflect the internal state of the system (e. g. the industrial plant) considered; typically, simple tests based on inequalities are then carried out on these figures in order to determine whether any risk-related threshold is passed, in which case a timely intervention is taken by actuators initiating some effective counter-measure.

Most basic operations, due to non-bijectivity, cause a certain amount of reduction: different classes of information loss were investigated in [1]. This loss as such would not represent a severe problem, in view of the fact that system protection is ensured by knowledge of the final results and in general does not require the original operands. Nonetheless, the impact of this aspect can have crucial consequences in different ways: one of the disagreeable effects of information reduction involves a high degree of failure dependency among diverse versions, even if the variants are conceptually dissimilar as well as their faults: common failures may be caused by different faults which, due to information reduction, are more likely to propagate into identical directions. This interesting point has been raised in [2] and will not (except few sporadic comments) be the topic of this article. Here we consider a further impact of information loss, namely on the effectiveness of checkpointing (by a non-specified mechanism, be it acceptance testing or diversity voting).

As each predefined checkpoint requires a time-consuming cross-examination of a corresponding checkvector (demanding in general also further resources), intermediate results should be checked as seldom as possible; on the other hand, to avoid fault propagation (e.g. to future program cycles), operands have to be verified as soon as required to enable a timely fault detection.

Thus, decision on checkpointing may be taken in terms of a trade-off: depending on the amount of information getting reduced in the course of data processing, checks should be performed just before an information loss prevents the checker from inferring (from correct checkvectors) the correctness of previous states. To support decision-making during operation, a conventional analysis of complex Boolean functions would involve procedures of intractable complexity. In order to overcome this limitation, the paper proposes to apply Reduced Ordered Binary Decision Diagrams: this yields yet another useful approach offered by a relatively novel data structure, in addition to its several efficient applications already available to safety engineers, which are briefly surveyed in the course of the presentation.

Formal Problem. The problem considered here is the following: given a binary function $f_1(x_1, ..., x_k)$ to be evaluated in the course of a program, and given a further Boolean mapping $f_2(f_1(x_1, ..., x_k), x_{k+1}, ..., x_r)$ based on the first one, the question is, whether the former value should be cross-checked in time or whether it is enough to verify only the latter result, trusting that its correctness ensures a good f_1-value. For specific binary variables $(x_1, ..., x_r)$ the second solution evidently suffices if and only if f_2 is able to discriminate between correct and incorrect f_1's, i.e. iff the following equation $(*)$ holds:

$$f_2(f_1(x_1, ..., x_k), x_{k+1}, ..., x_r) \oplus f_2(\neg f_1(x_1, ..., x_k), x_{k+1}, ..., x_r) = 1$$

This equation is the basis of the dynamic and automatic procedure proposed: as soon as the assignments to the variables are known, the system is enabled to decide whether to stop and check (last chance to find a fault) or whether to continue execution and check later (possibly allowing for a rollback). To implement this decision routine, the data structure introduced next is considered as most advantageous.

2 Reduced Ordered Binary Decision Diagrams (ROBDDs)

The particular data structure introduced in this chapter by successive refinement aims at representing Boolean functions in a compact way such as to permit a number of efficient analysis and manipulation procedures. A more general class was originally proposed in [3] and was then refined by supplementary constraints in [4].

2.1 Definition

2.1.1 Binary Decision Trees (BDTs)

It is well-known that each Boolean function f may be expanded by means of a so-called "Shannon decomposition" as follows:

$$f \equiv x_1 \wedge f \mid_{x_1 = 1} \vee \neg x_1 \wedge f \mid_{x_1 = 0}$$

The functions

$$g := f \mid_{x_1 = 1} \text{ and } h := f \mid_{x_1 = 0}$$

being independent from x_1, the above expression is usually abbreviated by $f \equiv \text{ite}(x_1, g, h)$, where $\text{ite}(x_1, g, h)$ stands for "if x_1 then g else h". This yields the classical graphical representation of f as a binary decision tree with tree root x_1 and decision subtrees representing subfunctions g and h. All inner vertices of the tree are marked with variable names x_i and have two outgoing edges denoting the two possible assignments. On the other hand, all leafs are marked with a binary value: namely the result of applying function f to the values assigned to the variables by each path marking. Evidently, such a representation is extremely redundant; therefore, a first step towards compactness is described in the next paragraph.

2.1.2 Binary Decision Diagrams (BDDs)

Like BDTs, also BDDs have exactly one source node (namely the root of the decision tree). They lose, however, the original tree property by merging all sinks with equal marking into one single node. Thus BDDs contain (at most) 2 sinks, marked with 0 and 1, denoting the outcomes of the underlying Boolean function.

2.1.3 Ordered Binary Decision Diagrams (OBDDs)

The property distinguishing OBDDs from mere BDDs is the additional specification of a particular total ordering "<" on the set of binary variables; without loss of generality let us assume that the variable numbering has already been arranged such that $x_1 < \cdots < x_n$. The predefined ordering has an essential impact on the resulting OBDD, in that it determines a unique order, in which the corresponding variable marking occurs on any path from the source to a sink. In other words, the OBDDs representing subfunctions g and h have to be based on the same ordering $x_2 < \cdots < x_n$.

2.1.4 Reduced Ordered Binary Decision Diagrams (ROBDDs)

Finally, representation compactness can be fully achieved by repeatedly applying (as often as possible) any of the two following reduction steps.

Step 1: Elimination of "don't care"-vertices. This step consists of removing redundant vertices (i. e. vertices with both outgoing edges pointing to the same subtree).

Step 2: Merging of isomorphic subgraphs. This step consists of merging more isomorphic subgraphs into one single copy.

In particular, a Reduced Ordered Binary Decision Diagram (ROBDD) is a directed, acyclic and connected graph, each vertex representing a different Boolean function.

2.2 Required Effort

2.2.1 Implementation

To implement $f = \text{ite}(x_1, g, h)$ usually two tables are used:

Ite-table. This is a recursive structure consisting of triples of the form:

$$(x_1, \text{ROBDD}_g, \text{ROBDD}_h)$$

where x_1 is the lowest variable of f (w. r. t. relation "<"), while the second and third entries refer to the ite-table-addresses ROBDD_g resp. ROBDD_h for ROBDD-representations of subfunctions g and h.

Computation Table. For reasons of efficiency a further table is applied in order to avoid the repeated evaluation of identical expressions; this table consists of quadruples for each binary operation $\Diamond$ performed on ROBDDs: the symbol $\Diamond$ of the operation, followed by the ite-table-addresses of both operands and of their result:

$$(\Diamond, \text{ROBDD}_g, \text{ROBDD}_h, \text{ROBDD}_{g\Diamond h})$$

Among the available tools implementing ROBDDs (e. g. [5]), there are packages permitting operations on ROBDDs with over 1 million vertices to be routinely performed on workstation computers (see [6]).

2.2.2 Synthesis

The application of an arbitrary algebraic operation $\Diamond$ relies on the fact that such operations "commute" with the Shannon expansion for any variable x:

$$f_1 \Diamond f_2 = \text{ite}\,(x, (f_1 \mid _{x=1}) \Diamond (f_2 \mid _{x=1}), (f_1 \mid _{x=0}) \Diamond (f_2 \mid _{x=0}))$$

This yields a recursive procedure to compute the ROBDD representation of $f_1 \Diamond f_2$.

The use of a computation table avoiding multiple evaluations bounds the synthesis complexity by the order $O(|ROBDD_{f_1}| \cdot |ROBDD_{f_2}|)$, where $|ROBDD|$ is the size of the ROBDD-graph in terms of the number of its inner vertices (see [6]).

2.2.3 Reduction

Reduction as a separate step takes linear time (see [7]), but can also be achieved directly during synthesis with the help of the computation table (see [6]).

2.3 Benefits of ROBDDs

Apart from the limited amount of memory space required by a compact representation, ROBDDs also allow simple analysis and manipulation procedures in the context of various problems, some of which are described in what follows.

2.3.1 Evaluation

Each path from the source of a ROBDD to one of both sinks corresponds to an evaluation for the specific variable assignment given by the corresponding path marking; in case some variables do not occur on a given path, their values do not contribute to the final result, so that for an evaluation purpose they may be ignored.

2.3.2 Uniqueness of Representation

For a given ordering, the ROBDD representation of a function is canonical, i.e. the resulting ROBDD is unique (up to isomorphisms), and minimal with respect to the number of nodes (see [4]).

2.3.3 Equivalence / Non-Equivalence of Boolean Functions

Functional equivalence / non-equivalence of Boolean functions can be easily tested by checking whether their canonical ROBDD representations agree for a given ordering.

2.3.4 Satisfiability / Tautology Problems

A function is satisfiable if its ROBDD representation does not correspond to the single terminal vertex labeled 0. Any tautological function must have the terminal vertex labeled 1 as its ROBDD representation.

2.4 Limitations of ROBDDs

2.4.1 Variable Ordering

The problem of determining the existence of a variable ordering permitting a ROBDD representation with a predefined maximum number of nodes is NP-complete (see [8]). Nonetheless, in practice acceptable approximations to this problem are often achieved by starting with application-related heuristics and by improving them dynamically by local search algorithms (see for example [9]).

2.4.2 Diagram Size

As satisfiability can be efficiently solved for ROBDDs representations of Boolean functions, the transformation of Boolean functions with NP-complete SAT-tests on ROBDD-form must necessarily be NP-hard for arbitrary variable orderings. In fact, there are functions (e. g. the one representing the middle two outputs of an n-bit multiplier) requiring exponential ROBDD representations regardless of the variable ordering. Nonetheless, for a large number of real-world applications upper bounds for ROBDD complexity can be derived based on the structural properties of the logic network realization, thus providing insight into design applications with efficient ROBDD representations (see [6]).

2.5 Applications to Safety Engineering

ROBDDs were already applied to numerous hard problems arising in the context of system analysis and verification procedures, thus permitting to approach complex fields, considered up to then as numerically intractable. Some among the most important applications to safety engineering are briefly surveyed here, before deriving in more detail the novel approach proposed in this article.

2.5.1 Verification of Digital Circuits

An immediate exploitation of the advantages offered by ROBDDs is achieved when testing the equivalence of two combinational-logic circuits. A real-world example of this potential is reported in [10]: the formal verification of a PowerPC microprocessor carried out by comparing the register-transfer level specification (derived in VHDL from an informal architectural specification) with the actual circuit implementation at transistor level; the equivalence of both views is either formally confirmed or rejected by means of automatically produced counter-examples.

2.5.2 Model Checking

Model checking can make use of ROBDDs to permit the exhaustive analysis of very large finite state systems by systematically verifying that given properties (e.g. in a temporal logic) are fulfilled for any of its reachable states (see [11]). Any set of states (resp. any state transition graph) is encoded by a ROBDD representing the characteristic function of the corresponding set (resp. the corresponding relation). [12] makes use of this technique for the formal verification of a cache consistency protocol in the Encore Gigamax distributed shared-memory multiprocessor. The method allowed to discover faults which previous extensive simulations had not been able to reveal.

2.5.3 Test Case Generation

Conventional generation of test cases for digital circuits is usually based on sensitivity analysis: given a fault, its effect on altering signal values is studied. This (more or less) unsystematic activity is carried out until an assignment to primary inputs is found capable of exciting the fault by sensitizing a path to the outputs. The complexity involved in this procedure frequently renders the task absolutely intractable. The approach proposed in [13] to support automatic test generation makes use of symbolic fault simulation: good and bad circuits are seen as finite state machines given by ROBDDs; differences among their canonical representations determine input patterns capable of detecting specific faults (e.g. stuck-at-1 or stuck-at-0 faults).

2.5.4 Fault Tree Analysis

Safety-critical systems are usually analysed by means of fault trees in order to identify those system components having the strongest impact on the overall risk involved. The insight thus gained is used during the planning phase to optimize system architecture; during development it is applied to adequately distribute (implementation and verification) resources among components; finally, after development it helps to quantify system dependability during the final assessment phase. Essential to all these activities is the determination of minimal cut sets, i.e. minimal combinations of basic events capable of initiating system failure. In case of very complex systems with ten thousands of cuts, the conventional procedure based on logical manipulations of Boolean expressions is often condemned to be practically useless. In such cases [14] suggests an efficient procedure making use of ROBDDs to determine the minimal cut sets of a Boolean function by recursion on its both Shannon subfunctions.

3 Dynamic Decision on Checkpointing

3.1 Checkpointing by ROBDDs

After a brief survey on the advantages offered by Decision Diagrams, we return now to the original problem posed in the introductory paragraphs. To simplify problem representation, consider for fixed i $f := f_2$, $n := r-k+1$ and $y_1 := f_1(x_1, ..., x_k)$, $y_j := x_{k+j-1}$ for $j \in \{2,...,n\}$. Then equation ($*$) from section 1 reads:

$$f(y_1, y_2, ..., y_n) \oplus f(\neg y_1, y_2, ..., y_n) = 1.$$

We would like to evaluate this expression as efficiently as possible. To do so, let $f = \text{ite } (y_1, g, h)$ denote the ROBDD representing $f(y_1, y_2, ..., y_n)$; similarly, let $f' = \text{ite } (y_1, g', h')$ denote the ROBDD representing $f(\neg y_1, y_2, ..., y_n)$. Due to

$$f(\neg y_1, y_2, ..., y_n) \equiv \text{ite } (\neg y_1, g, h) = \text{ite } (y_1, h, g),$$

this implies

$$g' = h, \text{ and } h' = g.$$

On the other hand,

$$\neg f = \neg \text{ite } (y_1, g, h) = \text{ite } (y_1, \neg g, \neg h)$$

and

$$\neg f' = \neg \text{ite } (y_1, h, g) = \text{ite } (y_1, \neg h, \neg g)$$

yielding

$$f (y_1, y_2, ..., y_k) \oplus f (\neg y_1, y_2, ..., y_k) = f \oplus f' = f \wedge \neg f' \vee \neg f \wedge f' =$$

$$= \text{ite } (y_1, g, h) \wedge \text{ite } (y_1, \neg h, \neg g) \vee \text{ite } (y_1, \neg g, \neg h) \wedge \text{ite } (y_1, h, g) =$$

$$= \text{ite } (y_1, g \wedge \neg h \vee \neg g \wedge h , h \wedge \neg g \vee \neg h \wedge g) = g \oplus h.$$

Summarizing, to evaluate the original expression ($*$), we just have to evaluate both subfunctions g and h with respect to the same input vector $(y_2, ..., y_n)$ and to (mis-) compare their results. As the function to be evaluated is known in advance, the construction of the ROBDD representing $g \oplus h$ is performed once and for all before operation. During runtime, only its evaluation is (efficiently) carried out for any new input vector $(y_2, ..., y_n)$. Just in case of a non-positive evaluation (i. e. one yielding 0), the system will opt for immediate checkpointing, activating its redundant measures to verify the intermediate result y_1.

3.2 Examples

3.2.1 Efficiency of Dynamic Checkpointing

The first example is meant to illustrate the dramatic impact checkpointing can have on failure behaviour. The application considered here is the well-known launch interceptor system described in [15], which has undoubtedly contributed to stimulate scientific discussion throughout the last decade. This experiment had been conceived to analyse correlation in the failure behaviour of 27 program variants written in Pascal on the basis of the same specification.

Each program was required to read data representing radar reflections and, using a set of conditions, to decide whether the reflections came from a threatening object. If so, a signal to launch an interceptor had to be generated.

Failure Dependence. It was noted in several publications that common failure behaviour observed among diverse variants was impressively high, overcoming by 2 orders of magnitude the idealistic case of failure independence (see for example [16]). This extremely high failure dependence can be explained by the fact that the (intermediate and final) values checked were based on the evaluation of so-called "Launch Interceptor Conditions" (abbreviated LICs); each LIC expressed a functional requirement for a set of up to 100 planar points representing radar echoes; the conditions were of the form "there exists at least n points such that ..."

For example, considering the case of $n = 2$ consecutive points, the LIC would actually correspond to a disjunction of 99 conditions C_i referring to pairs $(i,i+1)$ of subsequent points $i \leq 100$:

$$C_1 \vee ... \vee C_{99}$$

Cross-checking only the final result of this disjunction causes an increase in common failure behaviour due to the pecularities of failure propagation by loss of good information: an incorrect C_1 is capable of propagating if and only if it is erroneously set to 1 and $C_2 \vee ... \vee C_{99} = 0$ (i. e. the correct information in $C_2, ... , C_{99}$ gets lost). Thus, checking C_1 is worth performing in case of $(C_1, ... ,C_{99}) = (1, 0, ..., 0)$.

Complexity. For this particularly simple case the suggested policy is intuitively appealing without requiring any compact data structure. In most real-world applications, however, the logical combination of intermediate values is usually too complex to be treated by intuition. In such cases a systematic approach by ROBDDs as reported in this article allows to automatize this strategy for arbitrary binary operations.

3.2.2 Efficiency of ROBDD Representation and Manipulation

The well-known "Odd Parity" function provides a nice example showing how effectively ROBDDs can reduce both representation size and manipulation effort. In this particular case, a classical evaluation by means of the disjunctive normal form

$$\text{odd parity } (x_1, x_2, ..., x_n) =$$

$$= \bigvee_{K \subseteq \{1,...,n-1\}} \left\{ \left(\bigwedge_{i \in K} x_i \right) \wedge \left[\bigwedge_{j \in \{1,...,n-1\} \setminus K} (\neg x_j) \right] \wedge \left[(\neg)^{|K|} x_n \right] \right\}$$

would require a prohibitive exponential complexity due to its 2^{n-1} minimal terms. Evaluation by ROBDDs, on the other hand, just involves a one-time construction of the Decision Diagram f

$$f \equiv \text{odd parity } (x_1, x_2, ..., x_n) = \text{ite } (x_1, g, h)$$

where

$$g \equiv \text{even parity } (x_2, ..., x_n), \ h \equiv \text{odd parity } (x_2, ..., x_n)$$

Its evaluation merely requires linear effort (due to $2n + 1$ vertices, see Figure 1).

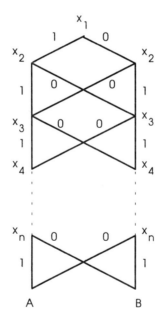

with $A = (\neg)^{n+1} 1$ and $B = (\neg)^n 1$

Figure 1: ROBDD representing odd parity function

4 Conclusion

Checking intermediate results has pro and cons: on the one hand, it reduces fault propagation (and common failures) by a timely identification of erroneous values; on the other hand, it requires additional resources, which for most checks usually reveal as superfluous where not prohibitive. For such reasons, dynamic checkpointing is suggested: input-dependent decisions are taken during operation on the basis of the momentary need for checkpoints. This allows an efficient expenditure of resources just when this is explicitly justified by the data presently processed. The choice of Reduced Ordered Binary Decision Diagrams to implement this strategy revealed as highly recommendable.

References

1. Saglietti F. Location of Checkpoints in Fault-Tolerant Software. Proc. 5th Jerusalem Conference on Information Technology (JCIT-5), IEEE Computer Society Press 1990

2. Bishop P, Pullen FD. Error Masking: a Source of Failure Dependency in Multi-Version Programs. Proc. Int. Work. Conf. on Dependable Computing for Critical Applications, Santa Barbara, USA, Springer-Verlag 1989

3. Akers SB. Binary Decision Diagrams. IEEE Trans. on Computers 1978; C-27 : 6

4. Bryant RE. Graph-Based Algorithms for Boolean Function Manipulation. IEEE Trans. on Computers 1986; C-35 : 8

5. Brace KS, Rudell RL, Bryant RE. Efficient Implementation of a BDD Package. Proc. 27th ACM / IEEE Design Automation Conference 1990

6. Bryant RE. Symbolic Boolean Manipulation with Ordered Binary Decision Diagrams. Communications of the ACM 1992

7. Sieling D, Wegener I. Reduction of OBDDs in Linear Time. Information Processing Letters 1993; 48

8. Bollig B, Wegener I. Improving the Variable Ordering of OBDDs is NP-complete. IEEE Transactions on Computers 1996; C-45 : 9

9. Butler KM, Ross DE, Kapur R, Mercer MR. Heuristics to Compute Variable Orderings for Efficient Manipulation of Ordered Binary Decision Diagrams. 28th ACM / IEEE Design Automation Conference 1991

10. Appenzeller DP, Kuehlmann A. Formal Verification of a PowerPC Microprocessor. Proc. Dagstuhl seminar 1995

11. Clarke EM, Emerson EA, Sistla AP. Automatic Verification of Finite-State Concurrent Systems Using Temporal Logic Specifications. ACM Trans. on Programming Languages & Systems 1986; 8:2

12. McMillan KL. Symbolic Model Checking - an Approach to the State Explosion. Doctoral Thesis, Carnegie Mellon, CMU-CS-92-131, 1992, Chapter 4: A Distributed Cache Protocol

13. Cho K, Bryant RE. Test Pattern Generation for Sequential MOS Circuits by Symbolic Fault Simulation. 26th ACM / IEEE Design Automation Conference 1989

14. Rauzy A. New Algorithms for Fault Tree Analysis. Reliability Engineering and System Safety 1993

15. Knight JC, Leveson NG. An Experimental Evaluation of the Assumption of Independence in Multiversion Programming. IEEE Trans. on Software Engineering 1986, SE-12:1

16. Saglietti F. Design and Assessment of Fault-Tolerant Software. Habilitationsschrift (post-doc thesis), Technische Universität München, Fakultät für Informatik, 1996

Practical Assessment of Neural Network Applications

Ian T Nabney*   Mickael J S Paven*   Richard C Eldridge[†]

Clive Lee[†]

Abstract

This paper reports the initial results of a joint research project carried out by Aston University and Lloyd's Register to develop a practical method of assessing neural network applications. A set of assessment guidelines for neural network applications were developed and tested on two applications. These case studies showed that it is practical to assess neural networks in a statistical pattern recognition framework. However there is need for more standardisation in neural network technology and a wider takeup of good development practice amongst the neural network community.

1 Introduction

Neural computing is a form of *inductive programming*: a task is performed by a general model which is trained using data that represents the task. Such an approach is particularly appropriate when applied to problems that involve modelling complex systems. As the use of neural networks becomes more common, with many live systems now commercially available, the question of how to assess and certify neural computing applications is becoming more important. In particular, if neural networks are to be used in safety related systems, it is essential for there to be an assessment methodology that is sound and accepted by regulatory authorities, end users, and developers. Even if neural networks are implemented in software on conventional computers, they correspond to a very different way of viewing computer programs, so it is not obvious that the classical methods used to develop and assess software are applicable to them. This paper reports the results of a joint research project carried out by the Neural Computing Research Group at Aston University and Lloyd's Register to develop a practical method of assessing neural network applications. Lloyd's Register provides commercial safety and quality assessment, and have been active in the field of software assessment and certification for many years. They provide the necessary experience and knowledge of assessment of conventional software.

The work carried out on the project so far has necessarily been limited in scope. We have only addressed certain sorts of problems and certain neural

---

*Neural Computing Research Group, Aston University, Birmingham, B4 7ET. Correspondence to first author at this address or by email at i.t.nabney@aston.ac.uk

[†]Safety Integrity and Risk Management, Lloyd's Register of Shipping, Lloyd's Register House, 29 Wellesley Road, Croydon CR0 2AJ

network architectures, and we have not looked at hardware issues. In particular, we have considered classification or regression problems that are tackled using multi-layer perceptron (MLP) or radial basis function (RBF) networks (see (2) for a good survey of statistical pattern recognition and neural networks). Approximately 70–80% of applications in the process modelling, monitoring and control industries (which are those of most interest to Lloyd's Register, since they represent the bulk of safety critical applications) are of this type.

In this paper we describe a practical method for assessing neural network applications based on current best practice. Neural computing is a field of very active research, so while we expect most of the *aims* and *principles* we describe here to remain valid, the *means* by which the aims are achieved may change in the future. Our work has also highlighted some new areas where further research is needed to provide developers with credible and *quantitative* tests suitable for assessment. During the project, we developed a set of guidelines and supporting technical information to allow people trained in the assessment of conventional software systems to assess neural network applications as well. Two case studies (involving real neural computing applications: one of which is live, and the other of which is at the prototype stage) were used to test the assessment method. To ensure conformance with assessment practice for conventional software systems, the case studies were carried out with the involvement of software assessors from Lloyd's Register.

Earlier papers on this subject (6; 8) have raised some of the important issues in the development process, but have not considered recent theoretical developments in the field that allow us to measure the dependability of neural network outputs. They have also been addressing the problem from the developer's, rather than the assessor's, point of view.

2 Neural Computing

While this paper is concerned with how to assess neural network applications and not with how to develop them, it is nevertheless important to consider some of the key issues in application development. This is because assessment is concerned with process ('was the system built using sound engineering principles?') as well as product ('does this system perform to specification?'). The emphasis in this section is on the principal differences between neural computing and conventional software engineering.

It is clear that neural computing represents a very different approach from the conventional view of software development, where an algorithmic solution can be specified in advance of writing the software. Because the performance and precision of the model cannot be determined in advance, the use of neural computing is best confined to applications where efficient algorithmic solutions are impossible or impractical. Such applications are typically complex, poorly understood, and imprecise. Understanding speech, reading handwritten documents, and modelling and controlling non-linear systems are all domains where neural computing and other statistical techniques outperform algorithmic methods.

2.1 A Comparison with Conventional Software Engineering

We can compare neural computing with a conventional approach to software development by considering a concrete example: the problem of developing a system model for a marine engine.

A conventional approach would involve determining the physical processes governing the engine, analysing these to generate mathematical equations that represent the system, and then programming some software to simulate these equations and their solution. In principle, this method could be used without the use of a physical engine.

An inductive approach involves gathering data from an engine and training a model (a neural network, for example) to reproduce the same relationships as are present in the data and determine a good approximation to the underlying function that has generated the data. The training process consists of adjusting some variable parameters in the model using the data ('parameter estimation' in statistical terminology). In our view, this process is best studied from the statistical pattern recognition point of view, placing neural networks in the framework of linear regression, time series models, and other statistical methods.

A consequence of the way in which neural networks are trained is that the parameters in the model are the only part of the model which is specific to a given application. The interpretation by humans of these parameters is considerably more difficult and less precise than the interpretation of algorithmic high level source code. This implies that the assessment of neural computing systems is necessarily statistical in nature. As safety cases are typically written in terms of limiting the probability of failure, this may actually be an advantage.

In principle, inductive learning involves no software development, as the software to run and train the model is independent of the application and data. In some respects, this software is analogous to a compiler in conventional software development, with the training process similar to compilation, and the parameters of the trained model comparable to machine code. This software is entirely algorithmic, and so can be certified for use in safety related applications with existing assessment methods. It is rather hard to develop high integrity compilers for languages of reasonable size (see (9) for an example); by comparison, neural network software is comparatively small and straightforward, so that it should be relatively straightforward to assess such software by conventional means.

In practice, the distinction between the two development approaches may not be so clear cut. When modelling any complex real world system, some data from the actual system is nearly always required, if only for model calibration and validation. Most of the issues discussed in this paper are relevant whenever real world data is used for such purposes. Equally, neural computing may only represent part of the solution to a problem: for example, conventional programming may be needed to pre-process the data before fitting a model.

Although there is little or no software development in a neural computing application, there are other important tasks to be carried out which have no real equivalent in conventional software engineering.

- Data collection. Adequate quantities of relevant data are essential.

- Data pre-processing. It is rare that the best performance is achieved when the data is presented in its raw form.

- Network training. This has to be carefully monitored to ensure that a good solution is reached.

- Performance assessment. The key question is not how well the network performs on the data it was trained on, but how well it generalises to unseen data.

The assessment guidelines have as their focus sound practice and testing for these aspects of development.

2.2   A Lifecycle Model

Most phases of a neural computing application development lifecycle will be familiar from those used for conventional software engineering. The main differences arise for three reasons:

- a precise functional specification is not possible at the start of development;

- the use of data means that extra tasks must be carried out;

- development is *necessarily* iterative.

Although there is no definitive lifecycle model (just as for conventional software engineering), the following is a principled approach which has been successfully used in practice.

1. Problem Definition: what are the aims? How can you measure success? This document is key to credible performance assessment.

2. Data collection: data sampled from the system to be modelled, cost measures, prior information (for example, how smooth the function should be, operational constraints on variables). In neural computing, particularly with a Bayesian approach, we attempt to quantify and formalise the assumptions (or prior knowledge). This makes it easier to test whether these assumptions are valid, and is an important part of verifying the performance of the trained system.

3. Preliminary data analysis: visualisation to understand the data, feature extraction, missing and corrupt data, pre-processing.

4. Model development: model design is based on prior knowledge and data analysis. A range of models should be trained: simple models as benchmarks and more complex models to attempt to capture more features of the problem and to improve accuracy.

5. Integration: interface with other software.

6. Operation and maintenance: ongoing model validation and retraining.

Note that data collection and pre-processing can take up to 40% of the development time (4). This lifecycle model (see Figure 1) is quite general, and is similar to others in the literature (see, for example, (8)). However, there are two important points to note about the lifecycle defined above and that are often omitted. Firstly, data is not just collected from the system to be modelled. Prior information can and should be used to structure and constrain the solution. Secondly, during operation, the model must be validated and retrained when necessary. Techniques recently developed allow us to measure, and therefore monitor, the quality of neural network performance during operation. For example error bars (see (3) amongst others) allow us to assign a *confidence* in the neural network prediction.

2.3 Training and Generalisation

Learning for a neural network means adjusting the parameters (usually called 'weights') to approximate an unknown function, based on a data set sampled from that function. The weights are adjusted during the training process by minimising an error (or cost) function. This error function is a global measure of the discrepancy between the target values and the values predicted by the neural network.

The error function is often very complex (since for neural networks it depends on the weights in a highly non-linear way). Thus finding the minimum is not easy. Most algorithms are based on the fact that the global minimum of a function is a point where all the partial derivatives of the function equal zero. However, this is a necessary but not sufficient condition. These points can be local minima (i.e. at this point the function value is a minimum for a small region around the point), local maxima, or other 'flat' regions. Being trapped in a bad local minimum implies that the solution is sub-optimal, which may result in non-compliance to the specification. Most optimisation algorithms find a local minimum close to their starting point: thus it is important to carry out multiple training runs with different random starting points.

Often the data used for training is corrupted by noise: for example, owing to the imprecision of measuring instruments. The aim is to avoid learning the noise but to learn the underlying structure so that the model *generalises* to previously unseen inputs. Thus if a neural network learns the training data and fits it perfectly, it is said to *overfit* the training data. This usually leads to poor generalisation performance, as can be seen by testing the model on an independent set of data. Often overfitting is associated with a complex model

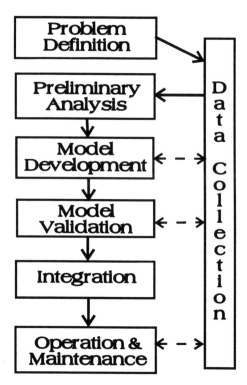

Figure 1: Lifecycle Model. The solid line denotes the main path through the lifecycle; dotted lines denote points at which which more data may be required and the development may return to an earlier stage.

for which the computed function may vary greatly between the training data points. We usually have a prior expectation that the function should vary in a relatively smooth fashion and this can be incorporated into the model training (by *regularisation* techniques) and usually improves the generalisation of the trained model.

2.4   Interpolation/Extrapolation and Data Density

Understanding the distinction between interpolation and extrapolation is fundamental to neural network reliability. Typically neural networks (and other data models) are much more accurate when interpolating than when extrapolating. The usual definitions of these terms (that the new data point lies in the interior or exterior respectively of the region of input space containing the training data) are not accurate or easy to measure in more than one dimension.

Instead, we say that areas of the input space where the training data density is high are interpolation regions, while areas of the input space where the training data density is low are extrapolation regions. Intuitively the idea is that in the areas where the model has a lot of information its behaviour is constrained, while in areas where there is little or no information its functionality is unconstrained and therefore unreliable.

Another way to measure the reliability of the neural network predictions is to generate 'error bars' which give an interval of 'likely' values which take into account possible sources of variation around the predicted output. There are different sorts of error bars corresponding to different source of variation: input noise, output noise, and parameter uncertainty. The wider the error bars, the less certain the network is about its output. It has been shown in (3) that Bayesian error bars (which take into account the uncertainty of the network weights due to the use of a sample of data in training) are related to the input data density, which links error bars with novelty detection.

We conclude that for safety critical neural network applications, the novelty of the input data should be monitored (as suggested in (1)), so that outputs that are likely to be unreliable can be identified. This would form part of a monitoring system which would be a quantitative way of assessing performance and testing the assumptions made during development on-line. In addition, most neural network systems make the assumption that the data generator is *stationary* (i.e. it does not change with time). This assumption can also be tested by monitoring the novelty of the input data and assessing the accuracy of the network's output.

3 Assessment Guidelines

The basic principles of the assessment guidelines are the same as those in conventional software:

- Check that the neural network function has been developed in a controlled and planned way (i.e. the quality of the processes and methodology used).

- Check that the neural network function has successfully passed the tests and complies with its specification.

Neither of these two aspects, if applied alone, is sufficient to assess a neural system: the two are complementary. Although the principles of conventional software development methods still apply, their practical application may differ. For example, repeatability means that random seeds used in initialising models and splitting data must be recorded so that experimental results can be confirmed at a later date.

The fact that neural systems are data based has many implications for development and assessment. The data becomes part of the 'program', and therefore needs to be subject to the same control as other project documents. More fundamentally, the data needs to be of good quality, and representative of the problem. This can be difficult to test (and therefore assess), as there are few objective statistical tests for these properties. As in any system, certain assumptions are made during development. One advantage of neural networks is that it is possible to quantify many of these assumptions and test them before deployment.

It should be noted that the assessment guidelines are not prescriptive: they do not, in general, mandate particular methods for developing applications. We can compare this with statement 3.3.2.4 from the MISRA guidelines (5): "Many diverse methods may be used to assess stability. No one method may be identified as preferred. It should not be assumed that similar results will be obtained from different methods for a given solution".

Most of the issues in neural network development apply also to many systems already in use. For example, in control theory the stability of linear controllers for linear systems can be mathematically analysed. However, developing a linear controller for a real system requires a system model (involving some parameter estimation from data). This model is not exact (for example, it may be a linear approximation to a non-linear plant, and may ignore system noise) and this inexactness affects the controller's performance: it will not exactly match theory and stability is no longer necessarily guaranteed. Thus practical systems are typically designed with large margins from the boundary conditions predicted by theory. Thus 'rules of thumb' are used now in safety critical systems, and some of the questions raised about the use of neural networks and other new technologies can also be asked of conventional development practice.

4 Case Studies

4.1 Questar

The first case study was based on the Questar product developed by Oxford University in collaboration with Oxford Instruments Ltd. The product monitors EEG traces to detect sleep disorders (7). It tracks the sleep/wake continuum on a 1 second time interval. Prior to the development of this instrument, a *hypnogram* would be constructed by hand from an EEG trace with a 30 second time interval. To analyse a whole night of sleep manually takes a considerable length of time (about 1 hour). Extensive trials have demonstrated that the system correctly automates a labour intensive process and improves the quality of the results (both through improved time resolution and with consistent and repeatable analysis). An analysis of a night of data by Questar takes just 10 seconds. The system is now used as a diagnostic aid for clinicians.

The problem is expressed as a classification problem (with 3 classes) which is mapped to a wakefulness score in the range $[-1, 1]$ which is the clinical users' preferred format. RBF networks were used and compared with linear models, over which they showed a significant improvement.

The main finding of the assessment was that although the development had generally been carried out in a principled way, the documentation was not as complete as could be desired. The Functional Specification had been written early in the project: however the performance targets were only determined at the end of the project. The developers agreed that it would have been useful to set concrete targets earlier in the development. The users and scope of the system were not explicitly defined: although end users had been consulted, particularly concerning the way in which the results should be presented, these reviews were not documented.

Testing was commendably thorough, involving comparisons with hypnograms (using 7,200 test samples) and diagnostic tests under clinical conditions. It has been shown to correlate with a by-hand analysis as well as one carried out by a second expert. The risks (i.e. misclassification costs) have not been elicited from clinicians: this information is important to make optimal choices in the decision theoretic framework.

Confidence measures, such as error bars, were constructed for the models, but they proved not to be robust (i.e. the confidence intervals themselves did not generalise well). A known problem with the system is that novel data tends to be classified as 'wakefulness', but there is no specific monitoring for novel data in the operational system. The assessors also had some concerns about how representative the data is. For example, the effect of different types of EEG recorder is unknown, and the impact of any variations has not been analysed. There was a good use of visualisation and a considerable body of prior knowledge from 30 years of clinical experience to understand the data and select relevant features. A systematic search over the order of the preprocessing AR model and the size of the network means that we can have confidence that the selected architecture is near optimal. Good use was made of script files so that all experiments are repeatable.

4.2 Engine Management System

The second case study is an ongoing project carried out by Aston University in collaboration with a company that manufactures engine management systems. At the time when the case study was carried out, the project was only in its early stages: that is, its feasibility had been shown on a sub-problem.

In normal engine operation, away from idle speed, the ignition timing and fuel injection volume is determined from a set of look up tables as a function of several variables, such as load, speed, engine temperature, etc. These look up tables are obtained on the basis of labour intensive experiments which involve tuning engine parameters until the engineer is satisfied that the engine is running optimally in a steady state. Typically, the input variables are quantised into 16 bands, and the resulting matrix is quite sparsely populated with experimental data. The criteria for 'optimal' values are complex, involving tradeoffs between performance, emissions, economy and driveability. There are many such look up tables in modern engine management systems governing all parts of an engine operating envelope. Usually a simple linear interpolation method is used to estimate values away from the measured data, which gives rise to unsmooth (non-differentiable) control surfaces. The aim of this project was to replace this interpolation scheme by a neural network.

Overall there was a good level of conformance with the guidelines especially after taking into account the early stage of development. The technical standard of the work was generally high, with a particularly thorough exploration of suitable error bars. The main findings were:

- Specification. The performance requirements were not fully specified and although core objectives had been identified, there was no priority order. This is important since it strongly influences the choice of cost function.

- Documentation. The activities and findings from the initial data collection and analysis were distributed in notebooks and could usefully have been summarised in a report. This report would form part of the system specification. It was also difficult to trace design features to the specification requirements.

- Testing of assumptions. An assumption of constant variance Gaussian noise was made (leading to a sum of squares error function) but the validity of this assumption and the sensitivity of the neural network to it had not been investigated.

5 Discussion

As with conventional software, providing a formal proof of the correctness of a neural network application is in general impractical. However, both case studies suggest that if a neural network application is developed in a controlled and methodical way and properly tested, then it should be possible to validate and verify it with an effectiveness comparable to conventional software. In both cases the technology had been applied in a principled and well engineered way. We note that assessment of such applications requires a good understanding of the basic properties of neural networks.

Both case studies have shown that during the development of a neural network application, three issues seem to be generally neglected: documentation, specification and testing of assumptions. For instance, both applications no quantitative targets were defined in the specification, and a standard noise model (leading to a sum of squares error function) was used without examining how appropriate this was for the data.

The main reasons for this neglect are probably:

1. The iterative nature of the development lifecycle and the fact that system performance cannot be predicted in advance mean that it is often inappropriate to define a concrete specification at the start of the project. Lower limits on performance can be derived from safety arguments and cost/benefit analysis. After the feasibility stage the specification *should* be reviewed to make it more precise, but this often does not happen.

2. As neural networks correspond to a novel way of viewing software, no standards currently exist. For instance, there is no clear definition of what should appear in a specification for a neural network application.

3. Although neural network technology is currently moving from research to products, many neural network applications are developed by academics. While they generally have a very good understanding of the technology, they usually do not have the same objectives and experience in software development as commercial software houses.

However, we believe that these problems are temporary and are due to the relative youth of the technology. Furthermore, there are many conventional software applications that are poorly specified and documented, so these problems are by no means unique to neural networks.

As was the case in the early days of conventional software development, there is a need for standardisation for neural networks. There are several motivations for standardisation:

1. Providing guidelines to develop successful neural network applications makes the technology more accessible.

2. Application development is easier to control if it is done in a systematic way. Moreover, better control over development is (usually) synonymous with higher dependability.

3. A standardised development method enables verification and validation to be standardised as well. This is not completely achievable (even for conventional software), but is a goal to aim for.

The two lead engineers on the case studies found the assessment useful and the procedure convincing. As these are two of the leading neural network application developers in the UK, this suggests that the process we have proposed would meet with widespread acceptance in the technical community.

Our current work is addressing four areas:

- Quantitative results. For some rules of good practice there is no standard technique to test their correct application in a quantitative way. So, for some aspects of the current guidelines, their assessment involves making sure that 'rules of thumb' and accepted good practice have been applied. This is not desirable for applications requiring the highest levels of integrity, although it is tolerated by some existing standards (e.g. (5)).

- Data quality and characterisation. This is essential for successful applications, but there are few, if any, useful tests for determining any weaknesses in this regard.

- Safety integrity levels. In principle, since neural networks are statistical models that make probabilistic predictions, they should be well suited to incorporation into safety cases. We shall investigate how this could be done and what the implications for specification of neural network systems are.

- Neural controllers. Some applications use neural networks as part of a closed loop control system. To train a neural network to perform this task is quite different from the usual supervised training regime we have considered up to now, and also raises questions of stability.

6 Acknowledgements

We are grateful to Lionel Tarassenko and James Pardey of Oxford University and David Lowe and Chris Zapart of Aston University for their assistance with the case studies.

References

[1] C. M. Bishop. Novelty detection and neural network validation. *IEE Proc.-Vis. Image Signal Process.*, 141:217–222, 1994.

[2] C. M. Bishop. *Neural Networks for Pattern Recognition*. Oxford University Press, 1995.

[3] C. M. Bishop, C. Qazaz, C. K. I. Williams, and H. Zhu. On the relationship between bayesian error bars and the input data density. In *4th IEE Conference on Artificial Neural Networks*, pages 160–165, 1995.

[4] DTI. *Best Practice Guidelines for Neural Computing Applications*, 1994.

[5] MISRA Report 4. *Software in Control Systems*, 1994.

[6] G. Morgan and J. Austin. Safety critical neural networks. In *4th IEE Conference on Artificial Neural Networks*, pages 212–217. IEE, 1995.

[7] J. Pardey, S. Roberts, L. Tarassenko, and J. Stradling. A new approach to the analysis of the human sleep/wakefulness continuum. *J. Sleep Res.*, 5:201–210, 1996.

[8] D. Partridge and W. B. Yates. Engineering reliable neural networks. In *4th IEE Conference on Artificial Neural Networks*, pages 352–357. IEE, 1995.

[9] S. Stepney. *High Integrity Compilation: A Case Study*. Prentice Hall, 1993.

Software Test Techniques for System Fault-Tree Analysis

John C. Knight & Luís G. Nakano

Department of Computer Science, University of Virginia

Charlottesville, VA 22903-2442, USA

Abstract

System fault-tree analysis is a technique for modeling dependability that is in widespread use. For systems that include software, the integration of software data into fault trees has proved problematic. In this paper we discuss a number of techniques that can be used to make the assessment of software dependability by testing both more tractable and more suitable for use in system fault-tree analysis. Some of the techniques are illustrated using an experimental control system for a research nuclear reactor as an example.

1 Introduction

Computers are introduced into applications for the many advantages that they provide. But these advantages do not come without a price. The price is the complexity that the computer system brings with it. In addition to providing several advantages, the increased complexity has the potential for decreasing the dependability of the overall system. This can be dangerous in safety-critical systems where incorrect computer operation can be catastrophic [14].

For safety-critical systems, it is essential that various aspects of the dependability of the complete system, e.g., probability of failure per unit time, either be assessed or predicted before deployment. Assessment is usually performed by observing the system operating in a test environment. Predictions are usually obtained from mathematical models.

The treatment of software has been a source of difficulty in the development of predictive models of computer-based systems. Acceptable quantification of a system's software components has proved elusive. In this paper we consider the problem of making system dependability predictions using system fault-tree models that include appropriate analysis of software. We focus in particular on how the results of software testing can be made a practical source of probabilistic data for fault-tree analysis. By employing a variety of techniques including restricting software's functionality and a very rigid software architecture, we show how various limitations in previous models can be overcome, and useful dependability predictions of complex systems produced. We illustrate the concepts using a small research nuclear reactor as an example.

The reactor system example is reviewed in the next section. Following that, the issues in fault-tree analysis and the issues surrounding software are discussed. In the

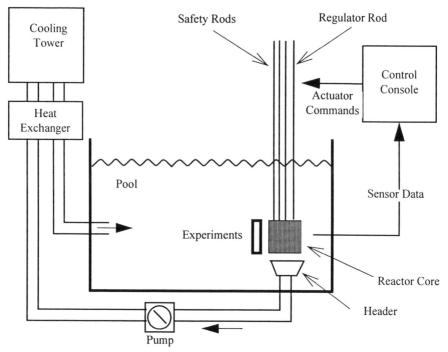

Figure 1: The University of Virginia reactor system.

following two sections we discuss two components of our overall approach, and then we present examples of their use. In the final section, we present our conclusions.

2 Example System

The *University of Virginia Reactor* (UVAR) is a research reactor that is used for the training of nuclear engineering students, service work in the areas of neutron activation analysis and radioisotope generation, neutron radiography, radiation damage studies, and other research [15].

The UVAR is a "swimming pool" reactor, i.e., the reactor core is submerged in a very large tank of water. The water is used for cooling, shielding, and neutron moderation. The core uses low-enriched uranium fuel elements and is located under approximately 20 feet of water on an 8x8 grid-plate that is suspended from the top of the reactor pool. The reactor core is made up of a variable number of fuel elements and in-core experiments, and always includes four control rod elements. Three of these control rods provide gross control and safety. They are coupled magnetically to their drive mechanisms, and they drop into the core by gravity if power fails or a safety shutdown signal (known as a "scram") is generated either by the operator or the reactor protection system. The fourth rod is a regulating rod that is fixed to a drive mechanism and is therefore non-scramable. The regulating rod is moved automatically by the drive mechanism to maintain fine control of the power level to compensate for small changes in reactivity associated with normal operations [15].

The heat capacity of the pool is sufficient for steady-state operation at 200 kW with natural convection cooling. When the reactor is operated above 200 kW, the water in the pool is drawn down through the core by a pump via a header located beneath the grid-plate to a heat exchanger that transfers the heat generated in the water to a secondary system. A cooling tower located on the roof of the facility exhausts the heat and the cooled primary water is returned to the pool. The overall organization of the system is shown in Figure 1.

Among the various safety systems used by the reactor, there are two that we will use for illustration in this paper. The first is a set of checks that shut the reactor down automatically (scram the reactor) if a specified condition arises. A scram occurs, for example, if the power level of the reactor exceeds a preset threshold. The second safety system is a set of operator alarms that alert the operator to a specified condition. Some alarms are coupled to the scram system thereby shutting the reactor down if the alarm condition arises.

As part of a research program in software engineering, an experimental (non-operational) digital control system is being developed for the UVAR that is currently in the specification stage. It is as part of this project that we are investigating the effect of software on system fault-tree analysis.

3   Fault Tree Analysis

System-fault-tree analysis is an important and widely used safety analysis technique [16], and is also the subject of active research [8]. Using the design of a system and the failure probabilities (due to degradation faults) of its components, a system fault-tree model is constructed and used to estimate the probability of occurrence of the various hazards that are of interest to the systems' designers.

The failure probabilities of a system's components are either measured or estimated. The probability is estimated when it cannot be easily measured using life testing. An estimate is developed by viewing the component itself as a system made up of simpler components whose failure probabilities can be measured by life testing. These probabilities are then used in a model (frequently a Markov model) of the component of interest to produce the required estimate [9].

Fault-tree analysis of systems that include computers can treat the computer hardware much like other components. Computer systems can fail, however, as a result of software defects as well as hardware defects, and this raises the question about how the software "components" of a system can be included in a fault-tree model. In practice, this has proved difficult.

Fault-tree analysis is an important technology in the overall assessment of safety-critical systems. For it to be applied to computer based systems, however, software must be included in the fault-tree models. With software excluded or not treated appropriately, the results of fault-tree analysis is conditional on the system's software always working correctly—an assumption that is unwarranted.

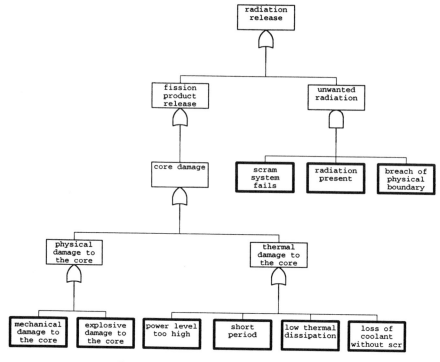

Figure 2: Top level reactor fault tree.

We are developing a comprehensive fault-tree model of the reactor as part of the research project mentioned earlier. The upper part of the fault tree we are using[1] showing the hazards and some of the events that can cause them is shown in Figure 2.

The portion of the fault tree that is shown is just a small part of the whole model. Extensive subtrees are associated with the lowest level nodes shown in the figure, and within these subtrees are many nodes—*many* nodes—whose proper analysis is critical to safe operation. The solid borders on the fault-tree nodes indicate that the associated node is not a leaf node.

The quantification associated with these nodes requires parametric information from software (in our experimental digital control system only) because the associated events occur as a result of software failure. The subtree associated with the event "loss of coolant without scram" (see Figure 2), for example, has events that arise because of failures in the software that implements the following: *the scram logic*; *management of several sensors*; *sensor signal processing*; *shutdown logic*; and *shutdown device control*. These events are used for illustration later in the paper.

---

1. This fault tree is an unofficial one developed by the authors and their colleagues for purposes of experimentation in software engineering and is neither an official safety document nor used in the reactor's safety case.

4   Software In System Fault Trees

In order to obtain the probabilistic data needed for fault-tree analysis, it is tempting to analyze software in the same way that hardware is analyzed—either as a black-box component whose failure probability can be measured by sampling the input space, i.e., life testing, or as a component whose structure permits modeling of its failure probability from its design.

Unfortunately, the quantification of software dependability by life testing has been shown to be infeasible in general for safety-critical systems [4, 12]. The reason is that an infeasible number of tests are required to establish a useful bound on the probability of failure in the ultra-dependable range. The large number of tests derives from the number of combinations of input values that can occur. It is quite literally the case that for most realistic systems the number of tests required would take thousands of years to complete even under the most optimistic circumstances.

Also unfortunate is the fact that there are no general models that predict software dependability from the software's design—the type of Markov models used in hardware analysis do not apply in most cases. The reason for this is that the basic assumptions underlying Markov analysis of hardware systems do not apply to software systems. In particular the assumption that independent components in a system fail independently does not apply.

Faced with this situation, there are three directions that can be followed. The first is to somehow limit the effect that software can have on a system so that the system is less dependent on software for meeting its safety goals. We refer to this technique as *robust design*. If this could be done, satisfactory fault-tree analysis could be performed and satisfactorily safe systems developed without requiring that software meet extreme dependability goals and without having to show that such goals have in fact been met.

The second technique is to obtain the parameters needed for fault-tree analysis by some means other than testing or modeling. Many techniques exist, usually within the field of *formal methods* [5], that can show that a particular software system possesses useful properties without executing the software. If these properties could be used to establish the parameters necessary for fault-tree analysis, then the requirement of using testing and Markov models would be avoided.

Finally, the third technique to dealing with the problems of quantifying software performance for fault-tree analysis is to try to modify the test process in some way (or ways) so that what is now infeasible becomes feasible by changing the details of what has to be quantified by testing. We refer to this technique as *restricted testing*.

We are developing a comprehensive approach to the treatment of software in system fault trees that exploits all three of these techniques—each in several ways. The overall approach is illustrated in Figure 3, and the various methods used within the three techniques are shown beneath them. We examine two of the three techniques that make up the approach in the following sections. Robust design is discussed only for completeness and therefore only briefly, and formal methods are omitted for the sake of brevity. Our primary topic in the remainder of this paper is restricted testing.

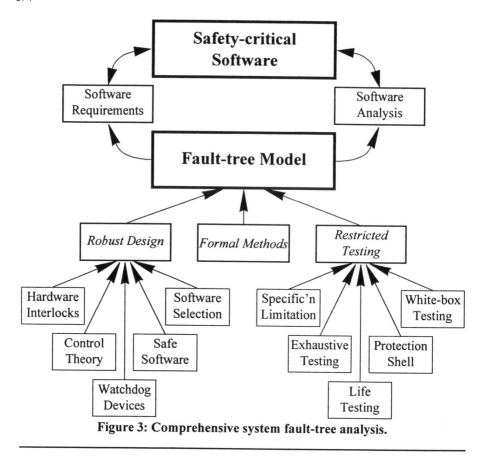

Figure 3: Comprehensive system fault-tree analysis.

5 Robust Design

Refinement of a system's overall design is often undertaken with fault-tree analysis. If the hazard probabilities computed using a system fault tree are determined to be unacceptably high, system design changes or component replacements can be undertaken until the predicted probabilities are acceptable.

The goal that we have with robust design is to use the *system-level* design to minimize the importance of software in the dependability analysis of the system. We illustrate this point using the following aspects of robust design:

- *Software selection.*

  The process of design refinement includes the determination of which aspects of a system will be implemented in software. Although it is stating the obvious, we observe that where a function can be implemented satisfactorily using some technology other than software, the analytic challenges that software presents are reduced. In other words, step one is not to use software to the extent that this makes sense.

- *Avoidance of software-only nodes.*
  Requiring that both a software failure and some other failure occur before a haz-ard can arise introduces an AND operator into a fault tree. This structure ensures that a software failure alone cannot lead to a hazard and reduces the dependabil-ity requirement on the software correspondingly. Various ways of introducing such conditions exist including hardware interlocks, watchdog devices such as timers, and various types of control-theory techniques that are stable even in the face of various types of implementation failure [10, 11].

- *Safe programming.*
  Changing the specification of a software element from requiring correct func-tionality to requiring either correct functionality *or no action* is a powerful tool in robust design. This technique is known as Safe Programming [2], and it per-mits software to be designed to be self checking rather than correct. Safe pro-gramming is far easier to implement and verify than full functionality.

6 Restricted Testing

We now turn our attention to our main concern in this paper, the issue of testing. The two aspects of the problem—too many tests required and no suitable predictive mod-els—are both significant and very difficult to deal with. But for testing to be able to play a role in providing material for fault-tree analysis, these two problems have to be tackled.

A major part of the problem derives from the size of modern software systems. Correct operation of the digital control system that we are developing for the UVAR, for example, depends, in principle, on the correct operation of an operating system, a windowing mechanism, a network interface, and a large application. This represents hundreds of thousands if not millions of lines of software source code.

The combination of five concepts—protection-shell architectures, exhaustive testing, specification limitation, life testing and conditional models—provides a test-ing framework that can yield useful information for many systems. We discuss each of these concepts in the remainder of this section.

6.1 Protection-Shell Architecture

A *protection shell*[1] [3, 13, 18, 19] can be used to limit severely the amount of soft-ware upon which a system depends for correct operation. As a result, the amount of critical software that has to be tested can be reduced significantly.

The detailed description and analysis of this architecture have appeared else-where [3, 18, 19] but the basic idea, shown in Figure 4, is to restrict the majority of the implementation of safety and thereby the dependability analysis of a system to a conceptual shell that surrounds the application. Provided the shell is not starved of

---

1. The term *protection shell* that we use here is relatively new. It was introduced to more accurately characterize the architecture to which we refer. This architecture is also known as a *safety kernel*.

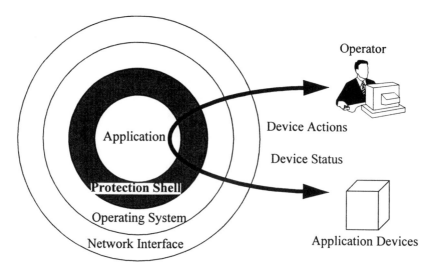

Figure 4: Protection-shell architecture.

processor resources (by the an operating system defect, for example), the shell ensures that safety policies are enforced no matter what action is taken by the rest of the software. In other words, provided the shell itself is dependable and can execute, safety will not be compromised by defects in the remainder of the software including the operating system and the application. The possibility of starving the shell is dealt with by an external watchdog timer (see Wika [19] for further details).

With a protection shell in place, the testing of a system can be focused on the shell. It is no longer necessary to undertake testing to demonstrate ultra-dependability of the entire system. For many systems, this alone might bring the number of test cases required down to a feasible value.

6.2 Specification Limitation

To further reduce the number of required test cases, we include the use of *specification limitation* [6]. This technique deliberately limits the range of values that an input to a system can take to the smallest possible set that is consistent with safe operation. In many cases, the range of values that an input can take is determined by an external physical device, such as a sensor, and the range might be unnecessarily wide. It is the combination of the ranges of input values that leads to the unrealistic number of test cases in the ultra-dependable range. Specification limitation reduces the number of inputs to the minimum possible.

6.3 Exhaustive Testing

There are many circumstances in which it is possible to test all possible inputs that a piece of software could ever receive, i.e., to test exhaustively. Despite the relative simplicity of the idea, it is entirely equivalent to a proof of correct operation.

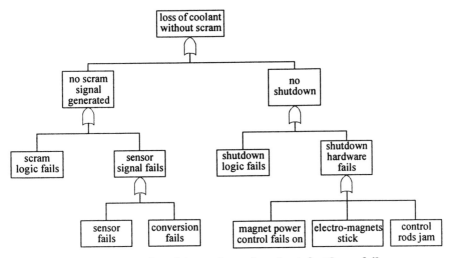

Figure 5: Example subtree—loss-of-coolant shutdown failure

If a piece of software can be tested exhaustively and that testing can be trusted (and that is not always the case [1]), then the quantification needed in fault-tree analysis of the system, including that software, is complete—the probability of failure of the software is zero.

6.4 Life Testing

Although initially we had to reject life testing as infeasible, with the application of the elements of restricted testing that we have already mentioned, for many software components it is likely that life testing becomes feasible. What is required is that the sample space presented by the software's inputs be "small enough" that adequate samples can be taken to estimate the required probability with sufficient confidence, i.e., sufficient tests executed to estimate the software's probability of failure.

7 Application To The Case Study

We illustrate the ideas discussed in the previous sections using the "loss of coolant without scram" circumstance in the reactor example. This event appears at the bottom of the high-level fault tree shown in Figure 2, and the subtree for this event is shown in Figure 5.

The problem that this subtree is addressing is the possibility that there could be a loss of coolant (i.e., loss of water from the pool) and that the essential scram associated with this event not occur. Such a situation obviously could lead to the reactor remaining in operation without adequate cooling.

The fault-tree fragment shown in Figure 5 indicates:

- that loss of coolant and a shutdown failure occurs if there is no scram signal or the shutdown fails,

- that there is no scram signal if the scram logic fails or the sensor processing fails,

- that a shutdown fails to occur if the shutdown logic fails or the shutdown hardware fails,

- that the shutdown hardware fails if the control rods jam, the control-rods-attachment electro-magnets "stick" or the power switch to the magnets fails,

- and so on.

In our experimental UVAR control system design, software is required to perform the following functions related to this subtree and so the probability of failure of each of these functions has to be determined:

1. evaluation of the relevant scram logic,
2. management of cooling-level sensors,
3. conversion of the sensor value to engineering units,
4. evaluation of the shutdown logic,
5. control of the electro-magnets that keep the control rods out of the core.

A protection-shell architecture is being developed for the experimental system. The policies that this shell has to enforce, the extent of the safety case that can be made this way, and degree of isolation from the remaining software that this provides has been documented elsewhere [18, 19].

With the protection shell in place, the software functions listed above are safety functions that are effected in part by the protection shell and in part by the application—the latter using a shell technique called "weakened policies" [18]. This permits testing to focus on these specific functions.

Items 1 and 4 amount to decision procedures that are fairly simple. Values have to be compared with preset limits and simple logic functions evaluated. Clearly, these items can be tested exhaustively.

Item 5 is similar to items 1 and 4 except that this software function requires in addition the setting of an analog value—the electro-magnet current. The logic of this component can be tested exhaustively. The analog computation can be simplified and its testing made tractable by specification limitation.

Item 3 in the list above is a case where specification limitation can be applied effectively. Level monitors typically return data that is far more accurate than it needs to be for safe operation. Indeed the present UVAR control system uses two independent sensors—one yields a conventional analog value but the second merely returns a discrete value based on coolant height dropping below a threshold. If the values returned by the sensors used for this type of application yield 16-bit values for a distance in the range zero to 20 feet, then safe operation is assured even if only the most-significant eight bits are used. This reduces the test-input space by eight binary orders of magnitude, i.e., by a *factor of 256*.

Item 2 is more complex because, in practice, the sensor array of a system of this type requires triplicated sensors (at least) and long-term sensor modeling to try to detect impending failures. This is a case in which life testing, i.e., basing a prediction of the probability of failure on sampling the input space, is probably feasible because of the relatively small size of the software concerned and because the input space can be limited with specification limitation.

As noted above, the alarm system of the UVAR is also a significant safety mechanism. There are alarms, for example, that are generated from a variety of breaches of physical security since such breaches can lead to human exposure to radiation (see Figure 2, right hand side). The subtrees of the system fault tree that deal with possible failures within the alarm system are very similar to those modeling the scram system. The software issues raised and approaches to testing are also similar.

8   Conclusion

We have presented some of the techniques used in a comprehensive approach to dealing with software in system fault trees. These techniques can assist in the design of systems that depend for their correct operation on software and whose dependability can be modeled using system fault tree analysis.

The ways in which these techniques might be used have been discussed using a realistic example—a research nuclear reactor.

Acknowledgments

It is a pleasure to acknowledge many helpful discussion about the safety requirements for UVAR with a variety of our colleagues including Bo Hosticka, Don Krause, and Bob Mulder. This work was supported in part by the National Science Foundation under grant number CCR-9213427, in part by NASA under grant number NAG1-1123-FDP, and in part by the U.S. Nuclear Regulatory Commission under grant number NRC-04-94-093. This work was performed under the auspices of the U.S. Nuclear Regulatory Commission. The views expressed are those of the authors and do not necessarily reflect any position or policy of the U.S. Nuclear Regulatory Commission.

References

1.   Amman, P.E., S.S. Brilliant, and J.C. Knight, *The Effect of Imperfect Error Detection on Life Testing*. **IEEE Transactions on Software Engineering**, Feb. 1994, 20(2), pp. 142–148.

2.   Anderson, T.; Witty, R. W. *Safe programming*. **BIT (Nordisk Tidskrift for Informationsbehandling)**, 1978, 18(1), pp. 1–8.

3.   Burns, A, and A.J. Wellings, *Safety Kernels: Specification and Implementation,* **Journal of High Integrity Systems**, 1995, 1(3), pp. 287–300.

4.   Butler, R. W.; Finelli, G. B. *The infeasibility of quantifying the reliability of life-critical real-time software*. **IEEE Transactions on Software Engineering**, Jan. 1991, 19(1), pp. 3–12.

5.   Diller, A., **Z: An Introduction to Formal Methods**. ed. 2, John Wiley & Sons, New York, NY, 1994.

6. Knight, John C., Aaron G. Cass, Antonio M. Fernández, Kevin G. Wika, *Testing A Safety-critical Application*, **Proceedings: International Symposium on Software Testing and Analysis (ISSTA)**, Seattle, WA, August 1994, p. 199.

7. Leveson, N. G.; *Software Safety: Why, What, and How*. **ACM Computing Surveys**, June 1986 18(2), p. 125–163.

8. Liu, S.; McDermid, J. A. *A model-oriented approach to safety analysis using fault trees and a support system*. **Journal of Systems Software**, Nov. 1996, 35(2), p. 151–64.

9. Modarres, M. **What Every Engineer Should Know About Reliability and Risk Analysis**. Marcel Dekker, New York, NY, 1993.

10. Ogata, K. **Modern Control Engineering**. Prentice-Hall, Englewood Cliffs, NJ, 1970.

11. Ogata, K. **Discrete-Time Control Systems**, ed. 2. Prentice-Hall, Englewood Cliffs, NJ, 1995.

12. Parnas, D. L. *Evaluation of safety-critical software*. **Communications of the ACM**, June 1990, 33(6), p. 636–48.

13. Rushby, J. *Kernels for safety?* In: Anderson, T. (ed.). **Safe and Secure Computing Systems**, Blackwell Scientific Publications, 1989. p. 210–20.

14. Storey, N. **Safety-Critical Computer Systems**. Addison Wesley Longman, Harlow, England, ed. 1, 1996.

15. University of Virginia Reactor, *The University of Virginia Nuclear Reactor Facility Tour Information Booklet,* http://minerva.acc.virginia.edu/~reactor.

16. Vesely, W.E., F.F. Goldberg, N.H. Roberts, and D.F. Haasl. **Fault Tree Handbook**, NUREG-0492, U.S. Nuclear Regulatory Commission, Washington, DC, 1981.

17. Westphal, L. C. **Sourcebook of Control Systems Engineering**, Chapman & Hall, London, UK, 1995.

18. Wika, K.J., and J.C. Knight, *On The Enforcement of Software Safety Policies*, **Proceedings of the Tenth Annual Conference on Computer Assurance (COMPASS)**, Gaithersburg, MD, 1995, pp. 83–93.

19. Wika, K.J., **Safety Kernel Enforcement of Software Safety Policies**, Ph.D. dissertation, Department of Computer Science, University of Virginia, Charlottesville, VA, 1995.

Author Index